*LET MY PEOPLE GO*

# Southern Classics Series

*John G. Sproat, General Editor*

**King Cotton and His Retainers:**
*Financing and Marketing the Cotton Crop of the South, 1800–1925*
By Harold D. Woodman

**The South as a Conscious Minority, 1789–1861:**
*A Study in Political Thought*
By Jesse T. Carpenter

**Red Hills and Cotton:**
*An Upcountry Memory*
By Ben Robertson

**John C. Calhoun:**
*American Portrait*
By Margaret L. Coit

**The Southern Country Editor**
By Thomas D. Clark

**A Woman Rice Planter**
By Elizabeth Allston Pringle

**Let My People Go:**
*The Story of the Underground Railroad and
the Growth of the Abolition Movement*
By Henrietta Buckmaster

# Let My People Go

*The Story of
the Underground Railroad and
the Growth of the Abolition Movement*

by Henrietta Buckmaster

*with a new introduction*
by Darlene Clark Hine

University of South Carolina Press
Published in Cooperation with
The Institute for Southern Studies
and the South Caroliniana Society
of the University of South Carolina

Copyright, 1941, by Harper & Brothers

Copyright © 1992 University of South Carolina

Published in Columbia, South Carolina, by the
University of South Carolina Press in cooperation
with the Institute for Southern Studies and
the South Caroliniana Society

Manufactured in the United States of America


**Library of Congress Cataloging-in-Publication Data**

Buckmaster, Henrietta.
    Let my people go : the story of the underground railroad and the
growth of the abolition movement / by Henrietta Buckmaster ; with a
new introduction by Darlene Clark Hine.
        p.   cm. — (Southern classics series)
    Includes bibliographical references and index.
    ISBN 0–87249–865–4
    1. Underground railroad.   2. Fugitive slaves—United States.
3. Slavery—United States—Anti-slavery movements.   I. Title.
II. Series.
E450.B89   1992
    973.7'115—dc20                                      92–16843

# Contents

# Contents

# GENERAL EDITOR'S PREFACE

THE SOUTHERN CLASSICS SERIES returns to general circulation books of importance dealing with the history and culture of the American South. Under the sponsorship of the Institute for Southern Studies and the South Caroliniana Society of the University of South Carolina, the series is advised by a board of distinguished scholars, whose members suggest titles and editors of individual volumes to the general editor and help to establish priorities in publication.

Chronological age alone does not determine a title's designation as a Southern Classic. The criteria include, as well, significance in contributing to a broad understanding of the region, timeliness in relation to events and moments of peculiar interest to the American South, usefulness in the classroom, and suitability for inclusion in personal and institutional collections on the region.

\* \* \*

One of the most dramatic and heroic aspects of America's lamentable experience with the "peculiar institution" of slavery was the Underground Railroad. Drama was inherent in the very operations of this secret organization, with its network of "stations" through which runaway slaves made their way to free territory. Heroism abounds in the exploits of the "conductors"—especially the African-American ones, of whom Harriet Tubman is the classic representative—who risked their lives repeatedly in facilitating the dash to freedom. No one told the story better than Henrietta Buckmaster; and with Darlene Clark Hine's sensitive introduction, *Let My People Go* now takes on added significance as a poignant account of a unique undertaking in southern and American history.

John G. Sproat
General Editor, *Southern Classics Series*

# INTRODUCTION TO THE
# SOUTHERN CLASSICS EDITION

IN AN AGE of rampant historical specialization, Henrietta Buckmaster's riveting narrative of the Underground Railroad, the Abolition Movement, and
the relentless struggle of African Americans to be free is downright exhilarating. This magisterial synthesis of the momentous events that led to a Civil
War holocaust and a turbulent Reconstruction is history at its compelling
best. The never-ending black quest for freedom against an equally determined white opposition both before and after the Civil War resonates in
many respects with the twentieth century Civil Rights Movement. Buckmaster captures brilliantly, through attention to detail, mastery of chronology, and the diverse personalities, the passions and complex nuances of the
antislavery crusade. The grand design of her synthesis echoes that of the biblical story of Moses who challenged Egypt's Pharaoh to let his people go. Biblical allusions heavily infuse Buckmaster's entire corpus of work. *Let My
People Go* reveals her spiritualism and deeply held personal commitment to
racial peace and social justice. Indeed, the author's own affinities operate as
a potent subtext. Still, the mountainous research, the lyrical writing, the in-
terpretive focus, and the sheer story-telling brilliance in *Let My People Go: The
Story of the Underground Railroad and the Growth of the Abolition Movement* make
it such an exceptional work that, fifty years after its initial publication in
1941, it well deserves the designation "A Southern Classic."

So inextricably interwoven are Buckmaster's life experiences and her art
that it is pointless to attempt to separate the two. The author and the text
beg simultaneous approach. An examination of Henrietta Buckmaster's
background and writing career helps to illuminate both the major themes
and purpose of *Let My People Go* and the political and intellectual concerns
she embraced. Born Henrietta Henkle in Cleveland, Ohio, in 1909 to Rae D.
and Pearl (Wintermute) Henkle, she published under the pseudonym Henrietta Buckmaster. Her ancestors, small landowners, had settled in the South
in the early eighteenth century and eventually migrated to the western territories in search of greater opportunities. Continuing this migratory pattern, shortly after his daughter's birth Rae D. Henkle moved his family to
New York City where he became foreign editor of the *New York Herald-
Tribune*.

A child prodigy, Henrietta Henkle began writing at an early age and by
the time she was twelve had already published her first story in *Child Life*

magazine. After completing school, first at the Friends Seminary and then at the exclusive Brearley School, the seventeen-year-old followed her father's lead and commenced a long journalism career. She began as book reviewer for the *Christian Science Monitor*, the *New York Sun*, and the *Saturday Review of Literature* and went on to employment at various magazines, including *Harper's Bazaar* and *Reader's Digest*. At the time of her death, in 1983 at Chestnut Hill, Massachusetts, she was editor of the *Home Forum* and of the fine arts and literary page for the *Christian Science Monitor*.

Buckmaster's voluminous writings defy easy categorization. She thought of herself as a novelist yet achieved international recognition for her impressive nonfiction book, *Let My People Go*. This work is perhaps best described as a historical novel, but all the characters are real and the events discussed actually happened in the chronological sequences indicated. Some of the conversations between characters and descriptions of their appearances reflect, perhaps, more a creative imagination than reality.

It is interesting to note that when it was published in England in 1943, *Let My People Go* was titled *Out of the House of Bondage: The Story of the Famous Underground Railroad of the American Negro Slaves*. The new subtitle of the British version alerts the reader that the black slaves themselves were central to the Underground Railroad. In 1959 Beacon Press issued a paperback edition to capture a wider market. In the new preface, Buckmaster declares, "The struggle against slavery—however much one may relegate it to the past—is still the dominating pattern in our complex texture of civil rights, our interest in the economic development of the South, and that spiritual integrity which is so challengingly American." A year earlier, in 1958, the book had been shortened and revised to appeal to children, and it was published under yet another title, *Flight to Freedom: The Story of the Underground Railroad*. *Let My People Go* earned high praise and for Buckmaster a prized Guggenheim Fellowship.

In an interview about the book Buckmaster confided, "I was very young when I wrote *Let My People Go*, and each day became an extraordinary revelation of the horrors and injustices endured by the black people who were brought here as slaves, and even more important, their unwillingness to accept bondage and their fight against it."[1] Unlike many authors of the 1940s, Buckmaster boldly placed blacks at the center of the history of the Underground Railroad. Instead of portraying blacks as mere victims of slavery, she viewed them as leaders and active participants in their own liberation struggles. In light of the intense interest in the African background among today's students, Buckmaster's Afrocentric approach lends a special relevancy to *Let My People Go*. She writes of the African Americans:

They came from a people who for ten thousand years had
raised and destroyed empires, provided a powerful Negroid
culture which dominated the Mediterranean and gave full-
blooded blacks and mulatto Pharaohs to the thrones of
Egypt. Their ancestors were those who had given form to the
culture of Ethiopia, that ancient land which to the
Mediterranean world was the home "of gods and fairies,"
where Jove and Neptune banqueted each year among "the
blameless Ethiopians."

The extensive research conducted for *Let My People Go* enabled Buckmaster to write a sequel, *Deep River* (1944), that covered events in Georgia
between 1859 and Secession. This novel centers on the work of a purely fictitious young Abolitionist, Simon Bliss, who is married to the daughter, Sa-
vanna, of a slave owner. The book probes the heated conflict between the
slaveholding plantation owners and the mountaineers. Like *Let My People Go*,
this novel is thoroughly laced with Buckmaster's abiding hatred of slavery
and her respect for the dignity of the enslaved. A *New York Times* reviewer,
Ruth Page, judged the book "that rare thing, a historical novel in which
events have moral values and are in themselves founded on ideas."[2] For *Deep
River* Buckmaster received the Ohioana Medal for 1944.

When commenting on her own work, Buckmaster insisted, "My first two
historical novels had an American background. Both dealt with the opposition to slavery within the southern states. I knew that the present unfinished
business of civil rights was inextricably entangled with our misinformation
about the Negro before and after the Civil War."[3] She added elsewhere, "I
suppose moral issues have always interested me most of all. By moral I mean
'responsible.' My books have always come out of questions: how and why
people *are*, individually, collectively, in terms of their own self-concepts, in
terms of social change." Buckmaster believed that the historical novel should
enliven an era in order to make the past meaningful to present readers. "My
writing concern is with spirit and motivation," she elaborated. "Above all, my
interest is in characters who endeavor to fulfill some affirmative and dynamic progression of spirit as exemplified in some particular love of freedom."[4]

Buckmaster's advocacy for the rights of oppressed people included not
only African Americans but also Native Americans, women, and prisoners.
Her denunciation of the treatment that Native Americans received at the
hands of the United States military punctuates her *The Seminole Wars* (1966).
However, she carefully avoided depictions of oppressed groups as victims
lacking human agency for effecting social change. She wrote a number of

children's stories with historical themes that elucidated the struggles of the subordinate and frequently invisible members of the society, as for example, *The Fighting Congressmen: Biographies of Black and White Congressmen in the Post-Civil War Period* (1954) and *Women Who Shaped History* (1966). She described these works as concerned with "remarkable struggles against indignity and human violation."[5]

Encouraged by the success of *Let My People Go* and of *Deep River*, Buckmaster published several additional historical novels. *Bread from Heaven* (1952) was written after she returned, in the aftermath of World War II, from a visit to Germany where she went initially to do a series of articles on adults and children who had survived concentration camps. The book is an allegorical sermon on prejudice illuminated by the reactions of a New England village to a young woman who brings her maimed child to live there.

In *And Walk in Love* (1956) Buckmaster focused on Paul of Tarsus to satisfy questions about the essence of "spiritual genius." Her curiosity about the metamorphosis of Saul into Paul motivated yet another project, a nonfictional study, *Paul: A Man Who Changed the World*, published in 1965. In what appears to be a natural progression from her interest in spiritual genius, she turned to Shakespeare and wrote a book about one year, 1600, in his life. In *All the Living* (1962) she explored the essence of imaginative genius. About Paul and Shakespeare, Buckmaster pondered, "What distinguished them from other men? What gives them their special kind of courage and indestructibility?"[6] Similar questions must have reverberated in her imagination when she wrote those magnificent descriptions of Nat Turner and William Lloyd Garrison found in *Let My People Go*.

*Let My People Go* comprises nine chapters. The first three chapters describe the origins of the Underground Railroad. As Buckmaster declares, "The first fugitive slave who asked help from a member of his own race or the enemy race drove the first stake of that 'railroad.' " Resistance to slavery commenced at the inception of the slave trade and continued in various guises until the Civil War. It was not simply the individual fugitive slave or the occasional insurrectionist who resisted but also free blacks. Buckmaster correctly observes that "free Negroes were an anachronism to a slave society." Free blacks fought to improve their own lot, to carve out living space for themselves and their families. Even so, free blacks proved absolutely essential to the flowering of the culture of resistance as was manifested in the Underground Railroad. Buckmaster explores white resistance as well as black and sharply analyzes the critical role of Quakers in organizing practical assistance to runaway slaves. Against the backdrop of major events such as the Missouri Compromise of 1820, she deftly unravels the developing pattern of abolition, pausing to appreciate Denmark Vesey, who in 1821, led an abortive slave uprising: "He was handsome, impressive and intelligent, a free man of Charleston, South Carolina, who had a tremendous power over his race." Whereas a professional historian would hesitate to use quotation marks, Buckmaster proclaims that Vesey "spoke in the words of Zechariah: 'Behold the day of the Lord cometh, and thy spoil shall be divided in the midst of thee. For I will gather all nations against Jerusalem to battle; and the city shall be taken.'"

The massive vengeance of white South Carolinians—twenty-two slaves were hanged in the aftermath of Vesey—did not halt the black assault on slavery. In 1829 David Walker, another free black, issued his *Appeal*, urging the slaves to rise against their masters. The publication was, in Buckmaster's words, "a bare sword" to the slavocracy and the "seeping waters that weakened the dam" for the slaves. Walker's *Appeal* was a precursor to "The Black Prophet" or, as she described him, "the mighty, the fabulous, the fire-eating Nat Turner." The Nat Turner revolt climaxed white fear in the South, even as it emboldened those whites and blacks in the North who vowed to bring down the house of bondage.

Of the white Abolitionists none is more famous than William Lloyd Garrison, editor of *The Liberator*. Buckmaster places Garrison on the pedestal with Walker and Turner, viewing them as the triumvirate most responsible for making the South a "mighty fortress." Buckmaster clearly admires Garrison, who among "the rank and file of antislavery workers" was "'abolition personified and incarnate'" and to those daily engaged with him was "the living and unalterable symbol of devotion to a cause." But her obvious approval of his vision and commitment does not blind Buckmaster to Garrison's faults. She does not gloss over the internal factions and schisms that plagued the movement. Indeed, Buckmaster is careful to note the contributions of a veritable galaxy of lesser-known antislavery men and women. There is, for example, the young editor named Elijah Lovejoy who settled in Alton, Illinois, in search of free speech and free press and wound up the victim of an 1837 assassination when he railed against the barbaric lynching of a mulatto freeman named Francis McIntosh. Lovejoy's death bound abolition to the cause of free speech.

The late 1830s signaled a new dawn in the antislavery movement. In chapters four through seven of *Let My People Go* Buckmaster provides a panoramic overview of all the events, momentous and dramatic, that led the nation to irrepressible conflict. Buckmaster respects historical chronology, but she also uses it as a structure upon which to fasten riveting accounts of indomitable personalities and heroic escapades loaded with drama and suspense. The Underground Railroad, she reminds us, is now running through the best parlors.

With a casual assurance that few of her generation of writers and scholars would have dared, Buckmaster remarks that the most powerful weapons in the new era's abolitionism were the black antislavery agents. Armed with a natural dignity and eloquence, she argues that they collectively articulated the personal equation: "Am I ignorant and crude? Whose fault is it? May I have a chance? Is there a place in this democracy for a citizen with a black skin? The right to vote has been taken from me in nearly every state, free or slave. Why has this been done? Why even in the North must I sit in separate places and eat the bitter bread of inequality?"

Free black men and women never simply waited for whites to acknowledge their humanity and to give them freedom. Instead, free blacks became active agents for social change as they set in motion a "crusade of the conscience" that rested upon a separate parallel institutional and organizational infrastructure of struggle and resistance. They hosted national Negro conventions and created the Philadelphia Vigilance Committee. Indeed, the Philadelphia Association for the Moral and Mental Improvement of the People of Color raised money and provided food, clothes, transportation, shelter, and employment for the runaways whenever feasible. These efforts of disparate people in border and northern states gave the Underground Railroad its structure and coherence. Free blacks wrote pamphlets, edited newspapers, lectured, organized boycotts of products made by slaves, and mobilized to thwart the intentions of erstwhile slave-catchers.

This black pattern of antislavery involvement was not duplicated by white male and female Abolitionists. Among white women, Abby Kelly, Lucretia Mott, Elizabeth Cady Stanton, and the Grimké sisters courageously took to the lecture platform to battle slavery, but none were active in the Underground Railroad. There were, of course, exceptions. Buckmaster provides a reverent description of Laura Haviland as "a plain, prim-mouthed little Quakeress who lived in northern Michigan" and insisted that "No man could have shown more courage and enterprise." According to Buckmaster, in 1837 Haviland started Raisen Institute because "she believed in mixed education, both as to sex and color." For some time she had distinguished herself by running an Underground Railroad station; but "not entirely satisfied with the limitations of her plot of earth, she made several trips with fugitives into Canada to see them safely out of the eagle's claw, and braved slave-catchers' pistols on more than one occasion."

Because it was the "right" thing to do and in recognition of the invaluable role women played in the abolition crusade, both Garrison and the outstanding black Abolitionist Frederick Douglass championed the rights of women. Not all male Abolitionists shared their beliefs in the rights of women, and the introduction of women's issues into the antislavery movement had a devastating impact. A new group, the American and Foreign Antislavery Society, separated from the American Antislavery Society. This split and the subsequent embrace of third-party political involvement signaled the end of an exclusively moral abolitionism. As abolitionism became even more complex in the 1850s, Harriet Beecher Stowe's dramatic presentation of Eliza's escape to freedom across the icy river with a clinging child refocused the human tragedy of slavery.

Among the distinguished black Abolitionists a few names are especially luminous. In addition to Douglass, they include William Still, David Ruggles, William Wells Brown, and the daring Henry Highland Garnet who called for a general strike in an 1843 address to the slaves. Garnet exhorted: "Brethren, arise, arise! Strike for your lives and liberties. Now is the day and the hour. Let every slave throughout the land do this and the days of slavery are numbered. Rather die freemen than live to be slaves! In the name of God we ask, are you men? Where is the blood of your fathers? Awake, awake, millions of voices are calling you! Let your motto be resistance; no oppressed people have secured their liberty without resistance. Remember that you are four million!"

Of all the Abolitionists she considers—male and female, black and white—Buckmaster appears to have a special affinity for the white Underground Railroad stationmaster Thomas Garrett of Wilmington, Delaware. In 1848, after twenty-two years of such work, stripped of all his worldly possessions as repayment to a slave owner for assisting the escape of two slave children, Garrett remained steadfast. And in the end he was vindicated. To Buckmaster Garrett was the complete Abolitionist. "Life seemed to increase for him rather than diminish," she writes, "for with his public championship of the slave, he became an Abolitionist in the fullest sense: a champion of women's rights, an advocate of temperance, a defender of the Indians, and an agitator in behalf of white working men and women."

On numerous occasions Garrett lent a helping hand to the indefatigable Underground Railroad conductor, Harriet Tubman, who is reputed to have returned to Maryland's Eastern Shore over a dozen times to assist two to three hundred slaves make their journey to freedom. Buckmaster's lyrical retelling of the now familiar Tubman legend carries profound emotional power: "She had the ruthless courage, too, that enabled her to carry a pistol wherever she went and threaten to use it if any of her friends showed timidity or a desire to escape from unfamiliar terrors to the terrors which they knew. A finger around the trigger and a calm, 'Dead Negroes tell no tales' was all that was ever needed. The sound of a horse galloping in the dark meant a quick concealment by the side of the road, the cry of a slave baby meant an extra dose of paregoric so that it lay in a stupor in its mother's arms." Given conductors like Tubman, Buckmaster may be excused for calling the Underground Railroad "one of the greatest powers in the country."

As great a power as the Underground Railroad may have been, the power of the slavocracy packed a wallop. In 1857 the Supreme Court's decision in the Dred Scott case provided a shocking reminder of that power. While Chief Justice Roger B. Taney dealt with the social aspects of the slavery question, his final declaration seemed to draw firmly the lines between North and South. He insisted, Buckmaster reports, that " 'the black man has no rights which the white man is bound to respect'; the inalienable 'rights of the Declaration of Independence do not relate to the Negro for whom citizenship is impossible,' and finally, 'Congress has no power to abolish or prevent slavery in any of the territories.' "

It was Frederick Douglass who offered what was perhaps a propitious rejoinder to Taney. He declared: " 'My hopes were never brighter than now. The Supreme Court of the United States is not the only power in this world. We, the abolitionists and colored people, should meet this decision, unlooked for and monstrous as it appears, in a cheerful spirit. This very attempt to blot out forever the hopes of an enslaved people may be one necessary link in the chain of events preparatory to the complete overthrow of the whole slave system.' " Following on the heels of the Dred Scott decision was the aborted raid on the federal arsenal at Harpers Ferry by the implacable and resolute John Brown. The nation needed only one more shove to plunge into war and the election of Abraham Lincoln to the presidency of the United States accomplished that task.

Abolitionists were not surprised when the governor of South Carolina sent a message to the state legislature urging secession and advocating a volunteer force of ten thousand men. The die was cast as the mortars split the silence and their shells exploded over Fort Sumter. Although Lincoln adamantly insisted that the conflict was no abolition war, free blacks and slaves knew better. Within months seasoned antislavery workers launched benevolent, educational, and freedmen's aid associations that took over the duties of the federal government as slaves made their way to Union lines. The Underground Railroad now witnessed the transformation of a dream into reality. In Buckmaster's words, "A greater insurrection was going on among the slaves than had been dreamed of—an insurrection of rising bondmen, taking their masters' possessions and leaving the fields and granaries of the Confederacy, the labor battalions, and the factories. And what good were laws, pleas to loyalty, night riders? Five hundred thousand men, women and children coming into Union camps, were to find the answer that suited them."

Lincoln's ambivalence ended when the Emancipation Proclamation took effect. Although Abolitionists quickly warned that the proclamation left enslaved 830,000 slaves in border states and that, as Buckmaster phrased it, "it was a moral statement only with no power of implementation behind it," to the average Northerner, black or white, male or female, freedom for the slave had come at last. Some 200,000 black troops would turn the tide of the war in favor of the Union. In 1865 the country ratified the Thirteenth Amendment to the United States Constitution, ending slavery.

The last chapter of *Let My People Go* is aptly entitled "But We Haven't Found Peace." Lincoln's assassination along with President Andrew Johnson's lack of sympathy for the agenda of the radical Republicans and of the old-line Abolitionists doused the celebration of freedom. "So the war was not over!" With the example of Thaddeus Stevens, Buckmaster captures well the continued frustration: "The men in the North who were fighting the battle of emancipation were not doing so only to keep the Republican party in power. Stevens was an old man, burning out, but the flame that ate at his body also ate at his terrible fury. Of all the Radicals, this grim old man from Pennsylvania with the devastating and Voltairian humor was the true revolutionist. And these were days of revolution." The revolution was, however, destined to remain unfinished.

For the ex-slave the end of the Civil War brought a tenuous freedom as the reconstructed states enacted a series of crippling Black Codes. Buckmaster offers a succinct summary of this assault on black freedom:

> he [the Negro] could rent property or houses only in
> restricted areas; he must never be without his contract of
> labor or his license from the police; if he quit his work he
> could be arrested and sent to the house of correction for a
> year, or if he were captured and brought back, his captor
> would be paid a reward of five dollars, and ten cents a mile
> for travel. Over him his employer held a control as inflexible
> as the slave master's, while his children were re-enslaved by
> apprenticeship laws. To restrict the movements of the
> freedmen were vagrancy laws, carrying penalties of hard
> labor or long imprisonment.

Freedmen and freedwomen fought hard to negotiate with white southerners the terms of their freedom. They wanted what every citizen, without regard to race, color, or previous condition of servitude, wanted: free education; equal political rights; the right to serve on a jury; the right to hold office; and laws that would protect their right to sell their labor and protect

their families. Still, there were positive symbols of freedom. With the ratification of the Fourteenth Amendment in 1868 the slave became a person and
a citizen, and the Dred Scott decision was repudiated in fact if not in custom.
In March 1870, the Fifteenth Amendment made the Negro, in Buckmaster's
words, "a citizen before the world." But the triumph of Abolition did not last
long, as the Compromise of 1877 soon unleashed a new reign of oppression.
But that is another story.

*Let My People Go* resonates even today because of the methodology and
perspective that Buckmaster adopted when she placed African Americans at
the center of the story of the struggle against slavery. Her fundamental assumption that human beings, no matter how oppressed and degraded, still
desire freedom and maintain wills to resist elevates the text. For decades respectable academic scholars such as U. B. Philips had held that African-
American slave resistance was almost nonexistent, because slavery in the
United States was little more than a paternalistic institution. Moreover, conventional wisdom held that the enslaved were mere children who lacked the
intellectual ability to conceive of freedom. In keeping with the path-break-
ing work of Herbert Aptheker, to whom she acknowledges a tremendous
debt, Buckmaster paints a picture that would have to await the work of a new
generation of historians in order to gain widespread currency.

African Americans, in Buckmaster's admittedly partisan and somewhat ro-
manticized account of the Underground Railroad, assume a critical position
as active agents rather than as objects of history. Where other writers and
scholars obscured, neglected, or minimized the multifaceted contributions
of blacks, Buckmaster breaks rank. She elevates the importance of African
Americans in the Underground Railroad without diminishing or displacing
the contributions of outstanding white Abolitionists. This long and often
frustrating struggle had room for many players, each of whom offered special services, talents, and resources. The diversity of the participants whom
Buckmaster presents underscores how much there is to learn from the past.
In the end, Buckmaster's portrait of the history of the Underground Railroad and the movement to abolish slavery is much more sensitive to questions of race, gender, and class than the earnest efforts of professionally
trained historians.

At the outset, Buckmaster establishes the point that enslaved Africans
were entitled to freedom and as human beings they, like the white Americans, were equally endowed with the inalienable rights of life, liberty, and
the pursuit of happiness. About this Buckmaster is morally certain and it is a
point from which she never retreats. At heart, her story of the Underground
Railroad and of the whole struggle of blacks to be free is a universal morality
play. In this drama, the African Americans and their white allies resist the

unjust and dehumanizing social and political power of the slavocracy on the one hand and those hypocritical and reactionary elements in the North on the other. Their tenacity, abiding love of freedom, and ultimate destruction of slavery, against overwhelming odds, serve as a source of hope and encouragement to all peoples engaged in liberation struggles.

For Buckmaster African Americans are the best barometer of American democracy. The black struggle to be free, therefore, engaged her throughout her personal and professional life. Even after the demise of slavery, as shown in the latter chapters of her book, the forces of white southern reaction and northern indifference made necessary an ongoing struggle for the ever-elusive freedom. In this perpetual quest, Buckmaster sees the experience of black Americans as the metaphorical mirror reflecting the global human struggle against injustice and dehumanization, racism, sexism, and classism.

It is important to underscore why, in *Let My People Go* and elsewhere, Buckmaster refuses to place blacks in peripheral, marginal, or adjunct role in the story of American democracy. She makes us ponder how the history of American democracy could have ever been taught without sustained attention devoted to African Americans, not only as enslaved Africans, but as freedom seekers and fighters as well. And Buckmaster does not err by attempting to make blacks into carbon copies of whites. Rather, her study demonstrates considerable respect for dimensions of the oppositional culture and political consciousness that the blacks themselves created, dimensions that supported individual and collective efforts to escape slavery via the Underground Railroad, assume leadership in the Abolition Movement, and even to return repeatedly to the South in order to rescue other bondmen and bondwomen.

One of the superb features of the book is Buckmaster's skillful re-creation of the culture of the Abolition Movement. Specifically, she illuminates the ways in which the Underground Railroad symbolized the movement's culture replete with myths and legends, code words and signs, invisible agents and conductors, and the heroic adventures of black and white rescue squads. In short, her effective blending of culture, politics, and biography permits multiple points of entry for diverse readers from the general public to the high-school student and even to the senior scholar. Every reader is certain to find hope, and a resonant theme, individual, or event in this timeless saga of resistance, *Let My People Go*.

Darlene Clark Hine

## Notes

The author thanks Linda Werbish, Jacqueline McLeod, and Professor Stan
Harrold for their assistance in the preparation of this essay.

1. Interview with Buckmaster, *Contemporary Authors*, New Revision Series, vol.
   6 (Detroit: Gale, 1982), p. 493.
2. Ruth Page, "Liberal in Georgia," *New York Times Book Review*, October 8,
   1944, p. 6.
3. Interview with Buckmaster, *World Authors, 1950–1970*, ed. John Wakeman
   (New York: H. W. Wilson, 1975), p. 235.
4. Statement by Buckmaster, *American Novelists of Today*, ed. Harry R. Warfel
   (New York: American Book Co., 1951), pp. 60-61.
5. *Contemporary Authors* interview, p. 493.
6. Quoted in *Something About the Author*, vol. 6 (Detroit: Gale, 1974), p. 39.

## For Further Reading

Among some of the recently published or reissued historical studies and important documentary projects on antislavery and Reconstruction are:

Ira Berlin, et al., *The Destruction of Slavery*, Ser. I, Vol. 1 of *Freedom: A Docu-
mentary History of Emancipation* (Cambridge: Cambridge University Press,
1985).
R. J. M. Blackett, *Beating Against the Barriers: The Lives of Six Nineteenth-Cen-
tury Afro-Americans* (Baton Rouge: Louisiana State University Press, 1986).
_____ , *Building An Anti-Slavery Wall: Black Americans in the Atlantic Aboli-
tionist Movement, 1830–1860* (Baton Rouge: Louisiana State University
Press, 1983).
John W. Blassingame, ed., *The Frederick Douglass Papers*, Ser. I, Vols. 1 & 2
(New Haven: Yale University Press, 1979, 1982).
David W. Blight, *Frederick Douglass' Civil War: Keeping Faith in Jubilee* (Baton
Rouge: Louisiana State University Press, 1989).
Leon F. Litwack, *Been in the Storm So Long: The Aftermath of Slavery* (New York:
Alfred A. Knopf, 1979).
Waldo E. Martin, Jr., *The Mind of Frederick Douglass* (Chapel Hill: University
of North Carolina Press, 1984).
William S. McFeely, *Frederick Douglass* (New York: W.W. Norton, 1991).

Benjamin Quarles, *Black Abolitionists* (rpt., New York: DaCapo Press, 1991; originally published by Oxford University Press, 1969).

C. Peter Ripley, ed., *The Black Abolitionist Papers, Volume IV: The United States, 1847–1858* (Chapel Hill: University of North Carolina Press, 1991).

Older works deserving attention include:

Larry Gara, *The Liberty Line: The Legend of the Underground Railroad* (Lexington: University of Kentucky Press, 1961).

Willie Lee Rose, *Rehearsal for Reconstruction: The Port Royal Experiment* (Indianapolis: Bobbs-Merrill, 1964).

Wilbur H. Siebert, *The Underground Railroad from Slavery to Freedom* (New York, 1899).

## PREFACE TO THE 1959 EDITION

LET MY PEOPLE GO is a history of the antislavery movement in this country. I was exceedingly untried when the book was written. Having been born in Ohio, I had heard of the Underground Railroad most of my life — that daring, clandestine venture which smuggled slaves out of the South into Canada — but I had given it little thought. Then by a series of fortuities I wrote an article on the "railroad" for a large magazine. I was dazzled by the implications of the material; I was still so young I was idealistic. In the old newspaper files, court records, diaries, letters, and books with which I spent my days, I discovered something which might almost be called the *mystique* of the United States. It set me afire with the conviction that if we knew more about the courage, faith, idealism, and practical good sense which went into the fight against the monolithic slave power, we would be better equipped to deal with present problems.

In re-reading my book after seventeen years, I realize that any slight partisanship on the side of freedom probably did succeed in setting forth the moral climate of that time in relation to ours, and that it also tended to fulfill the only valid function of history: the illumination of a present experience.

The century preceding the Civil War, and the twenty years which followed it, are wise and shrewd guides to the unfinished business facing us today. The struggle against slavery — however much one may relegate it to the past — is still the dominating pattern in our complex texture of civil rights, our interest in the economic development of the South, and that spiritual integrity which is so challengingly American.

I am very glad that the book will now be reaching a larger public through this edition. For better or worse, we are all the heirs of the past. I think there are very few of us who cannot benefit from a long backward look at what we have attained, and some quiet rumination on the tasks we have still to complete.

## FOR PETER

Who loves the world
of expanding thought,
the dream of free men,
the hope and the actuality.

# APPRECIATION

To say an adequate "Thank you" for assistance such as I have received is quite impossible. It must remain in that realm of devotion to a task in which most historians—and artists—dwell. But I cannot let this book appear without paying my tribute to the pioneer and ultimate authority on the Underground Railroad, Dr. Wilbur H. Siebert of Ohio State University, whose "vacation investigation" of the nebulous "railroad" lasted through forty years. Had it not been for Dr. Siebert's painstaking labors much that we know of the "railroad" would have been lost, since its superb illegality made written records dangerous, and those whose memories were printed deeply were coming to the end of their lives when Dr. Siebert's "vacation" began.

Accuracy, amid the recreation of so romantic and adventurous an undertaking as the "railroad," was his greatest concern. "This material I classified," he says, "by states and counties, so as to group related and corroborative evidence. Wishing to show graphically the extent of the Underground Railroad system, I mapped it for all the participating states. In only a very few instances did I find 'conductors' who knew a secret line of travel and its 'station keepers' across the state in which they operated. Such knowledge was extremely dangerous to one possessing it, if he should be caught aiding a fugitive slave. Most 'station keepers' and 'conductors' deliberately confined their knowledge to the 'station' from which they received their 'passengers' and the one—or the several on divergent lines—to which they sent or delivered them. Divergent lines were a safeguard in case of close pursuit. Pursuers could be sent by one trail, while the fugitive was spirited away by another. Mapping was a test of the reliability of my evidence. Sometimes a gap would show on my map until I finally heard from the 'conductors' who had managed the 'station' where the gap existed.

"Corroboration of reminiscences already gathered in the states came also from a group of fugitive slaves whom I went to see in Ontario, across the river from Detroit. The memories of their adventurous escapes from slavery and of the 'station keepers' who helped them on their way was surprisingly accurate. They knew dates, names, and places, and when I remarked on it, they said they had to remember because they couldn't write, and it was a matter of life and death. Having talked or corresponded with the parties they named, I knew they were giving correct narratives. I have never listened to more thrilling stories."

Harriet Martineau, the well-known English writer, once wrote to her Abolition friends, that the romance of the United States did not lie with the Indians or the frontiersmen but with the fugitive slaves. By Dr. Siebert's testimony, this is true.

Secondly, but not in scholarship or generosity, comes my friend Herbert Aptheker whose special domain is that vast and obscure region of court records, buried items in newspapers—the whole, unembellished picture of Southern internal struggle, a subject sadly neglected in relation to its scope and importance, and only now beginning to emerge at the hands of such historians as he, in a living, vivid, and significant form. My thanks to him, both for his personal help and his distinguished scholarship can be only half expressed.

Thirdly, must I acknowledge the unfailing assistance of Mr. H. W. Parker, Librarian of the Mechanics Institute in New York City. He never found it too much trouble to obtain for me the most unlikely books, and seemed to accomplish the impossible with unfailing regularity.

And lastly, but overshadowingly, I must say a very humble word for my family who ran errands, typed, grubbed in libraries, listened patiently, used blue pencils ruthlessly, acted as chauffeurs and cooks. What a strange world it would be without them!

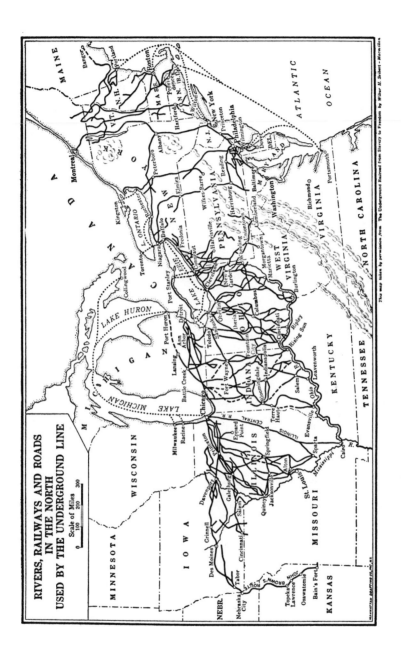

RIVERS, RAILWAYS AND ROADS
IN THE NORTH
USED BY THE UNDERGROUND LINE

Scale of Miles
0    100   200   300

This map taken by permission from The Underground Railroad from Slavery to Freedom by Wilbur H. Siebert - Macmillan

*LET MY PEOPLE GO*

*Go down Moses!  Way down in Egypt Land!*
*And tell old Pharaoh*
*To let my people go.*

This Negro spiritual came to be the slave's
hymn of freedom, and it was forbidden to sing
it. Harriet Tubman, one of the most heroic of
the colored Underground Railroad conductors, is said to have sung it to convey messages
to those groups of slaves who were gathering
to be led out to freedom by her.

# PROLOGUE

W E WHO live in America live here by the grace of revolution. Revolt is our heritage and the strength of our system.

The English immigrants rebelled against religious oppression, the Germans against political oppression, the Irish and the Italians against economic oppression. We cannot escape the deep roots which feed our branches.

The Africans also came to this country, but not to escape oppression. They came to be oppressed, to labor, to die, and to catch up their victimization into a blaze of revolt that burns as brightly in our national consciousness as those of the Germans who escaped the gallows, and the Irish who escaped the famines.

It is not a flattering picture that the black man makes of our country, but to those who love liberty it says again that Americans are not afraid to give their lives where equality is terrorized, where exploitation is not yet stamped out. It is not a picture, moreover, that is popular. Apparently there is something obnoxious about a black man defending himself, and for more than a hundred years we have been told, sternly or kindly, laughingly or threateningly that the black man is docile, tractable, stupid, sensuous, and dangerous to white civilization if—but of course that is impossible—he ever chose to assert himself.

There is a truth that cuts through the tissue of prejudice and fear, and, to those who care to listen, tells a story that stirs the heart and indicates a way for future peace to two races who for three centuries have built a continent together.

If "the negro on the whole yielded to the slave status with little show of resistance" as an eminent historian has said, how does one account for the fact that he employed sabotage, engaged in strikes, committed suicide, and mutilated himself; ran away, turned guerrilla, struck at his master through arson and murder? And more than anything kept the South in a real or imagined ferment? Why did armed men patrol the roads at night, or a Georgia woman write that she dared not trust her life with a single person on her plantation and never went to bed without an ax near her pillow? Why did state legislatures pass continuously repressive laws, taking away from the slave, one by one, the few privileges he had been allowed, until in 1860, when a flame of revolts broke out, he could hardly be classed as a human being with human rights?

How can the statement of docility be reconciled to the two hundred known revolts and conspiracies of over two hundred years, as revealed by the newspapers and the law courts of the South? These were not revolts of "drunken niggers" shouting imprecations, but armed conspiracies, carefully planned, nurtured for months, carried out with cold heads by those who desired, first freedom and then stark and complete revenge. The unknown conspiracies can only be imagined through the words of J. E. B. DeBow, the spokesman for the slavocracy, who maintained that the slaveholders kept their citadels well manned and seldom allowed disquieting news to cast a shadow on their autocracy.

How can the statement of submission be reconciled to the ingenuity and reckless courage that sent the Underground Railroad roaring through the best parlors in America or made the Abolition movement the conscience of the country? To understand these effects, one must understand the cause.

American slavery was a reign of violence, emotional as well as physical. It was a carefully devised and remorseless doctrine of racial inferiority. It halted the movement of progress for one half of the country, and brought the waste and destruction of a century, so that only today are we seeing the South emerge from a soil-exhausting, artificial economy.

There has been a long and honorable school of apologists for slavery, who still find it a matter of pressing concern to establish the fact that slavery was, on the whole, an agreeable and patriarchal manner of living, and draw gay pictures of Negroes singing at their work, and lovely women decorating the portico of classic plantations. But in that singularly uninhibited region of court records, newspaper items, plantation letters, and tales told by exhausted and defenseless fugitives, another picture is disclosed. The same weapons of tyranny, the same struggle to be free have not passed away, and now or then, they tell a story that is part of the world's cruelty and the world's perpetual desire to find a fuller way of life.

When slavery first came to America it did not have the open appearance of oppression. Much was said about the Christianization of the African voodoo worshipers; many plausible phrases were exchanged about the educational benefits that the heathen would receive at the hands of the colonial farmers. But these arguments scarcely concealed the only fact of importance; that a country was being built, and that men were needed, no matter how they came.

The first Negroes arrived officially in English America in 1619. They came from a people who for ten thousand years had raised and destroyed empires, provided a powerful Negroid culture which dominated the Mediterranean and gave full-blooded blacks and mulatto Pharaohs to the thrones of Egypt. Their ancestors were those who had given form to the culture of Ethiopia, that ancient land which to the Mediterranean world was the home "of gods and fairies," where Jove and Neptune banqueted each year among "the blameless Ethiopians." Their Negro empires had stretched from coast to coast and from Egypt to the tip of Africa. Black Africans first discovered the smelting of iron; under their influence music, painting, sculpture, and agriculture flourished for nine thousand years. The progenitors of the first American slaves were those who had fought against the battering tides of Romans, Persians, Byzantines, and at last with their empires weakened, had seen their civilization slowly collapse before the Moslems who brought religion and slave traders from the East, and the Christians who brought religion and slave traders from the West. Afro-Americans were themselves the children of a continent shattered by the political connivings of slave traders whose penetrations reached over a thousand miles into the interior, who made and unmade kings, who stirred up wars and bought the captives, and who cut a continent in half with their slave coffles. Between the Moslems and the Christians, over 100,000,000 Africans were taken from their land and a race degraded in a manner that history has never seen before or since.

Some of those first Africans were brought in as indentured servants. Sometimes they were men of considerable distinction—the erudition of a certain Job won him freedom and a place on the faculty of Cambridge University in England where he assisted in the translation of Oriental manuscripts. Their masters treated them with a benign paternalism, and many, at the end of their term of servitude, became small farmers or artisans. But, in time, the indentured period was transformed into perpetual servitude and by the middle of the eighteenth century, the Negro had ceased to be a man. He was now legally designated as a chattel and as such was subject to the restrictions of chattel. He could be used in transactions as a horse, a cow; he could be mortgaged like a house or furniture; if he escaped he could be advertised for like any other property. By the early nineteenth century when cotton had become a golden fiber, his judicial status had become a delicate blending of the grotesque and the practical. True he was a chattel, but could he not also be a person? If it were agreed to regard him as a man, untold embarrassment would follow; on the other hand to regard him as a thing without reason and responsibility would shift the burden of complicity in slave misdemeanors to the master, who was not prepared to support his principles thus far. The laws compromised, and a shifty and unstable balance that somehow managed to maintain itself with the skill of an acrobat became the acceptable status of a slave.

Yet to retain the slave's value, he must be stripped of his manhood, for otherwise his dependability would be subject to the instincts and actions of a human being. Long ago he had been told that he might not be the legal husband of any woman or the legal father of any children. Had legal relationships been allowed, husband, wives and children could not have been sold apart, and the profits of the slave trade would have been seriously impaired. He might no longer learn to read or write because only an unlettered and brutish man could fit himself into a brutish life. The laws that prevented his testimony against a white man were tightened, so that he had no practical protection against brutality, and actions of white men which were called misdemeanors were punishable by death when committed by him.

As time went on his movements were restricted by the pass which he must carry in his pocket, and any white man might arrest him if he did not give an acceptable account of himself. He could not assemble with his own race, unless a white man were present, nor might he trade or have intercourse with any white.

The vision of devoted and happy slaves was produced by the house servants whose contentment was frequently genuine, and who felt a close and affectionate concern for their masters. But house servants formed ten per cent of all the slaves and for the other ninety per cent, slavery meant inadequate food and clothing. "The weekly (food) allowance for a hand or full worker was a peck of corn and four quarts additional for every child, and a half bushel of sweet potatoes. This weekly fare the year round was with us supplemented in the season when the work was unusually heavy by rations of molasses or bacon or salt fish." James Madison allowed that nine dollars a year for food and clothing for a young slave was more than sufficient. For clothes, men were allowed one suit of pants and a shirt in the summer and one set in the winter, women two dresses a year. In South Carolina the working hours of a field hand were settled at fifteen hours for the summer and fourteen for the winter. Louisiana decreed two and a half hours rest in the twenty-four as obligatory on the master.

It was said that the Negro was stupid. Yet the slaveholder found it necessary to pass a formidable procession of laws, designed to fill up the gaps through which education might seep to him. The city of Savannah after repeated efforts to protect itself from "the great inconvenience" of educated slaves, was compelled to pass an ordinance "by which any person that teaches any person of color, slave or free, to read or write, or causes such person to be taught is subjected to a fine of thirty dollars for each offense; and every person of color who shall keep a school to teach reading and writing, is subject to a fine of thirty dollars, or to be imprisoned for ten days and whipped thirty-nine lashes."

The law was, of course, right. The hypothesis of the slave power was seldom at fault when dealing with its human chattels. The only hope for contentment in a slave was to keep him from detecting the inconsistencies of racial inferiority. It was established quite dispassionately that the law which curtailed religious instruction to the Negro came down from heaven. The church of the South followed politics in its subservience to the slavocracy, and Bishop Meade of Virginia placed the whole situation before his congregation of slaves clearly and without guile.

"Take care that you do not fret, or murmur, or grumble at your condition; for this will not only make your life uneasy, but will greatly offend God Almighty. Consider that it is not yourselves—it is not the people you belong to, but it is the will of God, who hath by his providence made you servants, because no doubt he knew that condition would be best for you in this world, and help you the better towards heaven if you would but do your duty in it. So that any discontentment at your not being free, or rich, or great, is quarreling with your heavenly Master and finding fault with God himself."

Such advice promulgated the ethics that were acceptable to the slavocracy, and the judiciary evolved an equally masterful code of law that bound the slave's body as completely as the slave church bound his soul.

"If more than seven slaves together are found in any road without a white person, twenty lashes apiece; for visiting a plantation without a written pass, ten lashes; for letting loose a boat from where it is made fast, thirty-nine lashes; for having any article for sale without a ticket from his master, ten lashes; for traveling in any other than the most usual and accustomed road, when going alone to any place, forty lashes; for traveling in the night without a pass, forty lashes; for being found in another person's Negro quarters, forty lashes; for hunting with dogs in the woods, thirty lashes; for being on horseback without the written permission of their master, twenty-five lashes; for riding or going abroad in the night, or riding horses in the daytime, without leave, a slave may be whipped, cropped, or branded in the cheek with the letter R, or otherwise punished, such punishment not extending to life, or so as to render him unfit for labor." In Virginia, a Negro could be executed for seventy-one crimes, a white man for three.

By no means was every slave whipped by every master for an offense, but the black man had no protection from the caprices of the white. The lash was the symbol of the slavocracy. The lash was never out of the overseer's hand, and it was used with a frequency that depended upon his temper and ambition. A good overseer was one whose only ambition was a greater production of crops. If he did not outstrip his employer's neighbor, his value was negligible to his employer. Frederick Law Omsted, quoting a small plantation owner in Mississippi, discovered "if they (the overseers) made plenty o' cotton, the owners never asked how many niggers they'd killed."

In the fast and ruthless effort to pour more cotton and sugar, rice and tobacco out of the South, it was no wonder "that the overseer presses everything at the end of the lash." Many masters held that a cruel overseer was not a competent one, but many masters did not know what was happening on their plantations or if they did, agreed with the verdict handed down in Tennessee, when an owner, claiming damages for the death of a pregnant slave, beaten by an overseer, was told by the court that the overseer's right to inflict punishment even if it resulted in death was inviolate if a question of obedience was involved.

Perhaps one wonders how valuable property could be treated in this way. We are assured by our modern apologists for slavery that cruelty seldom extended to murder, for what man would wantonly destroy his income? Yet men like Nehemiah Adams, earnest admirers of slavery, told of masters who killed their slaves or neglected them to the point of death. The most flagrant occurrences were brought to court, but the ones which fell short of death generally remained within the intimate obscurity of plantation life. Men with reputations as devils with their slaves were fully acceptable in the best society, although their acquaintances might not approve of their actions. After all, there were many subscribers to the belief—especially in the deep South—that it was more economical to work a slave to death in seven years and make a good profit than spare him and cut down on the income. The slave represented an investment, and from an investment, a good business man extracts the last possibility of gain. However, since the investment happened to be a rational being, subject to longings and bitterness, only force and cruelty seemed able to maintain him at the point of gain.

There were many kind masters who did not work their slaves unduly, who cared for them in sickness, who saw that they were well provided for, who felt a genuine and deep affection for certain individuals, and made their old age as comfortable as possible. Jefferson Davis established a form of self-government whereby his slaves settled their own difficulties and meted out their own punishments. He dismissed overseers if they were cruel, and he attached many of his slaves to him by kindness and generosity.

But the fact remained that a man like Jefferson Davis would be confused and troubled by a man like Frederick Douglass; that the most benign of slaveholders accepted without question the theory that the Negro was a natural object of slavery; that however kind and generous and tolerant they might be, they still held to the first premise of slavery —the inferiority of a race—and no benignancy, no tolerance, no kindness could wipe away this fact.

The apologists for slavery have maintained that every slave state had laws protecting the slave from hunger, cold and neglect. It is true that the laws were on the statute books, but each plantation was an isolated kingdom, and whether a law was obeyed or disobeyed depended on the humanity or ruthlessness of the master and overseer. Absentee ownership was a continuous blight in the latter days of slavery, and a kind master might not know what took place on his plantation. The cases of cruelty or negligence or violence that filled the courts were only those that broke through the cordon of the little empires. Lynch law was resorted to more times than court law, and as the estimable Mr. DeBow said on one occasion, "In our estates we dispense with the whole machinery of public police and public courts of justice. Thus we try, decide and execute the sentences in thousands of cases, which, in other countries, would go into the courts." The supreme courts were, on the whole, exceedingly fair to the slave and allowed him, on most occasions, the benefit of the doubt, but the local courts, controlled by slaveholding juries, recognized few "servile rights."

The very phraseology of certain laws makes one naturally question the ethics of a system which has found it necessary to prevent a master from "willfully cutting out the tongue, putting out the eye . . . or cruelly scalding, burning or depriving any slave of his limb or member, or inflicting any other cruel punishment other than by whipping or beating." In Louisiana the courts decided that if a man injured another's slave to the point where the slave was "entirely useless" and the owner recovered from the aggressor the full value of the slave, the slave by that transaction became the property of the man who rendered him useless, an extraordinary cynicism that even the law must have detected when it gave the slave, whose only remaining eye had been put out, into the compassionate hands of the man who had thus made him dependent on charity. As the judge who summed up the case observed: "The principle of humanity, which would lead us to suppose that the mistress whom he had long served, would treat her miserable blind

slave with more kindness than the defendant, to whom the judge-
ment . . . transfers him, cannot be taken into consideration in deciding
this case." The murder or mutilation of a slave was judged solely on
the basis of his impaired value. The humanitarian sentiments occasionally expressed in speeches, or the not infrequent compassion expressed by those slaveholders to whom bondage was increasingly dis-
tasteful, were merely gentle words with no alternative for action against
the stark rigidity and bloodlessness of the slave laws.

There is ample evidence to believe that Southern public feeling was
none too pleased by examples of slave cruelty; it was first, inhumane,
second, a reflection on the institution itself. One shocked newspaper of
Virginia in 1850 announced the general horror at an especially grue-
some slave murder in Clarke County and called triumphantly on Northerners to witness the swift course that justice would take. *The National
Era*, an Abolition paper, in its issue of November 6, 1851 announced,
with a certain grim satisfaction, that all the culprits had been tried
and acquitted. In slaveholding communities even the law could not
often rise above economic interests. It was of course impossible for two
things such as liberality and the frenzy for gain to live side by side.
Beyond that, in the deeper realm of the psychological, a small class of
slaveowners had been bred into a way of thought, had been reared
in an atmosphere of superiority, not only to the black man but also to
the poor white. It was taken in with the air, it was drawn in with the
milk of a black foster mother, it nourished the food, it went into the
whisky, it stung at the end of a lash. It was thundered from the pulpits,
it was blazoned in the newspapers, it was pounded into school books,
it was ground out with the law. It became bitterly impersonal; it
turned the South, as the slaves themselves said, into a great fortress,
with the guns trained on those within the fortress. It was a perpetual
state of war between the instincts of normal living and the artificial
necessity for conditioning and maintaining a state of mind which had
passed from the rest of the world with the eighteenth century.

Yet one cannot mistakenly assume that every brain in the South was
mesmerized by this mass hypnosis. The Negroes, who were its first
victims, never accepted a more degraded position without a struggle.
The poor whites, robbed of a future, in many instances broke through
their cultivated hatred and made common cause with the Negro. The
yeomanry, the middle class of tradesmen and small farmers, in spite
of their infatuation with the social prestige of the slavocracy, hated
the limitations it put upon themselves. They often spoke out in actions
or in words, but who heard them? Did the men who represented them

in the legislatures, or the men who sat for them in Congress, or the judges who entrenched the slave laws? Did the newspapers print their protests or the clergy support them? They were bitterly aware that all legislation and propaganda was for the exclusive benefit of slavery.

In Alabama, in South Carolina, in North Carolina, in Virginia, words that sounded very much like treason to the oligarchy were uttered by men whose names were famous in the state. William Gregg, speaking before the South Carolina Institute in 1851, credited the fact that "many a mother will tell you that her children are but scantily provided with bread, and much more scantily with meat," to the blight of slavery. "These may be startling statements but the members of our legislation who have traversed the state in electioneering campaigns can attest the truth."

There were also men whose names we do not know, small farmers in Tennessee, and the North Carolina hills, who hated the bitter competition of slavery and said so. Frederick Law Omsted, riding a horse from Texas to the seaboard states, reported his conversations night after night with his hosts along the way. "We're all poor folks here," one said, "nobody's got any black ones—only three or four." "It would be better," a friend interrupted, "if there warn't any at all . . . they ought to be in their own country and take care of themselves, that's what I believe and I don't care who hears it."

But with the rise of cotton from a petty despot to a tyrant, the conditioning of the South was effected at the end of the lash. It was quite impersonal. The big planters were no more personal devils than the members of any oligarchy, but the consequence of their actions, their dominance of the South, their control of thought, education and religion, their abrogation of a free press, free assembly and free speech, their calm and rationalized scrapping of the Bill of Rights and the Declaration of Independence make them fine progenitors of modern despots.

Here was no place for human values, either for the slave or the master. As long as the markets of the world demanded cotton, the human equation was reduced to the lowest minimum. Since the South was a vital part of the United States, the power of slavery dominated the country, and infected the North as well as the South. It was not, as Southern apologists thundered, a sectional problem off which the North must keep its hands. It controlled Congress, it controlled the Supreme Court, it controlled the army and navy. By 1860, eleven of our sixteen American Presidents had been slaveholders, seventeen of our twenty-eight judges of the Supreme Court, fourteen out of nineteen Attorney Generals, twenty-one out of thirty-three Speakers of the House, eighty out of one hundred thirty-four foreign ministers. Northern banking and shipping was bound up irrevocably with Southern economy, and without exception Federal laws were passed in favor of the South if a choice had to be made. Less than 400,000 slaveowners of the South had constituted themselves the spokesmen for the 11,000,000 inhabitants of the South; they called the Negro three-fifths of a man, which meant that although he could not vote, he increased the voting power which held him in bondage; they disfranchised the poor whites.

Yet in spite of this impregnable armor, slavery had within itself the seeds of its own destruction because it posited itself on the premise that one man could be the master of another, that the imposition of a will could stultify the expression of another's soul and govern the action of his body. It raised up as its natural consequence the forces that completed its destruction, for the Abolition movement represented the growth of theoretic freedom into fact.

It was inevitable that a deep moral and economic protest should expand into a vast concept of good for the greatest number and that Abolition should lead the way to an enlarged concept of life, capable of developing as far as human intelligence and intuition allowed, recognizing neither race, nor creed, nor sex nor previous condition of servitude as a bar to the highest accomplishments of the individual.

In the hands of the Abolitionists lay the morality of nineteenth-century America. Their principles were drawn from Jeffersonian radicalism and the Declaration of Independence. Their spiritual roots were sunk deep into a Christianity that repudiated orthodoxy, called slavery the Antichrist, and made the Bible a living instrument of freedom. Their development lay along the path of political progressiveness and marked its course by an unbroken movement through the antislavery societies, the Liberty party, the Free-Soil party, and reached its apex in Abraham Lincoln whose concern for the poor man's rights was a peak in our democracy.

This is the incomplete story of that spirit which endeavored to make freedom a living and unhampered reality, and succeeded only as far as the enlightenment of men allowed.

*Chapter 1*

# I WANT TO BE FREE

WHO laid the Underground Railroad? Perhaps a Paul Bunyan equipped with a frontier magic scooped up the earth with his fist and shot out his arm in tunnels north and south in the land. Perhaps a kind of voodooism made a display of black magic and transported a fugitive along rails that vaporized after him.

Nothing was wrong with these conjectures. They served an admirable purpose. They beclouded the facts, and the Underground Railroad depended for its life on mystification. But none of these things made it. The first fugitive slave who asked help from a member of his own race or the enemy race drove the first stake of that "railroad." And each one, as he followed, whether he went to the North, the South, the East, the West, added another tie until in the course of moral development the "railroad" extended to the lengths of necessity and assumed the shape of righteous indignation.

The hatred of enslavement came with the first slave and did not wane until the end of slavery. In 1526, when Spanish explorers landed with Negroes in what is now South Carolina, the first armed Negro uprising took place and established a continuity of action that found its climax in the swath of slave conspiracies and insurrections, cutting across the South of 1860.

The first slaves came to the American colonies in 1619. Within twenty-four years the problem of fugitives had reached such a pass that serious precautions were needed. The slaves, Negro and Indian, had found that the divergent loyalties of the Dutch, the French, the British provided them with unexpected friends. By 1643 the New England Confederation of Plymouth, Massachusetts, Connecticut, and New Haven, found the situation so precarious that their best legal parlance was invoked to assure mutual assistance and no harboring of another's slave.

Sometime before, New Netherlands had found it necessary to have an understanding with Maryland for the return of fugitives who fled into the South. The Dutch were not always polite about their restive servants. In 1659 they threatened, if more care was not taken to return their persistently absconding slaves, "to publish free liberty, access and recess to all servants, negroes, fugitives and runaways which may go into New Netherlands." Nor did they find any relief to the North, and scolded the French in Canada for passively maintaining a haven for runaways.

This understanding of freedom was so simple and catholic that laws against the white man and the free Negro were soon found to be insufficient. They must include the Indian as well.

The relations of the Negro and the Indian had begun before the arrival of the white man in the Western world. Balboa had found Negroes among the Indians of Darien. Perhaps they sprang from the African voyagers who were reported to have preceded Columbus in the discovery of the New World. Perhaps they were descendants of African pirates who were said to have been wrecked off the American coast. Although the Negro-Indian tie was not always strong or friendly, it persisted through marriage, through social relations, through occasional partnerships against the common enemy who seized and enslaved them both.

It persisted in the North, where the fugitives were absorbed into Canadian tribes, or the Northeast, where they found such sanctuary that the British, attempting to solve the problem, made a treaty with the Six Nations which included a clause of forfeiture. The chiefs signed, smiled, exchanged gifts, shook hands, and neglected to return the fugitives. There seemed to be no way to force them to give over Negroes who were by now friends or relatives or servants. It persisted in the South where the epic story of the Seminoles unwound itself nearly two hundred years after that day, in the early eighteenth century, when slaves of South Carolina learned of the lush land below the slaveless colony of Georgia, that warm, exotic land called Spanish Florida, where they were greeted by friendly Florida tribes, and the Spanish government gave them land in exchange for patrolling the border.

If the feet of Negro rebellion was the "railroad"—which as yet had no name—its fists were the armed revolts. In the seventeenth century, Negroes rose against white masters several times in Massachusetts and Virginia. In 1712 sentries were placed around the island of Manhattan because black men were in rebellion, and twenty-one slaves were either burned, hanged, broken on the wheel or hung alive in chains, while six committed suicide.

Black men revolted on shipboard; they made common cause with the Indian; in the first forty years of the eighteenth century, they raised thirty insurrections. Always for liberty. They never obscured their purpose. With "colors displayed and two drums beating," close to one hundred slaves of South Carolina marched one Sunday toward the free land of Florida, "calling out liberty."

Perhaps the New York slaves knew of the two hundred who, near Charleston in 1740, had a hope beyond their station. Probably they did, for one of the inexplicable and dismaying characteristics of slaves, which lent strength to the Underground Railroad, was their grapevine, their telepathy, their intercommunication, call it what you will. The lone fact remains that New York was terrorized. Fires appeared all over the city. Panic seized the inhabitants, and all those who were able to load their possessions into wagons started to safer ground in the country. The atmosphere of justice was so thick with fears and remembrances of the 1712 uprising that the trials of one hundred and forty-four Negroes, two white men, two white women and a Catholic priest became a circus. While the trials were going on, the fascinated watchers in New York saw barns burning across the Hudson River, and learned with the singular swiftness of terror that two—perhaps more—slaves had been executed and for what? For arson possibly—but more probably for the master's fear.

Still there was no peace. Within the next twenty-four years, the flames leaped up in New Jersey, in Virginia, in South Carolina, five times; aboard ships, in continued destruction of master's property, in sabotage, in poisonings, in self-mutilations when fingers or toes were cut off to lower that individual's value, in abortions with the express determination to bring no more slave children into the world, in killings by mothers of their children when they heard they were to be sold apart, in repeated suicides, in more and more daring escapes, in the first tenuous outlines of what would become the Underground Railroad.

There had always been antislavery sentiment in the country. Even in the days when slavery began to show a profit some men were set against it from humane, religious or economic reasons.

In the regions of domestic slavery it was quite evident, to those who cared to see, that two or three generations in America had blurred Africa in the mind of the Negro, and that his thoughts and influences were American. It was evident also that he breathed the same air as the whites, the air of the eighteenth century—that progenitor of liberal thought, of the end of the medieval mind, that harbinger of equal rights for all.

The revolutionary impulses of thirteen unhappy colonies tended to cut through the paradoxes of enslavement and open the eyes of many to the slavery in their midst. Men like Benjamin Franklin, Patrick Henry, Thomas Jefferson, while crying against the despotism of a foreign king, did not forget that they were despots. Abigail Adams, writing to her husband John, found herself wishing "most sincerely there was not a slave in the province; it always appeared a most iniquitous scheme to me to fight ourselves for what we are daily robbing and plundering from those who have as good a right to freedom as we have," while George Buchanan added stoutly that the Negro had already proven his ability in the arts, mathematics and philosophy, and that his inferior status was entirely due to the condition under which he lived.

In a world restless with a new age, slavery sat like a gaunt specter at the feast. Jefferson, reading the French Abbé Gregoire's extollation of the Negro's cultural achievements which stirred many questioning Americans, added the period to this discourse by drafting a denunciation of the slave trade for the Declaration of Independence.

But radicals must be put in their place. To "hold these truths self-evident; that all men are created equal, that they are endowed with certain inalienable rights; that among these are life, liberty and the pursuit of happiness" was as far as they were allowed to go, while prudent men explained their caution on the basis of the inevitable self-destruction of slavery within another generation.

Yet the conscience of many white men read a new meaning into their own insurrection. In Virginia alone ten thousand slaves were emancipated, and several Northern slaveholding states acted on the assumption that their slaves were free coincidental with the Declaration of Independence.

And black men, hearing as clearly as any the avowals of the rights of man, incendiary speeches and cries of liberty, struck seven times in their own behalf, in Georgia, in New Jersey, Massachusetts and the Carolinas. While the Continental Congress was attempting to solve the problem of Negro enlistment—the lessons they might learn with a gun in their hands were none too agreeable to the slaveholders— black men were deserting by the scores of thousands to the British who promised complete emancipation. Jefferson said that Virginia alone lost thirty thousand slaves in this manner. The North, less rigid in its traditions, promised emancipation to any slave who took up arms against the enemy, but the South still clung to its fears and its property, and left the British to liberate its slaves until, in 1779, Georgia and South Carolina provided for enlistment and eventual emancipation in order to lay at rest their great fears of potential insurrections.

But this did not halt the desertions to the British and the flights to Canada. For many slaves, wise beyond their station, doubted their masters' good intentions when the revolutionary spirit had died away. And they were right.

With the spirit of revolt triumphant but spent, many former masters found a curious gap in their lives which could only be filled by re-enslaving the property which they had relinquished in such a fine fever of patriotism. The epidemic of re-enslavement became so flagrant that the legislature of Virginia felt it prudent to pass an act of protection for the black soldiers.

Within those magnetized years three shadows were cast, the insurrectionist, the fugitive, and the free Negro, and the same form cast them all. But how many recognized this fact? How many saw the whole question mark of race free from the ossification of prejudice? Certain men of good will, humanitarians, immigrants, religionists, believed that a moral responsibility was due the black man, and they comprehended in a vague and individual manner the impulses of self-assertion, flight and rebellion. The religionist grieved that the slave knew nothing of Jesus; the humanitarian was troubled that emancipation would be delayed through his ignorance. Both situations could be remedied by education, and within and without the ranks of the slaveholders, reading and writing was given to the Negro. In some cases he gained enough knowledge to become tutor to his master's children. Here and there a school was started: in 1787 the Manumission Society opened the African Free School in New York to give to the colored children the opportunities of free education, and it was not for some years that a similar organization was available to white children. It was all very small, too small; the help came from individuals, not as an instrument of social good.

But this was the period of the Negroes' greatest hope, with the future shaping a promise of breathless liberality. They reared up leaders, men like Jacob Bishop who became pastor to white communicants in a Baptist church at Portsmouth, Virginia; men like Benjamin Banneker who helped to lay out the city of Washington; women like the slave Phillis Wheatley who became an advanced scholar of Latin and history and wrote poetry that was outstanding in her time; men like Richard Allen who bought himself from his master, became a preacher of great power to both the whites and the blacks, and established the independent Negro church. They came up quickly, individuals who asked nothing that they could not prove in accomplishment. To forget that there were blacks and whites or, if the whites found that impossible, to be allowed to live their own lives within the framework of their common country.

They established schools, churches, they became doctors, artists, merchants, artisans, soldiers, scholars, with the cloud of slavery hanging over them. Free Negroes, in spite of the laws against them, persisted in regarding themselves as citizens, paid taxes, founded their benevolent, masonic and insurance societies, sent out their own missionaries and, above everything, never lost sight of their desire for that anonymous liberty which would permit them, without the constant traps of prejudice, to be men and women.

Driven by economic discrimination, by the white laws which were designed to make the condition of the free Negro too unattractive for the slave to covet, the free Negroes still made fools of themselves over freedom and sweated like field hands to buy their wives or their husbands or their children before they were sold out of their reach. As the laws against manumission—the freeing of a slave—became more ruthless, the wife might remain her husband's slave or the husband his wife's, but their objective had been accomplished; they could not legally be separated. As an occasional free Negro grew rich and prospered he too bought slaves. When the law permitted, he freed them, and when the law stood in the way he allowed them to live as free men, separated only by a technicality.

But free Negroes were an anachronism to a slave society. To individual benevolence and individual efforts at self-assertion, the slavocracy had only one answer—suppression—and eventually the only difference between the slave and the freeman lay in the ability of the free Negro to hold property. In all other ways his degradation was complete. His so-called freedom became as hard to preserve as it had been to acquire. For any number of small offenses he might be sold back into slavery with no redress, no appeal. The free Negro was the whipping boy for every insurrection. He was the despised and the feared. Yet how could it be explained that the degradation of the free Negro stimulated flight? That every act of oppression, damming one outlet, broadened another?

Every flight represented from the personal point of view the bravest and most reckless of actions. If a slave proposed to run away, where would he go, how would he reach that mythical land of freedom? Let us assume that he struck out blindly, determined on one thing only, to leave the hated confines of the plantation. To him white men were enemies, the world away from the plantation an uncontemplated wilderness. Perhaps the roads around the plantation had been his only world. But he struck out, whenever the chance presented itself, usually without premeditation. Possibly he would slip into a thicket during his work; perhaps the overseer's back was turned when the slaves were going to their quarters at the end of the day; maybe he would disappear into the night and find his way like a cat with eyes in the dark. Often a friend or a brother went with him, for this action in duplicate might mean mutual protection.

When his loss was discovered and the cry raised, he was perhaps lying within a mile of the house; he might be lying even closer where he could see the slaves running, the dogs barking, the overseer and the master gesticulating with the motions of men who have been hoodwinked.

Perhaps the woods and the swamps near the plantation would be the closest to freedom he would ever come. In the wind, rain and cold he might lie out on small islands or in the mountains for months or years, getting his food by hunting or fishing or stealing. There he might build a cabin or live in a cave, and lead a wild and not unpleasant life. He might conceivably find life so congenial that he slipped back through the mountains, through valleys and all the danger spots, and got his wife and children, perhaps even a friend or two. And always a few provisions, stolen under the eyes of a household slave who said nothing, did nothing but open her eyes wide till all the whites showed, and, after the first startled recognition, bundle the meal, the side of a hog, the molasses into a bag and push the wanderer out into the darkness again.

The inner, unspoken lives of the slaves were as deep and unexplored as the waters of a well. A white man would see his own reflection and be satisfied. But in the dark unmoving waters which the light did not reach there was no reflection whatever of the master. He was as far from their lives and thoughts as India is from the Arctic. It took the white man several generations to accept this fact, and many never learned it and only cursed "the flighty niggers" who one week swore they had no desire for freedom and the next week disappeared. So now, when the slave in the kitchen was questioned about the lost side of hog, she giggled with chagrin, but she knew nothing; her stupidity was abysmal, her imagination fruitful and loquacious, and in the end she was scolded or given a few cuts with the lash because she was so stupid.

The bayous of Louisiana and the swamps of Florida, the mountains of the Atlantic states and the backlands of Mississippi and Alabama all sucked in the fugitive like a man-eating plant. He was called a maroon, and as such was the legal victim of any man who cared to track him down. It did not matter whether he stayed within his deeply concealed community, built houses, raised cattle or became a farmer, or whether he became a desperado and raided farms and villages at night. He was an unredeemed Negro; and his success was a constant inducement to other slaves who knew, out of the trees, from the air, God knows where, that he was cleverer than his master. More than that, having accomplished his freedom, he was apt to become infected with a desire to share it, or a desire for vengeance, or a desire to set at nothing the things that had in the past set themselves over him, or any of the other desires that made an insurrectionist. Nothing could rouse a slaveholder to action more quickly than this thought.

Some of the maroon encampments were small countries in themselves. The Exiles in Florida were maroons. Coming from the Carolinas, Alabama, and Georgia they remained deep in the luxuriant wilderness of northern Florida, where their canoes could follow the course of a river far into the bayous that frightened and bewildered a white man, where they could raise their crops on the broad flat plains that ran toward the border of Georgia, and watch the Andalusian cattle, inherited from the Spaniards, grazing on the flat pasture lands. The dwellers in the Dismal Swamp of Virginia were maroons, two thousand of them, lying between North Carolina and Virginia. Many of them, born in the recesses of the swamp, had never seen a white man. Those who lived nearer the outside world, traded regularly with the Negroes or the white people who lived on the edge of the swamp, although to do so was illegal.

But these encampments were few and hard to find; the slave could only hear of them by vague report. When he set out blindly for freedom anything might lie to the north or the south, the east or the west. Beyond the confines of his plantation world was only what rumor, imagination, or his own intelligence created.

When, one by one, the Northern States inclined away from slavery, the slaves knew it almost as soon as the master, and the North then coalesced into a gigantic outstretched hand. But the fugitive slave was helpless—or nearly so. He might perform the initial act of escape— he might even stumble on the information that acted as a compass to uncounted slaves, that moss grew only on the north side of trees— but unless he wished to become a maroon, he might wander about until starvation overtook him or the slave catchers laid hands on him unless he could find a friend.

As fugitives began to spread like a long dark trickle that was presently to broaden into a stream, new laws sprang up—new laws that must be circumvented. This could not be done from within, for the slave had exhausted his *resources* by running away. It could not be done from the rim, for the free people of color could not escape their black skins. It could only be done from the outside by men of good will who loved righteousness more than the laws of men. And who, in that greedy, eager, expanding country, loved righteousness more than the laws of men?

There were some individual answers—the Scotch-Irish settlers and the German immigrants, the isolated handful of Jews, certain religionists. But only one seemed to lift itself into a generalization—the Quakers. They said, "He has made of one blood all nations of men for to dwell on all the face of the earth." They also said, "The stranger that dwelleth with you shall be unto you as one born among you and thou shalt love him as thyself."

Many of the Quakers who settled in the South freed their slaves and set up schools for them. In addition they reasoned with their recalcitrant members who had become wealthy with slaves, and they attempted to provide compensation for the slave when he was freed and see that he was securely settled in his new way of life. For Friends in the South this meant social ostracism, for a decent white man did not work with his hands.

But how was a runaway to know these friends, since the consciences of the Quakers would not allow them to entice slaves from their masters? Occasionally word filtered through the slave quarters of planta-tions that men who wore a certain dress were their friends. The word even penetrated beyond the slaves, for the first mention of any sys-tematic aid to slaves came in two letters written by George Washing-ton in 1786. Speaking of an escaped slave belonging to Mr. Dalby of Alexandria, he observed, that "a society of Quakers formed for such purposes, have attempted to liberate him." Later in the same year he wrote of one of his own slaves who had escaped, "The gentleman in whose care I sent him has promised every endeavor to apprehend him; but it is not easy to do this, when there are numbers who would rather facilitate the escape of slaves than apprehend them when run away."

This everlasting preoccupation with freedom of antislavery men, black and white, helped to make rigid the slaveowner's mind. And the failure of a new country to be consistent to its principles meant that laws must be pressed down on a people who had been concerned only with remedying inconsistencies. The Fugitive Slave Law of 1793 was a triumph of this inversion.

It had come as the result of a plea from the Pennsylvania Society for the Abolition of Slavery for the extradition of three kidnapers who had seized a free Negro in Washington, Pennsylvania, in 1791 and taken him to Virginia. The governor of Virginia found that no extradition proceedings had been provided for in the law. The governor of Pennsylvania promptly called the attention of Congress to this oversight, and a committee was formed to bring in a bill that would permit the seizure of any person "charged in any state with treason, felony or other crime." But with this provision went the joker, showing how incapable the slavocracy was of withholding its coloring from any legal matter. The law also provided "the mode by which a person held to service or labor in one state under the laws thereof, escaping into another, shall be delivered up on the claim of the party to whom such labor may be due." It so happened that if the magistrate, dealing with the case, dismissed the alleged fugitive for want of evidence, he received no fee; but if he found him to be a slave, he received from five to twenty dollars for his effort. Moreover a fine of five hundred dollars for harboring or preventing the arrest of a fugitive was extracted from the friend of the victim.

Now such a law would split wide men's opinions. A law which permitted no evidence by the Negro and accepted a white man's word as final would startle a man into partisanship. Local ordinances were soon necessary to put teeth into the law, for an extraordinary diffidence sprang up about the apprehension of fugitives. And every new provision of the law seemed only to offend men who had a respect for justice, as Mr. Washington—a paternal but persistent slaveholder—had ample proof when he withheld a demand for the return of his fugitive from Portsmouth, New Hampshire, having been advised that the town was in no mood to give him up, even if he were the property of the President.

The Negro should have been glad of the law of 1793. Without the emotions which it engendered, he might have continued to pitch headlong into the North and find no friends, for the Yankee stock—the New Englanders of Ohio, the Anglo-Saxons and Dutch of the middle states— were notoriously fond of minding their own business unless they were assaulted in their most vulnerable spot—their conscience. And this conscience was most effectively manipulated by the law of 1793.

Slaves leapt into rebellion again at the word of San Domingo. There, in the wash of the French Revolution, an island full of slaves rose like one man, slaughtered the whites and established a Black Republic.

The effect of this cannot be exaggerated. It was a loud voice in the night, terrifying people from their sleep; it was the most gigantic and successful bid for freedom that the black man had made. The horrors of the massacre made the slaveholders of the United States beat out repressive laws and forget the liberality of their rebellious days. It was the worst thing that could have happened to the slavocracy in the United States. Within six hundred miles of the slaveholders was a government of Negroes, established through the overthrow of white supremacy and maintaining itself as well as many white governments. The sentiments that it had made into facts were more contagious than the plague. Toussaint L'Ouverture was the black man's Napoleon.

His heroism rang in slave cabins; slaves meeting on the road exchanged his name; educated Negroes used him and his exploits to tell of the wrongs done the colored man and whisper the word of escape. Refugees from San Domingo, settling in Baltimore, Norfolk, Charleston, New Orleans, brought stories of black vengeance that made the flesh of the master creep and the scalp of the slave tingle.

The revolutionary words, liberty, fraternity, equality, fed the fires of servile insurrection, which had been lighted by the depression and the famines which had numbed the South in those years between 1791 and 1802. From New Jersey to Louisiana the uprisings spread. Arsons, murders, and suicides grew, and the long irregular line of fugitives shaped into less dreamy form the outlines of the Underground Railroad.

In 1800, one, who in another land and under different circumstances would have been called a hero, made his name ring through the South. He was called Gabriel and he was a Virginia slave. He loved liberty more than his life and he had planned "to purchase a piece of silk for a flag, on which they would have written 'death or liberty.'" By his testimony he and his lieutenants, who, for four months had been meeting under the guise of religious worship, had raised ten thousand slaves. Every white man, woman and child encountered on their march to Richmond was to pay for the enslavement of the blacks. Every man, woman and child, that is, except the French who had taught them the words, "Liberty, equality, fraternity," the Quakers and the Methodists who were lovers of liberty, and the poor white men whose privations lay at the same door as the Negroes.

One thousand slaves met at a brook on an August night, armed with the weapons that had been made under the tutelage of Gabriel's brother. Under Gabriel, who had some knowledge of military science, they had planned their strategy, and before morning they intended to send out their message to "their fellow Negroes and the friends of humanity throughout the continent," increase their force to 50,000, and take possession of the countryside.

How near they came! Only a torrent of rain from which "every animal took shelter," and two timid house slaves who betrayed them, stood between them and their revenge. Richmond, shaken by what she had escaped, demanded military protection, and then her vengeance. Gabriel, captured on board a ship, declined to reveal the pattern of his revolt. That he bore himself with dignity seemed to astonish those who saw him. The New York *Commercial Advertiser* told the story more willingly than the Virginia newspapers which, for "prudence," had submitted to a censorship. "The trials of the Negroes are suspended until the opinion of the Legislature can be had on the subject. This measure is said to be owing to the immense numbers who are interested in the plot, whose death should they all be found guilty and be executed will nearly produce the annihilation of the blacks in this part of the country."

The state said that between two thousand and ten thousand slaves were involved, but it could only find evidence to hang thirty-five and banish ten. Jefferson, writing to Monroe, had tried to stem the tide of vengeance. "The world will forever condemn us if we indulge a principle of revenge, or go one step beyond absolute necessity. [The world] cannot lose sight of the rights of the two parties, and the object of the unsuccessful one."

But revenge against Gabriel did not end the revolts. The years 1801-1802 found white men making common cause with the Negroes. One slave named Arthur made the issue clear. "I have taken it on myself to let this country be at liberty . . . both blacks and whites will join with me to help free the country. I mean to lose my life in this if they will take it."

As the revolts were increasing at the very time that returning prosperity was making cotton king, retribution became swifter and more inexorable. The era of lynch law began.

Unrest, amounting to violence, licked up again and again in the years before and after the War of 1812. Soil exhaustion, which led to depression, the blockades that came with the war, the revolutions in South America and in Mexico and the antislavery agitation sweeping in with Bolivar, were felt or known by the slaves, and added to their tugging restlessness.

New Orleans, one afternoon in 1811, was thrown into a panic by a straggling procession of carts filled with terrified country people who told of a great uprising to the north. Troops sent out found five hundred slaves armed with scythes, "determined no longer to submit to their situation." They were led by a West Indian who had received his baptism in San Domingo. With a crude military strategy, they held off the soldiers for eleven days. When at length they were subdued, sixty-six were executed on the spot, seventeen were missing and sixteen were subsequently beheaded and their heads impaled along the road for sixty miles.

During the War of 1812, the dilemma that had plagued the slave masters during the Revolution came upon them once again. The British offered emancipation; the slaves went to them by the thousand score. Would the masters dare put guns in their hands and ask them to turn against the British? Only if emancipation were promised by the Americans as well. The promise was made; thousands came into the American army.

But insurrections continued and were crushed in Virginia, Louisiana and Kentucky in 1812, in the District of Columbia, South Carolina, Virginia in 1813, in Maryland and Virginia in 1814. Secret societies for freedom were uncovered and a song, said to have been written by a slave, "Arise! Arise! Shake off your chains!" was sung by conspirators.

In the deep wide stream of Negro consciousness the expression of unrest had become as fluid as the imagination. Conspiracies, uprisings, violence, were not the only weapons. There was a peaceful weapon as well, and men began to believe with something like a superstitious awe in the rumors of a mysterious system of escape.

The year 1804 emerges as the date of the "incorporation" of the Underground Railroad, because, from the occurrences in Columbia, Pennsylvania, it seemed, that year, to gather force and speed, and to assume a shape that would allow future historians to satisfy their tidy spirits with a ring around that date. However, to prove the exposed position of the historian, it should be added that this underground system did not receive its official name for twenty-seven years.

The "incorporation" came about through the purchase by General Thomas Boude, a revolutionary officer, of a slave named Stephen Smith whom he brought back to his home in Columbia in 1804. After a few months, Stephen Smith's mother ran away and came to find her son. The Boudes took her in and gave her a home. In a few weeks a determined spinster arrived on horseback, and marched into the Boude kitchen without knocking. Seeing her fugitive property, she ordered Stephen's mother to pack up her things and come along. Surprised at opposition, she seized the mother and attempted to carry her bodily to her horse. Young Stephen, hearing his mother's cries, rallied General Boude who arrived on the run and ordered the woman off.

The ruthless and arrogant manner of the slaveholding spinster helped to rouse the townsmen who had already become conscious of the activities of slaveholders' spies. Their indignation mounted when fugitives, attempting to reach the safety of the town, were seized or shot. Finally their sympathy was consolidated by the arrival of fifty-six slaves who had been manumitted by a Virginia planter but were now the frightened objects of litigation by his heirs. For two years the heirs had tried, without success, to persuade the courts to return them to slavery. Their cause became the cause of the slow-acting but justice-loving Columbians, most of whom were Quakers or the descendants of Quakers.

With such poundings on their consciences, friends of the Negro could do nothing less than organize their sympathy in practical ways.

In these first few years at the turn of the century, white friends began to pave the road to freedom—friends who were strong enough to protect them; friends who would grow with the next sixty years, lie for them, go to prison for them, be put out of the church for them, die for them. And, what was probably more important than all the others put together, see nothing strange in working side by side with them and attempting to create a common heritage out of the confusions, the nobilities, the greediness and the grandeur of the American dream.

*Chapter 2*

## WHERE ARE MY FRIENDS?

MR. ISAAC TATUM HOPPER was twenty-six when he went to see a certain imperious and distinguished visitor to Philadelphia upon whom he had never clapped his eyes. Mr. Hopper was not only young but inexperienced, and he had a not unnatural dread of a wealthy and potentially indignant slaveowner. But Mr. Hopper was a Quaker and consequently he put his duty before his personal feelings.

It must have been a painful situation for the slaveowner as well, for after Mr. Hopper's diffidence had been overcome, he lost no time in revealing himself as the emissary of his host's slave. Mr. X's slave, Charles, had some months before learned that if he stayed in Philadelphia for six months he would become free, but his master had apparently overlooked this detail. Mr. Hopper modestly made little of his own share in the proceedings; he merely informed Mr. X that a lawyer had drawn up the proper papers and Charles himself would presently serve them on his former master.

Mr. X was very angry; he expressed himself vituperatively on the subject of men who stole gentlemen's property. Did Mr. X know what he was facing? Did he know that he stood with one foot on the slippery roadway that ran underground and that Mr. Hopper was one of those mysterious devils who would in time be called "conductors"? Probably Mr. X had a faint suspicion, for slaveowners were seldom naïve fellows. Yet Mr. Hopper had acted within the confines of the law, and Mr. X could only chaff in impotent rage. Mr. Hopper always worked within the confines of the law, and in a long and spectacular career was never known to make a conspicuous mistake.

In the frame of this room in an unknown house in Philadelphia about the year 1800 one may see in this Quaker all the elements that were to compose the answer to the fugitive's need; the friend who could not be intimidated by the rage of the slavocracy, the religionist whose conscience made him a permanent advocate of freedom, the man whose wits were quicker than action and his action quicker than thought.

In time Charles arrived, a "nigger" no longer—now a free man. He

25

delivered the lawyer's note to his former master, and the latter, caught in a position which had no precedent for him, was obliged to admit that he had been outmaneuvered. That did not mean, however, that he could not outmaneuver Charles. So he proposed that since Charles was now free, he allow himself to be hired to drive his former master back to Virginia. But Charles, who had had sufficient experience with the slaveholding temperament, refused; Virginia would be no place for him. Then Mr. X in a final fury ordered Charles to take off his clothes immediately, as every stitch belonged to him. Mr. Hopper, one imagines, was rather proud to watch the aptness of his protégé and considerably amused to see him start out the door onto the street as naked as the day that he was born. Mr. X, who was a modest man, roared in dismay and seizing him violently, dragged him back into the room and ordered him to put on his clothes again.

When Charles finally emerged onto the street, Mr. Hopper was with him. Another rail had been laid on the "road."

Isaac Hopper had become the friend of the colored man when he was nine. He had loved an old colored man and had been deeply touched by his story of home and family torn from him. By the time he was seventeen, Isaac was giving what assistance he could, and before long he had joined the Philadelphia Manumission Society. His duty here was to give advice and legal protection to the Negroes who applied to the society. The operations of the work were public and scrupulously legal with only an occasional assistance to the letter of the law. The preliminaries were underground—at night in the home of a friend when a frightened fugitive clung to the shadows and at any hour when a quick peremptory tap on Hopper's door meant that one of the colored people of the town was seeking assistance for a hidden runaway who had reached the end of his resources.

Pennsylvania, on the edge of the slave states, was not only an objective of fugitives but also the prowling place of kidnapers, and outrages were constantly occurring. These outrages became the special concern of Friend Hopper. In time he became such a master of the loophole that a slaveowner would rather deal with the plague than with him.

He always employed the simplest devices first, the direct action. On one occasion he learned from a distracted mother that her child had been kidnaped and taken on board a ship that was to sail immediately for a Southern port. It was early in the morning, but he scrambled into his clothes and set off for the river. There he commandeered a horse and galloped as fast as he could along the bank until, with a slow wind assisting him, he came almost abreast the boat. A ferry house lay at this point and while the ship moved opposite him in the river, he cajoled and browbeat the ferry man to take him aboard and intercept the ship in the center of the stream.

The ship, believing another passenger was coming aboard, sent down a rope, and the redoubtable Isaac Hopper drew himself up, hand over hand. On deck, he wasted no time. He wished to see the captain, and he pushed his way to the forecastle through the perplexed crew and the slightly apprehensive passengers. He demanded the child without any waste of words. The captain shrugged, disclaimed any responsibility, and said quite plainly that he did not intend to interfere between a man and his property. Isaac Hopper, spreading his legs to steady himself against the swell, settling his hat more firmly against the rising wind, drew from his pocket the volume which contained the laws of Pennsylvania and read them then and there to the captain as though he were exhorting him from Scripture. The law of Pennsylvania protected the free Negro, and a child followed the condition of its mother, hence this child was free. The law of Pennsylvania, moreover, penalized the aider and abettor in a kidnaping. The captain, not to be outdone in respect for the law, gave hurried orders to remove the child from the boat. The ferryboat man, waiting with a slightly opened mouth below, was reaching out his hands to help the child aboard.

The indignation of the kidnapers was in proportion to their indifference to the law. They became noisy and violent, and attempted to throw Friend Hopper overboard. As there were five or six of them, it looked as though they would succeed. Mr. Hopper had no friends but the boatman and the child, who could only fish him out after he was ducked. But he wasted no time in alarm; he caught one of the kidnapers by the coat and cheerfully announced that this gentleman would have to come along if he went into the river. The other assailants pounded his hand with their canes, but he promptly seized the skirt of another coat. The boatman, meanwhile, roused by such a fine sight, maneuvered his boat into a position directly below the struggle, and Friend Hopper, releasing his hold on the coat as abruptly as he had obtained it, sprawled the kidnaper on the deck and himself tumbled into the ferry.

It was the colored people who knew first when a calamity had befallen one of their own race and it was Isaac Hopper who knew it second. If we might arrest him in the action most characteristic of his love of justice it would be as he forced in a door and cut the cords that held a fugitive. He performed this operation so many times that he must finally have been able to do it with little preparation.

On one occasion he was roused in the very early morning and told by his colored emissaries that a fugitive had been seized by a master and was to be sent out of the state as quickly as possible. When Hopper reached the tavern where the fugitive was held, the landlord blocked his way. But Hopper pushed the landlord aside and flew up the stairs to the room where the captive was held. He found Levin, the fugitive, with his hands bound and a guard of six men.

"What are you going to do with this man?" he cried before he had gotten beyond the open door. The answer descended on him like a cyclone. In less time than he had taken to mount the stairs he found himself hurtling through the window. His state of mind, he related later, was so feverish with excitement that he barely knew what happened to him. Time was precious. He picked himself up, his clothes torn, his body bruised, and while his attackers were still brushing their hands over his summary despatch, rushed around to the front door and darted up the stairs. But this time the door was locked. With time pressing so hot against his mind, he flew to the yard again, climbed to the roof of a pent house by means of a high board fence, and forced his way into an adjoining room. He re-entered the fugitive's room in full possession of himself, for he had his penknife open and while he exclaimed, "Let me see if you will get me out so soon again!" cut the cords that bound Levin and crying "follow me!" opened the door and dashed down the stairs as fast as he could go. His startling reappearance had struck the guards like an apparition. By the time they moved, Hopper and the fugitive were halfway down the street. The guards could only join the mob that had quickly started after them. The two fugitives ran, and the rest shouted, "Stop thief!" hot on their heels for half a mile, until they reached the office of a justice of the peace.

The justice looked at the energetic little man with the same disbelief as the guards had done. "Good heavens, Mr. Hopper!" he cried, "what brings you here this time of the morning in such a trim and with such a rabble at your heels." And when it had been explained to him, he could only say between his laughter, "They don't know you as well as we do, Friend Hopper."

That statement could not be taken too literally, for slaveholders grew to know him all too well. When the worst came to the worst, he might keep a case in court for three or four years until the claimants were sick to death of it, and willing to make any settlement. The law possessed an elemental clarity until submitted to the benign scrutiny of Mr. Hopper. Then it became a strange and plagued instrument designed for the harassment of slaveholders.

In his person, Isaac Hopper represented the quintessence of the

Underground Railroad—which was neither a railroad nor underground, but merely a conviction set to action. He was no more and no less devoted than certain obscure partisans, but his duties forced a more intense light upon him, since Philadelphia was the hub of this movement which was spreading like veins through the body of the state.

In these early days, it operated with great simplicity and directness. When a man emerged from slavery, weak and gasping, a friend opened his door to him, hid him from his pursuers until his fatigue and weakness were past, and then hurried him along in the protection of the night across fields, through woods, over rivers, to the house of the next friend. Or, if more than two or three needed help, loaded them into wagons, and covered them with bags or farm produce, and carried them to the next "station" in the daylight as though merely traveling on his own business.

The need for skill and resourcefulness is evident when one realizes that arrest would mean bankruptcy, for few of these friends were in a position to pay a $500 fine. They learned very early the advantage of discretion; many times information was conveyed from one friend to another by innuendo so that no names need be mentioned and no information given which could be used against them if arrested. Strangers were tapped for their sentiments in ways as varied as the imagination. A Mr. Coines on one occasion took it upon himself to lead a fugitive to the next friendly house. It was an all-night trip. Coines and the Negro took turns walking and riding their lone horse. When daylight came, they were still some ten miles from their destination, and danger might spring out at them from any house. Coines concealed the fugitive in a cornfield until he discovered the sentiments of the farmer who owned the land on which they stood. While hanging over the gate, he saw the farmer approaching and called out to him a question about stray "niggers," letting it be guessed that he was a slave catcher. The farmer gave him a cold and unfriendly look and answered sharply that Negro-catching was a bad business. Coines then told him with a great show of bluster that he was within his rights according to the law and ought to have his "nigger." The farmer, thereupon, set down his pails and repeated to him the golden rule. That was all Coines needed to know. He jumped over the gate and explained to the farmer that a fugitive was hiding in his cornfield who was badly in need of help. The farmer fed two strangers that morning and when Coines returned to his home, a new "station" on the underground road was in operation.

Southeastern Pennsylvania was full of those who though not habitual lawbreakers were willing to help a fugitive who, in the dangers he endured, made a simple and impressive appeal. To the Quakers, respectful of law and order, this meant a fine and skillful juggling with the truth. The letter was not broken, but it found itself in many strange and unexpected postures. The Quaker could not lie; he was also a believer in nonresistance. John and Mary Smith showed how such a problem could be handled without compromising their principles.

Two women fugitives appealed to them for protection. The agents of their owners were close behind and not a moment could be lost. Without a word, Mary drew them into the house and John stationed himself by the door. Taking the girls into the bedchamber, she pulled her bed apart and lifting the mattress told the girls to lie upon the ropes. She then replaced the mattress, made up the bed and smoothed the counterpane so that not a wrinkle betrayed a hiding place. John, meanwhile, was struggling to master not only his temper but the agents of the slaveowner who were peremptorily demanding to search his house. His principles of nonresistance were being sorely tried when his wife appeared in the doorway and said, "Let them come in, John. Thee knows there are no slaves here." She told no lie. To the Quakers, no such creature as a slave existed.

Against these humble friends the slaveowner had a singular paucity of weapons, being forced to alternate between violence and new laws, and after the new laws wavered, violence. By 1806 it was evident that all amendments, intended to give force to the law, were delusions, so violence struck again. A large piece of iron was thrown at James Lindley, a Pennsylvanian, as he walked through the streets of Havre de Grace. He was then beaten until three of his ribs were broken, a number of teeth knocked out, and he, unconscious, left on the street for dead. Mr. Lindley happened to be an innocent man. He had been mistaken for Jacob Lindley, a Quaker who was an active guide on the underground road.

In 1809 the Reverend George Bourne of Virginia felt it his duty to put in print his deeply righteous indignation against slavery. Mr. Bourne did not stay very long in his home after that. He and his family were soon forced onto the dark and unfamiliar road of the fugitives. They finally reached Pennsylvania where by 1816 Mr. Bourne's hatred of slavery had blossomed into one of the first vigorous Abolition volumes: *The Book and Slavery Irreconcilable* in which he advocated immediate abolition of slavery as the price of saving the Union.

Two years later the slaveholders drew up their third and most damning line: a repudiation of the Declaration of Independence. Their own rebellion must still have been lying on the horizon of their minds, yet when the Reverend Mr. Gruber, a Methodist minister of Maryland, preached a sermon against slavery, supporting his words by quoting from the Declaration of Independence, he was arrested and tried for inciting insurrection.

His young attorney spoke with great feeling. "Slavery is a blot upon our national character, and every real lover of freedom confidentially hopes that it will be effectually wiped away. And until the time shall come when we can point without a blush to the language held in the Declaration of Independence, every friend of humanity will seek to lighten the galling chains of slavery."

Thirty-eight years later, this attorney, become Chief Justice Taney of the Supreme Court, handed down the Dred Scott decision and observed with singular irony that "the enslaved African race were not intended to be included in the Declaration of Independence."

By 1807 the dilemma of slaveowners was acute. The Constitution had provided that in this year legislation should be undertaken to bring an end to slave importation. With the pronunciamentos of Washington, Jefferson, and Madison against the whole system of enslavement, with the worn-out earth and the slow indifferent labor of the slaves, many had foreseen in this year the beginning of the end of slavery.

The framers of the Constitution had set this year apart for that purpose. No one had told them that Eli Whitney would take the slow ginning of cotton out of the hands of slaves in 1794 and run it through his fabulous machine. They had not foreseen that five hundred pounds of cotton would now be cleaned a day instead of the five to which they had been accustomed. Nor that in England Arkwright would build a spinning machine and Hargreaves a weaving machine which would turn Southern cotton into pure gold.

Why, without slavery this golden age would be impossible! Cheap labor, fast breeding of new labor, importations, were all needed to meet the twenty-thousandfold increase promised by these new miracles. Yet there was the Constitution . . .

The law against the slave trade was passed in March, 1807, and promptly started down the slippery shoot that would make it a dead letter and create so profitable an enterprise out of slave smuggling that a systematic chain of outposts could be established from Fernandina, Florida, to Galveston.

Illegality merely increased the barbarisms of the trade, since the profit now was large enough to cover the loss of nine Africans out of ten, while around the necks of slaves, profits fastened an era of darkness and violence that would mount with the climax of the years.

President Madison might speak of "violation of the laws of humanity," emancipationists might be jarred out of their apathy, but there was no turning back the whirr of spinning machines and the cloudy bales that grew high on harbor wharfs. Colonization began to fill the thoughts of many different types of men.

The idea of colonization was not new. When Negroes could still be called Africans, they and their friends had longed for a homeland on the continent from which they had been snatched. Certain friends of the slave, especially the indefatigable Quakers, advocated colonization on the American continent, and on a number of occasions manumitted their slaves, sold out their holdings, and moved bag and baggage to the Northwest Territory where slavery was forbidden. But the joys of freedom were so short-lived, the discriminations against the Negroes so acute—segregated, disfranchised, without schools, and limited to certain trades for a living—that their thoughts turned more and more to a sentimental homeland.

But now colonization assumed a new aspect. The slaveowner saw in it advantages unrecognized before. His thoughts ran on a straight line: to make a profit out of slavery it must be undisturbed, no hope of freedom must distract the slave; but where free Negroes lived unrest was multiplied.

Within a relatively short time colonization became, not a means of benefiting the Negro but a means of getting rid of troublesome elements which would weaken slavery.

It took many years for its real nature to become apparent. The American Colonization Society was formed; branches sprang up in many parts of the country; a philanthropic zeal warmed the hearts of many advocates of freedom. In 1816, land was bought in Africa and given the sanguine name of Liberia. But all the while a ghost stalked the feast. To make a success of the colony, educated Negroes must be put in charge, and education of the Negroes had been forbidden. The society soon found itself in the unfortunate position of claiming at one time that free Negroes were such a depraved class that they were incapable of education or of assimilation into their own country, and claiming at another time that they were capable of sufficient education to rule themselves. As time went on the society became so ridden with the slaveholding ideals that a certain editorial in the *African Repository*, its official organ, did not seem out of place. Referring to the Negro as "ignorant, degraded, mentally diseased, broken-spirited, and scarcely reached in their debasement by heavenly light," it concluded with the melancholy information that, "They must be forever debased, forever useless, forever a nuisance from which it were a blessing to society to be rid."

Such pithy words were not needed to convince the Negroes that the colonization scheme was a benevolent and soft-spoken swindle. Three thousand Negroes in Philadelphia maintained that since it was their fathers who had first successfully cultivated the earth of this country, *they* were the true Americans and could not be sent away from their homes. Although families were bribed and coerced to fill the contingents that were painfully gathering for Liberia, the organizers found that a competitor was gathering most of their passengers, a competitor whose service was improving hour by hour, who operated in the darkness, unseen beneath men's noses.

Out in the young West they were coming to understand these underground matters very well. New Englanders, settling in the Western Reserve of Ohio, had brought their Puritan way of thought; Southern colonizers, who had broken the ground of lower Ohio, had come like warring brothers, some bringing their devotion to slavery in one hand and their inability to fend for themselves in the midst of slavery in the other, and the rest bringing their contempt for slavery and their determination to injure it in every way they could. Between the northern and the southern parts of the state stretched a wilderness, still inhabited by Indians. If the slaves could get from the scattered Emancipationists in the south of Ohio to the scattered Emancipationists in the north only the expanse of Erie would separate them from Canada.

Yet in 1810, they learned how weak and uninitiated were their forces. In that year their heads crashed for the first time against the Fugitive Slave Law.

Jane was a slave who belonged to a gentleman of Wellsburg, Virginia. One night she entered a shop and stole goods amounting to four dollars. For this she was condemned to be hanged. Before Jane could be executed, however, the door of her cell mysteriously swung open one night, and out she walked. Two days later she crossed the river to Marietta, Ohio, where she found employment. Her sentence in due course, was changed from hanging to transportation, that is, sale beyond the boundaries of the United States, but for close to a year no one felt sufficient concern for the majesty of the law to attempt to bring her back. But that indifference was suddenly jolted when it was learned that Jane, now a married woman, had given birth to a child. Two pieces of merchandise were now available in place of one. At this point a gentleman by the name of Jacob Beeson appeared in Marietta to claim the runaway Jane.

The citizens of Marietta, when notified, had a good deal to say about this claim, and used mostly simple words that could be clearly understood. Mr. Beeson was shocked. He protested to the governor of Ohio. "It is with great concern that the people of Virginia look forward to the evils that will grow out of this course of conduct pursued by the people of your state residing on or near the Ohio. The idea of emancipation is propagated, and that such will fire the breast of every slave no one will doubt."

Mr. Beeson was quite right. He stood like a small and rather petulant godling attempting to destroy the mold that was already shaping the hearts of men. He had thought that there was nothing stronger than the law of 1793, but the governor of Ohio, speaking over his head to the governor of Virginia, informed him that the law did not authorize the governor of a state to aid in the seizure of a slave. Mr. Beeson then pulled what he needed from his sleeve. He demanded Jane as a fugitive from justice. What could the governor of Ohio do? The excellent people of Marietta were novices at this game. Later they would have spirited her away. Now they equivocated, not yet stiffened by the scenes of life and death that were to confound their sons and grandsons. Mr. Beeson had obtained executive pardon from the governor so that Jane and her child might be sold at a neat profit with no danger of an unfulfilled sentence to interfere with the smart accomplishments of slavery.

Jane and her child went back to bondage, but it is not hard to imagine that there was a great examining of motives, a variety of silences, while men looked into their hearts and said, with a sudden fire, "When that happens again . . ."

When that happens again—decisive actions—deeds, not words, certain Presbyterian ministers who had helped to settle southern counties of Ohio, decreed with grim lips. Most of these ministers were from the South. They lost no time affirming their friendship for the slaves, and one and all kept their eyes fixed on the Ohio River.

It was at the hands of these Covenanters and their organized secret work, that the structure of the Underground Railroad took shape in Ohio. They were all men accustomed to leadership, grimly familiar with the slaveholding mentality and therefore charged with disgust and, more important, the capacity to make practical their disgust. Previous to their systematic work, a fugitive might look vainly for help and find only an occasional meal to eat or a barn in which to sleep.

A brief glance at a map is sufficient to explain their preoccupation with the Ohio River. Many of the black men and women who lived along the banks of the Mississippi found it a simple pathway to the Ohio. Ships, sailing up the eastern extremity of the Ohio came to within a hundred miles of the Great Lakes, the shortest distance in the whole United States to freedom or if the fugitive chose to leave the ship in the southern part of the state, he could find a friend at almost any point along the shore and be passed from house to house until he reached the wilderness of central and western Ohio where the Ottawa Indians gave him assistance. From there he would be sent into the Western Reserve where the pioneer town of Hudson, still fresh with New England traditions, was being formed to an antislavery refrain by men like David Hudson, and Owen Brown and his young son, John. Or he might go up through the Firelands where Jabez Wright lived in Huron Township and merged his legal acumen—he was an associate justice—with the sagacity necessary for the protection of fugitives. Perhaps if the slave escaped at the mouth of the Ohio River, he would come to Salem in the eastern section, a Quaker community, strongly fortified to withstand the blandishments of slave catchers. All these routes led to the Lake, and whether the fugitive would be concealed on a sailing ship bound for Canada or would be sent by land as far as Buffalo and Niagara depended entirely on circumstances.

Canada was the goal in every case. There was no real security south of Canada. Yet, in spite of the haven it had represented since the days of the Dutch, English and French, its reliability was not generally known until after the War of 1812. Soldiers returning to Kentucky and Virginia, revealed in the hearing of the slaves that the enemy of the United States who lived to the north of them lived in a land of freedom. Their astonishment at discovering former slaves fighting in the Canadian ranks was enough to indicate to the listening slaves that fugitives had found a haven. The new runaways acted on nothing more concrete than that.

In Canada the intensity of their desire for freedom was very soon evident. The hardships they endured must have made them, in unguarded moments, question whether they had merely exchanged one state of wretchedness for another. A cruel climate, a desolate wilderness from which homes must be wrested, loneliness—yet so few went back to slavery that a return was a matter of extravagant comment. For here, in spite of suffering, land was available, opportunities were equal; there was neither color prejudice nor wage differences.

Using these materials—routes, sympathies, haven—a loose organization of the underground road had, by 1818, come into being. Since secrecy was its strength, the slaveowners learned of it only through the results it achieved. We know of it now through recollections written immediately after the Civil War, when secrecy was no longer necessary, through court records, through celebrated rescue cases, through Abolition writings, through the reports of the slaveowners, through a few casual diaries. For it was rare that those engaged in helping the fugitives considered their activities apart from a line of duty. The few whose temperament or perspicacity led them to describe their underground work were forced to destroy these writings when the increased pressure of the law made such evidence dangerous to keep.

These freedom-loving men followed their dangerous avocation along the path of Christian indignation. They were nurtured in a passionate conviction of man's equality before God. They suffered, with a conscientious fury, from the repeated kidnapings which took place all along the borders of the Northern States. Their moral sense was outraged by the treachery to which the fugitives were subjected in the North, by the prejudice which led to stonings and terrorization, by the subterfuges of many Northern masters who re-enslaved their chattels, freed by state laws. Their final commitment usually followed the inescapable evidences of slavery: a fugitive's back, still torn by the whip, a toe with the nail torn out because an earlier unsuccessful flight, another and then another story of flight decided upon when the slave learned that he was to be sold to the deep South where the rice fields and malarial swamps cut life short and where families would never be seen again; of flight resorted to when a master died before he could execute his promise of freedom.

Men could not be indifferent at such times. They dealt briskly with their sense of law obedience, using all degrees of rationalization from the jugglery of a certain Elder Shepherd's daughter who, seeing a fugitive in her doorway, mutely begging for help, laid bread and money on the table and then left the room, to the uncomplicated espousal of a law, higher than the law of the land, which was a conclusive argument for many faithful spirits. In all cases the impulsion brought its own heroism with it.

The white friend must always go on the assumption that there was no hope for the Negro beyond this haven which he had reached. When Hannah Gibbons, a Quakeress, took a weary, sick, and filthy fugitive into her home, she ministered to him as she conceived a Christian woman would. When in a few days he manifested all the symptoms of smallpox, she nursed him for six weeks, tenderly as she might her son, letting no one near him save herself. To Hannah Gibbons this was loving one's brother.

It was these people who first heard Benjamin Lundy's voice in 1815. And it is against their scattered, disorganized, fervent background that Lundy's small but intense light shone.

This little Quaker was a kind of Peter the Hermit. "I heard the wail of the captive," he said simply. "I felt his pang of distress, and the iron entered my soul." In other men he believed he could kindle this same fire. With no money, he started a small newspaper with a large name, *The Genius of Universal Emancipation*. The first issue was read by six subscribers. The only available press was at Mount Pleasant, Ohio, twenty miles from his home, and he walked between the two towns, his edition on his back. Within six months, the subscribers had increased to five hundred and his mission became clear. He must spread the news of freedom. He started off on his long journey, a knapsack on his back. Traveling mostly by foot, he cried out his message wherever people gathered. Wherever he found a press he stopped long enough to produce another issue of his paper.

In ten years he traveled twenty-five thousand miles, and five thousand of them were on foot. His devotion was indefatigable. His brother, the colored man, was his life. He went to Canada to see for himself the condition of the fugitives; twice he went through the wild Mexican province of Texas into Mexico itself, seeking a grant of land where fugitives might settle. He suffered from hunger, thirst and exposure, but he had a conviction and a burning zeal.

Small as were his accomplishments, limited as was his scope, he represented with a homely grandeur the love of justice that made great men of these obscure partisans. With the acceleration of zeal, their work was spreading like the tentacles of a benign octopus, gathering in, sheltering, sending forth. An inevitable concomitant was the discovery and utilization of the Negro organizations which had grown simultaneously with the new paths of flight. The Negro had known that it was impossible for him to rely on his white friends alone. They might fail him at any time; circumstances might alter their capacity to help. At many important points, the Negro had opened up new outlets and handled the flow of fugitives without the assistance of white men. Sandusky, Ohio, was a vital center of activity because of its position on the lake. For many years—well into 1837—the fugitives who came to Sandusky were conducted and assisted almost exclusively by Negroes.

One of the natural consequences of the interdependence between the colored and the white "conductors" was the desire of the whites to raise the educational standard of the Negroes. It was a fight, hampered at every step. The friends were a small group; the Negrophobes were very

large. When it was seen that the children of the colored people were
unwelcome in the public schools, the Quakers, the Presbyterians, the
Methodists attempted to teach them in their own homes or their churches.
But it was the colored people of Cincinnati who finally decided in 1820
to give their children a school. They raised a small subscription among
themselves, they hired a teacher, they rented a room, and they approached
the fabulous, the marvelous touchstone of enlightenment through their
children. But what could they substitute for money? In a few weeks
the school was closed, and for the next ten years it opened and closed,
the barometer of the desires and the financial limitations of the Negroes.

The same thing was happening in the states which harbored the fugitives. Where free Negroes were gathered, a brief fire of learning glowed
and then was extinguished; a longer glimpse of freedom, a brighter
hope, a patient waiting in the darkness once again. No one knew the
importance of this, not even the students themselves, until much later,
until, in the turbulent years ahead, these students emerged as leaders,
prepared to speak for the uneducated and inarticulate mass of Negroes
who were sure only of their longings and had few spokesmen to clarify
their hopes to an indifferent world.

The pattern of Abolition was beginning to take form. The sympathies
that little Lundy, wandering up and down the country, had found
were beginning to coalesce, beginning to reach out veins like underground
tunnels. Yet how nebulous they seemed, how tentative, how washed by
their own illegality—too irresponsible to deal with the sweeping power
of the slavocracy.

For the slavocracy possessed everything. In these 1810's and 1820's,
it had all the Presidents but one on its side. It had the Supreme Court
and Congress. It almost had Illinois and it got Missouri.

The Missouri Compromise is part of our schoolbooks and there, except
for the shock it roused in the small band of antislavery men, it must
remain. To them, watching the finesse of the Southern politicians, it
did not seem possible that slavery could really perpetuate itself in this
highhanded manner. The Abolitionists had acquired none of their later
bitter wisdom; they still believed that emancipation could come gradually, that slavery would wear itself out. With what weapons could they
fight men who had with miraculous dexterity succeeded in having all
states hereafter admitted in pairs, one slave, one free, so that their
political power—their Congressional representation—could not be lost
while at the same time their cotton lands could be extended; who
had supplemented this with an additional amendment, giving them the

right to recapture their fugitives in the free territory, north of the compromise line?

John Quincy Adams, knowing that the decision was irrevocable, called it bitterly "the title page of a great, tragic volume." The freedom-loving farmers of Ohio and the artisans of New England and the small business men of Pennsylvania, reading about it in their newspapers, could not understand how the slaveowners had learned such smartness. To the next fugitive they gave extra care and a special sympathy. Were they not attacking the slaveholder more directly in this manner than he was attacking them? Action was their only comfort. "Stations" on the road increased.

This decade of the twenties rang all the treble notes of the prelude. By 1821, Kentucky was cajoling and cannonading Congress with petitions for help in restraining her runaway slaves. She was merely following the example of Maryland who, that same year, had issued another petition against underground operators. This petition, like the rest, was valueless, for how, she finally asked, can one redeem stiff-necked Negro-lovers, fanatical with knight errantry? From that time on it was a state of war between the slaveholders of Maryland, who were turning more and more to the breeding of slaves for the markets of the deep South, and the practical emancipationists of Pennsylvania who were busy suiting their actions to their words. Into this world of rising enmity came the haunting impact of Denmark Vesey. For Vesey envisioned a greater overturning of the slave power than had yet been dreamed of in these United States.

He was handsome, impressive and intelligent, a free man of Charleston, South Carolina, who had a tremendous power over his race. He read the Bible frequently, and spoke in the words of Zechariah: "Behold the day of the Lord cometh, and thy spoil shall be divided in the midst of thee. For I will gather all nations against Jerusalem to battle; and the city shall be taken." He read smuggled pamphlets and he became an implacable hater of slavery. He knew that the Missouri Compromise had, in 1820, extended the power of slavery, and he hated those who had given slavery this impetus. He was also familiar with the history of the San Domingo uprising, and entered into a correspondence with the heads of the Black Republic. His personality and his physical strength drew Negroes to him, and he instructed them in zeal and in the struggle for liberty. In the words of a comrade, "If a colored man bowed to a white person he would rebuke him, and observe that all men were born equal, and that he was surprised that anyone would degrade himself by such conduct."

Four years before his plans matured Vesey had been possessed with a vision of insurrection. When, in 1821, the time for action came, he and his men worked in such stealth that no rumor broke through their secrecy. They chose a farm for their meetings which could be reached by water and so avoid patrols. They shaped their own weapons, and recruited slaves from all the plantations. He chose his lieutenants well, men of mental and physical stature who in their own land would have been called heroes. The number of recruits reached the thousands— 6600 some said, 9000 according to others. Only what was evident was known exactly. After the betrayal of their plans, the leaders conducted themselves so calmly that their jailers were deceived and freed them, and their revolt came within a striking distance of delivering its blow. At last 131 Negroes were arrested, and the judges labored like Hercules to obtain confessions. But what could they do against that impenetrable, gaping silence of which a Negro is the master? Or against a man like Peter Poyas who raised himself on his elbow as one of the slaves weakened under torture, and said, "Die like a man."

Vesey, standing in court with his arms folded across his chest, was a picture of awful scorn. He had given an ideal of liberty to the bondsmen of his race, and only human frailty had entered between it and its success.

The white men's vengeance was sweeping. Only those slaveholders who protested against the destruction of their property, prevented a slaughter. Twenty-two slaves were hanged together on the same gallows. With the rope around their necks, many cried out to their fellow slaves to revolt without ceasing until freedom came.

No South Carolinian could find repose with those words ringing in his ears. He asked himself with the docility of the badly frghtened, why his slaves desired freedom. An official report was drawn, attempting to explain this phenomenon—political speeches were responsible; slaves had been ruined by kindness; they had been spoiled by the "mistaken benevolence" of education. The Baptist Convention claimed it was because they were not Baptists, and an Episcopalian pamphleteer believed that it was because they had lacked the restraining influence of the Anglican Church. More laws were needed . . . The grand jury recommended that the large number of schools, kept within the city by "persons of color," should be suppressed. The legislature passed an act for the imprisonment of colored seamen on Northern or foreign boats, since colored crews were popularly supposed to introduce incendiary ideas. All this and more, painstakingly covered the sore which emitted the poison. That sore must not be acknowledged or discussed . . . Then freedom will pass from the minds of our slaves.

Some people might have thought it strange that a plot so thoroughly exposed could have sustained a wave of terror for so long. After all, this was an age of common sense.

It might be an age of common sense, but it was also the age of imperial cotton, and between commerce and philanthropy there is always an unequal battle. In 1791 the South had produced 9000 bales of cotton; in 1831 they were to produce 1,038,000 bales. Beneath the pressure of those increased bales of cotton, the status of the slave was being decided once and for all.

One cannot pretend that the North was shocked by the vengeance against men who wore the look of Vesey, by the wave of repressive laws, by the fists waved at Northern intercessors, if by the North is meant the growing capitalists. They understood the South; much of their money was invested in the South; they had, long ago, distinguished between business acumen and humanity. But the common man was astonished. What could a man like the Representative from South Carolina mean when he said on the floor of the House, "Much as we love our country, we would rather see our cities in flames, our plains drenched in blood, rather endure all the calamities of civil war, than parley for an instant upon the right of any power than our own to interfere with the regulation of our slaves"?

But the indignation, the dismay, of the common man was all a thousandfold too small. It needed to be brought to the point of combustion. It needed to invade the national consciousness, invade Congress where slavery slept, unappeased and undisturbed. And meanwhile the name of Vesey became a part of the language of every South Carolina slave. What he had put in their hearts could not be taken away by legal restrictions. The flames of revolt, supposedly subdued, licked up in widely separated regions while the whole South stirred with a profound restlessness, and fugitives trickling North, roused the hearts of men who were, when all was said and done, the children of a new age of reform. Deeds of Negro courage were stirring hesitant men. Wherever the slave catchers gathered, the free Negroes gathered as well. They bore the brunt of rescue, the terrible exposure of black skins which made them the natural targets of men with violent minds. But rescues were a pressing necessity for them, for in the end they trusted only themselves, and slave catchers had reason to dread the silent gathering of black men and women with their remorseless eyes, their taut bodies.

Free Negroes were not men of indifferent stature. For many, the effects of the short period of opportunity in the eighteenth century was beginning to bear fruit. John Russwurm, the first Negro to receive a degree from an American college, and Samuel Cornish, a Negro clergyman, began in New York in 1827 to publish and edit *Freedom's Journal*, the first Negro newspaper in the United States. It was dedicated to freedom and to citizenship for the Negro. Its appearance in the year in which New York slaves were finally emancipated was an event of great importance in the antislavery fight. It marked the first intellectual effort of a Negro or a white to put the struggle on militant lines. It outdistanced Lundy's *Genius* and it anticipated Garrison's *Liberator*. More than anything it gave a nucleus and a pivot to the young Negro leaders who were to bring to this evasive decade a firmness and a point of view, and it provided another hand outstretched to fugitives coming up the eastern seaboard.

New York was the logical place for it to appear since the activities of New York Negroes in their own behalf were organized on a wide basis. Their benevolent societies and churches had welcomed and passed along fugitives long before white emancipationists—such as Isaac Hopper, moving there from Philadelphia—joined forces with them.

The subtly changing elements, the new values that were passing before men's minds, the frail but persistent poundings against the conscience, shook the pragmatism of owners of men. Too many hands were reaching out, anonymous hands, women's hands, men's hands, black and white, and drawing a fugitive up out of a cultivated darkness; too many hands were receiving them across those lakes that were supposed to lie so protectingly between the United States and Canada.

Henry Clay, as Secretary of State, protested to the Canadian government in 1826. The Canadian answer was thin and unsatisfactory. The next year, Mr. Clay, prodded still by Kentucky, made another appeal. Without a word added, this appeal could only mean that the fugitives' friends were becoming more and more acquainted with the business at hand. For five months Mr. Clay and his friends waited, and then Canada replied, "It was utterly impossible to agree to a stipulation for the surrender of fugitive slaves."

In eight months the British authorities reaffirmed these words. Two such rejections would seem conclusive, but the next year the House of Representatives urged the President to make another attempt. Slaveowners were nervous and fidgety and played skillful politics, but the Canadians had not put themselves into a position to be magnetized. For a third time they refused.

peal in 1828. In 1829 David Walker,
s own. He did not bother to address
ht to the slaves. In plain language
r masters. He named their sorrows,
ditions there was no release except
estruction of the oppressors God may
ne Lord our God will bring other
requently will he cause them to rise
, divided, and to oppress each other,
ith sword in hand."
vocracy the *Appeal* was a bare sword;
nbarrassment and a pleasure. To the
t weakened the dam.
an through three editions, each more
though briefly—in the remotest por-
gue would have been comforting in
ttized the slaveholders' fears so well.
though something could be done.
North and South Carolina, Georgia, Virginia, and Louisiana made its
circulation a penal offense. Georgia, in addition, prohibited free colored
people from coming into the state, and in one day rushed through a law
prohibiting education to both the free and the enslaved blacks. Louisiana
passed similar laws, with a penalty of life imprisonment or death. On
the surface, what did Walker accomplish? He inspired a reward of
$10,000 from Georgia if taken alive and $1,000 if taken dead; his sudden
death raised the question of murder, he dragged down about the heads
of the slaves the thick noose of increased oppression and the bitter lashes
of deepening ignorance.

What he accomplished lay at subtle and deep levels. Five white men
might read the *Appeal* and be repelled; the sixth might find his moral
values changed by it. Five slaves might hear of the *Appeal* and go back
to the fields; the sixth might strike a deadly blow for freedom. Never in
the world has there been a system so dependent on peace, docility and
ignorance as slavery.

It is true that men still moved with extreme caution, few willing
to come to grips with the law; that they still worked in the tradition
of the past, in the tradition of liberalism, of manumission societies; that
they still wished to see change come gradually in the manner of the
antislavery societies of the South which had accomplished almost nothing
through education or through legislation in all the years of their en-
deavors, in the manner of the religious bodies which believed that

slavery would come to an eventual end if that end were peaceful and bloodless. But these same cautious men were finding it more and more difficult to shut out the sounds of a new age.

Little Lundy was still carrying his message of liberation up and down the land. In Boston he had met a young man, William Lloyd Garrison, who in a small boardinghouse sitting room listened to him exhort eight clergymen of various sects who nodded to his words. Garrison listened with that scalpel-like look upon his face which was soon to bare men's thoughts. Lundy, observing him, was in the next few weeks to walk to Bennington, Vermont, and convert him. A monumental thing happened thus simply, although Garrison was born with the spirit of an uncompromising man and was already feeling the chemical of reform.

Later in the year, 1828, Lundy went back on foot to Baltimore where he was issuing his paper, and Austin Woolfolk, meeting him on the street, beat him over the head and left him for dead. Woolfolk was a successful, and therefore a notorious, slave trader. He claimed that Lundy had libeled him. Arrested, he was convicted for assault and fined one dollar. Yet this was a clear omen, more unmistakable than many omens. Lundy, a kind of antislavery saint, was beaten by Woolfolk, the villain. This meant that iron must enter the souls of gentle people all over the land. The day when reason might have triumphed was past and the day of the rope and the faggot was at hand. Who better could be chosen than Woolfolk to announce it? Woolfolk was a man who, living, caused great suffering but dying, might soon have been forgotten had it not been his ill-fortune to reproduce himself a thousand times in the mentality of the slaveholding South. Until Lundy was reproduced a thousand times in the mentality of the free-thinking North, violence would be the order of the day. Men would not see for another fifty years that these events were closing one era and opening another, an era as well defined as though a stone had been set to mark the time. A changing world was all about. A new North was coming into existence. All the paraphernalia of modern industry was appearing in microcosm in the North. Factories were being built, immigrants were coming from all over Europe.

But with this came a concomitant evil. Free Negroes and fugitives in the North, battling with prejudice, forced to work for any hire, drove down the scale of wages until they became the victims not only of their own poverty but of the violence of their white competitors. The fugitive and the free Negro, degraded in the South, was unwanted in the North. The poison of the colonization idea infected the minds of those men who chose to see a solution to the problem only in the wholesale removal of Negroes from competition.

Many Cincinnatians looking across the river at Kentucky, saw the Negro with as much prejudice as the Southern masters. In these days, the enemy of the Negro was more loquacious and far more powerful than his friends. The results were inevitable. In 1829 the township of Cincinnati issued a proclamation that any colored man who did not fulfill the requirements of the law must leave immediately.

The requirements of the law demanded that any Negro, settling in Ohio, must within twenty days give bond of $5000. The laws had stood on the statute books for some time, but had not been enforced since the expulsion of the Negroes would evidently follow. Where could they go unless they chose to follow the path of the fugitive again? Only a small number left Cincinnati. A mob took over, and for three days the city was paralyzed by riots. The colored people appealed to the authorities, but the authorities had ordered their expulsion. Barricading themselves in their houses they defended themselves as well as they could, until the rioting had spent itself.

When peace came they took the only step they knew and sent a delegation to Canada. Would they be welcome? "Tell the Republicans," came the reply, "that we royalists do not know men by their color. Should you come to us, you will be entitled to all the privileges of the rest of Her Majesty's subjects."

In Canada the effect of persecution, North and South, was quickly seen. Negro colonies appeared where empty lands had been before. Negro farmers began to turn the soil and Negro teachers drew the children into schools. Negro parents realized for the first time what it meant to be entirely beyond the reach of slavery where none of its distortions could mark their children's lives. Men became possessed with the idea that they could not have all this alone. More and more of their friends or families must be brought out of slavery into this gruff harsh heaven that was Canada. Here that heroic story begins, which will tell itself a little later, when thousands of Negroes slipped back from Canada, across all the dangers, through all the fears, straight into the hand of that thing which they feared more than anything in the world, and then miraculously—one must agree—returned with friends and family.

In the free states through which they passed, they left a trail of admiration, enthusiasm and new recruits. Enthusiasm for the cause of the fugitive was as infectious as the corruption of slavery. When it began to dominate the mind, the Negroes' hope could rise. It needed coalescence. It needed fervor. It needed a battle cry and a sword. The young man who went to answer the call of Lundy in Baltimore and join him on the *Genius* did not look like a sword. Only the sharp keen eyes might have hewed out a question here and there.

Garrison was twenty-four years old. He had never, to one's knowledge, given in to a man or shaped his views in accordance with another man's ideas. His hatred of slavery had come swiftly and finally. A Boston audience, gathered in Park Street Church, heard him start upon his mission. "I am ashamed," he said, "of our country. I am sick of our unmeaning declamation of praise of liberty and equality. I could not for my right hand stand up before a European assembly and exult that I am an American citizen. Should I make the attempt, the recollection of my country's barbarity and despotism would blister my lips and cover my cheeks with burning blushes of shame."

These were new words. They chilled and challenged and would not lie quietly in the brain. Garrison carried his scorn with him to Baltimore where Lundy, a little afraid of this sword which he had begotten, urged that they sign their articles separately. But if he thought to curb a tide, which he must have watched with a kind of awful pleasure, he was mistaken. In Baltimore for the first time, Garrison saw the slave trade in operation. He saw New England boats starting off from Baltimore for the South, loaded with slaves, and he saw a native of his own Newburyport commanding such a ship. He could not remain silent. He denounced this Todd from Newburyport in language which Captain Todd called libelous. Garrison went to jail, a fine triumphant beginning.

He stayed in jail for seven weeks, and the country heard about his imprisonment through the pamphlets, sonnets, letters to editors, private letters, and public messages that poured from his cell. The rich patron of emancipation, Arthur Tappan of New York, arrested by the ferocity of Garrison's inspiration and the justice of his cause, paid the hundred dollars that released him.

Garrison was ready now for the future. His world had expanded. Even the shadowy limitations of gradual emancipation which hemmed him in with Lundy must be discarded.

He returned to Boston. In a small room he set up a printing press, a chair and a table. Impatient, as only Garrison could be, he did not bother to write his editorial. He set it up in type without putting it down on paper. It was as though he said, "No wasted time, no orthodoxy is going to stand between me and this revolution that is splitting me in two. I have a continent to fight, I have men's minds to remake, I have a system to destroy, and I have no time to waste."

What he wrote down was better. On January 1, 1831, the first issue of *The Liberator* appeared and across the front page lay his challenge:

I will be as harsh as truth and as uncompromising as justice. On this subject I do not want to think or speak or write with moderation. No! No! Tell a man whose house is on fire to give a moderate alarm; tell him to moderately rescue his wife from the hands of the ravisher; tell the mother to gradually extricate her babe from the fire into which it has fallen—but urge me not to use moderation in a cause like the present. I am in earnest—I will not equivocate, I will not excuse, I will not retreat a single inch—and I WILL BE HEARD!

## Chapter 3

## THE SOUND OF THUNDER

TO HEAR him was to hear thunder, threatening to blot out a bright day.

That year 1831 was for all purposes a bright day in Boston. Boston was a town of commerce and the home of great merchants. Ships lay in her harbor which carried the prestige of New England as far as the Orient. Cotton had built factories for Bostonians and bound them with practical and sentimental ties to the South. The South bought their cotton goods and their slave whips, and Boston—which of course fancied itself New England—responded with a compact philosophy that did eminent credit to its small commercialism and its worldly character. Slavery was unfortunate, it ran, but Heaven was responsible for it and the body politic nourished it. The Founding Fathers had accepted it, and good citizens did not go beyond the Constitution, nor speak one word that would question the sanctity of the Union. The churches received their instructions from Heaven and their incomes from the merchants, trade was a delicate blossom, subject to the ruinous effects of sectional controversy, and Boston society admired the glittering nabobs from the South and their exquisite ladies.

The first issue of *The Liberator* appeared without a cent of capital or a single subscriber. But Garrison had figured well. If Boston could be assaulted, the Bostonians would have to fulfill their adage: "Boston rules Massachusetts; Massachusetts rules New England, and New England rules the nation." When he and his partner, Isaac Knapp, added up the results of the first issue they found their assets had increased by twenty-five subscribers, mostly colored people, and a gift of fifty dollars from a Negro friend. Success had been suckled on less than this!

For a while the little storm center remained obscurely belligerent, but the genius of its editor, setting afire the pages, caught the eyes of other men whose hearts were not made of money. They climbed the three flights to the combined office-printing-shop-home and came away with a new horizon broadening before their eyes. All kinds of men came, men whose names were to shine very brightly in the long and bitter days ahead.

There was Samuel J. May of the gentle face and the loving temper who had insisted, two years before, on shaking the young Garrison's hand when he had spewed forth his first defiance in the Park Street Church; there was Ellis Gray Loring, young and respectable, who was to sharpen his lawyer's teeth in Garrison's behalf; Samuel Sewall who represented the patricians, all too small a band within the antislavery ranks; David Lee Child and his redoubtable wife, Lydia Maria, the foremost lady author of her day, who stood for the most excellent of Boston traditionalists, the intellectual; Amos A. Phelps, pastor of the Congregational Church on Pine Street who came to investigate, driven by the bitter censures of his fellow churchmen. Then there was John Greenleaf Whittier whom Garrison had, in a manner of speaking, "discovered" when he traced the source of the grubby poems which were thrust under his door when he was editing *The Newburyport Free Press*, and that other Quaker Arnold Buffum, the small merchant.

A young man with such excellent friends could hardly be disturbed by the frenzy that he was now creating. As a matter of fact it delighted him because he knew that he had, without waste of time, touched the raw spot on the conscience. His paper struck out with the hot incisive parade of reason that bound the hands of his opponents at the same time that it released their tempers. He took his strongest weapon from the slaveholders themselves. In every issue of *The Liberator* he reprinted, without comment, carefully selected news items from the Southern papers relating to slavery, and nothing he could have written would have struck at the heart as did these unpremeditated exposures: "The subscriber's servant has run away. He had one ear cropped off and his back was badly cut up," or "$50 reward. Ran away from the subscriber, his negro man Paul. I understand Gen. R. Y. Hayne has purchased his wife and children and has them on his estate where, no doubt, the fellow is frequently lurking," or "The undersigned, having bought the entire pack of negro dogs, now proposes to catch runaway negroes. His charge will be $3 per day for hunting and $15 for catching a runaway."

That substantial, conservative, successful Boston could have begotten such a viper seemed to the business men, the aristocrats, and the clergy a jest, too grisly to be contemplated. They could only apologize, only attempt to show through their actions that they too saw the Negro as an inferior, conditioned beyond hope to the benign restrictions of slavery.

Against them—against the slaveholding temperament in the North— Garrison unloosed his most homeric fury. He challenged them, he damned them, he turned his small bright light upon them and tormented them with it in a way that left no shadows in which they might conceal themselves. Male and female, he pursued them relentlessly, calling out names when he could but making even anonymity curiously transparent.

It was not that he desired to stir up strife—"I am sorry to disturb anyone," the thunderclap once exclaimed, "but the slaveholders have so many friends! I must be the friend of the slaves"—it was merely that his own identification with a new age collided with the settled theories of a complacent and flourishing society that had by no means worn out itself. William Ellery Channing, the celebrated clergyman, gave a name to these budding years and, whether he intended it or not, identified these ardent spirits.

"Every age teaches its own lesson," he said. "The lesson of this age is that of sympathy with the suffering, and of devotion to the progress of the whole human race."

Beneath the current of classes, of commerce, of orthodoxy, lay this unmistakable truth. Though to the minds of conservative men, all espousers of strange fanaticisms lived on a lunatic fringe, yet to the indifferent beholder they resembled very closely the plain men who came to town meetings, sat in the churches and cast their votes in the unrefined hurly-burly of election day.

They *were* the same. Women with their market baskets and their children were the same women who opened their mouths for temperance and pressed them tight for the runaway slave. Men who preached in shabby broadcloth from the pulpit were the same who agitated for peace societies and shook open *The Liberator* in the face of their neighbors.

It was natural that men who loved good militantly rallied to Garrison that winter. They were not only the children of the age which Channing had described, but were also the mold and the material of the new Abolition movement. (Observe that it had become Abolition, not antislavery. A world of difference lay between the command of the former and the theory of the latter.)

It was predominantly a "people's movement," finding its strength during the 1830's among nonindustrialized workers rather than in the churches or the schools. Plain men seemed to have more prodding consciences and a less complicated concern for dignity. In all its history, when intellectuals like Charles Follen and Ralph Waldo Emerson or dreamers like Bronson Alcott or Henry Thoreau or *élégants* like Edmund Quincy or Wendell Phillips joined the Abolition ranks there was no undemocratic excitement. Without the hatters, the cobblers, the ship captains, the farmers and the peddlers their backbone would have been broken.

And back of them stood the Negro Abolitionists. They held up Garrison's right arm. They nourished *The Liberator's* half-starved coffers. They paid his debts on more than one occasion. They established a parallel line of action which enabled their white friends to say, "You see, the Negro is a man, and that man is worth saving."

In June, 1831, a National Convention of Colored People, called by several distinguished free men and survivors of slavery, assembled in Philadelphia. Colored Abolitionists felt that they had come of age. They had reached the point of social development when they realized that certain states of mind could no longer be neglected among their people. They dealt forcefully with the mental conditioning of slavery, which accepted white superiority without a question and fell heir forthwith to all its concomitants of obsequiousness, confusion and false valuations. They took account of the fruits of the underground road and the colonies that had sprung up in Canada.

Many white Abolitionists came to hear, to see, and to speak. Garrison, the fanatic, never allowed himself an alternative language. "I never rise to address a colored audience," he said, "without feeling ashamed of my own color. To make atonement in part I am ready on all days, on all convenient occasions, in all suitable places, before any sect or party, at whatever perils to my person, character, or interest, to plead the cause of my colored countrymen in particular and of human rights in general."

Now it was very clear to sympathizers with slavery and the slaveholder that a man who spoke words like these to an enslaved race was a madman and an inciter, shaking the roots of established society. One wonders in what bright Nirvana they lived. The surge and underswell in the world must surely, sometime, have communicated itself to their vitals. The world was stirring with freedom. Ten years before Bolivar had proclaimed emancipation in New Granada and watched it spread through all of South America, except Brazil. Britain and her colonies were restless with their slaves, and would in two years, proclaim the Negroes' freedom. A white love of freedom would flame up in Germany, in Hungary, in Russia, in France before this generation was much older. "The age of sympathy" could not wait for the conservative, the mercantile and the orthodox to catch up with it.

Perhaps the slaveowners blinded themselves with fear, for at the beginning of this decade the South was like a man fighting perverse and evil dreams. "Poverty," said John Randolph, "is stalking through the land." Talk of emancipation pushed its way through the apprehension of falling prices and the low value of cotton. Extracts from Garrison's

*Liberator,* reprinted in Southern papers, stung the minds of slaveholders. The nerves of the South were raw with six years of continued slave unrest. Virginia was stirring with suspected conspiracies. She asked, in the spring of 1831, for additional Federal troops.

How fortunate they were there, when the Black Prophet struck!

The Black Prophet—whose name was Nat and who had belonged to a Mr. Turner—succeeded where Gabriel and Vesey failed, for his plans were not betrayed.

As a child he knew that his destiny lay apart from other men. As he grew older other slaves agreed with him, for he could read, he knew of a wider world than the plantation, a wider world even than their masters knew. Fasting, praying, preaching, he had none of the spinning violence of a fanatic. His face was calm, black, African. He heard voices when he plowed the fields, and his voices all told him one thing: Freedom. Freedom, he told the other slaves, and then he told them what he had seen—black and white angels contending in Heaven, signs of blood, Christ's work to be done.

A portent came to him in August, 1831, he said, and on the night of August 21st he and his friends spent eleven hours at a barbecue, until at last the firelight played on their faces. Their work would begin that night. And it would be a slaughter so complete that no long-drawn-out agony would remain behind to trap them. He had only Henry and Hank, Nelson and Sam, Will and Jack, but his followers would grow, he had no fear.

The next twenty-four hours were a comprehensive answer to slavery. Murder, murder, murder. No outrages, no rape, no mutilations—just a blow on the head of men, women or children who wore a white skin; all, that is, but a nonslaveholding white family whom Turner pointedly spared.

At every farm they took recruits. First they were fifteen, then forty, finally seventy. They took axes and guns and ammunition as they progressed, but they took nothing else. The work was swift and terrible and carried on through the day and another night. The white country-side lay, to all appearances, paralyzed. Against Turner's advice they stopped at a plantation the next day to seek out recruits, and were surprised by a patrol. They tried to defend themselves but their guns were antiquated. In the end they were forced to scatter. Nat lay in concealment for the night, waiting for his company to form again. Forty of them reassembled, and then an alarm broke them up once more. By daylight, the insurrection was over.

Nat lay in the woods for two days, believing that his men would be able to return to him. After that he knew they had been caught. For six weeks he lived in those woods, venturing out at night for water and food.

In the world outside was a wave of terror and terrorism. Every leaf rustle at night, every stone crunching under foot was the approach of death. A letter going to Harrison Gray Otis in Boston told that "some have died, others have become deranged from apprehension." But when the first terror abated, the work of revenge set in. A North Carolina correspondent wrote, "The massacre of the whites was over, and the white people had commenced the destruction of the Negroes which was continued after our men got there. Passengers by the Fayetteville stage say, that, by the latest accounts, one hundred and twenty negroes have been killed in one day's work." "Volunteers rode through the plantations," said *The National Intelligencer*, "running down negroes, while the more temperate elements in the community protested against an indiscriminate slaughter of the blacks who were suspected." Even owners had no redress and saw their property picked off like crows. Slaves were tortured, burned, maimed, their jaws broken, their hamstrings cut and finally their heads stuck on poles. Overseers, pointing out refractory slaves, had them done away with. The editor of the *Richmond Whig*, serving in the militia, saw a free Negro shot dead when he answered yes to the question if this were Southampton County. Yet in the words of an eyewitness many of them died declaring "they were going happy for that God had a hand in what they had been doing."

The number of slaves who had a formal trial was fifty-five, but still Nat Turner was uncaptured, and as long as he might appear again some dark night and murder the murderers, no one could sleep quietly. In Baltimore Negro houses were searched for arms. The accidental gunshot of a hunter sent inhabitants of Delaware flying to the fields for shelter. Raleigh and Fayetteville, North Carolina, were put under military guard. Slaves were shot in Wilmington and more heads were put on poles. Swift steps were taken in Mississippi against conspirators. In Alabama a revolt of Negroes and Indians was discovered. In Tennessee and Kentucky revolts were discovered at the combustion point. In Louisiana handbills were distributed, urging the slaves to rise. In Virginia and North Carolina it was significantly rumored that the uprisings were "not altogether confined to slaves."

And still Nat Turner was free. He was seen here, there, everywhere. A thousand men were under arms in Southampton County. Two army regiments were there, and units of artillery and cavalry and detachments of sailors. Terror filled the nights, desolation lay on those plantations which had been invaded. The constant dread of being unable to read the minds of faithful blacks who might at any moment become Nat Turners made the hands sweat and the scalps tingle. Rumors of Nat Turner's arrest filled the air, but in spite of a thousand men he was still unapprehended. And he lay, all this time, within a few miles of the heart of his rebellion. His home was a cave; he watched white patrols passing down the road; he saw white men in the woods. One day the dog of two slaves sniffed out his provisions, and when the slaves saw the fabulous Nat they took to their heels, and within a day the news was cracking through the air of Southampton County. When a posse arrived at the cave, the man had disappeared. And ten more days were spent in this kind of free enslavement with haystacks as his only protection.

One day the owner of the haystacks surprised him before he could get to cover and a load of buckshot was fired through his hat. Yet for five more days he wandered in this vague no man's land between the impossible and the inevitable. Then on a Sunday in October, a patrolman passing a clearing in the woods, saw a black face appear among the boughs, and there emerging from a hole in the earth, was the mighty, the fabulous, the fire-eating Nat Turner. He did not need the gun aimed at him. He was too exhausted from privation and suspense.

The news spread like a flood. They came from all parts of Virginia to see him. His trial was quick and as legal as the hysteria permitted. He was convicted on the 5th of November, and executed on the 11th. He never lost his sense of destiny. His body was given over to the surgeons for dissection. His skin was boiled down for grease.

Turner's revolt was the climax of fear. It gathered together all the apprehension and terror of the slavocracy. With the peculiar characteristic of those who are afraid, the slaveholders rationalized their revenge in a manner that could only stir the revolt at deeper levels. Nat Turner was educated. No Negro must henceforth be taught to read or write. Nat Turner was a preacher. No Negro shall be allowed to preach. Nat Turner had met no opposition along the road. Patrols must be increased. Vigilance must stalk the roads day and night, and invade the slave cabins.

But oddly enough an uprising of Negroes was reported in Louisiana, and two companies of infantry were sent to New Orleans. Had the slaves not heard that discontent was illegal? Apparently the word had not spread to the Carolinas, Maryland, Kentucky or Tennessee either, to Florida, Texas, Arkansas, where bands of armed slaves were preparing to terrorize the countryside. The nerves of the South were close to the surface. Many property owners left Virginia forever and moved farther South; others "were dreadfully frightened about the niggers," as a Mississippian told Frederick Law Olmsted. "Remember they built pens in the woods where they could hide, and Christmas time they went and got into the pens; 'fraid the niggers was risin'."

The Northern papers intoned the chant of their Southern brethren. Horror, stern deeds and stern words, vengeance, stirred men's wrath and bloody thoughts. Only Garrison, calmly setting up type, said that although he disapproved of Nat Turner's methods, yet "what we have so often predicted at the peril of being stigmatized as an alarmist and declaimer has commenced its fulfillment." The South was in terror of insurrection? Then the only answer was IMMEDIATE EMANCIPA-TION!

This, of course, was no answer for an aroused slavocracy, North and South. Garrison had warned against insurrection; this conversely meant that he had preached insurrection. From now on he was a marked man. Obscurity could no longer hide him. It was freely said at Nat Turner's trial that he had read *The Liberator*. Many sensible people doubted this, and no proof could be adduced.

But more than the menace of *The Liberator* were the internal convulsions, the unpredictable forces that might—God knows—be released. Governor Floyd of Virginia hinted at a never-quiet fear: the poor whites might make common cause with the Negroes. The vibrations of that revolt were making them stir restlessly. They had little to lose and a world to gain by the overthrow of slavery with its degradation of white labor. How near this was at the time of Turner might perhaps be seen in a letter written by a Virginian named Mann to a slave in this very August. He hoped, he said frankly, that through antislavery efforts, "we poor whites can get work as well as slaves."

Since the poor whites too often wrote down their feelings, the slave-owners were forced to legislate new laws. The poor whites complained of the crops or the poor soil or the inferior work of the Negroes—this was now classed as incendiary. Some told slaves that they had a right to be free. This was clearly insurrectionary. The first time a man was caught, he was to be given thirty-nine lashes; the second time he was to be put to death.

Old laws which had fallen into disuse were twisted into flails. Free Negroes might have slave wives or husbands or slave children, but now free Negroes who lingered in the state without permission were to be sold into slavery by the sheriff. In Alabama, free Negroes were prohibited from settling in the state.

The suffering of slaves deepened. If the eloquence of a colored minister could bring tears to the eyes of hardened white sinners, how much more dangerous must he be for his own people? The Negro preacher could tell the story of the children of Israel, of the struggles of the Jewish people, of the defiance of Nehemiah. Negro preachers were outlawed.

Any assemblage of colored people for the purpose of learning to read or write was unlawful and punishable by twenty lashes on the bare back. Were a white person to assemble Negroes for the purpose of teaching them, he collided with a fine of fifty dollars and three months in jail. Finally, the Negroes found that the law was broken when more than two of them stood together, unless a white man stood with them.

The Negro replied to these restrictions as best he could. Schools went underground. Here and there both whites and free Negroes conducted schools for slaves in secret. Frederika Bremer, the Swedish authoress, heard that there were secret schools in Charleston. After some difficulty she located one of them, a dark wretched hole with a half-dozen miserable black children being taught of a world singularly removed from their experience. The Union Army, when marching through Georgia, discovered that a colored woman named Deveaux had maintained a school in Savannah for thirty years, unknown to the slavocracy and therefore untroubled by the law. Some slaves still learned through indulgent masters who, as the sole law of a plantation, might ignore the state law if they chose. Many times mistresses taught slave children along with their own but this was regarded as a dangerous indulgence, for a brutalized slave was the only contented slave, and as time went on, property with learning brought lower prices. Some of the clergy who owned slaves wrestled with their consciences and emerged with the conviction that salvation would be a doubtful accomplishment if their servants were unfamiliar with the Scripture, and they opened up certain insurrectionary pages in the name of religious instruction.

But all these were exceptions. To most the law was adamant. Yet one out of every fifty slaves, it was said, learned by the path of surreptitious schooling. A dark head lingered within earshot of white children at their lessons. A dark hand stole a copybook, imitating the childish writing in it. A dark figure loitered in a shipyard, spelling out the symbols written on the bows of ships, or rescued scattered newspapers from the gutter and dried them, as Frederick Douglass did.

As for the illegality of assembly, there were always swamps and cleared places in the woods at night if slaves had a mind to risk the dangers of the patrol. Burial and beneficial societies took on a nebulous formation. In every city of any size in Virginia, an organization was said to have been formed for the purpose of aiding the sick and burying the dead. Since the laws made no allowance for such organizations, they assumed the guise of underground activity. Many times they met on the property of one of the white makers of slave laws. To the best of our knowledge their system called for the selection as president of a slave who was trusted by his master and who could therefore go and come freely, and as secretary, of a Negro with the rudiments of education. When the meeting place was decided on, the secretary waited there for the members who came in ones and twos—remaining thus within the framework of the law—paid their dues, and moved on. The records were often concealed in the bed of the secretary. Names were avoided as often as possible, and dues were paid by number.

The system gave not only comfort to the sick and reassurance to the dying, but also allowed a form of communication to be maintained, for when a death occurred, all the members of the society attempted to get permission to attend the funeral, and in this way meet together. Not only did this provide the first kind of insurance known to the Negro, but it allowed him to remain a part of a larger world, and even perhaps, find his way into that other world. For, from any organization of slaves and free Negroes, flight invariably resulted, insurrections were bred, or, at the least, the desire for freedom communicated and enlarged to the point where it could charge the imagination and the hope of a rebel.

When the blast of Turner, following so closely on the efforts of young Garrison, had hurtled itself away, the consequences to the Abolitionists were counted up. From the personal point of view danger and ostracism loomed very large, but from a wider sense, the attention given them by their enemies catapulted them into a prominence which the struggling *Liberator* and the scattered Abolitionists could have labored for years without attaining. The attorney general of North Carolina, for instance, submitted a flourishing indictment against Garrison and Knapp for the circulation and publication of *The Liberator* in that state. It was quite naturally assumed that the governor would demand their extradition, and the penalty, it was cheerfully recalled, was death since this was not their first offense.

The governor of South Carolina, amazed and indignant that there was no Massachusetts machinery for the suppression of *The Liberator*, pursued the usual course of the slavocracy and called the attention of the Massachusetts legislature to this oversight. The condition was disturbing to the Northern sycophants as well. When pressure was put on the mayor of Boston by a South Carolina Senator to procure evidence against the outrageous pair, he aided them to the best of his ability, but his thinly disguised visit to *The Liberator's* office for evidence roused the never gentle wrath of the young Mr. Garrison.

This was in October, 1831. By November, the slavocracy was impatient with the slow process of the law. The legislature of Georgia offered $4000 for the arrest of Garrison within the borders of Georgia, where he could be tried according to the sedition laws of the state. Certain respectable gentlemen of Columbia, South Carolina, who constituted a Vigilance Committee, added a further $1500 for the arrest of anyone distributing *The Liberator* or Walker's *Appeal* within the state.

Garrison called them "bribes to kidnapers." He looked about in the other papers of the country for some condemnation of this brigandry, and found nothing but tacit approval of the methods of the slaveholders. So "where," he demanded furiously, "is the liberty of the press and of speech? where the spirit of our fathers, where the immunities secured to us by our Bill of Rights? Is it treason to maintain the principles of the Declaration of Independence? Know this, ye Senatorial patrons of kidnapers! that we despise your threats as much as we deplore your infatuation; nay more—know that a hundred men stand ready to fill our place as soon as it is made vacant by violence."

These were the words of a man at war, and they were accepted as such both by his enemies and by those who heard him for the first time. Never again was there to be an equivocal struggle between the North and the South such as the old antislavery forces had waged. Men were to snarl at each other now across the border of what seemed at times to be two countries. Blood was to run, and violence take a frightful toll, families were to become divided, more and more slaves were to spew themselves out of the South and take that invisible road to an unknown destiny.

Garrison by no means spoke for all the Abolitionists in the country. There were many who did not agree with his ungloved methods, many who foresaw in his attacks a threat to the Union. Many individuals were still tainted with the fashionable philanthropy of colonization. But whatever meanings his words carried there was no denying the electricity that he generated, nor the mighty fortress that Walker, Turner, and he had made of the South.

The system of help, the illegal activities, the journeys in the dead of night had no name at this time. They were merely the passing on of fugitives, the outstretched hands. But when the naming finally came, the news spread gleefully on that invisible telegraph which spoke an intelligible language only to the men who knew its code. The hand, the system, the journeys had a name, and a slaveholder had given it—the Underground Road!

It came about, according to those who were best informed, around 1831. A fugitive named Tice Davids crossed the river at Ripley under the expert guidance of those river operators who worked within sight of slavery. He was escaping from his Kentucky master, who followed so closely on his heels that Tice Davids had no alternative when he reached the river but to swim. His master spent a little time searching for a skiff, but he never lost sight of his slave, bobbing about in the water. He kept him in sight all the way across the river and soon his skiff was closing the distance between them. He saw Tice Davids wade into shore, and then—he never saw him again. He searched everywhere, he asked everyone, he combed the slavery-hating town of Ripley where John Rankin kept so formidable a watch. Baffled and frustrated, he returned to Kentucky, and with wide eyes and shakings of the head he gave the only explanation possible for a sane man, "He must have gone on an underground road."

Wonderful! The phrase spread like a wind, and the friends of the fugitives completed the name in honor of the steam trains that were nine-day marvels in the country. Underground Railroad! Why the very phrase was a mystery! How could such things be? Was there really a long tunnel, dug miraculously, into which runaway slaves were poured? The mystification was enhanced logically by the good humor of the operators who forthwith called themselves "conductor," "stationmasters," "brakemen," and "firemen," called their houses "depots" and "stations," talked of "catching the next train," and began sedulously to cultivate a wonder and a marveling in the minds of the uninitiated.

The sequence of events was assuming an old and honorable pattern. Suppression in the South, increased flight, greater diligence of friends. There was, however, one difference: militant Abolition. It changed the whole picture. It promised to weld the opponents of slavery together and give them a unified strength. It promised to use weapons, undreamed of, to loosen the nuts and bolts which held the unwieldy structure of slavery together. Nat Turner proved again that the South would never relinquish its slaves, even in terror; the Underground Railroad proved the unquenchable desire for freedom of the enslaved. Abolition demanded, therefore, as the only conclusion to this warfare, the immediate emancipation of all slaves.

Garrison was seeing that palliatives were of no value. He attacked colonization furiously. It had confused the minds of many sincere men.

As long as it was unexposed it would seduce the unwary. We, now, have no measurement for this act of war. Colonization was the primary soporific of the day. To attack it was to attack the consciences of many worthy men. Even Garrison's faithful friend, May, took alarm. "You have gone too far," he said. "Your censure is too indiscriminate. I fear you have already injured greatly the cause."

But Garrison would not be put off. He had the courage to see what must be attacked, and the rectitude to attack it without regard for consequences. He announced in *The Liberator* that he intended to write a pamphlet on this "conspiracy against human rights." "It can be demonstrated," he wrote, "that the [Colonization] Society has inflicted a great injury upon the free and slave population; first by strengthening the prejudices of the people—secondly, by discouraging the education of those who are free—thirdly, by inducing the passage of severe legislative enactments—and, finally, by lulling the whole country into a deep sleep."

His *Thoughts on Colonization* would not be published before the next year, and in the meanwhile it was evidently his duty to sting the shins of slavery wherever it would be most profitable and public. He took up the Quakers' enthusiasm for free-labor products, and urged, as strongly as the small voice of *The Liberator* permitted, the boycott of all products of slave labor. He advocated the multiplication of free-labor societies in order to "strike at the root of slavery." He offered *The Liberator* as a clearing house for certain free-labor stores which then did business in New York and Philadelphia.

These were all small seeds in the wind and no one knew it better than Garrison. Almost from the beginning he had felt the need for a National Antislavery Society. It was evident that to accomplish anything Abolition must present a unified front, a base for action. In November, 1831, Garrison called a meeting. If eleven men could be brought together—twelve apostles—who would agree on immediate Abolition they could then form a society. Fifteen met together in Samuel Sewall's office, but six were opposed to "immediatism." Another meeting was called and this group was sufficiently united to draw up a constitution. At length in January, 1832, they came together for a third time, meeting in the Sunday-school room of an African Baptist Church in an obscure quarter of Boston known contemptuously as "Nigger Hill." No white clergyman would open the meeting for them. A Negro preacher volunteered, and lifting his hands over their heads, prayed for the salvation of his race, prayed that these men might remain in strength and devotion and brotherly love.

How sanguine they were! Not more than two or three of them, according to Oliver Johnson, one of their number, "could have put a hundred dollars into the treasury without bankrupting themselves." They drew their membership from Negro supporters, small tradesmen, teachers, underpaid clergymen. Seventy-two names appeared within a short time on the membership roll, perhaps a quarter of them colored men who could barely write. These seventy-two, small men even within their local framework, proposed to set themselves against not only the Southern oligarchy but also the respectable, conservative and honored body of the Colonization Society.

They organized committees to assist Negro youths to find jobs, they pressed for the admission of colored children into the public schools, they attempted to improve and multiply the schools already established, they set out to investigate all cases of New Englanders who had been kidnaped and returned to slavery and, at the society's expense, take every possible step to liberate them, they agitated for the repeal of the act which prohibited the intermarriage of whites and Negroes, they urged support of a free-produce grocery store in Boston and they undertook to raise $50,000 for a manual-training school for colored youth. Apart from this, they appointed agents to spread the word, to distribute and sell antislavery tracts, and to carry this new gospel into as many and diverse places as possible.

The fruits appeared soon, tough and resilient. Antislavery societies sprang up all over New England, although to stand forth in public places as an Abolitionist was to make oneself the natural victim of whoever chose to cast the stones. The Abolitionist was the helpless victim of cartoons and personal diatribes in an age which knew few libel laws, the victim of fantastic stories for which he had no redress. On the streets, he was followed by droves of boys, and he and his family were forced to accept whatever insults or significant gestures passers-by might choose. His children were shunned in schools. In public places he was greeted with real or affected aversion and terror. At town meetings he was hissed. In churches he was ignored. Everywhere he was treated as a communal outlaw.

Yet agents trudged from town to town, lecturers appeared, sometimes of doubtful learning, but of unquestioned zeal and strong devotion. All talents, however dubious, were wrung dry for the cause. Men laughed at the "impassioned illiterates," but Samuel May, with his exquisite sensibilities, championed them hotly when the great William Ellery Channing turned aside his head in mortification. "The very stones have cried out," he exclaimed, forgetting his accustomed awe of this man who had been like a father to him. "You must not wonder if many of those who have been left to take up this cause do not plead it in all the seemliness of phrase which the scholars and practised rhetoricians of our country might use. It is not our fault that those who might have conducted this great reform more prudently have left it to us to manage as we may. . . . We abolitionists are what we are—babes, sucklings, obscure men, silly women, publicans, sinners, and we shall manage this matter just as might be expected of such people. It is unbecoming in abler men who stood by and would do nothing to complain of us because we do no better."

To attack slavery was then as unpopular as to attack private property now. They argued, they exhorted, they convinced, they disgusted, they wiped bad eggs off their clothes and dodged bricks, they stirred up men's thoughts so that never again could they rest in the old molds. The society believed also in the power of the printed word, and with a pittance they produced thousands of tracts and cast them broadside. Despite precautions of every sort the tracts filled the country, penetrating even the buttresses of the South. Men who wavered without a leader now had guidance; men who had never thought of the matter now found themselves disturbingly alive; men who hated change felt the ground rock beneath their feet.

At the end of the first *Liberator* year Garrison could look forward to a newspaper that was able to enlarge its format and enjoy the blessings of an increase in circulation. The Antislavery Society had begun to bloom like a sturdy youth; men of substance were making friendly gestures, and Garrison himself was becoming the strongest man in America.

In these early days there were no other men to stand to the stature of Garrison. Because we still stand so close to the Abolition days—perhaps because the abolition of racial prejudice is not yet complete—we are not as moved by this phenomenon as we should be. What Luther was to the Protestant church, Garrison was to the cause of freedom. His merciless tongue and his scorching pen, his violent black and white of good and evil, his relentless logic and his fanatical egocentricity—for there was nothing of him beyond the cause of freedom—meant that men of softer fiber hated him and all his ways. He was the strongest man in America because all the thunderbolts of the next thirty years passed through his fingers, because he touched the mind of every man whether that man chose to agree with him or not, because he took all things that happened in this land and lo! they were transmuted to the cause —negative or positive—of Abolition. "Mr. Garrison," his friend May protested once, "you are too excited, you are on fire!" Garrison gave then the key that should lock away all hatred of him. "I have need to be on fire," he said with his sharp quick look, "for I have icebergs around me to melt."

The North hated him and all his followers. The South could hardly have expended more fury. A certain New York merchant expressed this Northern hatred clearly and succinctly to the ubiquitous May. "We are not such fools as not to know that slavery is a great evil; a great wrong," he said, "but it was consented to by the founders of our Republic. It was provided for in the Constitution of our Union. A great portion of the property of the southerners is invested under its sanction; and the business of the North as well as of the South has become adjusted to it. There are millions upon millions of dollars due from southerners to the merchants and mechanics of this city alone, the payment of which would be jeopardised by any rupture between the North and the South. We cannot afford to let you and your associates succeed in your endeavor to overthrow slavery. It is not a matter of principle with us. It is a matter of business necessity. I have called you to let you know, and to let your fellow-laborers know, that we do not mean to allow you to succeed. We mean to put you Abolitionists down—by fair means if we can, by foul means if we must."

The Abolitionists had never deceived themselves as to their enemy. Garrison frankly said, many years later, that he was not fighting the South, but its Northern allies. The challenge was accepted. It stung zeal and stiffened sinews. A fight, to be thoroughly enjoyed, must be clear-cut and unequivocal. Neither side was to be the least confused.

In the South the last vestige of democracy was about to go, and it went out on words that would henceforth be treason. When the Virginia Assembly met in December, 1831, the shadow of Nat Turner still lay on the state. The deep levels of fright had stirred a hatred of slavery into speech, and from many counties in Virginia had come petitions for Abolition or for the gradual emancipation of the slaves. From the free-thinking West, around Charleston and Wheeling where the nature of the land and the economic condition of the farmers had never given slavery a strong foothold, came men who, spurred by the terrors of these last months, made this Assembly memorable. They were not necessarily friends of the Negro, but they were small farmers who resented the power of the rich slaveowners in the East.

Bolling, Berry, Brodnax, in turn, plucked out of the forbidden chambers the subject which was insurrectionary in itself, and demanded some relief for their wives, their children and themselves. Brodnax said that he could no longer allow other nations to believe that "the state of Virginia was not willing even to think of an ultimate delivery from the greatest curse that God in his wrath ever inflicted upon a people. What a fine situation," he went on, "when a master bolts his doors at night and only opens them in the morning for his servants with a pistol in his hand!" Philip Bolling took up the cry. "We talk of freedom," he exclaimed, "while slavery exists in the land, and speak with horror of the tyranny of the Turk; but we foster an evil which the best interests of the community require shall be removed and to which we trace the cause of the depression of eastern Virginia."

Henry Berry added the final warning. "Pass as severe laws as you will to keep these unfortunate creatures in ignorance, it is in vain unless you can extinguish that spark of intellect which God has given them. We have, as far as possible, closed every avenue by which light might enter. We have only to extinguish the capacity to see light and our work will be complete. I am not certain we would not do it if we could find out the necessary process. But this is impossible; and can man be in the midst of freedom and not know what freedom is? A death struggle must come in which one or the other class is extinguished for ever."

Few rigid and implacable advocates of slavery spoke. The tide was too strong to battle openly, and yet the final totaling of the Assembly's work disclosed that the machine of the slavocracy had been well employed. All the heroic and devastating speeches became so many words recorded on the state calendar. A colonization bill—the most radical proposal— was defeated by a vote of 65-58.

Young Professor Thomas Dew, of William and Mary College, made the official pronunciamento. "The exclusive owners of property ever have been, ever will be and perhaps ever ought to be the virtual rulers of mankind. It is as much in the order of nature that men should enslave each other as that other animals should prey upon each other."

Such an argument had the incisiveness of class interests and the sweep of dialectics. Dew was a prophet honored in his own country. If this were a battle of positive good where the crasser elements of pure commercialism were forever swept away, men could defend their human property on the ground of culture and lofty aspirations. A not inconsiderable blessing since, according to Professor Dew, there was $100,000,-000's worth of slaves in Virginia alone.

To silence Christian apprehensions, Dr. Richard Furman of the Baptist Church fixed the seal of piety. "Liberty," he said, "consists not in the name but in the reality. While men remain in chains of ignorance and error or under the dominion of tyrant lusts and passions they cannot be free." What, in short, was chattel slavery compared with the groaning victims of political tyrants, the wage slaves of the North, the drunkards, fornicators, adulterers and murderers who are bound with chains far heavier than those worn by the happy runaways of the South?

Finally, let no man lift his voice against this sacred institution, let Congress understand that our word is settled for ever. Does the North wish to lose its business? Does the Union wish to be broken?

Let no white man in slaveland trust in the color of his skin. For free speech is ended.

Yet had all men heard? An individual named Robinson was lashed at Petersburg, Virginia, for expressing the belief that "black men have, in the abstract, a right to their freedom." He was ordered to leave the town and never come back if he did not want to be treated "worser." In Georgia a man named John Lamb was discovered to have subscribed to *The Liberator*. A mob gathered around his house, dragged him out, tarred and feathered him. After that they poured oil on his head and set him afire. Still recalcitrant, he was tied to a rail and ducked in the river. What had survived of him was then returned to a post and whipped. Word like this spread quickly. Every man and woman in the county would know about such a lynching before the sun went down, and every slave. It had an effect. White men kept silent. Only the slaves waited— for a time.

That spring of 1832, Theodore Weld journeyed to the South. Theodore Weld was one of those young men who combined an obliviousness to danger with a great sweetness of character and a remorseless conviction once his mind had set itself against an established order. He had about him, apparently, something of the apostolic manner. His mental endowments were said by Lyman Beecher to be "logic on fire." His charm was always mentioned as self-evident.

None of this would be of more than passing interest were it not that Theodore Weld represented the new order of Abolitionist. He had not been converted by Garrison, but he had dedicated himself to him, as far as his individualism allowed. The foundation of his training had been in the great revivals which had swept the country. We meet him for the first time when he is dining with an Alabama, cotton-raising, slaveholding, clergyman-lawyer, James Gillespie Birney. To Mr. Birney he put a question. By what right did he hold his slaves? Mr. Birney had been attempting to answer for some years, but Weld's logic made the conventional responses cold and frivolous. He asked Weld to meet him at his law office the next day. There he admitted that he had spent the night pacing his floor and endeavoring once more to find an answer to the question. There was none.

That summer Birney gave up his legal practice and his church and became an agent for the Colonization Society, the only organization to which antislavery men might belong in the South. He moved his family and his slaves to Kentucky, where the air was less oppressive, became a member of the legislature and set out to defy the oligarchy. By the end of 1833 he returned to his home, resigned from the Colonization Society and emancipated his slaves. He could not believe in slavery and there was no halfway of saying it. To go the whole way meant the embracing of Abolition. He bought a press and announced his intention of issuing an Abolition paper. A mob formed and Birney, with a matchless dignity, picked his way through the mob to Cincinnati. He had come a long distance from Alabama, but he had not yet found freedom.

James Birney was a man of substance to the cause, because within five years he would stand up to the arch-priest of Abolition, Garrison, and challenge his place.

The lessons of the South were well learned in the North. Ohio, which lay so close, seemed to enjoy the dangers. Ohioans had called themselves Abolitionists before Garrison appeared. Living across the river from the slavelands, what could they be taught? They had men like John Rankin, and like Levi Coffin, and soon they would have Birney — all Southerners, all enemies of their enemy.

Societies did not take root very well with Westerners. Although New Englanders worked more smoothly in groups (a wag spread the tale that when Boston once suffered from an epidemic, some of its leading citizens organized the anti-smallpox society), Westerners were more eager to deal with actualities than with theories. Where the spirit of Garrison manifested itself was in the unification, the close front, that Ohio Abolitionists began now to present to their enemies. Garrison, however, knew he was not their leader. He believed in moral suasion. They believed in force. To men who saw the rails of the Underground Railroad lying all about them, who knew that slave catchers lived not a day's journey away, action was as natural as were resolutions, officers, agents to the New England temperament. In their objectives, however, they saw eye to eye.

Their enemies in the North were the same. The Ohio mobs were to prove as bloody and tenacious as the mobs of Boston, of New York, of Philadelphia. In Ohio Negro-hatred burned with fierce intensity. By 1832, certain citizens of Waverly had, through terrorization, murder and burnings, driven every Negro from the town. White immigrants, finding their way to the West, took on the Negro-hate when jobs were scarce and clung to it, for fear of the future, when jobs were plentiful. Old settlers did not understand their own hatred, but before the alien blackness of the Negro they were restless, apprehensive and suspicious. Against white friends of the Negro an even fiercer indignation raged . . . Nigger-lovers who hurt business, stirred up strife!

Underground conductors were as sensitive to public opinion as dogs to the wind. They had no choice but to walk warily and allow the night to cover their deeds. They must be prepared to operate with hostile neighbors on either side of them, sometimes with hostile boarders in their house. No conductor ever knew when the familiar tap would not come at his window and the low question, "Who's there?" be answered by the accepted signal, "A friend with friends." Was it safe this time? Would the law be blind again? Would the enemies of the Negro betray him? His decisions had to be made in a moment, decisions that protected not only himself but the fugitives. He must, moreover, be prepared to risk not only himself but his wife or his child. In emergencies a child or a woman might escape detection where a man could not. Many a small boy or girl of ten or eleven had been set on a horse with a fugitive clutching his waist and told to go to Friend So-and-so's as fast as possible. One Ohio lad of ten was not familiar with the route which lay for eighteen miles to the next station, but the Abolition horse knew the journey well and, at the end of the eighteen miles, pushed open a gate with her nose and trotting down the lane, deposited her cargo safely among friends.

The offering of rewards for fugitives brought unpredictable results. Often they would stimulate the Yankee's zeal to prove that he was not amenable to bribes and drive a man with no Abolition sentiments to the aid of the fugitives. At other times, $500 or $1000 would make a greater appeal than a man's humanity. A reward of $2200 was offered on one occasion for a group of fugitives who had escaped from a Kentucky plantation, and a large force of armed slave catchers were sent over from Kentucky. Every road was picketed, and it was almost impossible for the conductors to get the fugitives beyond Red Oak which lay eleven miles from the Ohio River. The Reverend Mr. Rankin's eldest son had charge of the family of fugitives, and the entire Rankin family was experienced in the ways of guile. He stayed with them—man, woman and little boy—continuously for three days and nights, hiding in fields and friends' houses. They ran the picketing guards like a blockade, first from William Minnow's house to Mary Pogue's; then when the pursuers reached the Pogue house they made a dash for the Campbell family in the next town and from there across country to the James McCoys'; from James McCoy to his brother William and from William back to the Pogue house, hoping thus to bedevil the pursuers. From the Pogue place they started back on their tracks to the Minnows' and then across the woods to the Campbells'. They continued this for three days and nights and still the slave catchers hung close. There was apparently no way of breaking the blockade. On the third night as they were hiding in a "station," they heard a horse gallop to a halt in front of the house and the voice of a proslavery neighbor, the neighbor in fact who was entertaining the slave catchers. They had merely time to motion the fugitives to their feet before the door was flung open.

"It's all right, boys," the neighbor said. "I just came to tell you how to get them Negroes out of this neighborhood. When dark comes, just take them across the woods to my house. They will never suspect me of having anything to do with carrying them away, for I'm feeding the catchers." They trusted him for he had always been a good neighbor although he knew the Rankins' business well enough.

With the dark came a pelting rain. In the dark and the mud, they lost their way and wandered until two o'clock in the morning before they reached their new friend's house. The fugitives were smuggled upstairs, and the next day Rankin guilelessly took dinner with two of the catchers. The following evening they outflanked the pickets and brought the fugitives twenty miles to the next station.

There were plenty of ways to harry the pursuer, as many as the imagination could devise. Ingenuity and a fine humor were utilized in a similar emergency by a certain white "station keeper" of Bloomfield, Ohio, who was by vocation a tavern keeper. One Sunday, in his former capacity, he took in a father, mother and three children who were at the end of their resources and weak from their flight. He gave them a meal, allowed them to rest, and put them in the charge of a conductor.

That night their owner, his son, and a slave catcher arrived at the tavern. What direction had their slaves taken? they demanded, winded and dust-covered. The landlord, taking their measure with a practiced eye, was all jollity and helpfulness.

A tatterdemalion family was a bare mile ahead, worn and tired, so that capture would be a simple matter, he told them. Why not spend the night and catch them in the morning?

The owner, spirited by this lack of complication, tumbled off his horse, and clattered happily to bed. But somehow—who knows how?—everyone overslept in the morning. The landlord was deeply apologetic when roused by his guests. And breakfast—well, when one makes haste, strange things happen.

At last, breakfast swallowed, the landlord was desperately ordered to get the horses ready. He made the long journey out to the barn, only to discover that he had left the stable door key in the house! It took him ten minutes to find it. When the stable door was at length opened, the horses were all found to have lost a shoe and the hoof of one was badly broken. The only answer was the blacksmith, but the blacksmith's shop was locked, and no one knew where the blacksmith was. It took quite a show of searching to find him, and when he was at last uncovered, he had no nails or shoes. It was nearly noon before the slaveowners rode out of town without a good-by. By this time, the fugitives had vanished —one more score for the mystifying underground road.

In Ohio, the bitter struggle was asserting itself with increasing fury. These 1830's would see the mobbings of Rankin—over one hundred times he recalled feelingly—the terrorizing of Birney, the murder of Lovejoy. For Abolitionists, East or West, there was little to choose between in personal discomfort. The Garrisonian Abolitionists, however, assumed with little delay the burden of being the mouthpiece of the antislavery forces and, obliquely thereby, of the Underground Railroad.

Of Garrison's articulateness, there has never been a question. He was prepared, by temperament and capacity, to make Abolition the only question of any endurance in the United States of one hundred years ago. Calumny and inchoate rage accompanied him to England and back when, determined to blast the lingering power of the colonizers, he made a bid for the powerful support of the British Abolitionists and by that stroke destroyed the pretensions of the colonizers who professed to speak for the antislavery forces in America. He had done a daring and presumptuous thing, attacking conservatism at its most subtle and deceptive point. A wave of indignation blazoned his return from England.

"How dare he," the papers demanded, "wash our dirty linen in public?" Slavery was a family affair, to be dealt with out of sight of the mounting scorn of the world.

He was taken off the boat hastily so that the sight of him would not stir an unrestrainable wrath. Perhaps the New Yorkers would not have bothered him, however, for several thousand of them were occupied on the day of his arrival with chasing down the small band of Abolitionists who had announced their intention of forming a New York antislavery society. Garrison watched them from the crowd, thin, hawk-faced, his thick spectacles concealing the awful vigilance of his eyes, the deep painful expectation of terror from these shouting guardians of property. He had seen the notices signed *Many Southerners* which had appeared about the city, calling a meeting of the friends of slavery. He had read the incitements in the morning papers. He went with the mob as it swept to the meeting place which had been selected to coincide with the Abolitionists'. The Abolitionists were not there; permission to use the hall had been taken from them by the owners. Shouting and reckless, the mob poured through the streets in search of them, elbowing pedestrians, swelling its clamor with inflammatory speeches, heating its blood to the temperature of violence.

Arthur Tappan said later that the shouts of the mob, as it burst into the street where Chatham Street Chapel sat, timidly housing the unwanted Abolitionists, could be clearly heard in the room where he and his companions were launching their small bark on the sea. The shouts were a matter of singular indifference to them. It meant merely that they must gather the skirts of their coats about them and climb out a back window.

What a temper lay in this breed of men! How many others could have accepted vituperation so calmly? The mob seemed unwieldly and pitiful in the face of these fifty solid men who, unruffled, passed their resolutions, struck the small match of their hatred of slavery, looked without despair at the minute blaze it created and then made their way imperturbably into a noisome back alley as though they were going calmly out the front door.

An unnamed colored man put all that they might have said into words. The mob, breaking down the door but balked by the empty room, seized a Negro on the street, called him "Mr. Tappan" and insisted that he make a speech.

"Gentlemen," he faltered, with nudges against his shins, "I'm not used to making speeches. But I have heard of the Declaration of Independence and I have read the Bible. And the Declaration says all men are created equal and the Bible says God has made us all of one blood. I think, therefore, we are entitled to good treatment, that it is wrong to hold men in slavery, and that ——"

He was hauled down with a roar and thrown out onto the street again. The mob was worn out and frustrated. They kicked the furniture and went home. The little voice of the New York Antislavery Society was not heard again until some of the bedlam had subsided.

Yet it never succeeded in becoming respectable. In spite of the dignified figures of Arthur and Lewis Tappan, its association with Garrison's name blemished it in the eyes of well-behaved people. Lewis deplored this. In these days—ever since his brother had paid the fine to release Garrison from the Baltimore prison—he admired the hard diamond that was Garrison. He picked his way among the vast commercial interests of his trade—among the bankers and the business men who interwound their businesses with his own—with the deliberate fanaticism of a man who had organized a Society of Morals, Literature and Mechanical Arts for young colored people, who had established a high school for Negro youth, who depleted his income of $100,000 a year on enterprises which only for his wealth's sake were called no worse than eccentric. Now he wished very much that Garrison would moderate his words, deal with the enemies as though they were misguided men and women, not raging steers. Lewis Tappan was a business man and a churchman. By a curious perversity, this increased his Abolition zeal, but it also compelled him to see Garrison through the eyes of the enemies. With dexterity, the New York Antislavery Society balanced itself slightly to the right of the New England society and although acknowledging the parenthood of the latter, pursued its course with the individualism characteristic of the day.

The New York society was little richer and no more resourceful than all the other bands of Abolitionists, but in the manner of all ardent and poverty-stricken groups they had mastered the art of turning the enemy's ill-temper to their advantage. To be maligned was to gather new forces; a good proslavery attack brought them strength and what they must be satisfied to call popularity. They were all realists. Most of them were hardheaded men of small incomes who had had few opportunities to acquire illusions about the world. All, one might say, except Garrison, but him they needed to lash at ineptitude, to hurl his scorn at the impossible, to stand on a high place and challenge the toughest forces in the world. There were plenty of men willing to deal with the softer forces. Garrison was a lash, and a lash does not always choose its victims carefully. This was why he rankled.

In the fall of 1833, it was decided to organize a National Antislavery Society. How small it must have appeared—sixty men gathered together in Philadelphia! But the friends of slavery would do well to take care from this time on. The avalanche was growing.

Whittier and May were there, Beriah Green who was soon to start Oneida Institute and educate Negroes whether the lawmakers liked it or not, the Tappan brothers and some fifty-odd young men, white and colored, many of whom had come on foot from New England. They made their resolutions calmly. "With entire confidence in the overruling justice of God, we plant ourselves upon the Declaration of Independence and the truths of divine revelation . . . We shall organize anti-slavery societies, if possible, in every city, town and village in the land. We shall send forth agents to lift up the voice of remonstrance, of warning, of entreaty and rebuke. We shall circulate unsparingly and extensively anti-slavery tracts and periodicals." On the second day of the convention they supplemented this by the making of history.

On the invitation of certain Friends, four women had been invited. Now women had always been kept in their place. They had been allowed to have antislavery auxiliaries but were not allowed to partake of the same strong broth as their brothers. In the West, they liked this well enough, for segregation allowed them to carry on their Abolition work under guises that might otherwise have been impossible. They had "library associations," "reading circles," "sewing societies," and what proslavery faction in the town could possibly take exception? Within these gatherings, clothes were made for fugitives, fancy work was sewn which could be sold to raise money to keep the Underground Railroad well oiled, antislavery literature was read aloud, Abolition meetings had their inception and were carried through with extraordinary dispatch. But Lucretia Mott and three of her sisterhood were not content with such obscure partisanship, and when they took their seats in that convention, they jarred most painfully the delicate organism of equal rights. Some of the antislavery men were restive, but the Quaker men folk sat serenely by, satisfied to challenge all forms of bondage. Garrison was pleased; women belonged with men where the causes of humanity were being championed. He did not see in them the rift in his own ranks nor detect the bitter kinship that slaves and women would find in their common struggle in the years to come.

The phenomenally sensitive mechanism that was the slavery-dominated mind responded to any radicalism with violent fluctuations. It was quite right to assume that any deviation from the status quo, whether through women's rights, temperance, or human slavery, bore within itself the seeds of unpredictable social change, and more for this reason than another, the Lane Debates were seen as dangerous straws in the wind. Slavery was now a part of the national consciousness as it had never been before. Lane Seminary lay almost within the jurisdiction of the slavocracy, yet tantalizingly beyond its reach. Established in Cincinnati in 1830, it was a training ground for the ardent young men of the revivalist movement where they might learn the rudiments of orthodoxy. Arthur Tappan had provided a princely endowment; Lyman Beecher, the great cleric, had agreed to become president in order "to hold the West for Protestantism"; Theodore Weld, "the lion-hearted, the sagacious" with his "far-reaching active mind" and golden tongue was the magnet toward which the young men flocked.

They had come from all directions. Marius Robinson came from Tennessee and the sons of the Reverend Mr. Allen, at whose house Weld had spoken so glowingly with Birney, arrived from Alabama. From Kentucky came James Bradley, a Negro who had bought his own freedom, while H. B. Stanton and some of the young men from New York state poled themselves down the Ohio on a raft. None of them were Abolitionists except those few who had already come under the influence of Weld, and Bradley who had been a slave.

But it is not to be imagined that such a situation could last long with Weld at hand. Birney had said that in one year he would abolitionize Ohio. Apart from his own inclinations, Weld had promised Tappan that Abolition would be "prayerfully investigated." He soon found that in the opinion of the young men, Garrison and fanaticism were one and the same thing, and could only be answered by scorn. But Weld did not give up hope. Among his small band, it was agreed that each should choose a student to exhort and convert. So persuasive were their efforts that by the early part of 1834, the students resolved on a public debate of the slavery question.

For eighteen nights, Colonization versus Immediatism was debated with such glow, such fervor, such ringing words of reproof and exorcism, such sweet persuasion that the hearts of those who listened were wrung. Harriet Beecher heard with wide eyes and incredulous ears, and remembered all that had been said. So golden was the harvest that the slaveholding sons, shaken and contrite, bore witness on the seven last nights to the iniquities they now confessed to have seen.

The excitement of those debates spread from the seminary to Cincinnati, and from Cincinnati to the country, and stirred the restless question in the backways and the public places of the North. The Lane Debates became a kind of touchstone to determine the merits of peace with slavery or of strife with Abolition.

Lane Seminary itself underwent a metamorphosis. The new converts now sent out their own apostles, eloquent young men, who a year before could not have foreseen this change in the ordered pattern of their lives. Stanton and Thome, the son of a slaveholder, went to the spring meeting of the antislavery society to bear their testimony, and Thome, Exhibit A, made the speech of the convention.

Another student, Augustus Wattles, feeling a strong need to do and not to say, organized a school for the poor colored children of

Cincinnati, and Marius Robinson, the Tennessean, joined him in the enterprise; another student left the seminary in order to free his slaves, the income from whose labor was maintaining him in school.

The free Negroes of Cincinnati became the rallying point of the students. For them, they gave hundreds of dollars to equip a library and to conduct night classes as a supplement to the schools which they had created for themselves. They organized social clubs, temperance societies, employment services, and a "freedom bureau" where assistance could be given to free Negroes who wished to buy their families. Success was with them. Tappan, fired by their ardor, seeing his dearest hopes of educating the Negro realized, wrote to Weld, "Draw on me for whatever is necessary," and straightway sent him a thousand dollars.

But the trustees of the seminary were distraught. Conservatism was being swamped by Abolition. In the absence of Dr. Beecher, they ordered the dissolution of the seminary's new antislavery society as well as its older Colonization Society. They said that never again should the question of slavery be debated at Lane Seminary.

They rang their own knell. Freedom of speech had been attacked. Four-fifths of the students, whether or not they sympathized with the Abolitionists proposed to leave the seminary as a consequence. The trustees were adamant, Dr. Beecher helpless.

When Asa Mahan, one of the professors, also withdrew from the seminary, the students shook the dust finally from their feet and prepared to journey into the wilderness. For so small a number, their withdrawal made a mighty sound. For the first time a nonpartisan institution had split upon the rocks of Abolition.

They were earnest young men who wished to live within the confines of an organization, but they had no money to form their own institution. John Shipherd heard of them, unattached and wandering, and hurried to Cincinnati to tell them of the college, the "forest bivouac," the sanctuary for women students as well as men, which he had organized at Oberlin. The Lane rebels agreed to enroll if they might choose the president, the faculty and the rules. Shipherd agreed, and he found himself with Asa Mahan for president. But Asa Mahan, the Southerner, refused to be president unless Negroes were admitted. Shipherd's trustees protested, but the trustees were overruled.

By the summer of 1835, thirty of the fifty-four rebels were breaking the ground in the North for "immediatism." These thirty formed the spine of the new antislavery forces in the field, and as pioneers they bore the physical dangers, they were the logical victims of the mobs. To be such a pioneer meant to display no less than cold pure courage. When an antislavery lecturer named Eastman announced his arrival in the town of South Charlestown, Ohio, in 1835, barely a dozen sympathizers could be relied upon, while the newspapers and the clergy built up a rousing hysteria of dark warnings. When Mr. Eastman arrived, a delegation met him, headed by the best citizens. They told him that he was most undesirable and that the citizenry would never allow the slavery question to be debated from the Abolitionists' point of view. Mr. Eastman replied politely but warily that he had heard all this before—in fact, before he spoke he seldom heard anything else—but, "I recognize a higher law than you," he said. "I fear God more than man."

He proceeded on his customary rounds to find a lecture hall. The church, the schoolhouse, all public buildings were closed to him. "Very well," said Charles Paist, a conservative old Quaker who had not heretofore made the acquaintance of Mr. Eastman, "Thee may speak at my house." That evening Mr. Eastman appeared on the porch of Friend Paist's house and found a gratifying crowd. The fact that the crowd was composed largely of men and boys, armed with eggs supplied by the village grocers, meant very little to Mr. Eastman. From poorer seeds had stranger flowers sprung.

The wife of Friend Paist unobtrusively took a position in front of Mr. Eastman, and during the entire period of his lecture she managed to keep herself between him and the egg throwers. She was greatly esteemed in the village, and no one would dare to spatter her with eggs. When Mr. Eastman was finished, he was taken out the back door, led across a cornfield to the house of a Mr. Smith where he was concealed until he left town.

Twenty-one years later Mr. Eastman was able to pluck the flowers that grew from that night. The citizens of South Charlestown provided the arsenal that prevented the recapture of Addison White, probably the most famous fugitive of Ohio.

The rails of the invisible line stretched by now from Maine to Iowa and from Alabama to Canada. Many a capitalist who depended on iron rails for his fortune would have been glad had the service been as excellent or the spirit of his employees so high.

The stakes and switches of this invisible railroad were the colored people, and an excellent reason for their responsibility lay in the fugitives' fear, cultivated by masters, of white Abolitionists who were endowed by them with sadistic and cannibalistic tendencies. Many a hungry and desperate fugitive wandered for weeks within the orbit of white station keepers, so acute was his fear, and even with proof in his stomach of white kindness, he might still refuse to tell his name or his story. This forced colored conductors into activities "so extensive" as Birney wrote to Lewis Tappan, that many an Abolitionist was ignorant of a danger until it had passed.

Jane Lewis of New Lebanon, Ohio, rowed fugitives regularly across the Ohio River. John Parker, who had bought himself for $2000, tempted fate by working hand in glove with the Rankins. An old colored man of Martins Ferry, Ohio, haunted the Virginia shore, showing slaves the way to freedom and then displaying himself in a drunken condition—real or not, who is to say?—in order to escape suspicion. James Cummichael, whose wife had been sold into a coffle which was to go down the Mississippi to New Orleans had a personality that was both affable and cunning. He went, bold and friendly, jingling money which he had earned by hiring his extra time, and struck up a conversation with the crew of the vessel. During the course of the conversation, he merely confirmed what they already knew that "niggers had no feelings and didn't care whether they were slaves or not." He told them with his own mouth that he knew his wife would like "de souf" and that maybe he'd like to be bought too. This was the kind of conversation they enjoyed. They even played games with him, and being a decent "nigger" he paid for their liquor. Not too soon they were liquor-logged with sleep. It was a matter of no time at all before he had his wife and several other slaves off the boat and hidden in a grove until, with the night, they could start for the North.

John Mason, a Kentucky fugitive, left Canada to spread the news among his friends in Kentucky. In nineteen months he passed along 265 slaves, and before his work was finished, sent 1,300 of them on the Underground Railroad. One autumn day nearing the river with four escaping slaves, he heard the baying of hounds. He tried to rally the fugitives, but their terror of the dogs defeated him. He fought until both his arms were broken and his body ripped by the dogs. He was sold, without loss of time, to a New Orleans trader. Yet—how did he do it?—within one year and five months of his capture, an Ohio friend received a Canadian letter from him.

From the security of Canada more and more fugitives were returning for their families, and masters were finding their ruses more difficult to combat. Josiah Henson made his first return about this time, although that statement could have meant nothing to his contemporaries. Josiah Henson was the figure who, later transformed, went about the world as Uncle Tom between the covers of Mrs. Stowe's formidable attack on slavery. He had escaped, after a youth full of good deeds to his master, through the wilderness of Indiana and Ohio. Chased by wolves, pursued by starvation, with a wailing child and a sick wife, helped now and then when he came within the radius of the Underground Railroad but aided more substantially by a tribe of Indians living in northern Ohio, he had eventually reached Canada.

There he organized committees for the bewildered Negroes who were finding Canada a forbidding place. He instructed them on crop rotation to offset the ignorance of men who had been trained to the raising of a few staples; gave them homely lessons in economics so that they might understand something of wages and profits. After five years or so of security, he came back from Canada on the plea of a fugitive who wanted his family with him but could not face the dangers of return. Henson, with only a token to identify himself, set out through New York, Pennsylvania, Ohio, for Kentucky. After weeks on the road and continuous danger, he found the man's family too fearful of the risks to make the long journey to Canada. By the slave grapevine, he heard of a group, fifty miles away, who wished to escape if they could find a leader. He established contact with them, and led them out through Richmond, Indiana.

Back in Canada, his friend was still determined to have his family freed. Henson agreed to try once more. This time he was successful. Before he finished his work—before he went to England in 1840 and became the first fugitive slave seen by Queen Victoria—he had carried away over two hundred slaves, and found a fame commensurate with his love of freedom.

What was to be done with all such men, whether white or colored? Higher bribes? Even the Kentucky legislature agreed that since a certain opprobrium was attached to men who captured other men for money, the inducement must be worth the loss of character. By 1838 the reward was raised from $30 to $100.

Why was it then so singularly ineffective, even against men as conspicuous as John Rankin and Levi Coffin? John Rankin thought it had something to do with the Higher Law. Levi Coffin was more or less sure, and Levi Coffin had a more than passing right to answer in whatever way he chose, for through his fingers ran the "trains" that bore over 3,000 fugitives to freedom.

He had begun the work of passing on when a youth in North Carolina. After his removal to Indiana—following the example of many freedom-loving Southern Quakers—he had placed himself in a highly culpable position, but the law did not move.

Learning that the only protection for fugitives were the exposed and badly organized "stations" of their own people, he marched to his co-religionists. How could they stand so calmly by? They excused themselves. They were afraid of the law. Levi Coffin expounded the scriptures to them and then set them a good example by seeing without delay that his own "locomotive" was well oiled.

It was far from an easy life that he set for himself. Many proslavery customers stormed out of his shop. His business wavered for lack of patronage. But the neighborhood continued to prosper. New emigrants from the Quaker South were arriving, Abolition sympathizers. Levi Coffin soon found himself director of the local bank. Even the bitterest enemies of Abolition were, on occasions, not above bank loans. He exerted his influence adeptly for his cause. It was well for his underground activities that his business had begun to prosper. He needed ready money at all times, since he never knew when his "train" would be called into use.

Fugitives were sent to him from Cincinnati, from Madison and Jeffersonville, Indiana. A week seldom passed without travelers on this invisible road. The Coffins never knew at what hour of the night they would be wakened by a knock at the door—the signal to build a roaring fire and heat a meal for fugitives huddled in the wagons outside. But the Coffin "station" was used to large numbers. It was the converging point of several lines. Fugitives would be sent in batches from operators in the South, from operators in the East, in the West.

It was a Southerner who first called Levi Coffin "The President of the Underground Railroad." It came about when seventeen fugitives, men and women, escaped in a body from Kentucky. They lived through perils, were scattered by gunshot, came together again and finally reached the Underground Railroad north of the river. Seventeen flight-marked slaves filed into the Coffin kitchen late one night, brought in two wagons by conductors. Seventeen thousand dollars' worth of property sat at a long table and ate the breakfast that was hastily prepared. Early the next morning after the wagons had rumbled on, a message came to Coffin, saying that fifteen Kentuckians had arrived in the neighborhood, hell-bent on their property. Coffin sent the messenger as fast as he could ride to intercept the wagons and scatter the fugitives. Then he settled down to observe the antics of the catchers.

Chasing will-o'-the-wisps, they at length caught up with the name of Levi Coffin, "nigger-thief." Their rage was monumental, and their actions promised to be so specific that a friend of Coffin's arrived in the middle of the night, with two loaded pistols, to take up his post at the door.

The hunters hung about the town, refusing to believe that such tangible objects as seventeen slaves would not pass before their eyes if they looked hard enough. Their threats diminished as their prospects waned, and after some weeks they set out for home. As they passed the plain square home of Levi Coffin, they made a significant gesture, and one put it into words, "There's an Underground Railroad around here and Levi Coffin is its president."

This was repeated so often and spread so far that letters came to Newport, addressed to "Levi Coffin, President of the Underground Railroad."

What Coffin, what the unnamed "conductors" up and down these Western States, set afire was licking higher and higher. In their stern, solid, drab persons was the essence of drama lived secretly, exposed reluctantly. The drama of their avocation could run no further than their nearest neighbor—if he were trustworthy. The pyrotechnics must be pushed off onto the Garrisonians.

The antislavery case was straining against the obstacle of untrained agents, of an unresolved manner of attack. Amid all the running off of fugitives, the stress and verbiage of Abolition agents, the Cause must imprint itself on men's minds as holy; it must fire men as the great revivals fired them. It must not be all war, but peace—peace with one's conscience, piety translated into daily deeds. Men must exhort and lift the heart and convert. George Thompson of England, with the golden tongue, the persuasive ways, and the Abolition honors of his own country, was, Garrison believed, the very man to do it. In his personality, Thompson had everything to recommend him to American audiences. The strength of the British Abolitionists had become mighty right arms to the Americans, and the effect of British emancipation had been incalculable. Garrison announced in the fall of 1834 that Thompson had been invited to lecture in America.

But being Garrison, from all this he reaped only the whirlwind. It seemed as though the legions who hated him and all his works seized on this announcement with the avidity of people who had exhausted their usual sources of outrage and were only too glad to be supplied afresh. "A foreigner coming to tell us how to behave! That man Garrison washing our dirty linen again to amuse an Englishman!" Garrison pretended to ignore the outcry, setting it down to the rowdyism of the Northern slavocracy. Whether Garrison really understood the temper of the people is questionable. What he could have done, had he understood it, is more questionable. Combined with the natural proslavery sentiment of business men was a new and restless force that sprang from the changing economic values of the day. Two gigantic forces, meeting head on, were producing a combustion that lighted up the skies of many cities. Industrial capitalism and slavery were natural enemies and yet in the blind confusion of these years they made an ironically common cause against the Abolitionists.

With the growing power of an industrialized North, foreign laborers, especially the Irish, dreamed of riches and opportunity. They had no racial prejudices; they came merely to turn a hand for their own fortunes. But Negroes, free or fugitive, harried by a society that had no place for them, drove down the scale of wages to the desperation point. This, combined with an unemployment that was becoming chronic and a subhuman social and economic standard, caught white workers in a trap of hatred. Violence flared. The Irishman, accustomed to talk with his fists, saw no other way to defend himself. The employers of the North, proslavery almost to a man, agreed to give preference to the foreign laborer, if he would accept the same wage scale as the Negro. In this way the employer could placate the South and drive out the detested Negro. It shifted the burden from his own shoulders and meant nothing to him if the white laborer, bitter with starvation wages, hated the Negro even more and shouted out his desperation with a paving stone in his hand. Many a good employer, the child of a lawless age, led a mob on this vain, blind, violent effort to extirpate once and for all these dark invaders. It was all a poor passion-ridden longing and it is not to be wondered that the Abolitionists put blinders on their eyes and refused to be led down devious and treacherous paths away from their panacea of all social ills, the abolition of slavery. But in the eyes of the workers and the employers, the Abolitionists must bear the blame for stirring up the blacks, and the blacks must bear the blame for existing.

It was such irrationality that reduced New York to a battlefield for three days in the summer of 1834. Thirty-one houses and two churches were destroyed by a mob. They invaded the Bowery Theatre near Elizabeth Street and stampeded the audience; they broke into Lewis Tappan's house on Rose Street and threw his furniture out of the windows, building a mighty bonfire in the street with his bed linen and possessions. Placards appeared mysteriously when the fever waned, inciting to rasher and more awful deeds. Mounted police, riding into the mob, drove them back from burning buildings until they pressed, thousands deep, into all the streets within that momentary radius. Some tore down fences to use for clubs; others overturned carts to act as barricades against the horsemen. In two days, terror broke them up—terror of the law that so seldom acted against them, and for a night a kind of feverish calm fell upon the city.

But in the morning, there were the Abolitionists again; there were the Tappans, fat and prosperous; and there were the "niggers," leading the white fools about by the nose. Arthur Tappan, knowing the mark that sat on his brow, armed the clerks in his Pearl Street store with guns, and as the first stone crashed through the window and the shouts of the rioters grew to a roar, they stood at their counters and lifted their muskets. The leaders, breaking down the door, needed only a single glance. Their flight from the store pushed back the mob like a wave on the shore and with only a brief consultation, they swept about and made off for more amenable substitutes. They gutted a church on Spring Street in retaliation, tearing up the interior to use as weapons against the 27th Regiment which clattered through the streets in a halfhearted effort to bring the riot to an end. Later that day they sacked a Negro church and set fire to several more Negro homes. By the end of the fourth day, every regiment in the city was under arms to subdue the terror.

It was so hopeless, so futile, in the manner of violence. The Abolitionists were not weakened; the Negroes were not terrorized; the rioters had not cooled their blood. The fever spread across the river to New Jersey, up to Norwich, Connecticut, where Negroes were attacked and driven out of town, and an Abolition pastor drummed from his pulpit and out of his church; down to Philadelphia, where a mob broke into an anti-slavery meeting and threw vitriol on the gathering, then spread itself through the Negro quarters, and for three days paralyzed the city with riots.

To such welcomes George Thompson came. Committees waited on him in one town of every three, requesting him to leave before rioting broke out. On numerous occasions, brickbats and stones were thrown through windows as he addressed the audience. From one of his meetings, Samuel May escaped in time to see a posse dragging a cannon to use against the building. He was insulted in the streets and mobs broke up meetings where it was rumored he would be. The campaign of the newspapers, from Maine to Georgia, was an unending stream of vituperation. A private regiment, marching through Boston, carrying two targets; one a likeness of Thompson, the other a kneeling colored woman.

But Thompson bore no more than native Abolitionists. Whittier was made the target for bullets as he drove through the streets. Guns weighed down the pockets of hired ruffians. No act of violence was without its influential supporters.

Everyone had explanations for these murderous impulses, and everyone had some truth behind him. Some understood the belligerent fear of white laborers. Others sympathized with the bitter and defeated colonizers. Men of attenuated antislavery impulses deplored Garrison's language and his lack of compromise and claimed that they would have joined the antislavery ranks had it not been for him who, by his arrogance and violence, stirred up violence of another sort to make men's sleep uneasy. Still others, like William Jay, the son of the famous jurist, sensed something that ran like a hissing stream through the national consciousness and was compounded of all these elements and something more. "There is abroad in the land a spirit of lawless violence," he warned, "which means danger to civil and religious liberty."

Yet there could now be no turning back. In four years the Abolition movement had become the conscience of the country, and until the devil, slavery, was exorcised, no conscience could be still. "What have I done?" Garrison asked triumphantly. "In seizing the 'trump of God' I had indeed to blow a jarring blast—but it was necessary to wake up a nation slumbering in the lap of moral death . . . Within four years I have seen my principles embraced by thousands of the best men in the nation. I have seen prejudices which were deemed incurable utterly eradicated from the breasts of a great multitude. I have seen the press teeming with books, pamphlets, tracts, and periodicals, all in favor of the bondman and against his oppressors. I have seen crowds rushing to hear the tale of woe and of blood. I have seen discussions of slavery going on in public and in private, among all classes and in all parts of the land; and more spoken, and written and printed and circulated in one month than there formerly was in many years."

If he were partly right—and surely that must be allowed him!—the quality of those coming now to his support must have made his steel eyes glint for a moment. William Jay did not care greatly for Garrison, he did not hold altogether with "Immediatism," but he knew that it must be Abolition or the end of constitutional freedom and he brought his prestige to the cause. Edmund Quincy was a flower of Boston aristocracy, but he was willing to become a pariah—for this was the price they all must pay—if he might ring the doorbell for Mr. Garrison's Abolition. Cassius Clay was said to be the wealthiest young man in Kentucky, yet by 1841 his political life had been blasted because a single lecture of Garrison had brought him to a fever heat, and youth, ambition and money turned to the cause. The Grimké sisters, who some years before had—without exaggeration—fled from their aristocratic slaveowning family in Charleston, were ladies of extreme gentility, but they were willing for the sake of Garrisonism to sink their delicacy into the task

of becoming "female itinerants." "Female itinerants!" It demanded great
courage of male Abolitionists to assume this responsibility; it demanded
great courage on their part to blaze so untrodden a path for their sisterhood. But Abolition demanded it, and they paid the price of immediate
arrest in South Carolina with consummate cheerfulness.

The Abolitionists were beginning to concentrate their fire in pamphlets—pamphlets that touched the heart of the matter in as simple and
laconic a fashion as the age allowed. How many hundred thousand went
out from the New York office is difficult to say, for Elizur Wright who
was in charge of their distribution promised twenty to fifty thousand a
week. They were scatter sheets, left by the wayside, in parlors, barrooms,
stage coaches, railway cars, and boat decks; sent blindly through the
mails to all public addresses. Several thousand were posted at regular
intervals to governors and legislators, judges, lawyers, clergymen, editors.
Large bundles were dispatched to clergymen and postmasters, with a plea
to distribute them in their neighborhoods. As 1835 wore on, over a million tracts penetrated the buttresses of the South as well. The possibility
of reaching the Negroes was doubtful, but as long as a single Abolition
exhortation remained within their orbit, no slaveowner could be easy in
his mind for, as Calhoun said, the Negroes must never know of any
exertions in their behalf since they would surely meet them halfway.

Abolitionists were accused of smuggling handkerchiefs, printed with
antislavery cuts, into bales of goods designed for the Southern markets,
of relying not only on printed matter but on pictures and engravings
which showed the joys of freedom to uneducated Negroes. As though to
prove their accusations. Abolition papers were picked up on a North
Carolina road, evidently thrown out by a stage coach passenger. Georgia
warned against antislavery schoolbooks, and passed resolutions against
"preachers or teachers whom we find advocating or entertaining opinions
in any manner favorable to emancipation." The records of all men seeking political office were scrutinized with unprecedented care, while
Maryland provided ten to twenty years for anyone who circulated or
assisted in circulating newspapers or pictures calculated to stir slave
rebellion. Virginia passed a similar law, but without the same severity,
and Alabama strengthened its law of 1832 which punished by death
anyone distributing antislavery literature, whether written, printed, or
engraved, on paper, wood, cloth, metal or stone. Tennessee agreed that
from ten to twenty years at hard labor was a reasonable penalty for those
who by words, gestures or sermons, in the presence of slaves indicated
a hope beyond their station, and South Carolina, recognizing the most
baleful influence of all, that of one enlightened slave upon another,

forbade a South Carolinian or anyone from another state to bring within its borders slaves who had been north of the Potomac River, to the West Indies, or to Mexico. A violator must pay a fine of $1,000 and forfeit all contaminated slaves.

At last people began to question. How much of this was fear of insurrection and how much fear that the slaveless whites might be seduced by Abolition arguments? Slaveholding politicians were not prepared to lose what they had built up so miraculously. On political questions, the small man must be kept deaf, dumb and blind. To confuse him, to complicate the issues, to cast a great mantle of racial solidarity over matters which bred insurrection was the manifest duty of the oligarchy.

The governor of North Carolina spoke dark words that lifted for a moment the myth of racial distinction. The workers of a country, he said, whether *"bleached or unbleached"* were a perpetual menace to political power, and within twenty-five years the North might find it necessary to reduce their "bleached" servants to slavery.

In Mississippi, in July, 1835, twenty-one "bleached and unbleached" insurrectionists were hanged. In October, white lumbermen in Georgia were involved in a slave plot. In December, two whites were hanged in Louisiana for their share in a planned uprising.

The governor of South Carolina was convinced that Abolitionists provided the subversive stimuli, and suggested that the "laws of every community should punish this species of interference with death without benefit of clergy." His legislature passed a resolution demanding of Northern states the suppression of Abolition societies. Within that year, 1835, Virginia, Georgia, North Carolina, Alabama, Mississippi and Kentucky had followed the example of South Carolina, and the governors of all the free states received the resolutions. How indignant one would expect them to be! Go home and mind your own business! But they were quite humble. They promised to do what they could.

Only the Massachusetts legislature took definite steps. Early in the new year they attempted to legislate these bastard children of their intellectual glory out of existence. But the Abolitionists won, as they always did in a crisis. If, as a body, they ever failed in tactical success, it is not recorded. Against the gavel of the chairman, against the gagging by the committee, they presented their case of free speech or mob rule so stirringly that the committee had no alternative. The resolutions against them were tabled and never brought again into the open.

In the end, nothing more than obsequiousness took place in the North, although the New York Exchange did offer $5,000 for the head of

Arthur Tappan, and Elizur Wright found it judicious to live behind
iron bolts and barred windows.

In the South, the slavocracy continued to take action, independent
of the slow movements of democratic procedure. In July a young theological student named Amos Dresser, a Lane Seminary rebel, a Southerner, went to Tennessee to sell the Cottage Bible, a common enough
practice among young men who wished to make a modest living. He
was accused of preaching Abolition. The Vigilance Committee agreed
that the charge could not be sustained, but urged that since slavery had
no protection against opinion, the citizens must provide a penalty. He
was condemned to receive twenty lashes in the public square, and at
midnight, by the light of torches, before several thousand people, he
was stripped and flogged.

The story of Amos Dresser crackled through the North. The slaveholders replied to protests by tarring and feathering Aaron Kitchell, a
Northern schoolteacher who taught in Georgia, and riding him out of
town on a rail to the dirge of a drum. They killed three white men in
South Carolina and in Georgia for "association with Negroes," a penal
offense in both those states. Free Negroes were watched as foreigners
are in a country at war. Steamboats and railway trains were supervised.
Every stranger, every free Negro, every piece of mail from the North
was scrutinized with a cold and regimented zeal.

Post offices all over the South were complaining of the Abolition literature which passed through their helpless fingers. In this same July,
*The Southern Patriot* of Charleston cried that the ship *Columbia* had
arrived, loaded with antislavery newspapers. If the post office did not
act, the people would. The people acted. They broke into the post office,
carried the objectionable mail into the street and burned it publicly.
It made a large bonfire, bigger than the conscientious postmaster of
Charleston could curb. He wrote frantically to Postmaster General Kendall at Washington, asking how he might protect the mails. Kendall
delayed answering for nearly a week, and his equivocation was a masterpiece. Mails must be delivered, but "by no act or direction of mine,
official or private, could I be induced to aid knowingly in giving circulation to papers of this description. We owe an obligation to the laws,
but we owe a higher one to the communities in which we live."

The postmaster in Charleston appealed to the postmaster in New York
to hold up the antislavery mailings as long as he could and relieve the
tension at the Southern end. The postmaster in New York appealed to
the antislavery society to keep their literature out of the mails. The so-

ciety answered with the Bill of Rights. The postmaster expressed surprise and held the papers.

Some of the Northern papers were shocked by the whole affair and suggested that Mr. Kendall should retire to private life. The Postmaster General was in a bad tangle of politics since his appointment had not yet been confirmed. When he appealed to the President, Andrew Jackson rolled out an impressive stream of epithets and came out for the law, although he urged the drum court for Abolitionists. The next session of Congress, he promised, would consider the matter of a new law.

That bonfire in the square at Charleston lighted up many corners of the South. Not only had the well-bred mob been left unchastised, but the Charleston *Courier* publicly thanked the clergy who had attended an open meeting in support of this act and had voluntarily suspended the Sunday schools in which free Negroes were taught.

Within its own bailiwick, free speech and free assemblage had been entirely abolished, lynch law had taken on a new meaning and now carried the sting of death. The slavocracy could only utter a final malediction against the North for which the *Southern Patriot* provided the words: if the North wished to maintain her trade with the South, she must suppress her Abolitionists.

Perhaps this was a rash and shallow gesture, since every one knew that the South imported nearly everything it used, from slave whips to toothbrushes, but its moral effect quivered on the nerves of cautious people and gave another, however chimerical, reason for the Northern merchant to hate the Abolitionist. Certain citizens of Georgia were specific in their threats. Any who traded with the Tappans would become the special object of their indignation, and a merchant in Charleston who also had a store in New York was told that if suspicions that he had dealings with the Tappans could be proved, his Charleston store would be burned to the ground.

Arthur Tappan was in fact very much desired in certain sections of the South. *The Macon Messenger* announced that Georgia had raised a reward of $12,000 for the man who brought him across its border. New Orleans raised the bid to $20,000 and an unnamed state was reputed to have offered $3,000 for his ears alone. It was quite evident why the rewards for Tappan exceeded those for the archconspirator, Garrison. The Tappan brothers represented the solid, successful, conservative Northern business men, rich and honorable, the aristocrats of the new era of capitalism, the strength and sinews of the growing North. Who knew how soon their antislavery iconoclasm might permeate the business world of the North, the nervous system of that "other country" which the Southern slavocracy could not do without? If only the North would extradite the Abolition leaders . . . The South could then charge them with criminal offenses. . . . Alabama attempted it, demanding that the governor of New York return a certain R. G. Williams to Alabama "for inciting" slaves. The demand was made in the usual form, stating clearly that Williams was a fugitive from justice, wanted for certain Alabama crimes. The only difficulty for the governor of New York seemed to lie in the fact that Williams had never been in Alabama. The governor of Alabama admitted this freely, but argued that since his spirit had incited insubordination through the pages of the paper which he edited, the corporeal man could have done no more.

Effigies of Garrison, Dr. Cox, whose church had been burned in the New York riots, and Arthur Tappan were burned in Charleston. In New York Harbor, a small ship appeared with eighteen Charleston men aboard who made no effort to conceal their interest in the rewards offered for Tappan's body. Tappan's business suffered through the ostracism of his Northern associates who were alarmed at his presence in their midst. The Northern press called him an incendiary, a midnight murderer, an assassin, in the best imitation of their Southern brethren. Insurance companies refused to protect his property—and why should they, since an effort was made to burn him out every so often? Banks would not lend him money. A slave's ear arrived by post, and a piece of rope fell out of a morning letter. So wide and constant was his fame that country people, coming to the city would enter his store merely to have a look at him.

Every pressure was put upon him to give up his activities. A delegation of bankers and insurance men pleaded with him to tranquillize the public mind, to assure his credit, to protect his creditors who were bound to suffer if his business failed—and fail it must with such a burden laid upon it!—to restore his reputation by resigning from his consummate folly, the New York Antislavery Society. It was said that he thought for a long time and then he answered with admirable brevity, "I will be hanged first."

There was a kind of noble courage in those words. He might very well be hanged. No Abolitionist put this from his mind. The jumbled motives of the anti-Abolition firebrands, the fear of poverty-stricken workers, the determination to protect forever the property of Southern clients, the startling and disillusioning rejection of all that democracy implied, appeared again and again in that year. Mass meetings in New York—"We deplore slavery, but we deplore the Abolitionists more"—sinister meetings in Utica where the crowd declared for suppression of

Abolition speech and press—noisy crowds in Philadelphia and young men crying out that the legislature must pass such laws as would protect the South. In Boston, in Faneuil Hall, that bulwark of democratic glory, 1,300 of the most respectable citizens hurried together to inveigh against the radicals who were trying to separate a man from his property and at the same time split the Union. The spirits of Washington and Jefferson were invoked to sanction the diatribes against the Abolitionists. The threat to business was repeated. What might have sunk to the bottom was stirred up again.

The echoes spread throughout New England. Three hundred citizens of Canaan, New Hampshire, whipped a yoke of a hundred oxen and dragged the small Noyes Academy to a swamp. The Noyes Academy had opened its door to Henry Highland Garnet and Alexander Crummell, and they were black.

Samuel May was mobbed five times that October in Vermont. George Thompson, who had survived the vilifications and stones of respectable people, had to be smuggled to Garrison's house outside of Boston. Yet between dusk and dawn a gallows went up outside the Garrison house, and two ropes dangled there for him and his host.

Garrison heated his pen and spoke for both of them. It was evident, however, that George Thompson's three-year mission in the United States would be over within this year, if he could be smuggled aboard a ship without a mob.

Finally the match was struck to the pile when word got around that those Jezebels in trousered petticoats, the Boston Female Antislavery Society, had invited Thompson to address their meeting on October 21st. The ladies denied it, but placards appeared in the city—violent placards that called on all lovers of the Union to "snake out the infamous scoundrel." A purse of $100 was offered to the man who would seize him and bring him to "the tar kettle before dark." The chivalry of the city was determined to teach frail womanhood that her place was at home "attending to domestic concerns instead of sowing the seeds of discord in the antislavery rooms."

Yet Abolition women had as much contempt for unruly males as any other women. Thirty ladies, white and colored, met that day, and Garrison crossed the hall from his office to address them. The meeting opened with a Bible reading and a prayer. The prayer could barely be heard for the howling of the mob that had taken possession of the street. (The conservative papers guessed that between two and five thousand people composed that body.) The mayor appeared, distraught and a little frightened. He entreated the ladies to leave. They asked him why they should give over their constitutional rights. "Ladies, if you do not wish to see a scene of bloodshed and confusion, go home!" Mrs. Maria Weston Chapman, fashionable, beautiful and intellectual, answered calmly, "If this is the last bulwark of freedom, we may as well die here as anywhere."

Garrison said he would leave the building; the ladies would be safe if he were gone. The mayor, deeply agitated, urged them also to make a good retreat. The mob had broken down the door and was swarming up the stairs. Garrison's escape was cut off, and the mayor assisted him out a back window. The ladies, two by two, a white lady and a colored side by side, walked down the stairs, their hands folded in their cotton gloves, their eyes busily identifying the genteel leaders of the mob.

The mob, missing Garrison, spread about the neighborhood. He was found in a carpenter's shop, attempting to get through into the next street. The cries of the mob spread excitement like ripples from a stone, and many came on the run to see the end of the monster.

They tried to hurl Garrison from a second-story window, but a more level-headed mobster saved him from that fate. His clothes were half torn from his body, yet they tied a rope around him and dragged him into the street. What a sinister sight this was. In Boston, the cradle of liberty, a champion of equality wore a rope about his body.

"Don't hurt him!" some cried from the crowd. "He is an American!"

People, pouring from the side streets were shouting and pushing, and sometimes those by the curb could not see him for the closing tide. Again, pale women and flush-faced men saw him clearly, walking between the two men who held his arms, his thin, hawk face raised, and a slight smile on his lips. He wore the detached expression of a near-sighted man and he closed his eyes now and then against the light, for he had taken off his spectacles when first caught so that they would not be broken.

At the turn of State Street, near the City Hall, the mayor and his constables made a sortie on the mob. The constables brandished their sticks and forced a way through the crowd. Seizing Garrison from his captors, they hustled him up the steps of the City Hall. He sat in the mayor's office until night fell, looking down on the mob which stirred and shouted in the street outside. The mayor, plagued and uncertain, debated the advisability of keeping him in the same building which housed the post office. He remembered the Charleston mob and the burning of the mail. The Leverett Street Jail was not far away, and there, in spite of mobs and hell, Garrison must go. The mayor ordered a carriage brought to the back entrance, and went downstairs with his prisoner.

But the mob had had an opportunity to scent this new development. When they swept around the corner, Garrison sat in the carriage pale and rigid. They tried to unfasten the horses and break down the doors, but the constables and the driver beat them off, striking knuckles and lashing with a whip, and the horses galloped all the way to the jail. There, the sheriff, to make this incarceration legal, swore out a warrant that Garrison had been breaking the peace.

That evening, his friends came to talk to him through the bars— Whittier and Mr. and Mrs. Bronson Alcott, and others. The next day, the judge dismissed him.

On the wall of his cell, he had written, "William Lloyd Garrison was put into this cell on Monday afternoon, October 21, 1835, to save him from the violence of a respectable and influential mob, who sought to destroy him for preaching the abominable and dangerous doctrine that all men are created equal, and that all oppression is odious in the sight of God."

Oppression was never so oppressive in Boston again. Too many people were shocked out of their complacency. Two absorbed young men stood in the crowd that day: within two years, Wendell Phillips was to throw in his priceless lot with this man who wore a rope around his body; within fifteen years, Charles Sumner was to sit in the United States Senate as the champion of the slave. Perhaps they both had read the justification issued by those gentlemen from the counting houses of State Street and the parlors of Beacon Street, who frankly led the mob, "to assure our brethren of the South that we cherish rational and correct notions on the subject of slavery."

The next day, word came from Utica that at the hour when Garrison was finding a not inconsiderable glory, six hundred antislavery delegates had been attacked by an equally uncontrolled and respectable mob, who drove them from the Presbyterian Church straight into the arms of Gerrit Smith. In this case, as well, the mob served a highly desirable end. To draw Gerrit Smith into the Abolition ranks was to bring to their support a vast income and an immense prestige. He had been induced to attend the meeting as an onlooker, a convert from colonization. Before the day was over, he was chairman of an emergency committee and had invited four hundred delegates to meet on his estate at Peterboro, New York.

Gerrit Smith was, above everything, an honest man, zealous in his pursuit of righteousness. And righteousness to him was a strong church, revivals to shake the soul, equal rights for women, uncorrupted politics, world peace, and above all, emancipation. His family had been slaveholders, his wife's family were now slaveholders, the colored man was to him an object of immediate concern, not a theme for dialectics. He had given over one hundred and fifty thousand acres of his tremendous holdings to three thousand colored men and women and provided them with the means to settle into life on their own terms; he had established on his huge estate an efficient station of the Underground Railroad.

Gerrit Smith was a man who brought a new temper to the Abolition cause by reason of the vastness which he seemed to typify. Vast compassion, vast interests, vast estates, vast fortune; the little band of poverty-stricken zealots became now men of a wider world. With him the tight era of Garrisonism drew toward an end, an era that, whatever the enemies of Garrison might say, was in a tradition of heroism that Gerrit Smith could never approximate. Smith, Birney—who would the next year cross once and for all from the South into the North—and the Tappans already held somewhere in the recesses of their minds, a new era—an era of political Abolition.

The Boston mob, the Utica mob, all the rowdyism, all the bewilderment of "bleached" laborers, set the antislavery cause on its feet as no other event had done, except the challenge of *The Liberator*. The threat to the very basis of Americanism, the Bill of Rights, troubled many solid folk who had never seen a Negro. For a while, it is true, Garrison was forced to leave Boston, *The Liberator* went underground and printed its issues clandestinely, yet the voice of antislavery had become the voice of new recruits, organized and trained as they had never been before. Within the year, the National Antislavery Society had gathered the Seventy together, as Weld's new band of agents was called in all humility. They had been trained in ardor and in facts by the passionate Weld who made it his life's work to deal only in those two essentials. Most of the Seventy were clergymen or theological students who could speak directly to this church-respecting age.

Popular opinion was shifting toward them ever so slightly. The great Dr. Channing published a book called *Slavery* which, although an equivocation from Garrison's point of view, yet brought the imprecations of the South on the head of Channing who represented orthodoxy to more people, North and South, than any other man of his day. Theodore Weld, gathered the testimony of Southern newspapers and local witnesses into a book which he called *American Slavery As It Is*, and shocked the country as it would not be shocked again until *Uncle Tom's Cabin* broke upon them.

All such variegated testimony nurtured the antislavery sentiment. Ohio, in 1835, felt strong enough to organize a state society with John Rankin and his sons in the seats of honor, and the Lane Rebels attending in force from Oberlin. The report of that meeting makes lively reading. These men were Underground Railroad operators. They told in their plain speech of the courage they had witnessed, the fugitives they had helped, the kidnapings they had forestalled. They prepared a grim and detailed list of the violence in Ohio against the free Negroes, of the attacks on lives and property, of the oppression that the law worked upon them, so that one did not know whether he was in the South or in the North. The Oberlin students, invested with the robes of militant Abolition, had not only their wide field of antislavery agitation to expatiate upon, but also the enterprising "station" that was working on full schedule in Oberlin.

All such Abolition societies, born in the storm and grounded in the swell, strengthened the Underground Railroad. Each member became, willy-nilly, a candidate for station-keeper. An Abolitionist might be called upon at any time to help the fugitive, although every man who helped a fugitive was not necessarily an Abolitionist. That friend might be found suddenly in the man who, when not taken by surprise, was the stoutest champion of Southern rights. "I'm a Democrat," one rough, bearded fellow said, coming into a Quaker's store, "but I couldn't stand the pleading look in that fellow's eyes."

The full-time friends came by the same route. William Cratty in central Ohio, deeply moved by the sight of a fugitive with an iron band about his neck from which prongs curved up and over his head, began his operations in 1836 and continued them for nineteen years. He helped three thousand slaves to escape. His reputation spread so far that a reward of $3,000 was offered for him if delivered dead or alive below the Southern line. He eluded both the Federal law and the lynch law, although he said he never opened his door until he first knew the intention of his visitor.

Most of the points of danger were well marked by now. If the slave catchers knew where to find their fugitives, so did the men of the Underground Railroad. In New York City these danger zones centered around the ships which filled the harbor. On these ships were, many times, either domestic slaves who did not know of the New York laws under which they could claim their freedom, free Negroes who had fled from the

South, without free papers or proof of property, or kidnaped slaves who had been caught and stowed away for the voyage home. It became obvious by 1835 that a committee would have to be organized to give its sole time to the protection of these individuals.

This task fell to a handful of white and colored men. Against an evil of kidnaping, hoodwinking and exploitation that would have harried the Federal government, they set themselves. David Ruggles was the secretary of the group. He was an intelligent and enterprising Negro, an editor and doctor. And, most important in his new position, capable of dealing with all the intricacies of the law and the strategies that would entangle them. As a natural concomitant of these activities, he was a zealous station keeper of the Underground Railroad and piloted over six hundred fugitives through the dangers of the city and on to the next conductor.

The Vigilance Committee was a natural development of the Negroes' own social life, a development from the schools they had founded (by 1834 there were seven African Free Schools in New York), from the colored newspapers which were exerting a small but insistent power, and from the churches which were playing an increasingly important part in the struggle for emancipation. Not only were the colored clergy actively running off fugitives, but their churches were, in the North as well as in the South, the meeting places of conspirators for freedom. What they supported, they supported with the energy of people who knew that they had no time to lose.

In spite of the law of 1807, the slave trade had revived with all the energy of a refreshed monster. France, Spain and Portugal had carried on the trade until about 1830, when it began to fly again the American flag. The government gave its oblique consent to this by refusing to adhere to the international agreement of Right to Search, to which all other countries had subscribed, and by making an insufficient appropriation for ships to guard the African coast. Many of the slave ships came to New York; slave pens were built in private houses where the Africans were held until they could be shipped to the South. The committee knew that the law which forbade the holding of slaves in New York state was being violated, and they set their small strength against it. They sued, and they were thrown out of court. They sued again and met only the powerful proslavery forces that dominated the New York courts. The price of slaves was rising. They continued their agitation, they drew in the best legal talent of the Abolition movement. Bands of determined colored citizens again and again fought with the kidnapers and slave agents, snatching fugitives from under their noses or giving them up only after a struggle. David Ruggles, who bore the brunt because of his position, at last lost his eyesight from the strains and perils of his office.

The dangers of the cities, both physical and psychological, were evident at this time to all antislavery workers. Weld, coming to New York with the reports of his Seventy, urged vehemently that "everything in the shape of agents, papers, etc., be poured into the *country*, the villages and the smaller cities of the interior." The cities must be left alone to be burned down by the conflagrations that the small towns would fan.

The Abolitionists realized that they had perhaps outsailed the worst outbreaks of riot, they had perhaps strengthened their doors and girded their loins, but that the one force which they had not yet assailed would probably put them in peril of their lives. With perseverance they could outwit all the other agencies set against them, but they would not be able to outwit the kind of law that their political enemies threatened to legislate.

They had known their danger ever since the mail had been burned in Charleston. All future fights would have to be waged for the protection of their constitutional rights and to keep intact free speech, free press, and free assembly. Within their own body was the giant growth, Garrisonism, a phenomenon that was coming rapidly to a point of danger. With the adherence of sober, well-bred men to the antislavery cause, wider fields were opened for proselyting, but at the same time, problems were introduced that were delicate and complex and colored by that peculiar mingling of individualism and conservatism, characteristic of this age.

Garrison saw only compromise in this. To his zeal and his single purpose new problems did not exist. Immediate emancipation could be gained only by moral suasion. Because he was so sure, he kept the columns of *The Liberator* open to friends and enemies alike. He printed not only the vituperations against himself, but he chastised vigorously and sometimes painfully his friends and coworkers who were not, he believed, maintaining an undeviating spirit and striking at everything which violated not only the spirit but the letter of immediate emancipation.

He was a man of relentless logic, and many of his coworkers felt that relentless logic did not always encompass the perplexities and doubts of the average men who had only good will to offer. The great clanging bell that was Garrison should, they felt, be modulated to the sound of many little bells, calling persuasively, convincingly, disarmingly. No doubt they were right; the earth had yawned at the touch of Garrison; he was the voice of thunder and the shock of lightning, but the storm must give place to a calmer day.

To him the enemies were still in the North, and he struck without mercy at the New England churches. Their opposition to "Garrisonism" was complete. By 1836 the Congregationalists had closed their doors to every exponent of Immediate Abolition. They were willing to subscribe to moderation, they said, but not to the violent rending asunder of man from his property. The man Garrison was the spirit of the Antichrist. In 1836 also the Methodist church, which had at first attacked slavery, now disclaimed "any right, wish, or intention to interfere with the civil and political relation between master and slave." In two years the Presbyterians were to split, North and South, having refused to take a stand on slavery, calling it "political" rather than "divine."

The Abolition cause had drawn its most effective strength from pastors and preachers; its agents and the operators of the Underground Railroad were, almost to a man, members of a church. Outside of New England, the pattern of a pending crisis was beginning to show in the church bodies. To many observers, it seemed that more strength was being exercised by the churches to crush Abolition than to crush slavery. The church attacks were finally dramatized in a *Clerical Appeal*, signed by five New England clergymen, who attacked Garrison with almost as much ferocity as he himself might have used and stood out bitterly against the use of churches for Abolition meetings.

Now as schools and churches were the meeting places of nine-tenths of the people of this age, such a prohibition would act as a violent separator of the people from the Abolitionists. Garrison let loose his fury and attacked not only the churches as dwelling places of Satan but all institutions that were subject to the vagaries of men. Slavery was assuming for him, more and more, the guise of sectarianism, of prejudice, of orthodoxy, of bigotry. He had a vast and awful love for humankind, and he hated with the same intensity whatever stood between itself and freedom.

His language was as uncompromising as usual. He moved in a world of pure principle; there were few who had the temperament or the capacity to move there with him. Tact, common sense and worldly wisdom lay between their world and his. He strained his friends. He was too great a burden in a changing world.

The influential new adherents and even some of the older Abolitionists believed that everything should be subjugated to the cause. Not only personal animosities and personal attacks, but the impulse toward iconoclasm. Appease as far as one may honorably do so; do not antagonize. To Garrison, the sectarianism of the churches, the fierce attacks against women Abolitionists, the political expediencies, were all coins of the same stamp as slavery, all ropes twisted by the same hands.

Alarmed by his attacks on orthodoxy, Lewis Tappan wrote to him, "I do not like your language." The outspoken Elizur Wright said, "You exalt yourself too much. I pray to God that you may be brought to repent of it." William Goodell, who had stood by him from the earliest days, wrote in his paper, *The Friend of Man,* "Can the 'orthodox' abolitionists of New England continue to go with Mr. Garrison? Not if he must needs point his arrows against the great moral law which lies at the foundation of abolitionism." Yet to the rank and file of antislavery workers, Garrison was "abolition personified and incarnate . . . the god of their idolatry" as the writers of the *Appeal* had said, and to those who stood closest to him, day by day, he was the living and unalterable symbol of devotion to a cause.

The Abolitionists, making vigorous efforts to feed their doctrine to the public before their enemies could act, now had the record of nearly one new Abolition society a day. From these societies they must shoot their gunfire as long as possible. The only central point which could feel the effect of their bombardments was Congress, and their most effective Congressional ammunition was petitions; petitions for the total extinction of slavery. And then, to show that they could be practical as well as idealistic, petitions for the end of slavery in the District of Columbia. Perhaps Congress could not trespass on state's rights and free all slaves, but it could declare slavery illegal within its own bailiwick. The slave-pens within sight of the Capitol, the slave coffles dragging their chains through the dust and mud of the Washington streets were a visible and shocking cancer. To the Abolitionist, they indicated once and for all that the Federal government lay wantonly in the hands of the slavocracy.

The petitions poured in, a heady flood. Free the slaves in the District. Protect the rights of free Negroes. Give fugitives the protection of the courts. Fight against the admission of Arkansas as a slave state. Hold back aid from Texas in her proslavery fight with Mexico. By 1835, the wisdom of keeping petitions always before Congress and debates continually recurring on the floor was evident. Under the direction of Whittier, Weld and Henry B. Stanton, one session of Congress received four hundred thousand signatures.

To the unwieldy Congress with its tireless oratory and its inadequate rules of debates, the petitions represented a behemoth. But the orators of slavery were never apathetic in such emergencies. In February, 1835, Wise of Virginia wasted no artifice or pettifoggery. "Slavery, interwoven with our very political existence, is guaranteed by our Constitution and its consequences must be borne by our Northern brethren as resulting from our system of government, and they can not attack the institutions of slavery without attacking the institutions of the country, our safety, and welfare." He spoke to a nodding and acquiescent House. Only Slade of Vermont, a pariah in this temple, had a different word to say. "The progress of Abolition," was necessary, he protested, "to preserve the balance of the Constitution, or rather to restore it."

The Senate, too, housed only one champion of Abolition, Morris of Ohio, when in January, 1836 the skillful and brilliant Calhoun made a motion to table all petitions for the abolition of slavery presented by this same persistent Morris. The rest of the way was well oiled. By February the House had indicated the course to follow and had recommended that all petitions, relating in any way to slavery, be laid upon the table and "that no further action whatever shall be had thereon."

The debate, which raged for several weeks, was worth "a thousand dollars to the cause." Abolition had been Garrisonism. Now it was something else. If a choice must be made between slavery or the right of petition, the decision was not difficult even though it might be disagreeable. Many who were not Abolitionists joined the campaign of petition, and many went on from there to join the antislavery movement.

In the House, when the vote was taken, John Quincy Adams rose and, in place of voting, denounced the measure as a violation of the Constitution.

To Adams, ripe in dignity and heavy with honors, the Abolitionists had been irritants, but in this crisis something of that virus of Revolution into which he had been born stirred in his blood and made his voice take up a new and startling refrain. The gag rule had given to the Abolitionists what years of agitation could not win—"old man eloquent."

To the House he was their most venerable and honored member, the only man so skillful in debate that no rule hampered him, the only man in Congress who through his own prestige could lift the antislavery cause to the level of patriotism. He defied the gag. Freedom for the white man was the cry he raised in the House. The end of slavery was the cry he raised in the North. The remainder of his life, he said, would be devoted to this end. "Whether peaceably or by blood it shall be accomplished. By whatever way, I say let it come."

With the basis of the fight shifting in the public mind, the new Abolitionists drew more and more within the circle of the Constitution. They shaped not only their tactics by it but provided a new strategy for strengthening the Underground Railroad. The effectiveness of personal liberty laws for which they were responsible could only be gauged as famous case succeeded famous case, and each skirted with consummate skill that nemesis of the runaway and his friend, the Fugitive Slave Law of 1793. Personal liberty laws had been in the mind of the fugitive's friends for some time. As long as the fugitive had no redress from the sheriff and the warrant, his friends had to depend on their own resourcefulness which was not infallible. With the personal liberty laws the fugitive was granted the right of trial on the same basis as the white man. Indiana and Connecticut, Vermont and New York allowed a trial by jury, and Connecticut refused to allow state officials to have a share in fugitive slave cases.

Antislavery to the extent that it meant humanitarianism had penetrated Northern thought.

The personal liberty laws became a burning wound to the slavocracy. They could not touch these laws. There they stood, an enticement and a promise. The slaveowners' frenzy was reasonable for, with the trade in slaves reaching fantastic figures, every slave who escaped represented an investment of from $700 to $2,000. What could they do more than they had done to root out these changing times? The anticlimax of effort gave their methods a grim monotony. Missouri, so sensitive, so close to the North, drove two of her men across the border. A young editor named Elijah Lovejoy went first and after him, escaping in the manner of a fugitive, came Professor David Nelson.

Lovejoy was a young man from Maine who had been ordained in the Presbyterian church. He edited a religious journal called *The Observer* in St. Louis. The Abolitionists could not claim him because he believed that immediate emancipation was too reckless; but the slavocracy would have nothing to do with him since he believed that Missouri would profit by the elimination of slavery. The storm he raised among Missourians showed him the light. In the placards inciting a mob against him he recognized his own possible fate; in the Synod, frightened by the excitement he had stirred in St. Louis, he saw the withering debility of conservatism. He challenged them both. "I deem it my duty to take my stand upon the Constitution," he declared stoutly. "We have slaves it is true, but I am not one."

For free speech and free press he left Missouri and went to Illinois, but he was soon called back to his editorship. And there in the spring of 1836, a mulatto freeman named Francis McIntosh was lynched at a slow fire in a barbaric and revolting manner. Surely, Lovejoy insisted, pale with horror, the city of St. Louis, the state of Missouri, would find a punishment to fit this medieval sadism! When he heard the Judge's instructions to the grand jury he could not believe his ears. "Whether the grand jury shall act or not depends . . . on whether the destruction of McIntosh was the act of the 'few' or the act of the 'many.' If [his] destruction was not the act of numerable and ascertainable malefactors but of congregated thousands, seized upon and impelled by that mysterious, metaphysical and almost electric fury, then I say act not at all in the matter. The case then transcends your jurisdiction—it is beyond the reach of human laws."

Lovejoy was outraged, and his outrage crackled in his paper. For his flailing indignation, his office was stormed, his press was destroyed, and in the night he crossed over once again into Illinois.

Dr. Nelson was a Virginian and had been a slaveholder. In 1836 he was president of Marion College in Missouri. At a religious meeting he had misjudged the temper of his colleagues and read a paper which proposed the manumission of Missouri slaves and indemnity for their owners, a course allowed by the state constitution. The rejection was so violent that one man was badly wounded, and Dr. Nelson, without even waiting for his family, was forced to seek the doubtful hospitality of Illinois.

In Quincy, Illinois, Dr. Nelson founded his own college. By 1839 his college showed the effect of that flight from Missouri. Every Sunday night, a detail of students crossed the Mississippi River and patrolled the Missouri shore. What a strange sight they must have made, softly tapping stones together. Those who heard came out from the woods beside the river with the prescience of the fugitive, and were guided safely across the water and for sixteen miles inland to a red barn where the Underground Railroad conducted a "waiting room." This watch on the river was a regular assignment to the Abolition students, until in due time, Dr. Nelson's Institute was burned down about their ears.

When Birney was attacked in July of that same year in Cincinnati, the proceedings could not have been more alarming. Gentlemen of property, who made no effort to conceal their names, surrounded the mob like protecting genii. Nicholas Longworth was a wealthy landowner and a lawyer, Jacob Burnet was a Supreme Court Judge and a Senator; Josiah Lawrence and Robert Buchanan were presidents of banks, Oliver Spencer was a Methodist minister, William Burke was postmaster of the city and a minister.

Birney's paper *The Philanthropist* was a mild-tempered organ, with a slaveholder's column. It had a not inconsiderable subscription list, and was pursuing a well-ordered and persuasive course, a benign cousin to *The Liberator*. But on the night of July 12th all that was changed. At midnight, thirty or forty men, using a ladder and plank, reached the roof of the printing office. They dropped through a window onto the floor below and fastened the bedclothes about the head of an apprentice so that he could not identify them. They destroyed that week's issue of *The Philanthropist*, broke the containers of ink, took the press apart and carried off the principal parts. No one need think that this was done quietly. Achille Pugh, the printer, heard it all, but confederates saw that he raised no alarm. Their business took them nearly two hours; many neighbors were wakened from their sleep, but the night watch mysteriously heard nothing.

The editors next day cleaned up the mess, repaired the parts and printed the paper. Such an answer had not been foreseen. Public meetings were held, warnings were posted on the streets. Those gentlemen of property who did not conceal their names gave words to the public sentiment.

"Abolitionists. BEWARE.

"The citizens of Cincinnati, embracing every class, interested in the prosperity of the city, satisfied that the business of the place is receiving a vital stab from the wicked and misguided operations of the abolitionists, are resolved to arrest their course."

*The Philanthropist* refused to be throttled and the "firm, united and decided actions" promised by the Vigilance Committee struck like a hammer. The office was again broken into, this time in daylight, the property was destroyed, the office gutted, the type scattered in the streets and the press borne off to the river, where it was broken and hurled into the water. Young Salmon P. Chase, although no Abolitionist, hurried to Birney's house when he heard that Birney's life was in danger, helped him to escape, and then stationed himself, a giant of a young man, in the doorway facing the mob.

Since the mob wanted an uncontested fight, they took their guns and went into Church Alley where the black people lived. The blacks answered with gunfire, an unexpected development that scattered the mob. Rallying, the houses were broken into but the colored people had retreated by the back way and their possessions were all that held the field. These possessions were destroyed, and a march down Main Street was ordered. It was midnight. The mayor was standing there, a solemn and poker-faced man who told them that they might as well disperse. Some of them went to their homes, but the city did not quiet for three days. The publication of *The Philanthropist* continued for several years, surviving another riot in 1841 when the office was sacked, and forty lives were lost. As for Salmon Chase, he then and there fastened securely the thread that would lead him, as "attorney general for fugitives," to Abraham Lincoln and the Emancipation Cabinet.

The year 1837 saw a prosperous beginning for the slaveholder. Politically at the height of his strength, secure in a new proslavery President, with Abolition placed firmly in the trap of fanaticism, the price of slaves was at a peak. This man-commodity reflected the same elements as corporation stocks. Values were gauged not only by fluctuations of optimism and pessimism but also by the price of cotton. In 1837 cotton was selling for thirteen cents a pound and prime slaves, from the breeding fields of Virginia, were valued as high as $1,100.

But 1837 passed, and with its passing a swathe of ruin lay across the land. By 1845, cotton had sunk to five cents a pound and prime slaves commanded only $500. Between those years lay a long and desperate depression that left poverty stalking in the fields. The manipulation of stocks, the bankruptcy of states, Nicholas Biddle and the banks, closed mills, collapsed industries, starvation, belong here only as shadows against the wall. A North Carolinian starting off toward the Southwest in an effort to collect some debts, described the Southern scene in 1840. "Mississippi is ruined. Her rich men are poor and her poor men are beggars. . . . The people are running their Negroes to Texas and Alabama and leaving their real estate and perishable property to be sold. So great is the panic and so dreadful the distress that there are a great many farms prepared to receive crops, and some of them actually planted, and yet deserted, not a human being to be found upon them."

The effects soon showed themselves. Poor white men, driven deeper and deeper into poverty, white farmers stripped of land, slaves, hope, were jarred loose from their preoccupation with the slavocracy. In the mountains of Tennessee, in the hills of western Virginia, along the bayous of Louisiana, in the wagons that rumbled through the streets of North Carolina, bound for the West where a man might hope to live off something better than the stunted products of an exhausted soil, the voices of antislavery men were heard. They were not the voices of "poor white trash" as the slavocracy called them. They were the men and women of the middle class who knew that they could never work with their hands as long as a slave remained in the South, and they were leaving their homes by the thousands.

Depression bred unemployment and destitution among slaves. Slaves, hungry, ragged, bold with want, raised insurrections. In Rapides Parish, Louisiana, a regiment of soldiers was needed to bring an end to "the indiscriminate slaughter of Negroes who were accused of plotting an uprising." But the conspiracies in Georgia, Alabama, North Carolina, Virginia and Mississippi were dealt with by the local authorities.

A few slaveowners, bewildered or compassionate, set their slaves upon the faint rut paths of the Southern "railroad." Other slaves struck off without a leave-taking. A group of white men was said to transport fugitives, for a fee, from Louisiana across the Sabine into Texas from where they could make good their escape into Mexico.

From the central states and the Gulf states, they went down as well as up the Mississippi. New Orleans and its ocean ships received many of them and river steamboats were a constant path to freedom. Laws were passed, holding captains responsible for property which escaped in this way, but a Negro deck hand could easily deny all complicity and as for those slaves who were hired out as boat hands and found the distance from the deck to the wharf of a free city a very short trip, the courts declared, "We must presume that the owner is fully aware that every facility of escape is afforded by the very nature of the service."

The British, serene in their own consciences, added woe on woe by persistently disregarding the sanctity of slave ships, and when these vessels were driven by storms into British harbors or shipwrecked in British waters, the Negroes were regarded as ordinary fugitives, free men. The American government energetically protested, but the British saw no reason to change their policy. Calhoun prepared resolution after resolution in an effort to protect this American chattel property, but a country where emancipation was still a bright phenomenon, was not impressed by aged arguments. In the Senate Calhoun's voice rang out, challenging, everlastingly challenging by moral arguments the moralizings of opponents, and at length his challenge became the bright new dogma that cast a well-calculated radiance around the needs of the South. "Slavery," he admonished the Senate with final, awful solemnity, "slavery is, instead of an evil, a good—a positive good. Many in the South once believed that it was a moral and political evil, but that folly and delusion are gone. We now see it in its true light and regard it as the most safe and stable basis for free institutions."

Calhoun was the voice and the temper of the slavocracy. He under-estimated neither its strength nor the strength of its enemies. With this new triumph of strategy, he deliberately assaulted the emotions with the cry of "positive good," stretched tight and hard the power of the slave-holder, gave bold new words to Southern editors, built new support beneath the pulpits of the Southern churches, and wiped away for the bedazzled slavocracy the last justification for reform. Within the churches, the sin of slavery was washed clean, and a new redemption promised.

Slavery, by the testimony of the Reverend Mr. Postell of South Carolina, was now "a merciful visitation; it is the Lord's doing, and is marvelous in our eyes."

Under the impetus of this new visitation, the Bible was searched, not for moral redress or to "break the chains of the captive," but to verify a divine sanction for slavery; not by Southerners alone but by all who saw in slavery the chains that held the past to the present, and the future to that which had gone before.

Dr. Channing had said that one kidnaped or murdered Abolitionist could do more than a hundred societies. In November, 1837, Elijah Lovejoy was killed.

He had come to Alton, Illinois, the year before, when the mob drove him out of St. Louis, and here set up his *Observer*. But Southern Illinois was for all ethical purposes a Southern state, and the newspapers of St. Louis had delivered an ultimatum. Illinois' business with the slave-holding states would be over if she did not silence the nuisance who brayed so loudly against slavery. Certain men of Alton responded by throwing his press into the river. Lovejoy bought another press. It too was thrown into the river. He invested in a third, and the waters of the Mississippi closed over it as well.

Meetings were called by the citizens, and Lovejoy asked permission to defend himself. He spoke, they said, very well. He was a young man, his wife was an invalid, his conscience was too big for their peace. Many in his audience burst into tears. "You come together for the purpose of driving out a confessedly innocent man for no cause but that he dares to think and speak as his conscience and God dictates. Will conduct like this stand the scrutiny of your country? Of posterity? . . . If the civil authorities refuse to protect me, I must look to God, and if I die I am determined to make my grave in Alton."

Many were moved, but the Reverend Mr. Hogan took pains to show them how foolish was their leniency. Citizens' meetings sprayed the air with invectives. Lovejoy must have seen the shadow of the end.

His fourth press arrived that week. It came at three o'clock in the morning, and his enemies blew horns to communicate the news to their colleagues. Lovejoy's friends—some fifty of them, who had sworn that this press should not be seized—hustled it into a warehouse and barricaded the door. There it stayed all the next day, a keg of dynamite with a burning fuse beside it.

That night, some thirty gentlemen knocked upon the door and demanded the press. They were told that it would not be given up. The leader then drew a pistol, and announced that it would be had at any sacrifice. Stones appeared from the bosom of coats and satchels, pistols were fired at the building. The friends of Lovejoy answered with guns. The mayor interceded, praying the besieged to surrender the press. Some of the mob climbed by ladders to the roof and set it afire. Five of the besieged appeared at the door, fired on the mob and scattered them. There was silence. The mob had apparently been awed by the resistance. The building was afire. Lovejoy and a friend ventured out to see if the way were clear. From behind a pile of lumber, a flurry of shots broke the quietness. Lovejoy, with five bullets in his body, staggered back into the building and died close to the door.

Blood and death had done what words could not. Plain men understood. A man, defending his property, had been shot and killed. That shot touched the nerve centers of the country. The Abolitionists knew that what had happened to Lovejoy might happen to any one of them. Those men who could not make up their minds between good and evil saw themselves walk from a burning building to five shots lodging in their breast.

In Boston, the great Dr. Channing appealed to the citizens of Boston to meet in Faneuil Hall to protest an outrage that touched the deepest level of citizenry. This was not an Abolition meeting, but a defense of constitutional freedom. The hall was crowded. The meeting was decorous, indignant, patriotic. Then the attorney general of the State arose. Lovejoy, he said, with slow contempt, had died "as the fool dieth." His murderers were the kinsmen of those Bostonians who had cast aside the law and thrown the British tea into Boston Harbor. Abolitionists, he said, brought their own deaths with them.

Proslavery was there that night and cheered him. Suddenly a young man leaped upon the platform, and in a voice clear and outraged, called down horror on this "recreant American." His outrage stirred and swelled and swept about the hall. People listened because he was so handsome, so ardent and so deeply moved. Those who heard Wendell Phillips that afternoon never forgot, for "abolition's golden trumpet" had sounded its first note.

That speech, unplanned, passionate, carried him to fame. What was he thinking about as he stood there and fought an audience, no longer orderly but shouting with the fervor of their convictions? He was thinking only, he said later, of carrying resolutions. This meeting must be thrown to freedom. When his wonderful voice was silent, a vote was taken. Lovejoy's murderers were denounced.

People did not realize how deeply they had been stirred. A letter, going from Boston to England, spoke the words that only retrospection allowed. "Men came home that day and wept. Dr. Channing did not know how dangerous an experiment, as people count danger, he adventured. We knew that we must send our children out of town and sleep in our day garments that night unless free discussion prevailed."

Abolition was now bound to the cause of free speech. And stirring at such deep levels, it became at the same time as much a part of the American consciousness as church or politics. With the baptism of fire and the first martyr, an era had closed.

## Chapter 4

## CRUSADE OF THE CONSCIENCE

WHEN the new era opened, it was seen that a powerful weapon was coming into the hands of the Abolitionists. Negro antislavery agents were mining them pure gold. People would come to hear them out of curiosity and stay to be convinced. Theories might now be swept aside. Was the slave a man?—and the arm could sweep to the speaker on the platform.

They spoke with a natural dignity and eloquence. What they said bore the hot melting heat of the personal equation. Am I ignorant and crude? Whose fault is it? May I have a chance? Is there a place in this democracy for a citizen with a black skin? The right to vote has been taken from me in nearly every state, free or slave. Why has this been done? Why even in the North must I sit in separate places and eat the bitter bread of inequality?

Why indeed? people asked themselves when Charles Lenox Remond, small and spare and black, first climbed onto an Abolition platform. There was nothing in his appearance or manner to set him apart except his dark complexion. Why was he not a fully franchised citizen? A free-born New Englander, he pleaded not so much for the emancipation of slaves as for the emancipation of the free man. People heard him and were moved.

The leaven was working. If men's minds were stirred by questions, a thing could never be the same again. He who cared to see, looked about him and beheld a startling array of Negro newspapers, capably and sometimes stirringly edited; saw Negro clergymen battling with the poverty and unemployment of their race and holding their spiritual fortitude intact; saw Negro teachers sending out young men with the capacity of leadership. Pamphlets, written by Negro teachers on education and on peace were eagerly printed by the Abolition press. Fugitive slaves were induced to record their stories, and their books sold by the thousands.

Their national conventions were welding them into an integrated whole and the white man heard self-sufficiency ring in the counsels of their leaders. Fighting an unequal battle, they strengthened themselves by a pride in race. What white men, they asked, could absorb education as fast as fugitive Negroes, escaping from the mental darkness of slavery? Was there ever a race of men, they wanted to know, who could so soon forget the horrors of slavery as to become pastors to white congregations? Were there many white men who, after buying themselves out of slavery, could accumulate in a few years fifteen thousand dollars as Robert Gordon of Cincinnati had done?

Free colored men provided most of the Negro leadership within the United States. Ruggles in New York was a free man and so was the Reverend Charles B. Ray who edited *The Colored American*. Robert Purvis in Philadelphia, the son of a Moorish-Negro woman and a wealthy English father, had been brought out of the South before he had occasion to know much about slavery. It was in Canada that the fugitive slaves were providing leaders, although the day when the "eloquent fugitives" would stir the North was almost at hand.

Since Robert Purvis had committed his life to the cause of the Negroes—although his elegance, wealth and white skin would have allowed him to conceal his origin—since he had helped to organize the first National Negro Convention, and was one of the sixty who had signed the declaration of the American Antislavery Society, it seemed only fitting to put him in charge of the Philadelphia Vigilance Committee when it was formed in 1838. For this Vigilance Committee was exceptional. It was, in reality, the first formal effort to organize the Underground Railroad on a businesslike basis.

It is not known how this so-called organization of the Underground Railroad took place. Probably as the effect of irresistible causes. Philadelphia, honored since the days of Isaac Hopper as a haven for the fugitive, was haunted by the slave catcher, who could in case of need raise a mob. A city presented problems that a small town did not. Individual charity was unreliable. True, the colored Dorcas societies made clothing, organized fairs, aided in the boycotting of slave products; the Philadelphia Association for the Moral and Mental Improvement of the People of Color raised money, provided food, clothes and, as often as possible, employment for the runaways, but more than that was needed. With frayed tempers, and violence close to the surface, with Abolition a raw wound to many honest people, a frightened black face, mutely begging for assistance, might be the straw which broke the camel's back.

That this committee was an organization in the accepted sense of the word is doubtful. But it functioned under officers, chosen for certain responsibilities. It was sufficiently integrated to move swiftly and smoothly; it was the clearing place for fugitives, so that a tabulation could be kept on those who had escaped and an effort made to see that their freedom was secured. Robert Purvis kept a record of the number of fugitives he sent North, and the average, he said, was one a day—nine thousand slaves between his first interest in the cause in 1831 and the end of his work in 1861.

"The funds for carrying on this enterprise were raised from our antislavery friends as the cases came up and their needs demanded it," he said. "Many of the fugitives required no other help than advice and directions how to proceed. The most efficient helpers or agents we had were two market women who lived in Baltimore, one of whom was white, the other colored. By some means they obtained a number of genuine certificates of freedom which they gave to slaves who wished to escape. These were afterwards returned to them and used again by other fugitives. The general opinion that "all negroes looked alike" prevented too close a scrutiny by the officials.

"Another most efficient worker was a son of a slaveholder who lived at Newberne, North Carolina. Through his agency the slaves were forwarded by placing them on vessels engaged in the lumber trade which plied between Newberne and Philadelphia, and the captains of which had hearts."

The hint of an agency in the South is left to tantalize. Who was the slaveholder's son and how did he operate? It was made clear again, however, that the inception of the Underground Railroad lay in the South; that the slaveholders bred their own enemies. How many operated through the South, it was impossible to say. There were frequent glimpses of a man here or there, concealing and sending on a fugitive, but the indications of a positive association with the Northern terminus of the railroad were mostly confined to those who worked within the border states. For that reason the story of Jo Norton, explaining so graphically how the Southern "railroad" connected with the Northern and how the Southern conductors found it possible to operate, is a history in itself.

One Saturday morning, the latter part of October, 1839, a Washington newspaper carried this headline, "Underground Railroad mystery not yet solved," and then bluntly developed its alarming information:

The abolition incendiaries are undermining, not only our domestic institutions, but the very foundations of our capital. Our citizens will recollect that the boy, Jim, who was arrested while lurking about the Capitol in August, would disclose nothing until he was subjected to torture by screwing his fingers in a blacksmith's vice, when he acknowledged that he was to have been sent North by railroads; was to have started from near the place where he stood when discovered by the patrol. He refused to tell who was to aid him—said he did not know—and most likely he did not know. Nothing more could be got from him until they gave the screw another turn, when he said, *"the railroad went underground all the way to Boston."*

Now we learn that Colonel Hardy, a tobacco planter, residing in the district about five miles from the city, lost five slaves last Sunday evening. They were pursued by an excellent slave catcher, but no trace of them was discovered. The search was abandoned this morning, the Colonel having received a paper called *The Liberty Press*, printed in Albany, with an article marked, so as to attract his attention, which reads as follows: "Arrived this morning by our fast line three men and two women. They were claimed as slaves by Colonel Hardy of the District of Columbia, but became dissatisfied with the Colonel's ways and left the old fellow's premises last Sunday evening, arriving at our station by the quickest passage on record." The article goes on reciting certain incidents that have transpired in the Colonel's family, that correspond so exactly with the facts that the Colonel says, "Nobody but Kate would have told that story!" Said article closes by saying, "Now, Colonel Hardy, please give yourself no trouble about these friends of yours, for they will be safe under the protection of the British Lion before this meets your eye."

The stark, cold mystification of Colonel Hardy and the editors of the Washington paper must have been gratifying to this midnight-striking, masked devil that was neither man nor monster. But it was not the destiny of the editors or the Colonel to know the movements that took place behind their backs or the flawless mechanism that rolled the underground train to this record-breaking stop. That story came only afterwards, from one of those five slaves.

Jo Norton had a wife and child, and he longed to take them out of slavery. He had thought about it so long that his ears were ready when a stranger engaged him in conversation one Sunday night on a dark road. Jo realized from the gentleman's speech that he was a Northerner and he said afterwards that he felt in his bones that here was a friend. Escape was put in Jo's mind that night. For two weeks, he thought about it and at the end of that time had another secret meeting with his new friend, who explained to him some of the mysteries of the Underground Railroad. It was decided that Jo should go alone, prepare a home for his wife and child, and wait for their delivery by the same route.

Three weeks later, Jo came faithfully to the clump of bushes by the old cemetery which had been designated. A signal was heard—a whistle perhaps, or an owl's hoot—and Jo lifted himself from behind the bushes. As he did so, he saw four other heads appear like ghosts from among the tombstones, all friends, all slaves of Colonel Hardy. At a second signal, he and his four unexpected companions crept out onto the road and down in the direction toward which they had been told to walk.

They were terrified, Jo said later, afraid to whistle away "the spooks," liberty becoming less and less desirable as they approached the mysterious underground road which, they sincerely believed, would "just go down into the ground among the dead folks." They greeted the shadowy figure who emerged out of the trees with terror and suspicion. But after they had exchanged signals in a low voice, their fright began to subside, and his instructions were not as terrifying as they had expected. The "conductor" explained that they must continue down the turnpike until they came to the iron rails of a genuine railroad. They must follow the track until they saw a man standing in the middle of the track. Then they must stop and listen, and if he said, "Ben," they were to go with him and do as he told them. He gave all his instructions in whispers. The night was dark and they could not see his face. He appointed Harry as their leader, told them they had thirty miles to travel, took them out into the clear of the road and pointed out the North Star which was to serve as a compass, shook hands all around and said, "Godspeed."

The cocks were crowing before they saw "Ben" standing like a mysterious black archangel. They said not a word until Ben gave his name, and then they followed him, silent and shaking. He led them to a field and taking away some bundles of cornstalks, indicated a hiding place in the corn ricks.

In time they learned that Ben was a free man and that the Underground Railroad had rented his field in return for his care of fugitives. He had stacked his corn as close to the tracks as possible, on the assumption that no one would look for fugitives in such an exposed place. At nightfall the next day, another agent appeared and led the two women across the fields to the road where they were put into a carriage and started off toward Baltimore. The men remained in their hideaway for a time longer before they too were put on the road to Baltimore.

Now what Colonel Hardy did not know—while he and the Washington editors were attempting to solve the mystery of the lightning arrival of the fugitives in Albany—was the fact that the fugitive women were concealed in Baltimore and the fugitive men in Ben's corncrib until the misleading message had been sent to the Colonel, via *The Liberty Press*. Underground officials in Albany, learning that fugitives had taken off from Colonel Hardy's on a certain night, found it simple and relatively true to say that these fugitives were under the protection of the British Lion, since Colonel Hardy did as they anticipated—called off his slave hunters and left the road clear for the five slaves to get to the North in safety.

Jo, Robert, and Harry came to Baltimore between eight and nine in the evening. They had been instructed to walk openly through the more crowded streets, to act naturally and do whatever was spontaneous. They had been provided with money to buy peanuts and fruit, and had been told never to lose sight of their Baltimore guide, a sharp-faced colored boy of thirteen. They reached the outskirts of the city just before the Negro curfew, and there they met the girls in charge of a colored man who gave them their next directions and started them along the proper road.

Their journey to Philadelphia was taken by night. During the days they stopped at Quaker homes. From Philadelphia they were taken in a fishing boat to Bordentown, and from there to New York City on a puffing tangible train, the boys having been smuggled aboard and hidden among crates and bales; the girls, dressed as ladies with veils over their faces, put into first-class carriages just as the train was starting.

From New York, they passed on to Albany, where they separated, some to go to Canada, others like Jo to remain in the United States.

The skill with which they had been handled showed that the Underground Railroad made no allowances for failure. A conductor could usually depend on the crudities of the slave catcher whose profession had not trained him in the double meanings and subtleties of the Underground Railroad. Yet the alertness of conductors could never wane. Decoys were sent against them repeatedly, the most favored disguise being the words and ardor of an Abolitionist. A good antislavery speaker, though his heart was as black as slavery, was in a fine position to disarm his victims. But even disarmed, those victims proved a match for him. A Kentuckian named Carpenter appeared in Cass County, Indiana, in 1840, professing to be a zealous antislavery worker and an agent for Abolition newspapers. His industry and fine words opened up many secrets to him, and he soon learned where the objects of his guile—seven fugitives—were hidden. He sent his information promptly to their owners; they were seized and were on their way out of the county when the indignant Abolitionists jumped on their horses, seized their firearms and made both masters and fugitives their prisoners. The personal liberty laws were invoked, and the slaves set free.

Negro decoys were the most pitiful of all, for a man's black skin was regarded as sufficient introduction by the average conductor. In Pennsylvania, where slave catchers never slept, many conductors took the precaution of giving their passengers a talisman for the next station, and the next stationmaster would not give sanctuary until this assurance of integrity was forthcoming.

Success had come—a hypothetical success, some might say, but still measured in good round numbers. Two thousand Abolition societies, with two hundred thousand members, existed to startle the skeptic. Antislavery societies were built broad enough to include all idiosyncrasies and to operate free of sectarian or political bias. To Garrison it was inconceivable that an antislavery society should assume the limitations of political disputes.

Many antislavery men agreed on the propriety of this basis, but even Garrison could not prevent the immemorial impulse to cast a vote at the polls. Abolition votes elected William Seward, governor of New York in 1838, not because he was an Abolitionist but because he had answered certain questions satisfactorily, and was a step upward from his predecessor. In the same year, Joshua Giddings was sent to the House of Representatives from the Ohio Western Reserve. Joshua Giddings was an out-and-out Abolitionist, a conductor of the Underground Railroad. He had come under the influence of Weld, and no Garrisonian could find a flaw in his hatred of slavery. He came at an opportune time to lend a hand to John Quincy Adams who had by now thrown his prestige and his power, not to the Abolitionists, but to the antislavery crusade.

Giddings was fearless and loud-voiced. He pretended not to notice that no committee appointments were given him; that no one asked him out to dinner. He set himself with bland deliberation to evade the gag rule, and by some individual sleight of hand managed to introduce petition after petition into a restive Congress. He knew what he was doing; more important he knew how far his constituents would allow him to go, for in himself he expressed the slowly growing power of the Underground Railroad in the action-loving, speech-sparing Middle West.

Gerrit Smith was as aware as Garrison of the danger of Abolition in politics, and his remedy was disturbing and exhilarating—a new political party, four-square Abolition, with hand-picked candidates.

Many Abolitionists protested. They had no strength to show. The thing would be a farce. Wendell Phillips demanded in their name, how any Abolitionist could believe that a politician would be able to keep faith with his principles when his first action was an oath to uphold a slavery-tainted Constitution which allowed the slavocracy three-fifths representation, giving ten thousand slaveowning inhabitants of North Carolina, say, equal weight in the government with forty thousand inhabitants of Massachusetts. These constitutional provisions would make it impossible to hold office without being caught in the meshes of the slave power. Politics and morals could not mingle . . .

. . . Anymore, his Abolition opponents retorted, than morals and women's right which the Garrisonians did not hesitate to mingle.

Garrison's answer carried his usual impact. "As our object is universal emancipation—to redeem women as well as men from a servile to an equal condition—we shall go for the RIGHTS OF WOMEN to their utmost extent."

How could one avoid a reef like that?

Women were addressing "promiscuous assemblies" by now; they were working side by side with the men. Yet they were an embarrassment and a menace. The political wound might have healed; the policy of nonresistance might have died out under the bludgeoning of mobs, but there was no putting aside the women.

Abby Kelly, the fiery little Irish Quaker who had followed the Grimkés onto the lecture platform, Lucretia Mott, Elizabeth Cady Stanton, and all their sisterhood, were willing to work, able to talk, as clearly aware of the issues as the men and sometimes more skillful in tactical maneuver. Yet they were, the dissenters insisted, an extraneous topic by the introduction of which the cause of the slave was injured. Let us not champion two causes at one time and lose with both. The question was red-hot. It had seared fingers before this.

The problem only tightened nerves already taut. The Abolitionists had suffered painfully from the financial depression. The New York society was floundering in a sea of unpaid obligations. The Tappans, ruined by the crash, were attempting to rebuild themselves. All over the country, antislavery societies were faced with deficits and had no means of paying their agents or carrying on their work. A new organization split the Boston ranks as well, and its purpose was explained to the public. "The new organization proposes to overthrow slavery by the use of means, the old by simple truth."

Obscured and badly phrased, it nevertheless showed something of the heart of the matter. To Garrison, pure motives, action unentangled with mundane obligations, a vision wide enough to encompass the destruction of both moral and physical slavery, was the only platform desirable for an Abolitionist. To Garrison there was only black and white. "Who is not with us is against us." Either the two guardians of American morality, the Church and the State, must support immediate emancipation or they must be discredited and exposed. There could be no parleying.

Garrison was a deeply religious man, but the good pillars of the church, from whom the body of the Abolitionists was drawn, were horrified at his heresies. He refused to honor the Sabbath; he questioned the authority of the Church; he interested himself in anarchism; he discussed the problems of free love; he preached a strange kind of transcendentalism utterly at variance with orthodoxy. Such men are eternal misfits and must be put aside.

That Pennsylvania Hall should be burned to the ground at this junction seemed profoundly ironic. The conflagration within the Abolition ranks had taken place; this tended merely to show that, split or whole, their enemies still regarded them as undesirable.

Pennsylvania Hall had been built by the Abolitionists and Abolition sympathizers of Philadelphia at a cost of $40,000. It was to be open not only to Abolition lecturers, but to all petitioners for reform. It was dedicated, however, by an antislavery meeting, and this was enough for the pro-Unionists, the pro-slavers, the pro-business men and the advocates of peace-is-dull. Stones were thrown through the windows, a mob, several thousand strong, broke down the doors with axes, and within an hour the building was burning to the ground.

How many Abolitionists saw in this a confirmation that moral suasion had failed? Surely it worked against the Garrisonians. Many antislavery men felt that there had been enough of terrorism, lootings, burnings, and killings. Physical force must be met by a worldly strategy that spoke directly to the interests of the average man.

In an age when politics were the flavoring of every man's speech and the spice of his life, the suggestion advanced by Smith, Birney, Tappan spread through the minds of certain Abolitionists as the logical weapon. Although slavery and Abolition had, thanks to Garrison and his burning zealots, become the one question upon which every man had an opinion, Garrison himself must be shaken from his spectacular position; his reputation and his heresies which had become, in the words of Tappan, "a stench in the nostrils of the nation" superseded by the language of men who could speak in terms comprehensible to practical men.

By 1840 political action was stirring in every branch of the society. "I am in an antislavery convention," wrote Henry Wright from upper New York to Garrison's brother-in-law. "All is bustle and noise. To discuss the character of political candidates seems the great object of Myron Holley, Gerrit Smith, William L. Chaplin and others. The President, Agent and Committee [of the society] are all turned politicians. It is evident that H. B. Stanton, Birney and others in New York are determined to organize a great political party to regenerate the Government."

The new sectarianism appeared to Garrison as the supreme menace to the moral and religious strength of the antislavery cause. The crisis that would evidently arise at the anniversary meeting of the American Antislavery Society called for drastic action. A boat was chartered, and four hundred and fifty New England delegates, men and women, black and white, selected for their strong Garrisonism, were offered free passage to New York. Others came on foot or by train. They did not "pack" the meeting, however, since Birney, Tappan and Smith had their delegates as well, but a split took place without delay.

According to the bylaws, the president of the meeting must immediately appoint a business committee, and to the ten men chosen on this occasion, Abby Kelly's name was added. The appointments were put to a vote and carried by a slender margin. Lewis Tappan then arose and asked to be excused from serving, explaining that the "woman question" was "throwing a firebrand into the antislavery ranks; it is contrary to the usages of civilized society." Those who had voted against the committee appointments were asked to separate themselves and to form a new society, and the American and Foreign Antislavery Society came into being.

Hard on this split, the dissenting Abolitionists crossed their Rubicon. While still in New York City, the proposition of a third party was considered, and this time Birney accepted the nomination for President. The step had been taken that would lead in a straight line to Abraham Lincoln. Emancipation had ceased to be an exclusively moral question.

With the slavocracy firmly entrenched in the White House, holding both Houses in its hands, with its feet firmly planted on one half the country, with its sentiments expressed by every ambassador and representative abroad and its ethics expounded in the Supreme Court, the brave new Liberty party seemed a giddy jest, conceived by the light of the moon.

The Garrisonians saw the results of that year's elections with a grim complacency. Though probably fifty thousand voters were Abolitionists in 1840, the Liberty party polled a bare seventy-one hundred votes.

Yet, unimpressive and problematic, it foretold the eclipse of the antislavery societies. Those societies which had made antislavery a power in the country would soon cease to be the primary and ultimate factor in the antislavery agitation. The Abolition movement had assumed the complexities of manhood.

While all this was going on, fugitives had not delayed their flights. The Abolitionists were yet to learn that their brightest jewel had escaped. That Frederick Douglass had, two years before, taken the Underground Railroad.

He was in New Bedford now, working on the wharves or doing whatever odd jobs came his way, and omnivorously learning more of this strange new life that faced him on every side. He was ignorant and disillusioned, but fighting, determined that this cold, hard North would be the "land of Canaan" that he had dreamed of in the South.

Freedom had never been out of his thoughts since he was a boy. He had seen his family and his friends beaten to uphold the authority of a dissipated overseer, he had been separated from his mother who, many nights, walked twenty-four miles to teach him the bare rudiments of education, he had learned early that the plantation was "a little nation of its own, having its own language, its own rules, regulations and customs; the laws and institutions of the state touching it nowhere," that his owner—and his father—held that it was "worth but half a cent to kill a nigger and half a cent to bury him." Yet it took him nearly twenty years to reach the point of flight, years of cruel masters and kind masters, of plantation life when the lash was designated to break his spirit, of city life, where a new world opened up before his astonished eyes. When he persuaded his Baltimore master to allow him to hire his time, a common city practice whereby the owner was paid a certain sum each week by his slave who was allowed to pocket any surplus, he made his first move toward freedom. With money, with personal responsibility, the end of his slavery was inevitable.

However, the cordon around the railway stations, the boats, the roads leading North was too well built by laws to permit escape except by a ruse. For a long time he had weighed the possibility of borrowing the free papers of a friend, knowing the danger both to himself and the exposed, unprotected friend who could, before the papers were returned, be sold into slavery. Yet he was prepared to take the risk and his friend was willing to follow the example of thousands of other free Negroes all over the South and lend him the essential papers.

Disguised, as well, by a suit of sailor's clothes, Frederick went to the station, waited until a train was about to pull out and jumped aboard. Had he stopped to buy a ticket, he would have been scrutinized and the dissimilarity between himself and the description on the "protection" would have betrayed him.

He traveled openly all the way, taking the ferry across the Susquehanna River at Havre de Grace, the train to Wilmington, the steamboat to Philadelphia. He arrived in New York by train within twenty-four hours of the time he had left slavery.

He dared not speak to anyone nor look for work in the only trade he knew, shipbuilding, for fear of detection. Finally in desperation he told his troubles to a colored sailor, who provided the solution to all his problems by the simple expedient of fetching David Ruggles. Ruggles took him to his home, and kept him well hidden until the young free woman whom Frederick planned to marry reached New York.

David Ruggles decided that the safest place for Frederick—who as yet had no last name of his own—was in the shipping town of New Bedford. There Frederick turned himself and his wife over for safekeeping—since slave agents seemed to lurk in every shadow—to Nathan Johnson, a prosperous colored man. Nathan Johnson told him he must now select a name, and imbued with the romance of *The Lady of the Lake* which he had just been reading, offered "Douglass" to supplement the Frederick. Frederick found it pleasing, and combined thus the violent anonymity of slavery with a lush romanticism.

The questioning and logical mind of Douglass became plagued by many things. Exceedingly religious, he went to church immediately and he chose a white church as indication of the glorious equality that the state of Massachusetts promised him. But he discovered that the colored people had to sit in separate seats, that they were given communion last, that discrimination against them was as real and pointed as in the South. He never returned.

One day an agent approached him and asked him to subscribe to *The Liberator*. He confessed that he was a fugitive, that money was very scarce. The agent promptly told him that under those circumstances *The Liberator* would be sent to him without cost. Garrison and

*The Liberator* became the twin stars of his new world. Here, for the first time, he saw in solid print, in a newspaper which anyone could read, the claims of freedom which he himself put forth. Zeal consumed him. He spoke often and eloquently in his colored church. He groped for the words that would quickest win the heart of those who heard him, and stir them to his own zeal. Finally at a Nantucket antislavery meeting, he stood up and told a crude story of his sufferings and escape, but told it with such a radiance of feeling, such a natural eloquence, that Garrison who was present knew that a great man stood before him. "I think I never hated slavery so intensely," Garrison said recalling that occasion. "There stood one in physical proportions and stature, commanding and exact, in intellect, richly endowed, in natural eloquence, a prodigy—yet, a fugitive slave, trembling for his safety."

Garrison followed him that evening onto the platform, and all he said, pointing toward Douglass, was, "Is this a man or a thing?" Douglass snatched up that message and carried it wherever his magnificent voice was heard.

When he agreed to become an agent for the Massachusetts Antislavery Society, he went largely as the "graduate of the peculiar institution . . . with his diploma on his back," telling the unadorned tale of a fugitive. Garrison kept him under his supervision and tutelage, and his first lecture tour in 1843 was under the guidance of Charles Lenox Remond who had the bitter draught of soon discovering that when Douglass had once been heard, people were not as interested in him.

With the 1840's, the heyday of Negro leaders, springing up from the ranks of the fugitives, was beginning. Negroes were gaining distinction in the arts. Ira Aldridge, the son of a freedman, had left the United States for his fame on the European stage where he was to be acclaimed as one of the greatest of *Othellos* with Edmund Kean playing his *Iago*. Alexander Crummell, one of the two disputed colored students of the Noyes Academy, had gone to Cambridge in England to follow his study of the classics and of theology. Henry Highland Garnet, that other unwelcome student of the Noyes Academy, was making his strong mind and vigorous personality felt on Abolition platforms all over the East. The grandson of an African chief, he spoke with a terrible pride, a consuming kind of spirit, which showed him to be a kinsman of the insurrectionists of the South. James W. C. Pennington was soon to leave for Europe where he would be given an honorary degree at Heidelberg, although, the unhappy story goes, his return to the United States found him barred from the classroom of Yale. James McCune Smith had returned from Glasgow, where he graduated from the medical college, and had begun a long career as physician and lecturer in New York. Samuel Ringgold Ward, Garnet's cousin, was, in 1841, to come under the benevolent tutelage of Gerrit Smith and be transformed into a stirring orator, arguing for the social and political equality of the Negro.

When William Wells Brown appeared on the Abolition horizon in 1843, he forcefully asserted the black-white challenge that lay at the root of the slaveholder's morality. Slender, graceful and exceedingly handsome, he made a consistently agreeable impression on the audiences who heard him. Years before, his master had hired him to Elijah Lovejoy. Lovejoy had taught him what he knew of reading and writing —an asset that later led him to become a successful novelist and the best of the early Negro historians. His intelligence and his good looks had always provided his master with conspicuous jobs for him—coachman, sailor, printer—so that he was more equipped for freedom than most fugitives. One day at Cincinnati he walked off the boat on which he was hired and never returned. When he reached Sandusky, he hired himself out to a lake captain, whereupon, with promptness, he became an employee of the Underground Railroad. He said that the ship never put into Cleveland without finding a fresh contingent of fugitives, waiting with their conductor. The groups he handled were seldom large— for large groups were not common until the nerve-wracking 50's—but he carried over sixty-nine fugitives during eight months in 1842. The next year he discovered *The Liberator* and it kindled his mind as it had the mind of Douglass.

These men were coming thick and fast now. They made the issue painfully clear. Hypothetical discussions of freedom by free-born white men were pale beside these challenges of men who had suffered and thrown off the humiliations of slavery. Its effects were seen, persistent and unmistakable, in the enlarged audiences, in the steady, perceptible pressure on politicians, in the continued immunity of Underground Railroad conductors who, in the intense light that was now thrown on Abolition doings, might have suffered greatly at the hands of the law, in the increasing boldness of attack. In 1842, the *New York Tribune*, in great distress of mind, told its readers that at an Abolition meeting Gerrit Smith had advised the slaves to raise insurrections against their masters, and at the Buffalo Convention of Colored Citizens in 1843, Henry Highland Garnet made a flaming speech that was too much even for his colored brothers. He attacked the conventions which mourned over the slavery of their brethren and sent resolutions of sympathy. Now, he felt, was the time to speak directly to the slaves themselves. What he proposed was nothing less than a general strike.

"Brethren, arise, arise! Strike for your lives and liberties. Now is the day and the hour. Let every slave throughout the land do this and the days of slavery are numbered. Rather die freemen than live to be slaves! In the name of God we ask, are you men? Where is the blood of your fathers? Awake, awake, millions of voices are calling you! Let your motto be resistance; no oppressed people have secured their liberty without resistance. Remember that you are four million!"

To many free Negroes his exhortation was a thunderbolt. The resolution of the meeting summed up their perturbation: "that it was warlike and encouraged insurrection and that if the convention should adopt it, the delegates who lived near the border of the slave states would not dare to return to their homes." Yet this resolution was won by only a single vote.

Such advocacies brought about the same degree of comfort to the slavocracy as Queen Victoria's recent announcement that every fugitive from slavery came under the protection of British law the moment his foot touched her dominions. To the southeast and to the north lay her empire, and to the southwest lay the Republic of Mexico with even less cause to respect the integrity of the slavocracy.

Yet as the 1840's progressed, the value of slaves rose so high that the business of the "railroad" fell off. Vigilance, like a prison, clamped down upon the slaves. Many fugitives were seized before they could reach a free state, and so many free Negroes were reduced to slavery that a proposition was "seriously entertained in Virginia of enslaving the whole body of the free Negroes in that state by legislative enactment."

But restlessness surged like a terrible undertow, and the "railroad" compensated for the slack season by bringing through many valuable pieces of ammunition of which none had a greater value than a certain celebrated fugitive, known all over America and famous all over Europe —Eliza who escaped across the ice floes with her baby.

The first part of her story runs much as Mrs. Stowe recounted it. She was a slave woman with several children, the property of a kindly slaveowner who had fallen on difficult days. Learning that she was to be sold, she took her youngest child to whom she was deeply attached, and ran away although it was the middle of the winter.

She did not reach the river until daylight, and then she saw that the frozen surface had broken into floes. From a Scottish couple who lived not far from the bank she begged protection, and they allowed her to stay throughout the day. At night, hoping that the river had frozen again sufficiently to allow her to reach the "good man" who, they assured her, would give her shelter once she crossed the river, she went down to the shore with her baby. But the floes were still stirring sluggishly across that wide expanse of river, and she turned back to the Scotsman's hut. Then she saw the slave catchers clattering into town. Panic-stricken, she ran toward the river. Her only chance lay in the improbable, the fantastic. She wrapped her baby in her shawl, tied it about her neck, and stepped out onto the ice. She jumped from ice cake to ice cake, sometimes going down to her knees in the icy water, sometimes slipping so that she fell onto the floes. Sometimes the floe sank beneath her, and she was forced to lay the child on the cake and drag herself up by her hands. She was wet to the waist and her hands were numb when she reached the shore. A man, who had been watching her with unbelieving eyes, ran to the edge of the water and drew her, exhausted and shaking, up the bank. She asked insistently for the house of "the good man," and she was shown the straight, perpendicular cliff where the Rankins kept watch over the river.

The doors were not locked. She came into the kitchen, made a fire, dried herself and her baby, before she went in search of the family. When they heard her story, two of the Reverend Rankin's sons said that since slave catchers were in the neighborhood, she must be on her way immediately. By daylight they had brought her inland and put her in care of the next stationmaster.

In due course of time, passing from station to station, she arrived at Levi Coffin's where she was kept several days and given the name of Eliza Harris. A few days later, another group of fugitives arrived and she and her child were sent on with a wagonload to Sandusky.

Rush Sloane, a well-known Ohio lawyer and conductor of the Underground Railroad, said that she had cut her hair, dressed as a man and put boy's clothes on her child before she boarded the boat which was to carry her to Canada, and that on the wharf she saw her master, watching the dark passengers, but never recognizing her with her changed appearance.

That is all of the Eliza story that Mrs. Stowe made famous, but the real Eliza carried her heroism to a spectacular and dramatic conclusion. One of the Rankin sons completed her tale many years later.

She had told the family, according to the son, S. G. W. Rankin, that she would be back to fetch her other children, and she named a day in June of the following year. They discouraged her—a routine practice it seems to this remarkable family who never failed to be filled with admiration when their advice was disregarded—but on the June day she had designated, a man climbed the perpendicular hill and appeared in the Rankins' garden. Under the disguise was Eliza, and they helped her across the river, gently flowing now between the green hills on either side. She hid on the outskirts of the plantation and attracted the attention of her eldest daughter, who concealed her that night beneath the floor of her old cabin in the slaves' quarters. The next day was Sunday, and the master and mistress went some distance calling. Eliza promptly gathered together not only her five children but, following the advice of the Israelites and Gerrit Smith, some two hundred pounds of blankets and household goods. They were supposed to reach the river at two o'clock that morning when the Rankins would be waiting on the other bank, but the weight of possessions so overburdened them that they did not come to the river bank until the sun was well up in the sky, and a heavy fog was lifting.

The Rankins, strongly fortified on the other side, had waited through the dark early morning. The lifting fog now showed them that many men on horseback, with dogs and guns, were spreading out along the Kentucky shore, beating the bushes and attempting to persuade the dogs to pick up tracks that had mysteriously disappeared. The Rankins knew that Eliza had not crossed the river, and during the day they managed to send a man across to the place where their practical experience told them she would be hidden. There she was, her children's feet and hers still wet from the water in which they had stood all day in order to throw the bloodhounds off their tracks. She was given instructions, and the man rowed back to the Ohio shore again. Just at twilight, one of the Rankins, conveyed across to Kentucky, put on a slave woman's clothes which he had brought and made a feint to attract the attention of the hunters. He led them a lively chase in the opposite direction, and finally disappeared into the darkness while a confederate ferried Eliza and her children across the river.

They stayed with the Rankins two weeks, and Eliza had time to contemplate that long shining river that melted so exquisitely into the sky and had been so kind to her. At length they were packed into a wagon and, covered with bags of flour and bran, borne off to their first stop on the "railroad."

Mr. Rankin had the last word. "She was a heroic woman, if one ever lived."

The publicity value of these years was tremendous. Midnight stories vied with hairbreadth escapes at noon. Fugitives were snatched back under the noses of their rescuers and their rescuers recovered them at the point of a gun. This border warfare was no less dramatic because its actors were rawboned farmers, middle-aged ministers, and nonresisting Quakers.

The means of operation were changing now. The war was being carried into the South. Moral suasion was failing in all branches of Abolition. More and more zealots of the Underground Railroad were believing that slavery must be rendered so unstable as to destroy itself. To accomplish this, they must stiffen those faltering slaves who did not have the initiative for flight and give help on the spot to those who waited for only a word to make a break for freedom. With the era of Calvin Fairbanks, a new element asserted itself, and the tactics of invasion began to override the counsels of the cautious.

Fairbanks was a student at Oberlin, unswerving in his abomination of slavery. In the spring of 1837 he had been sent down the Ohio River by his father to sell a raft of lumber. At Wheeling, Virginia, he was attracted by a strong and active slave whose confidence he gained, whose desire for freedom he learned, and whom he soon set on the raft, poling for dear life toward Ohio. A few days later, Fairbanks reached Kentucky. There a slave woman, attracted by his friendliness, asked him if he would arrange for the escape of her seven children. He agreed and that night the seven children went across the river.

By 1842 he had become such a wizard at this sleight of hand that he was able to spirit an octoroon, who had been sold for prostitution, out of the garret in which she was kept in Covington, Kentucky. Sliding down the rope he provided, she changed into the boy's clothes he brought. As the girl was well known in Covington, they did not dare hire a boat to carry them across the river. But Fairbanks found a large log lying half in the water and half on the shore and put the girl and himself astride it. With a piece of board, he paddled them to freedom.

Fairbanks used many simple devices to run off his friends. He depended mostly on the unelaborate disguises—the masquerade of ladies and gentlemen, or of men in women's clothes and women in men's. He carried fugitives on foot and on horseback, in buggies, carriages, wagons "in and under loads of hay, straw, old furniture, boxes and bags"; he swam them across rivers or waded with them chin deep.

No fugitive of his was ever recaptured. When the worst came in 1844, it was he himself who was taken.

Lewis Hayden belonged to one Kentucky master, and his wife and son to another. Hayden had asked Fairbanks' assistance, and Fairbanks had, in turn, drawn in a young New England school ma'am who could hardly have foreseen the lively days she was to give herself when she left her Vermont town. They brought off the three slaves safely, Miss Webster disarming all suspicion in the rear seat of the hack, surrounded by her "servants." They safely crossed the ferry, changed horses and drove as far as a "station" at Hopkins, Ohio, where Hayden and his family were turned over to the "railroad."

Two days later, Fairbanks and Miss Webster returned to Lexington where they were teaching, and were promptly arrested by the master of Hayden's wife and son. Their trial served them and the cause they had joined no ill whatever. What did it disclose? That the Underground Railroad was now so powerful that it could snatch slaves from under the noses of their masters and drop them into that long deep tunnel which apparently had no beginning or end; that another martyr had been created for Abolition and that for five years, Abolitionists could point with pride to the Kentucky Penitentiary and Fairbanks, serving his term with an excellent grace.

The Prigg case, in 1842, also served the Underground Railroad as well as a phalanx of new adherents. In 1837, a fugitive from Maryland, named Margaret Morgan, had been found in Pennsylvania by Edward Prigg, an agent of her owner. He seized her, without troubling to secure his rights by law, and thus made himself liable to the Pennsylvania law against kidnaping. He was convicted, but he appealed his case to the Supreme Court which in 1842 handed down a decision characteristically equivocal in these days of divided loyalties: The master need not be restrained by state laws from seizing his slave, but in no way could the law of 1793 be interpreted to mean that the state authorities were obliged to lend a hand.

The effect of this ruling was tremendous. The danger of the law had always hung over the heads of the runaways' friends, but now, although the Federal law was no less stringent, they could offset it by a fresh crop of new personal liberty laws, prohibiting the state authorities from joining in the man hunt. Vermont, Pennsylvania and Rhode Island acted quickly. The hands and reputations of the Abolitionists were strengthened all over the country, and the prestige of the Supreme Court mellowed antagonisms in many quarters.

The case of George Latimer, a fugitive slave who had lived many years in the North until seized by a claimant, followed fast on the heels of the Prigg decision. So fast indeed that the Chief Justice of the Massachusetts Court refused to issue the *habeas corpus* provided by the state law, contending tnat the Prigg case had cast new interpretations on old laws. The Abolitionists protested as loudly as Faneuil Hall permitted. It was the first fugitive slave case in Boston—it was, in fact, the inauguration of new Abolition tactics whereby controversial fugitive cases would be well aired in the courts—and it roused all the indignation that city men feel who have not been exposed to the violence of border warfare and hair-breadth escapes.

Four thousand people were present, proslavery and Abolition. Sections of the audience were uncontrollable; Remond and Douglass had been howled down, and Wendell Phillips at last jumped to the platform in fury, and brought the meeting to a shocking and heretical conclusion. "We presume," he cried, "that the Bible outweighs the statute books. When I look upon these crowded thuosands and see them trample on their consciences and the rights of their fellow men at the bidding of a piece of parchment, I say, my curse be on the Constitution of the United States!"

Such horror as wracked the building! In this sacred Hall of Liberty, dedicated to the memory of the Founding Fathers, the buzzing was terrific. The madman Garrison and his mad henchman Phillips had blown against the fragile petals of the Constitution, and discoloration was bound to show.

But other men went out, stirred to their souls, and quickly raised the $400 that was necessary to buy Latimer back from the hell of a free man, made slave, while Boston Abolitionists, shocked that their colored friends were not safe in the calm, removed state of Massachusetts, hurriedly presented and saw passed, a personal liberty law.

Finally, in Ohio a farmer named Van Zandt dramatized the struggle against the federal law when, in penalty for giving a lift in his wagon to nine colored people — whom, he professed, he did not know were fugitives—he was bankrupted to the extent of $1,200. In all the years that the Underground Railroad had slipped through the Ohio scene, this was the first time that a slaveowner had been able to drag down the law upon the head of a fugitive's friend.

Since his case was of such vast importance, in the light of the Prigg decision, he was defended by the former Senator from Ohio, Thomas Morris and by Salmon P. Chase. When his fate was known, his case was carried to the Supreme Court where William Seward joined with Chase in the pleas. But the Supreme Court refused to overturn the verdict, and Mr. Van Zandt had the dubious pleasure of working twice as hard the rest of his life in payment for a short wagon ride.

The effect of these cases, inestimably important to the records of the Underground Railroad, not only strengthened the hand of the operator but strengthened the outraged zeal of the slaveowner. The latter could not rest now. He realized that these cases and these personal liberty laws had burst a seam in the law of 1793 and were, in effect, a green signal for the Underground Railroad. His one objective must be the sewing of that seam.

It was quite plain now to every employee of the Underground Railroad and to every Abolitionist and to every politician touched with the antislavery color that they were fighting a monopoly bigger than anything that could be measured. Incorporated by no law, it nevertheless formed a body of mutual interest that was greater than any possible and farfetched combination of the four greatest industries in our country today. With four million slaves, whose average individual value was $500 (but might be $2000), it is evident that the minority which controlled them controlled the country.

The two political parties drew their lives from the same blood stream. The Liberty party listened to the equivocations of the Whigs and the Democrats and put up Birney again for President. With the elections of 1844 approaching, the whole country strained to know whether a war would be waged for Texas and whether slavery would again be allowed to lengthen its borders. It was clearly the duty of the Liberty party to provide a mouthpiece. The case for political action was even more clear-cut now than it had been four years ago.

Sixty-two thousand Liberty party men came to the polls in contrast to the 7,100 who had voted four years before—enough to disrupt the balance of power and give a death blow to the Whigs. To most Underground Railroad men, the Quakers and the Garrisonians excepted, the Liberty party belonged to them, and speaking through it in convention as loudly as they dared, they flung down a formidable challenge. The words they chose were bold; in every syllable they said that the days of moral suasion were over.

"Wounded, writhing slavery still cries 'Let us alone!' But the people will not let it alone . . . God will not let it alone! His decree has gone forth, that slavery shall continue to be tortured, even unto DEATH! Lift up your heads then, brethren, for your redemption draweth nigh!"

## Chapter 5

## LET MY PEOPLE GO

TORTURED to death! We shall torture it "even unto DEATH!"
A cold shiver ran down the spines of those who heard. Then this
was a war between men of the same race—a civil war? The Underground
Railroad men, the Abolitionists saw it as civil war when they mentioned
the name of Texas.

Texas had been fitfully in and out of the national consciousness ever
since that day in 1836 when Mexico had recognized her independence and
Sam Houston had become first President of the new republic. The slavocracy had never forgotten her. Slaveowners regarded her as part of themselves, for were not her blood ties and her slave ties as close as two fingers
on a hand? And if Texas looked on Mexico, lying below the Rio Grande
as her enemy, neither did the South equivocate, for in Mexico slaves were
free. And if Texas were slow to see the sinister designs of a slaveless
England, offering her trade and treaties, the South was quick to show
her the dangers that lay with such Abolitionists. Clearly these two parts
of one whole must melt their destinies into each other!

Annexation—annexation. And on the wings of "annexation" came the
spades that would prepare the ground. All the darkest machinations of
the British Foreign Office were laid before the startled eyes of Americans.
The terrible web she was spinning from Canada down through Oregon
on one side and the West Indies on the other, would knot itself in Texas,
and the United States would be trapped, for with England, the small man
was told, came freed slaves, Negro insurrections and cotton competition.
Mexicans, moreover, were planning war. Border raids were magnified to
such an extent that Texas women were set to molding bullets and making cartridges. Northerners were whipped into concern over vast unde-
veloped markets which would be lost to them if England were allowed to
have her way.

These intrigues dazzled the Texans. They were swift to see the advantages of statehood in the Union. When Mexico threatened that
annexation "would be equivalent to a declaration of war," they merely
said that Mexico had threatened war before.

But the question was buzzing through the North. Was the United States willing to fight the war that would follow an annexation treaty? The offer of an annexation treaty was the answer. War was a small price to pay to keep the British threat of Abolition out of the Southwest and to open up those great plains for slavery.

President Tyler drew up the treaty, signed it, and in April, 1844, submitted it to the Senate. The Senate would have nothing to do with it. The Constitution forbade the acquisition of land by treaty. Well, said President Tyler, this is not my only plan. The people will decide.

The future of Texas obscured all other issues that election year. Abolitionists, unexcelled now in agitation, stirred many hearts with their warnings against the slavocracy, warnings that sprang from a deeper moral basis than all the justifications of imperialism, of westward destiny, of American investments in Texas. The South, wildly apprehensive, shouted itself hoarse at disunion meetings from Virginia to Louisiana. "The possession of Texas is infinitely more important to us than a longer connection with the Northern States, and if we have to yield either it cannot and shall not be Texas!" a manifesto read. The Democrats declared for annexation, the Whigs equivocated. That the Democrats won the election was all the answer needed by annexationists. "The will of the people had prevailed." This time Congress would obey.

Many people claimed that the Whig votes and the Liberty party votes, counted together, gave a majority against annexation. But the machine could not be stopped. Texas belonged to the slave power. Texas would be cut into four states and these multiplied representatives would be sent to speak for slavery in Congress.

This, said William Channing in a letter to Clay, "is but the first step of aggression." In the House, John Quincy Adams led the anti-Texans. In Detroit petitions were circulated demanding the annexation of Canada and a return of the balance of power. In Boston a large number of Whigs and a few Democrats called a meeting the first of the new year, 1845—an Anti-Texas Convention—to meet in Faneuil Hall. "The anti-slavery spirit of the convention was surprising," said Edmund Quincy. "The Address and the speeches of the gentlemen, not abolitionists, were such as caused Garrison to be mobbed ten years ago."

How quickly ten years had passed! To some who had seen a broadcloth mob lead Garrison bound through these very streets it seemed only yesterday. And yet here was a broadcloth convention cheering to the rafters that same Garrison and his words which fell like "fiery rain." He was elected a delegate from his ward, and there was but one thing they failed to do for him that day. They would not act on a certain proposal. But that proposal called for the dissolution of the Union.

It is probable that when Garrison sat down, his thin hawk face imperturbable, his eyes piercing through his spectacles, he was content for the time—*for the time*—to be the only revolutionist. But things would move fast now. Sixteen years would go past more quickly than one could believe.

NO UNION WITH SLAVEHOLDERS had lain across the masthead of *The Liberator* for a year or more. Garrison had made quite clear what he thought of the democratic paraphernalia which cradled slavery so comfortably. "The ballot box is not an antislavery but a proslavery argument, so long as it is surrounded by the U. S. Constitution, which forbids all approach to it except on condition that the voter shall surrender fugitive slaves—suppress Negro insurrections—sustain a piratical representation in Congress, and regard man-stealers as equally eligible with the truest friends of human freedom and equality."

Some of his coadjutors might disagree with him on this point—Ellis Gray Loring, Edmund Quincy—or some of those who accused him of leaving the Negroes in outer darkness while the slaveless North withdrew within its own borders. For them he had the words of John Quincy Adams, "If slavery be the destined sword in the hands of the destroying angel which is to sever the ties of the Union, the same sword will cut asunder the bonds of slavery itself." But to others his dogma of revolution did not need to be explained—to men with minds as hard and smashing as his own, men like Phillips who dazzled and pummeled with his brilliant invectives against the Union, "that unholy alliance of slavery and freedom"; men like Stephen Foster, the theological student, who invaded churches whose members would not come to antislavery lectures and interrupted the services with denunciations of their intrenched conservatism, their tacit consent to slavery, their "Brotherhood of Thieves." ("This hat was crushed for me," he would shout to an antislavery gathering, "in *a church in Portland!*" and his battered topper became the very symbol of the oppressed, the very fount of horror); men like Parker Pillsbury, great, black-bearded Pillsbury, "tearing up words like trees by the roots," as Lowell said, who would turn slowly about on the Abolition platform and show his coat, ripped from hem to collar by a pious mob.

The deadly apprehension, the sense almost of doom that harried antislavery men was not out of proportion to the facts. If the Missouri Compromise had troubled men's consciences, the treaty of annexation stirred them deeply, for the intervening years had laid a heavy hand upon the future. When, in March, 1845 the outgoing Tyler, with "indecent haste," signed a Senate resolution annexing Texas and left to his successor, the Tennessean, Polk, the disposition of military and naval forces to hold the prize, and when Polk, coolly informed his Cabinet that California would soon cease to be a Mexican possession, all the doubts and wonderings were over. The slavocracy had won. The Abolitionists acknowledged it with their customary realism. But did it mean that antislavery men would let the challenge pass? No indeed. It meant merely that they would make their cause clang like a fire bell in the North.

They were prepared for a challenge on any front. The diminishing membership of the antislavery societies showed that the fight was broadening its front, was assuming political action. All during the summer of 1845 they held meetings, agitated, kept the question alive, waiting, always, for that Mexican declaration of war. Their power to act was limited, but they could sting the conscience, they could make slavery the most hated thing in the country. On the Fourth of July and on August 1st, the anniversary of West Indian emancipation, they held great rallies. Eloquence was a golden torrent, intended to tear to pieces the pretensions of the slave power. Jonathan Walker was there, shocking, fit to be gazed at with round eyes, confirming in his own person all that they had said.

Jonathan Walker's story had sizzled through the North like the branding iron on his skin. Anyone there could have told you about him. How he, a New Englander, went to Florida to assist in the building of a railroad. How he treated his black workers in the manner of a Christian, allowing them to eat with him and pray with him, and how he won their friendship. Wasn't it natural—the story passing from ear to ear —for those black men to come to him when they wanted to leave the prison house of Florida? And wasn't it natural that such a man as Captain Walker would agree to help them? In 1844, seven of them, with the captain, pushed off in an open boat from Pensacola for a Bahaman island. They rounded the capes of Florida. But the beating sun prostrated the captain and the slaves knew nothing of navigation. A shipwrecking sloop found them, drifting and desperate, and seven black men and one white were hauled aboard. Walker was sent to Pensacola in chains where he lay in a jail, fastened to a ringbolt for fifteen days without bed or chair. After two trials he was stood in a pillory for an hour while a "renegade Northerner" threw rotten eggs at him, and then he was taken out and a branding iron heated. By order of the Federal court the letters SS were burned upon his hand, slave stealer, to bring him glory among the friends of the fugitive. Returned to prison, he was chained until the seven fines for the seven slaves and the costs of his trial were paid, and the seven terms of imprisonment for the seven slaves were served.

Within the year the fines were paid by the Abolitionists of the North and the imprisonments were waived. And Jonathan Walker was able to stand at an Abolition meeting in Massachusetts and raise his branded hand against the slavocracy. What if the meeting were emotional? Captain Walker, solid, blue-eyed, a son of their own, was asking them to give a hundred times less than he had.

In September they went to another convention—not of the Abolitionists but of the still uncertain Whigs. Yet the Abolitionists were the ones who saw the issue squarely, and made the best speeches. Everywhere anti-Texas men were hastily preparing a unified front against the awful juggernaut of the slavocracy. In Massachusetts, public meetings were held all over the state and some of her most distinguished men let their oratory mount to stirring heights. Petitions, signed by tens of thousands, were gathered and borne off to Washington by Henry Wilson and John Whittier.

It was a fine effort, but too many of the antislavery politicians had already admitted defeat. Seward wrote a public letter to Chase, submitting to the annexation, deploring the talk of disunion, and urging that the Abolition work be concentrated, not on whipping a dead horse, but on electing an "independent Congress" which would stem the slave trade. One by one they submitted, and by their submission sapped the courage of many brothers.

Yet New Englanders were aroused. Pride in their revolutionary antecedents had been stirred. Faneuil Hall was jammed in November; Palfrey, the secretary of state, was chairman of the meeting. On that day Charles Sumner rose in his seat and took his first public part in the fight that would carry him to the Senate, to the cause of "Bleeding Kansas," to the pummeling stick of Preston Brooks, to Emancipation. He fought valiantly on that occasion against the defeatism of those who professed antislavery principles and yet accepted the Texas annexation with a bowing of the head. The meeting was fervent. Committees were organized in the best New England fashion. There was something deeply stirring in their freshness, vitality and inexhaustible faith in good. Had Abolitionists ever accepted defeat before? Never! And they let the cry ring around Faneuil Hall, whip at lagging spirits, and sweep Garrison, the saturnine, onto the committee that was authorized to rouse the state into action. How true to himself Garrison always was.

The misfit, the radical, with the faint smile that rounded his lips, consented to the post as "an experiment to demonstrate the futiliy of any and every attempt to assail slavery in its incidents and details." Texas was a detail. He had larger game to catch. He had the whole slave power to fasten on the end of his hook.

When the emotions had subsided, when the cold days of winter arrived and Texas became a state, they saw that he was right. They saw that with the division among themselves—Whigs, Liberty men—the slave power could always seep in through the cracks.

When Congress convened, they waited to hear what John Quincy Adams, aged, the fire in him subsiding, had to say. There was not very much to say. He laid the petitions they had gathered, thousands of signatures, before the House and the House tabled them. Stephen Douglas, the cherubic little man from the West with the sly eyes and the barroom manners, presented a resolution to admit Texas to statehood. A majority of five to two agreed with him. Daniel Webster, with the ravages of ambition catching at his beetling brows, darkening his deep sunk eyes, protested in the name of Massachusetts. Others stood up, men dedicated to an expanding North, and solemnly voiced their condemnation, their words echoing with a hollow solemnity in the restive chamber, a consciousness possessing them that the day would come when their fine expanding North would outgrow scenes like this, would be strong enough to sit elbow to elbow with the slavocracy and speak with a lusty voice.

Antislavery men in the North might admit discouragement but the Abolitionists laughed. Garrison wrote jovially to a friend, "Apparently the slaveholding power has never been so strong—has never held such complete mastery over the whole country—as at the present time; and yet never has it in reality been so weak, never has it had so many uncompromising assailants, never has it been so filled with doubt and consternation, never has it been so near the downfall as at this moment." And Edmund Quincy writing to the same friend, took up the note. "Garrison is in good spirits as he always is, and as we all have a trick of being. Mrs. Follen says that when she wants to be put in spirits, she goes among the abolitionists, and there she is sure to find cheerfulness, wit, humor and fun. And who should be cheerful and merry in this country but the abolitionists?"

They knew why they were merry. Civic consciousness was roused. Agitation like this would make men realize that occasional voting was not the sum of their duty, that all the wide promises of freedom must be kept for others if they were to be kept for themselves. Garrison was not the only man to say that the slavocracy had overreached itself, that Texas with its million acres, slave-hungry, was the swan song of a swollen oligarchy.

Boston was deeply alive those days in the searching of its spirit. Men still made money on State Street, workers still sat fifteen and twenty hours a day at spinning looms, but New England was flowering in the deep places of the heart and mind and her great men were bringing her the exquisite immortality that was to lie like a balm on the brutality of a new industrial age. The Boston of the 1830's and '40's was a world of new ideas. German idealism, French enlightenment, Swedenborgian mysticism, spiritualism, possessed the underlying channels of thought and mingled with the doctrines of revolution—Communism, women's rights, temperance, protection for the insane, rehabilitation of prisoners —all social panaceas for a new age. Emerson, who had cut away from his church, searching for truth, had propounded his intellectual Declaration of Independence seven years before, and pulled at the roots of orthodoxy with his challenges. Young Theodore Parker, with the round formidable skull and the vigilant eyes, had found his "soul so aroused" by this "declaration . . . so beautiful, so terribly sublime," that within three years he had proclaimed his own iconoclasm and left his church —at its request. By 1845 he was preaching not to the handful who had filled his regularly appointed church but to the thousands who filled Melodeon Hall to enjoy the fine clear blast of his championship of freedom, of the soul, the mind and the body. That year, he joined the antislavery society and began fourteen years of agitation that was paralleled only by Garrison and Phillips. He made the North his parish and became a self-appointed conscience, his name and his fame spreading from Maine to Mississippi. Over the principle of Abolition he threw the fabric of transcendentalism, so that it became not merely a material agitation, but a profound intuition of the spirit; into its mouth he put his own inexhaustible erudition; finally to the cause itself he gave his vivacity, his humor and his love of action.

In Cambridge, Longfellow, the most popular author of his America, was writing thunderously on slavery, and what he said stood for awhile, although by 1848, when he refused to allow his Abolition poems to be included in his collected works, his thunder had muttered away and left him face to face with the indignant Abolitionists. James Russell Lowell, ecstatically a bridegroom, was a perfect zealot of a reformer, writing for a pittance a stream of antislavery articles and shouting gloriously while his fervor was still fresh. Alcott, happy, ardent, dreaming, could not keep himself from something that so closely touched on life, and lent his sweet unworldliness to a cause that seemed a whole soul removed from him, yet was in reality a deep spirituality translated into action. Thoreau, dwelling in a world where there was no slavery of black or white, quite naturally, with no struggling of the intellect or the conscience, reached out a hand to the fugitive.

In the antislavery world away from Boston, politics were more powerful than cultural philosophy.

In Congress Giddings and Adams were no longer fighting a solitary battle. Owen Lovejoy was there, the brother of the martyr. And Gates and Tilden from New York, Mixson from Ohio, Slade from Vermont as well as former Governor Crafts who was vice president of the Vermont Antislavery Society, Clarke of western New York, a section now becoming a roadbed for the "railroad." Ohio also sent a Tappan to the Senate, a brother of the redoubtable pair in New York City. They were all products of a rising political thought, yet all outcasts, all hated and abused.

What peculiar leaven then was knitting the small men of the North loosely—very loosely—into a new way of thinking? Had the slavocracy indeed overreached itself? Were industrial ambitions perhaps stronger than devotion to Southern interests? Yet the farmer of Ohio, where politics flourished in such congenial soil, had very little concern with the manufacturers of the East.

He must have sensed something that was blowing fresh across the Eastern hills and the Western prairie land—a new world that ran on iron rails and that gave to life a curious exhilaration. A generation ago someone's father had been the first man to nail two boards together and begin a house and a town out this way. That town had grown, whether it was called Springfield, Illinois or Akron, Ohio, and people had grown with it. They weren't sophisticated people; when an Abe Lincoln started off for the Illinois legislature and a Ben Wade started off for the Ohio legislature, and put on their shiny stovepipe hats, this did not mean that the world was coming in; it merely meant that two men were going to another town of mud streets where rooting pigs and cows contested the way with them. But there they learned something—learned maybe that a railroad had been built in Russia, that in England people were sending ships across the Atlantic to buy their corn and wheat. Russia and England weren't much farther off than the Alleghenies then? Just beyond those mountains, down those long iron rails, were people who needed the men of Ohio, of Indiana, of Illinois, even the men of that terribly faraway Pacific coast. The world was drawing very close. Railroads were beginning to shape the thoughts of men. They brought new things for the women, sewing machines and other curiously natural devices that the new power-driven factories of the East were producing, they brought tools to men—quick and cheaply—so that men no longer had to cut and shape their own implements. From Chicago they brought a new harvesting machine which a man named McCormick promised would mean riches for the farmers. Railroads were the explanation of a new life, a panacea for old ills.

All that railroads signified gave men a new attitude toward that huge commanding land below the Ohio River which had no railroads to speak of, which talked instead of its power in cotton, which made fractional representation out of their slaves in order to keep Congress jumping according to their plan. (They knew about it in Ohio and especially in Illinois because of the men who crossed over to make their homes among them.) Maybe those men in the South had a right to their slaves; they weren't going into that; but they were beginning not to like the airs they gave themselves. When a runaway came along, white-eyed with nerves, it was a slap at the high-and-mightiness of his master if space were made in the corncrib. After all, men of the North didn't need black boys to work for them. They weren't ashamed of their own two hands!

Into all this, Garrisonism was growing, in Ohio and Michigan where the Liberty party was strong, growing enough to make a pipeful of talk, perched on the rail of the crossroads store, for Garrison and nonresistance, Garrison and nonvoting had never found such root before in the Western temperament. Maybe it was the people who came preaching Garrisonism—Abby Kelly and Stephen Foster and Parker Pillsbury —nobody's fools, with voices as loud as any hecklers', plain people. Abby Kelly looked like one of their women, no furbelows, no foolishness, arms primly crossed above her stomach, a nice hot temper. And Pillsbury and Foster made dandy stump speeches and didn't mind the words they used, or those their audience used. You could laugh them down, but they just roared a little louder and threw in a story for good measure. Maybe most people went away laughing, but some did not. Some stayed to talk a little longer. In Salem, Ohio, where the Quakers were strong, they even founded a paper and called it *The Anti-Slavery Bugle*. It blew its little tune for twenty years, while other antislavery papers rose and fell, and its little tune never varied—"No Union with Slaveholders!"

Probably some of these things were unimportant—small people using small means to create a revolution—but they fell into the pattern of those years, and their small design added to a larger scroll, a big scroll that was just beginning to unwind itself in the Texas annexation.

The excitement had grown with the summer. Florida had come in as a slave state with a constitution that attempted to prohibit, *forever*, the possibility of freedom. Northern men hurriedly presented Iowa, and the balance was restored, precarious, artificial. The country was subtly, within its own heart and mind, preparing for war. The farmer in Ohio, the artisan in Pennsylvania, the schoolteacher in New England, might not have recognized war in the food they ate, the newspapers they read, the spinning looms they manipulated, the plow they guided; and the shopkeeper in Louisiana, the small planter in Georgia, might not have seen war in the cotton, going up the slow rivers and disappearing into the hungry doors of Northern factories, or in the rising price of slaves or the rising value of manufactured goods, but certainly they must all have known that the new quickening of the eyes, the pregnant silences and exchange of glances when free land was spoken of carried a threat as far as the Pacific, as far as the Rio Grande. Free Land! It brought a swifter response than Free Man had ever done. Whig turned against Whig, Democrat against Democrat.

The German immigrants, flying to America from political oppression took up the cry with a contagious zeal. The young and gangling trade-unions recognized in it the very shape and color of the proletariat. The Abolitionists saw in it the death blow to the slavocracy.

But the slavocracy had seen it too. Without slavery extension, the industrial North would outstrip it; the balance of power would be lost; the domination of the Supreme Court, the foreign service, the army, the navy and the administrative branches would be gone. Hysteria was strengthened by atrocity stories. When Mexico moved she must face a United States bound together by a common hatred of the dark men below the border. As the summer went on, many of the real issues were lost in the stimulated hatred.

But Mexico moved too slowly. When a "border incident" was invoked early in 1846, when Polk ordered General Zachary Taylor to advance into Mexican territory, the slavocracy, much as it might deplore the effect of war, drew a deep breath. The West would now be made safe for slavery.

The excitement was electric. Polk had moved adroitly and inconspicuously. Protests and acclamations were both anticlimaxes. He calmly declared that a state of war existed, and Congress without delay voted men and money. A year before, orders had gone to the commander of the Pacific fleet to seize California when the word was given, and the word was now given. More than half of Mexico was demanded by the United States.

Voices in Congress were a cheap commodity. Yet Giddings' roar filled the chamber, as he stalked rough-haired, bushy-browed up and down the aisles, shaking his fury under the nose of Southern Democrats. And Corwin of Ohio wrote his epitaph when he flung out his arms and shouted to a turbulent House, "If I were a Mexican, I would greet you with bloody hands and welcome you to hospitable graves!" But from their long thin friend Lincoln from Illinois, fell the counsel of the future, the "sacred right of the people . . . to rise up and shake off the existing government, and form a new one that suits them better [since] it is the quality of revolutions not to go by old lines or old laws, but to break up both and make new ones."

The Abolitionists—well, they were not surprised. Perhaps even, in the secret of their beds at night, they were a little glad that the hand of slavery had shown itself so clearly. Garrison merely reiterated with his inspired monotony, "What the people need is a new government—a free government—NO UNION WITH SLAVEHOLDERS!"

Garrison had had an invitation to go to an antislavery convention in London. He hesitated for a little while, for this was no time for leaders to be away from home, and Elizur Wright and Arnold Buffum were both absent, and Frederick Douglass was already triumphantly in England. But after all, there was nothing new here. A crisis would not arise from the Mexican War, although the Mexican War would lay the groundwork for a crisis. And he was needed in England. His friend George Thompson was making it evident that reactionary forces were slowly gaining control of Abolition sympathy in England, and English support was invaluable to the American Abolitionists. Some day there would be a showdown, and England must be on the side of freedom.

In the South, the recognition of war rose here and there among the slaves. In Pensacola, "as soon as a sufficient number of white men went off to war" they intended to rise, and martial law was declared in the navy yard, and patrols filled the city. In Louisiana, Solomon Northup, free colored man of New York, who had been kidnaped and lived for twelve years in slavery, found that "the news of victory filled the great house with rejoicing, but produced only sorrow and disappointment in the cabins."

All the while in Washington, that dusty, dirty city where soldiers on parade at the last inauguration had sprawled in the slippery mud, where pickpockets worked their trade at the best receptions, where every dialect could be heard, but mostly the soft or nasal tones of the South, where pigs rooted in the streets and slave coffles shuffled past the Capitol, here in this fierce town, the forensics rose and fell with the course of the war, and Lincoln, who hated the war, became an intimate of Alex Stephens, that "little pale star from Georgia" who saw, bound into the war, all that he believed. Here Andrew Johnson, come from Tennessee with the rooted bitterness which made one know him for a "poor white," sneered at that other poor man from Ohio, Josh Giddings, and the ex- quisites from Massachusetts listened with startled good manners to Steve Douglas who, by the testimony of Adams, "in the midst of his roaring stripped off and cast away his cravat, to save himself from choking, unbuttoned his waistcoat and had the air and aspect of a half-naked pugilist." Here men hated at the tops of their voices, and drew a fierce line, more visible than Mason and Dixon's, between their individual interests and concerns. Even the Southern Whigs, who were theoretically against annexation, saw the wisdom of adding their voices to the Demo- crats, for the only alternative was a denunciation of slavery expansion, and slavery politics were more important to them than a plank in a badly nailed platform. Only Calhoun, gaunt and burned out but mighty, was filled with dismay at the thing that he had done. This was the Texas he had maneuvered, as Secretary of State for Tyler, out of the hands of the British and therefore out of the hands of emancipationists. But he had not intended this, he had not meant to drown it in blood or bring slavery with the sword to a free half-breed population. Some of his Southern Whig disciples attempted to find a compromise, perhaps even a solution. "They were for their country right or wrong, but Con- gress had the right to declare War, and it was the President who had done it." But a new kind of politician, full of hot chauvinism, arrogant with thousands of miles of cotton furrows, was putting aside such men as Calhoun. At their hands the war was legalized.

By August, 1846, Polk was asking for more money "for the purpose of settling our difference with Mexico." He suggested that two million dollars would be an adequate sum. The dissident Whigs and those few Democrats who could not go with the war party, were not prepared to let such an opportunity pass. Voices were raised sharply. Party lines were broken. This Congressman would not vote for the appropriation unless he were assured that slavery would be limited. Another seconded him. Another rose to repeat the same thing in different words. Finally David Wilmot of Pennsylvania stood up with a carefully drafted amendment.

He moved that slavery should be forever barred from any territory taken in this war. The champions of slavery rose with a roar, yet the Proviso burned through all the questions of the war that session and the next. It lay on the lips of men and women everywhere for it had become a greater issue than the war itself. Sectional lines were broken through again and again. And meanwhile the war went on without the two-million-dollar appropriation.

Had the Northern forces been united, had the Proviso been acted upon quickly, some comfort might have been taken from the months of debate. But by January, 1847, it was evident that the slavocracy had recovered whatever ground was lost and set its machinery to work. Whatever fight was left was merely a matter of principle. On the last day of the session, Wilmot again offered his amendment as the appropriations bill came up, and 102 voted against it, 97 in its favor. The President now had two million dollars with which to negotiate a peace. And slavery was unrestricted.

For antislavery men who were not Abolitionists, it was a dark and disturbing moment. To the Garrisonians it was merely further proof that political action was futile. To other Abolitionists it was a clear call for a new political party. Soon—very soon—America must know its own mind.

That summer Garrison went on his first Western tour. It was not a pure triumph, for his reputation met him everywhere and sometimes he was not able to contend with it, but it was on the whole a remarkable success for Garrisonism, that strange flower in the Middle West. Edmund Quincy edited *The Liberator* while he was gone, and Frederick Douglass accompanied him. A Frederick Douglass now sure of himself, beginning to show his superb talents, infusing the facts in which he dealt with the warm splendor of a magnificent voice. England had done a great deal for him. He had traveled there alone, lecturing and being received without a trace of prejudice. To England he was a man of talent and virtue, and Englishmen did not seem in the least concerned by the color of his skin. It had been hard to come back to America where, on one occasion, he had been forced to tear up the plush seats of the general passengers' coach on his way to forceful exile in the Jim Crow car. Yet now he was a celebrity, and other celebrated men in the North were pleased to meet him, although lesser men still greeted him and other colored Abolitionists with stones.

The tour of Garrison coincided with the fall of Mexico City and the virtual end of the war. Garrison who missed nothing, who explained everything according to the undeviating pattern of his principles, carried the battle of disunion as far as Ohio where crowds pressed eagerly to hear him debate the question with Giddings, his outspoken admirer. Middle Westerners were not afraid of the rough-and-tumble; they were more realistic, more willing to admit that the possibility of a political upheaval might be closer upon them than they suspected. Farther West, in Indiana, the ground had been well covered by antislavery lecturers, telling their stories at meetings in log cabins, in schoolhouses, in places where ox teams were the only means of locomotion, where they had to carry their own supply of candles to light the poor back-country meeting houses, where tracks of split logs, unsoftened by earth, jogged their wagons to pieces as they looked for a night's hospitality.

The Mexican War had aided them. It had taken more time, cost more money, and given people more opportunity to study the purpose and mentality of the slavocracy than the war enthusiasts had anticipated. And the wind that was blowing carried the questions and the doubts not only to those Middle Western men who were making their own futures and knew well their own pasts, but to the settlers of the West, where modern industrialism was a far-fetched phenomenon, and to the God-hungry, trade-hungry men of New England and the Atlantic States. For they remembered things that the slave power had forgotten, remembered a country which had produced men like Jefferson, the revolutionist, and Franklin, the philosopher of freedom. The overflow meetings, come to hear the Fosters, Stephen and Abby Kelly, Burleigh with the head of a fierce and uncouth Jesus, Pillsbury, and now Garrison and Douglass, made these remembrances increasingly evident. "I have seen nothing like it," Garrison wrote his wife. "Yesterday we held three large meetings, two of them in the open air and concluded last night with the greatest enthusiasm. The place seems to be electrified, and the hearts of many are leaping with joy."

Abolition was not the only topic which drew the crowds, for Garrison was ready to expose the Church and the State, to preach the doctrine of disunion and combat the budding dogma that the Constitution was an antislavery document—an attitude of mind which he regarded as flagrant wishful thinking. A reshapen public opinion on all these matters would, he was convinced, break the mesmerism that made blind devotion to inflexible values seem the very form of integrity, the exact sum of patriotism. Garrison was not a man to see the minutiae of the future; he had no political training or social philosophy to allow him to prognosticate: he saw only an evil and its destruction. The vibrations in the air could not be identified by him. It is questionable if any man had the vision to see what lay so soon in the future.

By the summer of 1847, several inescapable facts had been established. Stung by the Mexican War, by the impact of fugitives on the emotions, and by the dynamics of Abolitionists which brought forth friends and enemies, fully grown, it was evident that antislavery sentiment had grown with startling impressiveness within the rigid limits of the Whigs and Democrats and would play a large part in the forthcoming Presidential campaign and provide a challenge that was bigger than the Liberty party had met in 1844. Yet the party itself was at a standstill. From Maine came word that it was merely holding its own, and anticipating "certain death" if something were not done to relieve its static condition. Gerrit Smith spoke frankly of a falling away on all sides, and proved this statement by carrying off the most influential of the Negro supporters, Henry Highland Garnet and Frederick Douglass (who had by now split irremediably with Garrison on the question of politics), into the new Liberty League.

In a Massachusetts by-election, the original Liberty party polled only ten thousand votes and in a similar New York election it fell from sixteen to twelve thousand. The strong political Abolitionists were still among the Whigs.

It was evident that political Abolition must find a new policy, adopt some method that would compete successfully with that political dreadnaught, the Democratic party and with the ailing but still sprightly Whig. Garrison, pleased by the small flowering buds of his Western trip, stopped over in Buffalo long enough to heap scorn on the Liberty party convention which was attempting to find a solution for this restive problem. To him, the dilemma had been easily anticipated and was now justifying the jeremiads of himself and Phillips. They had predicted that antislavery alone would prove insufficient for a political group and this fact was now being discovered by the very men who had found Garrison's reform movements too scattered for concentrated loyalty. Birney, Smith, Goodell, Beriah Green were urging free trade, direct taxation, government monopoly of mails, disbandment of the army and navy, distribution of public lands, as necessary concomitants of a sound reformation party. (Women's Suffrage was still too much for them. That must be left to the women themselves, meeting at Seneca Falls the next year and to the colored conventions meeting a few weeks after that at Cleveland and Philadelphia. At Seneca Falls, the women recognized their common interests with the slaves by nearly electing Frederick Douglass chairman; at Cleveland and Philadelphia, resolutions of feminine equality were among the first to be passed.) Discontented Whigs and Democrats would thus be disarmed and absorbed, and would find themselves imbibing antislavery with other advanced ideas. This was still heresy to the original framers of the party, yet the two factions came together at Worcester, Massachusetts, in September, and mended their breaches for a few months until bigger things and larger issues wiped out the Liberty party forever.

Seen with even a limited vision, these events were all of a single design; they all made antislavery a fitfully sleeping giant in the land. To some observers the antislavery forces might appear disturbed and breaking, to others they might appear to be losing their pure absorption in the liberation of the black man and his unequivocal right to citizenship. From an absolute point of view both were perhaps right. That which came from political and economic necessities could not have the same pure altruism, the same infinite compassion as that which had come with the early zealots. Expediency might bring the end of slavery, but would expediency build a strong world for the Negro? Yet antislavery, a bare ten years after the gag rule, was in the consciousness of all Americans.

Even some of the border states were roused over the further extension of slavery. Delaware came so close to legislation providing for gradual emancipation that Calhoun, prophesying a new balancing of power, cast Delaware on the side of the free states. Western Virginia, where slaves were proving a bad economic investment, allowed the antislavery forces a power that threatened for the time to draw it from the orbit of the slavocracy. While in Kentucky, Cassius Clay, the scion who had heard Garrison speak in New Haven, was agitating with all the powers of his impeccable Southern name and his unassailable social position for the abolition of slavery, although his life was scarcely worth a farthing, his vicissitudes being taken from the same book as those of Birney, or of Daniel Goodloe who was waging the fight in North Carolina.

In every case the oligarchic machine worked fast and ruthlessly, but there was a not unnatural perturbation in the very swiftness forced upon it. Many straws were in this now new and unpredictable wind. Passage or attempted passage of laws protecting the Negro from slave hunters were rousing the legislatures of all states which did not have personal liberty laws. The boycott of slave produce was growing with small but impressive strides. Levi Coffin had been forced to leave his Indiana home and move to the larger city of Cincinnati in order to act upon the money subscriptions and resolutions passed by free labor conventions which authorized immediate organization of free labor associations in the West.

For some time Westerners had been faithful supporters of free labor products, but their demand for sheeting, yarn, muslin, exceeded the cotton supply of free labor planters. As a Southerner, Coffin knew that the South was filled with small farmers, nonslaveholders, whose small patches of cotton were in hopeless competition with the great plantations. By correspondence, he now learned that contacts might be made with some of these small farmers for free-grown cotton. But that was not enough since slave labor ginned and baled it. At last, with the co-operation of the Philadelphia Free Labor Association, a gin was bought and shipped to a Quaker farmer in Mississippi who agreed that the entire process should be done by himself and his hired labor. The associations agreed to buy all the cotton in reach of that "Abolition gin" provided it were shipped to Memphis, the nearest shipping point that used free labor. In Memphis it was to be handled by a well-recommended commission merchant who used no slave labor, and shipped up the river on boats, manned by free men. Large quantities of cotton were thus made available, and the Philadelphia Association was able not only to keep Levi Coffin supplied and through him the mills and the free-labor consumers of the West, but to ship good quantities to the Manchester mills of England in exchange for a finer grade of goods than they were then producing. A Quaker agent was hired to keep a continuous check on the producers and middlemen in the South, and local agents were employed to pay for the cotton on the spot and arrange for its shipping to Memphis.

Coffin himself went as far south as Mississippi, carrying with him his staunch Abolition views, his fearlessness, and his humor. His Quaker dress set him apart. Men accepted the fact that he probably did not believe in slavery, and many times a stranger fastened himself to Coffin with an eager volubility, curious to hear the statements of an Abolitionist, eager to argue against them, or, as Coffin had occasion to discover a number of times, eager to agree that slavery was the greatest curse of the South.

He was thankful, he said to his Abolition friends later, that he had found such an open field for spreading antislavery principles. Every journey through the South to buy free-labor cotton, every encourage-ment to paid labor, was in reality a plea for the cause of the slave.

His free-labor business grew so rapidly that difficulties were soon upon him. The demand for free-labor goods had spread so far that he was receiving orders from all the free states west of the Alleghenies, from Canada, and from Kentucky and western Virginia. His supply was not equal to the demand, and neither he nor the Philadelphia Associa-tion had the equipment to fill orders. He needed a larger capital in-vestment, and men with money were not interested in free-labor prod-ucts. The Free Labor Association in Indiana attempted to organize a stock company, but antislavery men were not the ones with money to invest. It was a tantalizing uphill struggle, but he was able to fight for his growing business for ten years, while the market for free-labor goods developed all over the free states and in England.

When he left Indiana for Cincinnati, he had fondly believed that his Underground Railroad work was over. He had been a conductor for twenty years, and other aspects of the cause seemed now to demand his time and energies. Familiar with the Abolitionists of Cincinnati, he had believed that the work was in good hands. It took him only a short time to discover that the fugitives were mainly dependent on their own endangered and exposed people, and that the "railroad" was in much the same condition here as it had once been in Newport, Indiana. Cincinnati, that half-Southern city, was consistently hostile to Abolitionists; they were ostracized in religious and political associations, and it took courage to assume the work of underground activities. It was a foregone conclusion that Coffin would not be able to leave the situation as he found it. He resumed his acquaintanceship with the Abolition workers of Cincinnati, and organized a more successful resistance to the slave catcher as well as a lively and active station for the Underground Railroad. The word spread rapidly, in that inexplicable manner which characterizes all underground activity, and it was only a matter of days before the fugitives were finding their way once more to a Coffin house.

They came from directly across the river and from Ohio River boats. They also came, now and then, from Rankin's famous "Abolition college" at Ripley, where that indefatigable little man with his spotless white stock, unending geniality, and nine sons, was doing a thriving and dangerous business.

What effect the Mexican War had on the underground work is undetermined. When he moved to Cincinnati, Coffin was struck by the increase of runaways. How much of this was due to the position of the city itself on the banks of the river, and how much to the underswell of restlessness in the South cannot be said. In any case, the work intensified to such an extent that the need for vigilance deepened in proportion, and Coffin was obliged to nip off more and more time from his business in order to supervise the concealment and safe conveyance of the runaways.

With runaways multiplying, the cost of the work increased. More material must be supplied to the antislavery sewing circles, more wagons and teams hired to make the journey to the next station, twenty or thirty miles away. A two-horse team cost ten dollars, and often two or three teams were required at one time. Coffin dealt with a German livery stable, sending an innocent colored man to transact the business and pay in advance for the wagons. The German seemed to understand that no questions were expected, and Coffin counted on this discretion. It was necessary to take every precaution in order to keep clear of the law. He himself seldom saw the colored man who hired the wagons, but gave the money and instructions to an intermediary. The drivers of the wagons were generally chosen in the same way from colored men who owned no property and therefore would lose nothing if they became entangled with the law. These drivers must, first of all, have courage and resourcefulness, for although they always left at night, their drive might not be completed until the early hours of the daylight, and with daylight came all the dangers of discovery and arrest.

But the danger of the underground work did not, apparently, put any limits on the sex or previous condition of the workers. No man could have shown more courage and enterprise than Laura Haviland. She was a plain, prim-mouthed little Quakeress who lived in northern Michigan, and brought up her children with a brisk concern for the details of integrity and self-reliance. But domesticity was not enough for her. Her energy needed wider scope. In 1837 she had started Raisen Institute because she believed in mixed education, both as to sex and color. For some time she had followed the example of other energetic Abolition women by running an Underground Railroad station. Not entirely satisfied with the limitations of her plot of earth, she made several trips with fugitives into Canada to see them safely out of the eagle's claw, and braved slave-catchers' pistols on more than one occasion. To her, Levi Coffin was the leader and the guiding mind of these enterprises, and she thought nothing of packing her small reticule and going to Ohio to consult with him.

She went to see him promptly when, in 1847, a fugitive named John White who worked on a farm near Raisen Institute begged her to do something to rescue his wife from slavery. The Vigilance Committee of Cincinnati seemed the natural consultants, and Coffin, never surprised by any exploit, suggested that she go to Rising Sun, Indiana, and consult several colored friends of John White who had escaped from the neighborhood of his plantation and settled in that neighborhood.

They conferred for several days. Mrs. Haviland, in her prim sober Quaker dress, her prim little lips folded meditatively, her prim little finger following the black figures, young and old, that traced a path for her, her bright eyes looking into black ones and disposing of the dangers beforehand, finally nodded her head, snapped shut her reticule, shook hands all around and returned to Cincinnati. Coffin heard her plans, offered only tentative advice and saw her onto the ferry that carried her to the Kentucky shore.

In Kentucky she made her way, in as conventional a manner as possible, to the neighborhood of the Stevens' plantation where Jane White was a slave. A free mulatto woman named Rachel, who showed no trace of her colored blood, agreed to pass her off as the aunt whom she was expecting from Georgia. Dressed in shabby clothes, with berry pails over their arms, "Aunt Smith" and Rachel walked up boldly to the Stevens' plantation and joined the slaves at their noonday meal. "Aunt Smith" did not have much to say as her Yankee twang would have turned her into a doubtful Georgian, but Rachel asked permission of Mrs. Stevens to take Jane with them berrypicking. Bending over the bushes, heads close together, voices low, Mrs. Haviland gave Jane her husband's message and attempted to cover up the wild storm of weeping that seized the girl. When she had been calmed, Mrs. Haviland told her to be ready when plans for escape had ripened. Berry pail filled, she slipped away, and before the day was over, had resumed her Quaker clothes and was on her way back to Michigan.

Within a few weeks, there she was in Kentucky again, as ladylike as you please, busy establishing a contact with a slave friend of John White whom John had selected as the pilot of the enterprise. But she found the countryside in an unexpected ferment. In every stranger a counterfeiter was seen, for the countryside had taken upon itself the task of uncovering a predatory ring. Even the self-possessed little woman in the Quaker dress was regarded with deep suspicion. Because of this enforced conspicuousness, she could not speak for more than a moment with John's friend. But he said that when the excitement had died down he thought the escape could be made. She did not leave Kentucky emptyhanded though, for she arranged for the immediate escape of a slave woman and her children, an exploit that was a blessing to everyone but the Indiana station keeper into whose hands she gave the family. The law closed down upon him, and he lost his farm and lands.

The weeks went by, and still Jane did not come. Impatient, apprehensive, John started alone for Kentucky and weathering the unabated excitement of the neighborhood, smuggled Jane and a friend to the Indiana shore. This was almost freedom—almost. By nightfall they would reach a depot. But between noon and nightfall the slave catcher fell upon them, and three fine prizes were returned to Kentucky.

Jane and John were separated. Through an intermediary he managed to send word to his Michigan friends. A price of $400 had been set on him; his wife's fate he did not know. Soon he learned that she was dead.

In Levi Coffin's "council room," the Vigilance Committee of Cincinnati discussed the situation. Three hundred and fifty dollars was raised before the next day, and within three weeks Mrs. Haviland was returning to Raisen Institute under the escort of John White.

This war within a war showed how illusory were any lasting triumphs of arms for the slavocracy. With Levi Coffins, and, to a lesser extent, Laura Havilands duplicated in action over and over in the North, and with small or mighty Garrisons to echo the words of their prototype in Boston, "If you come to us and are hungry, we will feed you; if thirsty we will give you drink; if naked, we will clothe you; if you need a hiding place from the face of the pursuer, we will provide one that even bloodhounds will not scent out," there was little to calm and reassure the more coolheaded of the slavery champions. They tried again in Congress, as they had tried at frequent intervals for fifty years, to procure a law that would protect their absconding property. Now, in 1847, Kentucky again asked Congress to frame new laws that would allow her citizens to reclaim their slaves after they had reached the relative security of the North. The Senate bill never got beyond its second reading. Something bigger was in store—something much bigger.

By the close of 1847 the end of the Mexican War was in sight, with hundreds of miles of new territory with the look and spirit of cotton upon it. Upper California, New Mexico, Arizona, parts of Nevada and Colorado—territory almost as large as the original thirteen colonies— was to be given to the United States; $15,000,000 was to be paid to Mexico. Mexico tried vainly to include in the treaty she was about to sign an agreement to keep this vast land free of slavery, but Nicholas Trist, the agent of President Polk, told the Mexican commissioners "that if it were in their power to offer the whole territory, increased tenfold in value, and in addition to that covered a foot thick with pure gold, upon the single condition that slavery be excluded, he could not entertain the offer for a moment, nor even think of communicating it to Washington."

In February, 1848, a formal treaty was signed and over one-half of what had been the Mexican Empire came under the moral suasion of slavery. Moral suasion it remained for a suitable time, as even the politicians in Washington could not arrive at a compromise that would not be a complete submission to the demands of the slavocracy. The Southern politicians fought stubbornly. Jefferson Davis, a tall handsome war hero, was sent from Mississippi as Senator to persuade, exhort, but there were antislavery representatives now to keep the issue ablaze, to keep alive in the minds of Northern voters the arguments against the extension of slavery. Compromises were offered—specious compromises such as the proposal to admit New Mexico, California, and the new acquisition, British-dominated Oregon, in one measure, leaving the Supreme Court—five slaveholders to four nonslaveholders—to decide whether slavery should be admitted as well.

The politicians of slavery were a-dream with arrogance. All the country would be theirs. Adams spoke darkly of secession; Northern members looked from under their brows and wondered whether peace was not more desirable than union. To placate the South meant not compromises but complete capitulation. There was California, for example. While Trist was still wrangling with the Mexican commissioners, gold had been discovered in California. A wilderness of Mexican villages turned suddenly into a settlement of a hundred thousand lovers of free labor. Could anything persuade them to give California to the slave power? The slave power said, "Yes."

But while the masters fought up and down the halls of Congress to make their "Yes" a valid fact, the California legislature, emboldened by the streams of fortune seekers from the North, from Europe, where competition with slave labor was an economic horror, ratified a constitution which forbade slavery or involuntary servitude forever from the territory. Constitution in hand, they asked admission as a state.

They came at a singularly inopportune moment. The glamor and the chivalry of the Mexican War, the troops and the bands and the tearful pride of the Southern women—for the Northern women saw it in a different light—had been transformed into a chimera. The Wilmot Proviso had not been laid to rest. It hung like a sword over the seats of Southern Congressmen. They had never lost a fight before—were they prepared to lose one now? No, they cried almost as one man and prepared to use the time-honored weapons that had always insured their victory.

Victory was more sweet and necessary than ever. Had not the South fought and paid for the gold fields of California, had not the price of slaves risen as a result of the war and the prospects of new territory? Fine things had been gained by the slavocracy; the brightest days of its civilization lay ahead . . . then let us say so in words and prove it in deeds, and the violence of the deeds will not matter so long as the proof is clear.

The slavocracy was hypersensitive these days. Its power had not been questioned in this manner before. Antislavery men, however prudent or moderate, felt the full weight of its displeasure. Mobs, violence and suppression had supplemented this displeasure before. They were called upon again.

Yet they faced a subtle difference now, a difference which the slave power had not anticipated and which it was unable to subdue. When its wrath fell on Gameliel Bailey who had founded a Liberty party paper, *The National Era*, in Washington it discovered that Mr. Bailey was using a new kind of worldliness—a worldliness that bore little relation to the heroic martyrdom of Lovejoy—and that his political astuteness baffled all the efforts to suppress his journal. Within sight of the Capitol building it was inadvisable to call out a mob.

In Baltimore, an antislavery newspaper, *The Saturday Visitor*, has been established, and citizens set out to suppress it. They called on its editor Dr. Snodgrass and presented their demands. Then and there one saw what the 1830's had done for the Abolition cause. The battle for a free press had been fought and Dr. Snodgrass could enjoy the fruits. He defied the citizen's delegation, proclaimed his right to publish and, probably to his own surprise, lived to see the day of emancipation.

Yet John H. Pleasants—the editor of *The Richmond Whig*, a partisan paper as its name will indicate, was not so fortunate. He had inserted a few articles on the economic aspects of slavery. The machinery of opposition moved with precision, and Mr. Pleasants found himself in a cold world, outside the editorial offices. He was challenged to a duel by the son of a proslavery editor, and fell in the futile exchange that followed.

In Wilmington, they caught up at last with that doughty miracle worker, Thomas Garrett. Thomas Garrett is a story and a song and a legend, and he should share no page with any other. But he was always one to find great enjoyment on the fringes of lesser people's mighty trivialities.

Born a Pennsylvania Quaker, hatred of slavery was in his blood. When he was twenty-four he had followed the kidnapers of a colored woman employed by his family halfway across the state and rescued her without ado. During that ride, he later said, the horror of slavery had so beat upon his brain that he seemed to hear a voice, telling him that his life's work must be devoted to the persecuted and enslaved. Through the heart of a slave state he accordingly passed over twenty-seven hundred fugitives.

He had come to Wilmington, Delaware, in 1822. His work had begun immediately. It took only a short time for slave and master to know that Thomas Garrett's house was a station of the Underground Railroad. And yet the consummate skill of the man was such that for over twenty years he was able to carry on his avocation just outside the reaches of the law. No evidence could be obtained against him. His business reputation was so impeccable that he made friends against their will. His house was continuously under the surveillance of the police and the slaveowners.

His calmness and his physical impressiveness added weight to his refusal to be intimidated. He never denied that he aided fugitives, but he usually received only those fugitives of whom he had been notified by a conductor farther South, forestalling, by the advance precautions he was able to take, any damaging proofs against himself.

He had, at the start, assumed a share of the dangerous burden borne by certain free colored people, and as the work increased, white friends were drawn in to lend a hand when they least expected it. "Even numbering," as one of his biographers put it, "singular as it may seem, some ardent Democrats." When he heard that Maryland had offered $10,000 for his capture, he wrote an open letter saying that he was worth at least $20,000, and if that sum were forthcoming he would collect in person. Threats of murder were so frequent that many of his colored friends established a watch in his front yard and took turns guarding him at night, although his expostulations could be heard clearly through the window.

The success of his work depended—as truly it did with every conductor —on the fertility of his imagination. He prescribed like a doctor according to an individual's need. Often he would give a fugitive man a scythe, a hoe, a rake, and send him onto the street with instructions to walk calmly, as though he were going to work, to a certain bridge near the outskirts of the town. There he was to conceal his implement and from that point follow implicit directions to the next station, the implement being recovered by one of Garrett's friends and used again. Several times he dressed a woman fugitive in his wife's clothes, leading her to their carriage and driving off, smiling comfortably at the stragglers who were invariably about his door.

Sometimes he would direct fugitives to the home of Isaac and Dinah Mendenhall, ten miles from Wilmington. His directions were brief. "Go on and on until you come to a stone gatepost and then turn in." Frequently (as times grew more dangerous and spies lurked along the underground line) he gave them a note for the next station keeper, saying sometimes, "I send thee two [or four or six as the case might be] bales of black wool," and at other times openly, "This man needs help." Now and then he sent fugitives to Chandler and Hannah Darlington, over the line in Pennsylvania. Their house was too exposed for frequent use and too generally filled with boarders of undetermined sympathies to be more than a switchhouse on the line, but the Darlingtons recognized an emergency when a tap, generally around eleven at night, came at their window and the voice of a conductor called softly, "Can you care for these people?" They seldom saw the conductor, transacting their business in the dark, in order to claim truly, if the need arose, that they did not know the personnel of the line.

Garrett knew that these friends and others, whom he had tested, could be trusted to outmaneuver the law as well as any. Better than he, he might have thought with a wry smile when, in 1848, at a moment of extreme caution on his part, the law descended upon him in all its majesty. Why it came then and not sooner no one was prepared to say. But it is not unlikely that it sought him out at a time when the crisis in the South was reaching a climax, when for the first time the slavocracy doubted the invincibility of its power and determined to make an example, through a Federal law, of a man who had flouted it for twenty years.

His trial, for aiding two slave children, was called in the spring of 1848 in Newcastle, Delaware, with Garrett and a fellow conductor, John Hunn in the defendant's box. When the verdict was returned, every cent of his property had been swept away. Every cent of John Hunn's property had been swept away, but John Hunn was a younger man. Thomas Garrett was sixty years old.

When his sentence had been pronounced, he rose in the courtroom, a tall rather stooping old figure with white hair, soft as a baby's, and drooping lids that did not conceal the fire that suddenly blazed in his eyes. "Judge," he said, "now that thee hast relieved me of what little I possessed, I will go home and put another story on my house. I want room to accommodate more of God's poor." After a bare glance at him Garrett turned to the courtroom, and for an hour expounded on the evils of slavery. He spared no one. He spoke in this room, dominated by slave laws, as men seldom had the courage to speak. Mostly he was listened to in silence, occasionally someone applauded, now and then a hiss cut across his words. When at length he sat down, breathing only a little more deeply than when he had begun, one of the jurors who had convicted him ran across the courtroom and seized his hand. "Give me your forgiveness," he said, "and let me be your friend." "Freely given," said Garrett, his stiff little smile breaking across his lips, "if thee cease to be an advocate of the iniquitous system of slavery."

Everything was sold. He watched his household goods and his merchandise carried out to the auctioneer. When the sale was over the auctioneer turned to him and said with a glint of righteousness, "Thomas, I hope you'll never be caught as this again." Only as quickly as it took him to put the words together, Garrett answered, "Friend, I haven't a dollar in the world, but if thee knows a fugitive who needs a breakfast, send him to me."

Thus at sixty he was forced to remake a life not only for himself but for "God's poor." In the twenty-one years that were left him, he found a greater success in business than in the forty-odd years of adulthood behind him. His friends bought his possessions and returned them to him. With great pride he told Wendell Phillips that, proslavery as Wilmington was, his credit was so good that he got an immediate loan at the bank. He built the extra story to his house, true to his promise, and his name penetrated more deeply into the South. Persecution was excellent publicity for the underground road. Fugitives came in greater numbers. Friends in England sent him money, and every penny he paid back. Life seemed to increase for him rather than diminish, for with his public championship of the slave, he became an Abolitionist in the fullest sense: a champion of women's rights, an advocate of temperance, a defender of the Indians, and an agitator in behalf of white working men and women. He even performed the miracle of turning Negro-hating Irishmen into conductors, for the poor Irish of Wilmington knew that he was their friend and if "Father Garrett" wanted them to help a fugitive, they asked no questions.

Thus Garrett became an Abolition hero, and in a few months, Daniel Drayton was catapulted after him. Daniel Drayton represented that hardy specimen, a seafaring hater of slavery. It was a wonder that all seamen who carried the dull and torpid slaves in their bottoms were not antislavery men, but most of the sea captains were tough men who cared more for the prize in their holds than for the pros and cons of humanity. Daniel Drayton admitted that once he thought Negroes were fit only for slavery, that he had often turned away from thinly veiled pleas for assistance. Methodist meetings were the only gatherings he frequented and, as he said, "Nothing was heard there about slavery." But one night, when his ship lay tied to a Washington wharf, a strange thing happened to him. A colored man came on board as Drayton was idly smoking his pipe, and began to talk to him. The Negro was a man with easy manners, and his white teeth shone in his dark face as he talked with apparently aimless garrulity. Presently he slipped in, "Cap'n seemed to be from the No't'. I s'pose they is all pretty much Ab'litionists up th-yah?" Drayton looked at him a moment, and turned over in his mind how such information could have come to so poorly appearing a slave. He put his pipe back into his mouth and nodded. The black man hesitated, then stumbling a little, he came to the point. A woman and her five children wanted to escape to her husband, a free colored man. The woman had been working under an agreement with her master for her freedom, but when she asked for a settlement, the master threatened to sell her.

"Cap'n," the black face bent close, "will yah talk t' her? Kin ah bring her on the bo't?" Drayton took one puff and then nodded abruptly.

He did not know what had moved him, and he did not understand why he agreed to the woman's importunities. Later, when he saw the woman caught in the arms of her husband, he admitted that something got into his blood. He went back to his home in Philadelphia to muse about it for several months. He mused about it until he received a letter from a person whose name he did not know but who asked him to come to a certain place at such and such a time. He did so, a weathered eye, no doubt, looking behind and before him. He learned, at the meeting, that word of his exploit had filtered through Washington, and here was a messenger from that city, asking if he could be persuaded to help two other families who expected hourly to be sold. The letter that he brought was touching, and Drayton pulled on his pipe while the intermediary anxiously folded up the sheet of paper. Finally Drayton shook his head. It can't be done, he said, he had no vessel and he could not take another man's through the dangers of the stormy season.

He must have left the matter open, though, for he saw the intermediary again a fortnight later and agreed to go to Washington to see what arrangements could be made. In the secretive channels of underground work in Washington—for Washington was an increasingly important junction of the Underground Railroad—he met the colored friends who were attempting to negotiate the escape of the slaves, and promised that he would find a vessel and see what he could do.

Washington, one evening in April, was aflame with torchlight. The White House and the homes of Secretaries and prominent politicians were illuminated inside and out as for a fête. Crowds swarmed through the streets, splashing through the spring mud. Bands played all the fine marching tunes they had ever learned and the torchlight procession, impatiently gathering, stamped off at length to the stir and rattle of the drums and the whistles and huzzas of transported watchers. Dignitaries as well as common people dirtied their trouser hems as they wheeled down Pennsylvania Avenue, past the government buildings where people waved flags and shouted lustily, past the militia drawn up impressively, to a speaker's stand where more notables were setting aside their silk hats and fumbling with the speeches which were to make this occasion ring in the annals of republican history.

For—glory of glories—that nurse of revolution, that sister across the sea had sent her king into exile. Revolution had triumphed. France had now taken her place among the democracies of the world.

As dusk came, the excitement mounted with the rising torchlight and the crescendo of eloquence. Senator Foote of Mississippi was stirred to strange words: "The age of tyrants and slavery is rapidly drawing to a close. The happy period, to be signalized by the universal emancipation of man from the fetters of civil oppression and the recognition in all countries of the great principles of popular sovereignty, equality and brotherhood, is visibly commencing."

"Visibly commencing . . ." Drayton had stayed on board his ship that night, and to all those with a dark skin who came up the ship's plank, he promised this fulsomely praised liberty if they were aboard by eleven o'clock, three nights hence.

Three nights hence, Drayton's eyes swept over the low fields that ran down to the river. Darkness had barely set in when he saw the first figure coming across the field, stooping low, running fast, darting swiftly up the plank that stretched to the vessel, and disappearing without a word into the shadows of the ship.

Several times he went aboard the vessel and learned from his mate that the hold was filling rapidly as several additional slaves had taken literally the enthusiasm for liberty that was filling Washington. Sometime past ten o'clock, seventy-eight had run swiftly up the plank onto the vessel, and Drayton now went aboard. Around eleven, Sayres, who was to pilot his own ship came aboard, and it was evident that they must start immediately as a dead calm had settled and it was necessary to maneuver the vessel into the river in order to pick up whatever wind sprang up. Toward midnight a wind began to stir, setting the halyards to creaking faintly, and Drayton and those on deck watched the low shores going slowly past. So far—*fine.*

All the next day they moved under a restless, sporadic wind; the next night Drayton went to his bunk and fell asleep to the slow roll of the ship, and he did not waken until the cries of a boarding crew rang in his ears.

They were taken back in triumph to a Washington still intoxicated by French liberty. The fugitive men had begged to be allowed to fight the boarding party but Drayton had refused, knowing that no firearms were aboard. They came back to a crowd of several thousand spread out along the road that led to the jail, for the city of Washington was wildly concerned to see the $100,000 worth of property which had slid down the river in the night and only been recovered through the betrayal of a hackman who had carried a fugitive to the wharf. The fugitive men were driven by whips through the city, tied together two by two, the women following. The crowd shouted itself hoarse in taunts and jeers, although here and there a long wail rose above the noise, and once a relative fell insensible.

Congress was immediately reassembled, and Giddings, who had been warned to keep out of sight, swung hurriedly into action, drawing his antislavery colleagues with him as fast as they would go. He went first, with Hamlin of Ohio, to offer his services to Drayton and Sayres. Then he demanded a Congressional investigation to determine why the jail was being used to house eighty individuals who had as yet been convicted of no crime.

But neither Congress nor Washington was prepared to take a judicious view of the affair. Within two days mobs had taken possession of the city, attacked the office of *The National Era* where the press and the papers were saved only by the gifted tongue of its editor, Gameliel Bailey, and the stubbornness of the captain of police, and were threatening members of Congress. While in Congress, for three days the uproar drowned out everything but the personal vilifications and the shouted challenges to bloody combat that made a journey down the aisles an unpredictable adventure.

By the second day, fifty of the runaways had been sold to Hope Slatter, the principal slave dealer of the neighborhood, and silent Congressmen, watching from the windows, saw the coffle marching by the Capitol.

The Southern members realized that the tide was running in the wrong direction—the antislavery members were using this occasion to introduce a resolution against the rule of mobs. In such a resolution the slave-owners saw only a threat to the reclamation of fugitives, and Calhoun, more superbly the politician as age dug great rivers in his face, rose like Jeremiah to foretell the end of things. Slavery was the only question— he repeated himself deliberately *the only question*—that could divide the Union, and a crisis was not far away. If at one grasp, seventy-eight of their slaves could be carried off, the apathy of the public must be roused. He promised insurrections as terrible as San Domingo if the fanaticism of certain antislavery Congressmen was not rebuked. But he offered no remedy for the rift that was separating the minority of antislavery men from the great body of their opponents, a rift that was deeper than politics . . . as deep as the past and the future.

Forty-one indictments were drawn against Drayton. Bail for him, Sayres, and the mate of *The Pearl* was set at $228,000, and seventy-five additional indictments hung perilously above his head. Horace Mann, the successor of Adams in the House, Seward, and Chase had offered themselves as counsel and fought stubbornly, although the verdict was evident from the start. Some of the indictments were dismissed, but when sentence was pronounced, the hungry-faced and taciturn Daniel Drayton had accumulated a lifetime in jail, for his fines amounted to over $10,000.

Perhaps the slavocracy gained from all of this. It renewed its demand for a competent Fugitive Slave Law, it raised again the threat of disunion in Congress, it threw the weak-spirited into a frenzy of conciliation. But certain things had been observed that neither time nor words could alter. *The Pearl* had tried to escape when liberty-loving speeches filled the air. The effect of this was not lost. 1848 was "the year of revolutions." Kings had been overthrown; Garibaldi, Mazzini, Kossuth were heroes on every tongue; freedom had become a taut word not to be used idly.

From the pulpit of Plymouth Church, Brooklyn, young Henry Ward Beecher, newly come out of the West, was selling slaves into freedom. To denounce slavery in this open manner was to make him as popular as is one who denounces private property today, and his more conventional parishioners urged him for his own success to leave such dangerous topics alone. "I don't know what it is," he replied, "but the moment you tell me that a thing is unpopular I am right there every time." And they had to bear the sight of a small black girl being auctioned off on a Sunday morning. It was shocking, true. Sobbing was heard all over the church, but her freedom was guaranteed when the collection plates were quickly passed.

Of course it was sensational, but no one can rightly speak against the dramatizing of the dramatic. As Beecher himself observed, "He is the best fisherman who catches the most fish whatever epithet may be flung at him about the kind of bait he uses."

Abolitionists were only too glad to cry out the drama of freedom if in this way the imagination could be stirred. When the Crafts escaped, a thrill went through the cohorts of Boston such as Greece must have felt when Phidippides ran from Marathon to Athens.

William and Ellen Craft were Georgia slaves who had determined that no matter what the hazards, they would make the dash from the deep South to freedom. They considered and rejected ways of escape, until they finally decided on a daring disguise that might succeed because of its boldness. Ellen's skin was white; William's was dark. Ellen would, therefore, become a young planter and William would become the gentleman's servant. The plan seemed foolproof until Ellen's womanliness promised to betray them. But perhaps the young planter had a toothache and could muffle half his beardless face in linen! Perhaps he had weak eyes and needed the protection of green glasses! Their plan, predicated on boldness, necessitated stopping openly at the best hotels on the way North and registering their names, yet neither of them could write.

Neuritis—or a sprain—would dispose of the young gentleman's right hand. William was ideally suited to act the part of the alert, devoted servant whose sole desire was to be the eyes, ears, hands and feet of his debilitated young master, a devotion which would encourage only the kindliest co-operation from all whom they encountered.

The strain of the trip was immense, but William was always at hand to explain the unsociability of his young master when a stranger attempted to make his acquaintance. Perhaps, as slaves, they had been allowed to hire their time, perhaps they had made a little money by vegetable or cotton raising after dark—in any case they had sufficient funds to allow them to stop at the best hotel in Charleston, while they waited for their train, and at a first-class hotel in Richmond. Toward nightfall they arrived in Baltimore and went immediately to the station to buy tickets for Philadelphia and the end of the journey.

William handled the matter of tickets, and apparently he gave away none of his dismay when told by the ticket man that his master might have a ticket, but that a bond must be posted for him as required for all Negroes journeying north through Baltimore. William had to reverse this decision then and there, with other ticket buyers pressing with impatience behind him. "My master is in a very delicate state of health. We are afraid he may not be able to hold out until he reaches Philadelphia where he is going for medical treatment. It's out of the question to post a bond and he cannot be detained." He waved toward his young master, sitting ill and drooping close at hand, and the ticket seller took a brief look and pushed two tickets toward him.

How feebly that poor young master got into the train, how tenderly his servant supported him, brought him water, arranged his blankets. Only a few more hours . . .

The Vigilance Committee in Philadelphia never forgot the first few moments of their arrival—the pale young man and his solicitous servant. First the tall hat was removed, then the green glasses and linen muffler. Finally the arm was freed from the sling and a few experimental dancing steps were attempted. When the final metamorphoses had taken place in an adjoining room, they were able to appreciate the full effect of ingenuity and courage.

They wished to send them on immediately, as such fine specimens would bring a swarm of interested slave catchers, but Ellen's nerves had gone to pieces. For several days she was prostrate. Yet the word of their exploit went ahead to Boston, and when she was well enough to travel, the Boston Abolitionists greeted them as heroes, and took care to spread their story North and South, as well as to England and to Europe. Antislavery workers, men and women, came to shake their hands. These were the kind of people we have been fighting for, they said. Isn't the battle worth the powder?

That William and Ellen Craft provided so spontaneous a reunion of dissident Abolitionists showed that differences of opinion did not penetrate to the heart of the cause. Beyond that, it indicated how things should be, and wakened grief in many hearts that by their discords an excuse was given men who held aloof from the antislavery fight. Yet, if one took the trouble to examine the reasons for these factions, they would have been found, not caprices, not the result of some leader's inflated ego, but rather an expression of deep perplexity, a perplexity that wondered a thousand times how a handful of men and women could render powerless a power that had laid its mark on the compromises of the Founding Fathers, and then had bound itself inextricably to the governing function of the country, interweaving itself with every aspect of society—political, commercial, social and religious. To agree how to disentangle such a monster from the mazes of the national house without bringing down the entire structure must have seemed impossible. And yet they did agree, fundamentally, on the means of accomplishment. "The formation of a new republic, that shall be such not in name only, but in full living reality and truth," was what the Garrisonians envisioned, and the political Abolitionists found their hopes embodied in the same dream. They differed only on the interpretation of the Constitution. If it was a "Covenant with Death and an Agreement with Hell," as the Garrisonians maintained, then it must be utterly repudiated, and to accustom minds to such iconoclasm all the pernicious growths which hampered freedom and kept the mind in a mold of antiquated forms must be uprooted. Everything that perpetuated slavery—the degradation of women, the rigidity of the churches, the poor-spirited social reforms, the economic, intellectual and social orthodoxies, the devotion to the ballot and to political and religious organizations—must be condemned.

If, on the other hand, the Constitution was read as an antislavery document, polluted by the proslavery forces which had gained control of national policies, then action on a political front, the unremitting use of the ballot, the tireless support of antislavery men in Congress, were all that could wipe out such a national disgrace. Perhaps only a national calamity would show which one was right.

The recriminations which passed between the antislavery camps made unhappy dissonances in friendly ears. Men from the old political parties, watching with experienced and worldly eyes, saw that in spite of the golden eloquence of the Garrisonians and the inspired writings of their faithful, in spite of the belief that "Duty is ours, results are God's" of the new Liberty League, in spite of the bold words of the emaciated Liberty party, the slave power was going on from victory to victory. Nothing had stopped it yet; appeals to reason were useless, consciences had been invoked in vain. Impassioned and brilliant as the Garrisonians might be, it was unlikely that the country would ever be brought to an espousal of disunion; the political Abolitionists therefore held the stronger position, for ballots could be made to carry an unequivocal message. Even though the Liberty party had sickened because its platform was too narrow for men of different minds to stand upon and even though orthodox politicians were still evading *the* issue and pouring out a stream of demagoguery to cover their omission, there were still abundant signs to show that the balances were settling in favor of a new political party. "Conscience" Whigs were in revolt against the "Cotton" Whigs, who by adroit maneuvering had hung upon them, as Presidential nominee, a Mexican War hero, a Louisiana slaveholder, General Zachary Taylor, and had not even given the "Conscience" Whigs assurance that he would support the Wilmot Proviso or oppose the extension of slavery. The Democratic Convention had been forced to trample swiftly on its own rebels, the "Barnburners," who disclaimed being Abolitionists but claimed a right to protest against corruption and patronage and urge the Proviso. How furiously the revolt was flaming was proved when the Barnburners called their own convention, offered their own candidate, Martin Van Buren, in opposition to Lewis Cass of Michigan, the choice of the Southern Democrats, and made their platform one of undeviating hostility to the extension of slavery. The "Conscience" Whigs, fanning the flames, saw what they believed was a more practical solution. If a new party was formed, it could absorb the dissidents of the old parties and be in a position to take an uncompromising stand for freedom. For seven years they had worked for this moment, when the powerful Democrats and Whigs, fed by the same blood stream, could be cut in two. Nothing must now be left to chance or faulty leadership. They looked among the "Barnburners" and the "Conscience" Whigs for their leaders; that is to say, to men like Hale, King and Wilmot among the Democrats, Giddings, Palfrey, Seward, and Mann among the Whigs. Free soil, the defeat of Taylor and Cass, the nonextension of slavery were to be the cries calculated to draw delegates to the convention set for Buffalo.

In August the delegates assembled, divided with representative equality between the Whigs, Democrats and Liberty party men. Many famous names were there—Dana, Giddings, Lovejoy, Adams, Sumner, Fletcher

Webster, as well as Samuel Ringgold Ward and certain eminent "station keepers." Salmon Chase was chairman, and the keynote of the convention was quickly struck. Unity—Unity!

Their purposes were set forth quickly: the Constitution was an anti-slavery document, promulgated in the spirit of Thomas Jefferson and the Northwest Ordinance which forbade the spread of slavery; states rights, which prevented the abolition of slavery must be circumvented by the admission of free states only.

They added other things as well to make their platform roomy; cheap postage, government economy, land grants to settlers, a settlement of the national debt, an adequate but not proscriptive tariff. "On our banners we inscribe, 'Free Soil, Free Speech, Free Labor, and Free Men,' and under it we will fight on and fight ever, until triumphant victory shall reward our exertions."

Of course, the matter of candidates tickled the sensibilities. And, in the matter of candidates, this political party showed the fundamental weakness it shared with all its kind. The Massachusetts "Conscience" Whigs had determined that they would accept only the ballot which swung in the Barnburners and forced them to share the burden of election. When candidates had been proposed and the rolls were called, the Democrats voted for Van Buren, and the Whigs took the hint. The men of the Liberty party with few exceptions stood by John Hale. When the delegates had responded, Van Buren had a clear majority.

This ironic choice must have made the terrible days of the 1830's seem like hazy figments. Was no Abolitionist prepared to remind the convention that Van Buren, as President, had been such a faithful servant of the slave power that he had been known as "a Northern man with Southern principles," that his sudden devotion to antislavery was due to his dereliction over the matter of Texas annexation which had lost him the Democratic nomination?

But enthusiasm and satisfaction were all that the delegates displayed. They went home to call for state conventions and the whirlwind campaigning that characterized such an election year. The state conventions even reached within the bulwarks of the enemy, for local conventions and small meetings took place in Delaware, Virginia, North Carolina, Kentucky and Missouri, and antislavery men in the border states wrote fervently and daringly of the paralyzing effect of slavery on industry, of the degradation of labor, of the stifling of education.

The Free-Soil party entered the fight, unencumbered by any "Southern wing." They could say what they chose, in conformity with their platform, and potential voters knew that it held no hidden meanings, unless

Van Buren could be construed as a hidden meaning. The center plank had now been laid which was to lead the voters to that significant day, a few years hence, when the Free-Soil party would consign its spirit and its purposes to the larger scope of the Republican party, and when the slavocracy would, with negligible prompting, foretell its own end.

There was little doubt that the Free-Soil party was a child of the Abolitionists. And yet, could Garrison bring himself to believe that any Abolition promise lay in that direction? He wrote to Edmund Quincy directly after the convention, and his argument had the sting of truth behind it.

> As for the Free Soil movement, I feel that great care is demanded of us Disunionists in giving credit to whom credit is due, and yet in no case even seeming to be satisfied with it. It is only placing the country in precisely the same condition, on the subject of slavery, that it occupied a quarter of a century since—to wit, that slavery ought not to be extended to new territories; that it ought to be abolished (when or how is not stated in the new creed) in all our territorial possession—(nothing, I believe, is said about its abolition in the District of Columbia): and that Congress has no Constitutional power to meddle with it in the several states.
>
> Our Disunion ground is invulnerable, and to it all parties at the North must come e'er long. The temptation to vote, however, at the coming election, will be so great that I fear a considerable number of Disunionists, and even of professed non-resistants, will fall into the snare, and try to persuade themselves that, for this once, they may innocently, and even laudably, "bow down to the house of Rimmon." Calm yet earnest appeals must be made to our friends to preserve their integrity, and not to lose sight of the true issue. Already, in this region, I hear it said that a number of those who have hitherto acted with us think they can now vote, even for Martin Van Buren. What infatuation!

The infatuation swept through the ranks like a wind. In Ohio, Chase with all his impressive skill organized mass meetings, drafted resolutions, delivered his slow methodical speeches, wrote stirring addresses for others. The importance of this Free-Soil campaigning could not be exaggerated. In Ohio, where men drew in politics with their breath, the Free-Soil doctrines found a surprisingly rich reward. Young Whigs went over to their camp by the hundreds, nonvoting antislavery men were caught in the fervent belief that this was indeed their party. As the day of election drew closer, Edmund Quincy wrote to his friend Webb in Ireland that

Free Soilism "has carried off multitudes of our abolitionists, and it is to be feared that many of them will never recover themselves."

They came to the polls that November two hundred and ninety thousand strong; prognosticators of the future, whether they knew it or not, untutored prophets of a new economic order. Even Garrison was moved by this drama of political revolt. "I am for hailing it as a cheering sign of the times, and an unmistakable proof of the progress we have made, under God, in changing public sentiment. Those who have left the Whig and the Democratic parties, for conscience sake, and joined that movement, deserve our commendation and sympathy." Yet, spectacular as this rebellion was—"unprecedented" was Quincy's word "taking into consideration its brief existence and formidable foes"—it had not delivered the anticipated blow. Van Buren carried no state in the Union, and only in New York, Vermont and Massachusetts did the Free-Soil ticket climb beyond third place. They gained no electoral votes, and sent only five members to Congress. But the election of Taylor—an enigma with no political views which could be ascertained—and the consequent defeat of the powerful Democratic machine were unmistakable attacks on the slavocracy.

In Ohio, Free Soil accomplished its greatest moral triumph in the repeal of the "Black Laws" which had lain like a canker on the statute books. Now the Negroes of Ohio needed no longer to give bonds before making their homes in the state, their children were no longer excluded from the schools, they might testify in court against a white man. And from Ohio, "the attorney-general for the fugitives," Salmon Chase took the long and dusty journey to the Senate, where he met William Seward, elected on a freedom platform from New York. Although politicians first of all—rivals between whom no love was lost—their devotion to individual fugitives had been proven on numerous occasions.

The slavocracy which was seldom guilty of self-deception was beginning to realize that its gains had been ephemeral. Within the Southern States, a renewed oppression struck at the free colored people. Old laws which had become inoperative were revived again, new laws were framed. The border states attempted to quell their white dissenters and bolt their doors. But their arguments were less persuasive than usual. Although their dogma remained the same, counterbalancing forces were disturbing the minds of many Southern men, who questioned: Once you said that slavery was an entailed evil, something acquired by an earlier generation, something sectional, yet now you say that slavery is a positive good, that it is permanent, that it is national. What is true?

The men who questioned were mostly small clergy, living in the western parts of Virginia and North Carolina, the eastern parts of Tennessee and Kentucky—in the mountains—where slavery had never gained a hold. This subdued struggle, born to defeat, rubbed the raw wounds of those Southerners who wondered and could not understand what had happened to the fine imperial sway of the slavocracy. General Taylor— what had they acquired with General Taylor? One might have justifiably expected a slaveowner with a son-in-law like Jefferson Davis to be the very thing they needed. Yet they were discovering that he did not intend to be unduly swayed by his Southern attachments or his natural concerns with slavery. The tumult in the South was deeply seated. It raged like a furnace now that the Whigs were in power. The Wilmot Proviso, the Missouri Compromise, were living monsters bent on destroying the slaveowner's concept of freedom: the right to take his property and settle in any district which he chose. He was fit to stifle in the South with all the vast broad plains of the West closed, by moral suasion, to him. The governor of Georgia in a burst of sectional devotion, proposed that his people should embark on a holy march to Washington and dissolve the government. Southern legislatures and newspapers were sending up a single chorus—disunion—disunion—if the tide did not soon turn in their direction.

Disunion came onto the floors of the Senate through the voice of Calhoun. The whip, which had always kept the ranks in good order, now seemed to have lost some of its immediate potency. Calhoun's usual adroit and brilliant persuasion offered no remedy for the threat of secession; he contented himself mostly with an attack on emancipation, picturing the horrors of racial equality in the South. When Congress adjourned, nothing had been decided. California was still waiting on the doorstep. Although no action had been taken to admit her with her free constitution, no effort had been made to bar her demands. Armed settlers started out from the South for the disputed territories, carrying their slaves with them, willy-nilly. Disunion conventions intensified the heat of the Southern summer, and just before the reassembling of Congress, committees of the Georgia and South Carolina legislatures made quite sure that certain Northern "doughfaces" understood the position of the slavocracy on the question of secession if, by an unforeseen chance, the new Congress should prove as unpredictable as the last.

Many people, in 1849, looked for war before the year was out.

Although, in terms of all who were enslaved, the number of successful fugitives might be slight, its proportion nevertheless reached figures that were alarming to the master. And at all the doors in the North their recovery was blocked by personal liberty laws. Masters of Maryland, Virginia and the Ohio Valley were turned back time and time again. The Virginia legislature wildly denounced Pennsylvania when she withdrew state aid to kidnapers, and cried that such actions might "lead to war between independent nations." From Virginia and from Missouri went insistent pleas to other states to lend all their pressure to a new Fugitive Slave Law which would give to Federal postmasters or Federal collectors of custom the same authority to arrest, hold, convict and return fugitives as was possessed by the courts, and the governor of Virginia added a further plea for a system of taxation by license "so arranged as to transfer entirely the trade from those states which have trampled under the foot the Constitution of the United States [in the matter of fugitive slaves] to those which are still willing to abide by its compromises and recognize our rights under it." At the same time Kentucky shifted her desperate, continuous complaints against Ohio to Michigan which, she claimed, was blocking every effort to recover fugitives.

All this made Garrison proud and perhaps a little overconfident. "The times have indeed changed, and a radical alteration has taken place in public opinion on this subject," he exclaimed. "Probably not another slave will be allowed to be seized on the soil of New England, to say nothing of the other free states." At the Antislavery Convention in May, Edmund Quincy supplemented this by maintaining that the duty of the Abolitionists was to keep the subject of slavery agitated in New England, to fight with all their power against any law which prevented New England from giving asylum to any fugitive from oppression. A few days later at the same convention, Wendell Phillips pointed to the fruits of their earlier proclamation in the presence on the platform of William and Ellen Craft and the amazing Henry Box Brown whose exploit was a nine-day wonder.

Probably five people out of six at that convention would have pinned you firmly against a wall while these stories were told again, and you would not have been able to choose which was the more remarkable— the stark bravery of the Crafts or the utter recklessness of Henry Box Brown whose middle name told in one word his story. A Virginia slave of no little inventive ability, as his master had discovered to his advantage, he had found none of the usual avenues of freedom open. He therefore hit upon a plan that would mean either death or liberty. He would have himself nailed in a box and shipped as freight to Philadelphia! He made the box according to specifications that would allow him a modicum of comfort. In it he carried a bladder of water and a few small biscuits. The friend who nailed him in the box and took charge of this peculiar freight was a shoe dealer by the name of Smith, a white man who for many years had been helping fugitive slaves to the North. The box was addressed to a member of the Philadelphia Vigilance Committee, William H. Johnson, and sent to Adams Express Office in a dray.

Word came cryptically to the Philadelphia committee, hinting that a box might be expected on the three o'clock morning train from the South and in the box would be—could it be a *man?* The members of the committee looked at each other.

They were quite willing to agree later that the strain of the next few hours was more than they enjoyed. When the box was carried in by a drayman they looked at this uncanny object with an apprehensive silence. What would be inside? Would it be alive or dead? Several friends had gathered to witness the "resurrection," and when the door had been locked, James McKim rapped quickly on the lid of the box and called out, "All right?" "All right, sir," came the muffled answer.

The witnesses never forgot that moment. With saw and hatchet they cut the hickory loops that bound the box and pried out the nails. Brown sat up quickly but shakily and no one said a word. Then, with all the aplomb of a Stanley meeting a Livingston, he reached out his hand. "How do you do, gentlemen."

The effect of Brown's escape spread north and south. In Boston, where he was promptly sent, he was greeted as the Crafts had been—a hero. In Richmond, where his friend Smith plied his inconspicuous shoe trade, the news was received with such incredulity as to allow Smith to repeat the exploit with two other slaves. But this repetition had unfortunate results, for the fugitives and Smith were betrayed, the fugitives recaptured and Smith sent to eight years confinement in the state penitentiary.

When Congress came together again in December, 1849, only the most dreamy believed that a clash could be avoided. A crisis hung over the Capitol, and no man going into the Houses could help but give a quick and harried look where trouble sat. Was this the end of the Union—a Union conceived in revolution and born in a fight for freedom? It took three weeks of violence that amounted sometimes to blows to elect a Speaker in the House. The balance of power hung like a thread. The South won.

The country was transfixed that winter; every ear from California to Maine strained to hear the forensics that swelled and battered against the walls of Congress. Was this a death struggle? How soon would the South or the North be brought to its knees? Words of the burning arguments that raged from day to day filtered through to the ears of the country. The Whigs were vacillating—could they be trusted? When the Wilmot Proviso was tabled—and thereby killed for the time at least—fourteen of the thirty-two Northern members who presided at the execution were Whigs. You see? . . . and what did Inge of Alabama say? He prophesied with infinite scorn that when the Democrats came to power they would hold the Mississippi River and demand tribute of all states, west and east, which sought to reach the oceans. Cuba, too, Congress was reminded, was ready for the Southern signal. With her in their embrace, and all the fields south and west of the Rio Grande, "with all these views of future wealth and grandeur lighting up the path of our destiny, can you feel that we fear to tread alone?" Robert Toombs of Georgia added the final curl of arrogance, "We have the right to call on you to give your blood to maintain the slaves of the South in bondage. Deceive not yourselves; you cannot deceive others. This is a proslavery government. Slavery is stamped on its heart!"

The small men of the North looked at each other, sitting in their shoe shops, leaning over their plows. The Whigs of the North looked at each other in their law offices and their dry-goods stores. The Democrats of the North looked at each other in their factories and their shipping offices.

Ears straining from the law offices and dry-goods stores heard Mr. Root of Ohio declare solemnly, "So help me God, I never will be a compromising man." God and the country must decide whether new territory was to be slave or free. Some, in the factories or shipping offices, held the corners of their ledgers and listened with a sick dropping of the heart to the attacks on Northern integrity. But there must be no recriminations, no stormy words to break the delicate cords that bound the factories and the cotton fields, the cotton fields and the shipping offices. Some, in the shoe shops and plowed fields, waited, waited, and heard Horace Mann speak up with a terrible directness of the horrors that the South would know if it persisted in disunion talk. "The South fosters in its home three millions of latent rebellions. Is there no Spartacus among them? Is the race of Nat Turner extinct?" And all of them, Whigs, Democrats and Abolitionists heard a fearful new voice raised for the first time in those halls.

A man's maiden speech should be decorous, tentative, but for Thaddeus Stevens it was merely an occasion for a blow as hard as his devastating wit and passion for equality could make it. "These Southern gentlemen" whose "well defined object is partly to intimidate Congress and partly to occupy its time so that no legislation could be matured obnoxious to Southern gentlemen," found their most honorable pretensions exposed to the withering scorn of this dour-faced gentleman from Pennsylvania. "During the present session we have been told amid raving excitement that if we dared to legislate a certain way, the South would teach the North a lesson . . . Are the representatives of free men to be thus treated? You have too often intimidated Congress. You have more than once frightened the tame North from its propriety and found 'doughfaces' enough to be your tools. But I hope that the race of 'doughfaces' is extinct!" His voice was harsh and crisp. He refused to glance at the "Southern gentlemen" who had formed a ring about his desk, were putting their hands significantly into their pockets and interspersing his speech with such clearly articulated oaths that Stevens' friends heard little of his speech for watching over him.

The Abolitionists greeted him with cries of joy. Northern papers were in an ecstasy of excitement. Here was a power which they needed badly—if it had not come too late.

When Mr. Mason of Virginia rose one January afternoon in 1850, no very impressive representation was in the Senate to hear him offer an amendment to the Fugitive Slave Law of 1793. Antislavery men listened with a single ear, no more. His amendment sounded like a child of all those other efforts to bind slavery to the North, varying only slightly from the law of 1793. It merely reduced a man to bankruptcy for befriending a fugitive and left no possible loophole for a fugitive's escape if he were caught. But, as Mr. Mason pointed out, under the existing laws "you may as well go down into the sea and endeavor to recover from his native element a fish which had escaped from you as expect to recover a fugitive. Every difficulty is thrown in your way by the population." And Mr. Yulee of Alabama raised his hand insistently to tell about a convention, meeting *at that moment* in a church in Cazenovia, New York, called by the New York Vigilance Committee to consider ways of escape that could be passed on to restless slaves. One by one representatives stood up and told the number of the slaves in his state lost to the Underground Railroad—Kentucky, "hundreds of thousands of dollars'" worth each year, Maryland, $80,000 worth a year, Virginia, "losses too heavy to be endured . . . increasing year by year . . . already more than $100,000 a year." South Carolina and her neighbors, $200,000. From the District of Columbia, in ten years, the number of slaves had melted from 4,694 to 650 because of "Underground Railroads and felonious abductions." And Mr. Clingman of North Carolina summed it up angrily, when he snapped that 30,000 fugitives were living in the North; at current prices they were worth $15,000,000. What did the North propose to do about it? Thirty million dollars' indemnity was due for all that the underground lines had carried off in the last forty years.

Of course the figures were shocking. Antislavery Congressmen wakened abruptly to the fact that if property losses were to be emphasized they must be on their guard. Northern men in Congress were taking occasion to shake hands sorrowfully with Southern colleagues and to insist, over a toddy, that as men of property themselves they would have to see that some protection was offered to their friends.

The ball was rolling fast. The South had presented a justifiable grievance. Around this grievance was built the session that followed, that dark turbulent period that was identified so disarmingly as a search for compromise. Before much time had passed compromise was a phrase found big enough to include every grievance that had festered North and South since the days of the Missouri Compromise. Perhaps the South did need protection for her slaves, but the North remembered that she needed protection for her free men. An empire of free men was waiting to stretch from the Atlantic to the Pacific. A slave empire was waiting to reach from one ocean to the other. What was to be given here to be gotten there?

The question was laid in the hands of three dying giants, bowed with age and honor and ambitions, whose search for an answer was to set fire to the fears and apprehensions of their countrymen.

Calhoun, from the deep South, gaunt and spectral, Clay from the border states, surviving from the age of compromise to the age of violence, Webster from the North, seeing still his dreams before his eyes, the Presidency almost within his grasp, were giants all, who had held the destinies of the country in their hands before.

Clay spoke first, Clay, the compromiser, Clay the union-lover, Clay who stood in the middle of the road, but with his eyes fixed on the fields of the South. Clay proposed his compromises to the moving refrain of patriotism, moderation, liberalism. Tears flowed freely.

How did this advocate of liberalism propose to heal the wounds of the country? He proposed it on the basis of the sacrifices that the North should be prepared to make. California should be admitted, and the question of slavery settled later; territorial governments should be without restriction or prejudice; the western boundary of Texas should be the Rio Grande; the abolition of slavery should be declared "inexpedient" in the District of Columbia, although the slave trader should be barred from the capital in order that he might not "establish his jails and put on his chains and sometimes mock the sensibilities of our natures by a long train of slaves passing through that avenue from the Capitol to

the residence of the Chief Magistrate": and finally, although the power
to obstruct the slave trade between states should be unequivocally denied
to Congress, the recapture of fugitive slaves should be made more effective
as Mr. Mason and other gentlemen had pointed out.

Yet some of his Southern colleagues objected. He did not go far
enough. He did not say that slavery was a positive necessity. He compromised. Clay answered sharply, the equivocator baring himself with
sudden cynicism: "Coming from a slave state, I owe it to myself, I owe
it to truth, I owe it to the subject, to say that no earthly power could
induce me to vote for a specific measure for the introduction of slavery
where it had not before existed, either South or North of that line." He
was visibly agitated. Perhaps for the first time he realized that a new
South had risen which had no use for compromise.

Could anyone discuss these proposals calmly? Those who did not say
so, sensed that an ultimatum had been delivered. Would it be compromise again, would the North take what Clay had selected for her, and
allow the slavocracy to have the rest? Would the doughfaces, the Northern
lovers of the slavocracy, bow—bow and vote as the South told them?

The debates raged in the newspapers, they spilled into the legislatures
of the North, they whipped at the Abolitionists, who knew that only a
great miracle could snatch the power from the Southern masters of Congress and at the same time prevent disunion. Of twenty-seven standing
committees in Congress, Southern chairmen presided over sixteen, while
"doughfaces" chairmanned most of the others. From all important committees the irreconcilables, Hale, Seward and Chase had been excluded;
Giddings after nearly fifteen years still had no committee of any kind. The
House was slavery-dominated; the Senate compliant. The Supreme Court
would uphold any doubtful legislation; the foreign service would explain
with urbanity any singular results.

And yet through those winter days, the South rocked and tore at Clay's
proposals. The South had been betrayed! California was to be given to
the North—California which was larger than Georgia, the Carolinas and
Virginia—and what was the South to get? A fugitive slave law that could
not be enforced! A few hundred thousand dollars' worth of recaptured
property, while free men staked out claims in gold fields and valleys
rich in cotton-growing soil but richer still in representatives who would
drag their greasy boots across the floor of Congress and vote for the
North.

When word came that the giant of the South was to speak and that
the third enigmatic giant was to answer for the North, the country held

its breath. Calhoun and Webster, and the whole vast country between them!

Calhoun spoke first, and when he dragged himself into the Senate that day, wrapped in his long black cloak, one saw something of a dying age; one might have foretold that when his harsh brilliant fire became extinguished the death of a civilization would have begun. He himself could not speak; Mason of Virginia read his speech for him, but the huddled, black-shrouded figure with the face of death and the burning eyes of life, opening now and then to sear the awe-struck chamber, arrested friend and enemy and bade all men be still.

The younger voice of Mason rang out the vindication of a system, the challenge to advancing times. Calhoun had forgotten nothing from a lifetime—the unchallenged power of the South, the sweep of a slave empire, the rise of a North which followed another way of life, a life that tore at the vitals of the slavocracy and showed its power like brazen youth. He remembered the Ordinance of 1787, the Missouri Compromise, the exclusion of slavery from Oregon, revenues and disbursements that did not coincide with slavery needs, a growing centralization of power that could only operate for the benefit of the North. And who was to blame for all this? From small beginnings, "a fanatical party" had grown, now "become an object of courtship to both the great parties." (How his smoldering eyes must have opened and his black cloak stirred as he looked at the faces of the Free-Soil Senators!) Mr. Clay's proposals he repudiated. They were no compromise. What was the answer? And his long withered fingers lay for a moment against his black shroud. Disunion—*disunion*—two presidents for two sections of the country— disunion in the manner of the churches, in the manner of the Methodists and the Presbyterians and the Baptists who had made their choice, and split peacefully North and South. (In the manner of the Quakers who were disciplining their radicals like Levi Coffin.) The North must decide, and Mason's voice took on fresh vigor. Either the North must give in, agree to an equal balance of power, admit California with no restrictions, cease her slavery agitations, and respect the law by returning fugitives, or the South would understand that the end of the United States had come.

There was no demonstration. That black figure had sat in his seat for thirty years, and in another month he would be dead. Perhaps he was the South. Perhaps it meant civil war. Many men's eyes passed that day, to the other giant who had also sat in these halls for thirty years and seen his ambition pass him by as it had passed Calhoun. What would Webster answer? Would he speak for the North? There was uneasiness that night. What if Webster did not speak for the North? What if the South had won again?

His hour came on the seventh of March, and so momentous was that day that Webster's speech was ever after called by its name. When he rose, sunken-cheeked, black Daniel of the cavernous eyes, the Senate Chamber overflowed into all the halls about it, and an awful breathlessness hung in that moment of silence before he began to speak.

He spoke as a patriot—he chose his words with his customary test of their golden quality—"for the preservation of the Union. 'Hear me for my cause.' " Men remembered afterwards quite clearly what he said, but for the lovers of the antislavery cause it would have been a blessing to forget. For the slavocracy had won again.

If he had held something back, if he had conceded one thing for the antislavery cause, if he had agreed by a scintilla that the Southern demands were preposterous . . . but everything was given away. The hopes that had been laid in him went on a wind that bore two names—love of the Union and a last determined hand toward that Presidential election which lay two brief years away. Ambition had consumed him since he was a young man: his reputation had been built on his devotion to the Union. Between those two his friends and his enemies might choose.

The slavocrats had listened to him with scorn, to his pleadings to the North that it had everything in any case, that slavery would never take root in California or the mountains of New Mexico. "He thinks to get the Southern delegates with a speech like *that*," Toombs cried, "but, by God, how he'll find he's mistaken!" Yet they knew that they would not have won if Webster had not filled the breach for them.

Antislavery men could not find words for this perfidy. Emerson said for them sadly, "His finely developed understanding only works truly with all its force when it stands for animal good; that is, for property."

It was men of property who greeted him the day he returned to Boston. Nearly a thousand gentlemen signed their public thanks to a memorial, assuring him that "he had convinced the understanding and touched the conscience of the nation." Massachusetts divided very much as the country divided. The minority saw in him the betrayer of humanity, and huzzaed when Faneuil Hall was denied his friends for a reception; the majority saw him in his well-worn role of defender of the Constitution.

As for Webster, his deep-seated conservatism, his distrust of all innovation and change, his well-known dedication to the interests of those friends whom he instinctively found among the bankers and the industrialists, led him to see only the hundreds of letters of congratulation from men of property, the letter from William Corcoran which spilled out canceled notes for $6,000 and an additional check for $1,000. He had for the time forgotten the manner in which Calhoun had analyzed the political strength of the North.

> Abolitionists—about 5% of the voting population. Sober people, willing to see slavery abolished, but not by overthrowing the Constitution—70%. Highly respectable people who sympathize with the South—5%. The remainder—20%, who care less for principles than for spoils. Yet the abolitionists hold the balance of power from the nearly equal division of Democrats and Whigs. Hence the danger to the South should any party unite with the abolitionists.

He was not aware that those, East and West, who held the balance of power now despised the name of Daniel Webster. The Seventh of March had brought no peace to the Senate. Awful visions had been conjured up by extremists of both sides, of a country bleeding, paralyzed and wantonly defaced. Public men were face to face with what had yesterday been mere political expediency but today was the very shape of terror. Could they reduce this terror to its former innocence or had a new day truly come? The fight that consumed another six months showed that they had found no answer.

Violence flared again and again. In the Senate, Foote, of Mississippi, his back against the President's desk, had flourished a pistol at Benton of Missouri who had dramatically flung back his long coat and cried out to be assassinated. "Harry of the West," the great Clay, had cajoled, implored, argued and maneuvered with a tirelessness that put to shame men less than his seventy years. Seward had sent shivers down the spines of Constitution-deifiers when he shouted that "there is a higher law than the Constitution which regulates our authority!" In the House, antislavery was vociferous. Giddings was fighting as he had never fought before, casting aside party lines, leading the antislavery representatives, who were strengthened now by his son-in-law, George Julian of Indiana, and by Thad Stevens, whose remorseless wit and logic were more devastating than Gidding's bludgeons.

Blood had been rising all these months. The Abolitionists had believed the days of mobs were over, but a nervous and apprehensive country turned upon them once again as natural scapegoats.

When, in May, Garrison went to New York for an antislavery convention, violence seemed to fill every corner of a violent city. The New York *Herald* had James Gordon Bennett for its publisher, and Bennett was freely presumed to have the devil in him.

He was busy now exhorting "the merchants, men of business, and men of property to frown down the meetings of these mad people, if they would save themselves." Each day his fine choice of words—"look at the black and white brethren and sisters, fraternizing, slobbering over each other, speaking, singing, praying, blaspheming and cursing the Constitution of our glorious Union"—grew more violent, each day they crept nearer to mob exhortation. *The Globe* was judicious rather than impulsive. It propounded one of demagoguery's favorite arguments:—"The right to assemble peaceably for the overthrow of the Government is nowhere guaranteed by the Constitution."

A picked crew answered the exhortations, and filtered into the hall of the antislavery convention to bring again the bloody days of the 1830's. Garrison knew they were there, above his head in the galleries, sitting in the backmost seats. But it was not in his nature to give them any dignity. He began without preamble. The proposed Fugitive Slave Bill was a monstrosity. Abolition was *the* Christian movement in the country, and he proved it, to his satisfaction, by a recital of the defections of organized sects. Dr. Furness felt a little rustling in the audience. "What does it mean?" he asked Wendell Phillips who sat next to him. "It means there's going to be a row," that imperturbable gentleman answered, crossing one leg over the other and folding his arms. Someone hissed from the gallery. Douglass and Phillips looked up, faint smiles ringing their mouths. Samuel Ringgold Ward sat, black as night, only the whites of his eyes showing. ". . . A belief in Jesus is no evidence of goodness," Garrison's voice was continuing. The hissing materialized when a man stood up in the gallery. Mr. Phillips may have given Dr. Furness a gentle nudge. It did not take farsighted eyes to recognize the bulk and shape of Isaiah Rynders, professional gambler, Tammany district leader, organizer of "roughs and desperados." "Are you aware," said Captain Rynders letting his thunder bruise the head of Mr. Garrison, "that the slaves in the South have their prayer meetings in honor of Christ?"

Mr. Garrison, with his voice only slightly raised, sent a shock coursing down the spines of the respectable listeners who sat close to the platform. "Not a slaveholding or a slave-breeding Jesus. The slaves believe in a Jesus that strikes off chains. In this country Jesus has become obsolete. A profession in him is no longer a test. Jesus is the most respectable person in the United States."

The outcry was tremendous. Only the phalanx of Abolitionists did not move an eye. Captain Rynders let out a roar, and forsaking his detached post in the gallery, pelted down the stairs, up the aisles, his pack at his heels. A visible agitation went over the audience as they heard the shouts, but no panic was evident. Mr. Garrison, with his tantalizing tranquillity, replied to the fist under his nose, "We go upon the principle of hearing everybody. If you wish to speak, I will keep order and you shall be heard." Francis Jackson, the impeccable gentleman, who was presiding, coldly offered Rynders a seat on the platform and plenty of vocal opportunity as soon as Mr. Garrison had finished. The "roughs and desperados" hid their momentary failure by fulminating noisily and spitting on their hands. Garrison was very soon finished with one of his resolutions that was casually produced to bring down the house: ". . . indifference or hostility to this [Abolition] movement indicates a state of mind more culpable than was manifested by the Jewish nation in rejecting Jesus as the Messiah, eighteen hundred years ago."

Captain Rynders with his uncomfortable new piety, was thrown into a frenzy. "He vociferated and harangued," a witness said, "at one time on the platform, and then pushing down into the aisles, like a madman followed by his keepers." There was no stirring this gathering. Several hundred people sat quietly. Antislavery sentiment was not the despised, the outcast that it was when an earlier New York mob descended on a handful of men. Someone called out loudly for Douglass—Douglass of the lordly head. Rynders had the platform. He had taken it over without preamble and was prepared to administer business as he saw fit. "All right," he said to Douglass, "you can speak, but mind what I say, if you speak disrespectfully, I'll knock you off the stage."

Douglass only intended to use his logic. A few words would sum up what he had to say. "The gentleman who has spoken has undertaken to prove that blacks are not human beings. I offer myself for your examination. Am I a man?"

The affirmations rolled to him in a roar. Rynders tried to shout above them. "You're not a black man; you're only half a nigger!" Douglass turned with the blandest of smiles and a kind of half-affectionate bow. "Then, I am a half brother to Captain Rynders." The place was beside itself with joy. Whatever Douglass chose to say after that was oracular. He spoke with passion of the unemployment and despair of his colored brothers, he tantalized Rynders with half asides, he finished his words with a gesture to call up Samuel Ringgold Ward, that inky black man who came up like a dark cloud from the rear of the stage, and startled the audience by the very drama of his color.

His speech was the climax of the evening, for he put a period after every sentence of Douglass. "Never," said Dr. Furness later, "was there a grander triumph of intelligence over brute force. Two colored men whose claims to be considered human were denied had, by mere force of intellect, overwhelmed their maligners with confusion."

There were no more sessions in New York after that. The trustees of the Hall forbade it. "Thus closed," said the New York *Tribune*, "antislavery free discussion in New York for 1850." ". . . The great battle for free speech and free assembling," Whittier wrote Garrison a few days later, "is to be fought over. The signal has been given at Washington, and commercial cupidity at the North is once more marshaling its mobs against us." From Boston, Channing wrote to Theodore Parker that if they persisted in clinging to the old ways of giving help to the fugitives they would be crushed. An office must be rented, he urged, and kept open continually with a Negro with the intelligence of—say—William Nell, the historian, in charge. It would also be a wise move to print a small paper called *The Slave Catcher* to be issued when important fugitive cases were being discussed.

They were then not unprepared when the word finally came, one morning in September. Ominous political moves had been taking place, which had presaged some disturbing climax: the unending fight in Congress, the fear of the Northern politicians, even the death of Taylor, who as the crisis deepened had hinted that he would have nothing to do with compromises, especially if they emanated from Mr. Henry Clay.

Only a few weeks before, Fillmore had become President, and he was a man of small prejudices and determined conservatism, and conservatism in those days meant only one thing—proslavery bias. He had brought Webster with him into his Cabinet and Webster had taken care to denounce the Abolitionists in one of his last Senatorial declamations.

What weapons did Abolition possess with which to fight so powerful a government campaign, a campaign calculated for only one purpose: to drive through the program of compromise and appeasement? The program had become the frenzied concern of politicians who made it their business to see in the threats and the cries of the South a break in the Union, a disruption of trade, a financial debacle. The country had not been so prosperous within the memory of this generation. Fat years were blessing it and the violence of a schism was unbearable. Business men had made no effort to conceal their share in organizing the procompromise meetings held in large cities of the North. Antislavery Congressmen recognized the dimensions of the fight. They had seen government patronage violently utilized, the press whipped into line, and even the pulpits of the country invaded in such a manner that Simon Draper of New York observed caustically. "No Whig could have the confidence of the administration unless his heel was bathed in Negro blood." They had heard the endless forensics of the slavery champions, giving their fierce opinion that the adulterated and sickly dish of compromises would never nourish the extreme requirements of the South, and all the while secession became a darker and more bitter threat.

The fight had absorbed six months, and words that had, at the beginning, an honest meaning—"Union," "patriotism," "emancipation"—became fierce assaults on personal liberty and constitutional rights. The nemesis of all had been Henry Clay, cajoling the timid, persuading the stubborn, conceding here to gain there, altering his course until it became an inexplicable maze to some of his most devoted followers, all in an effort to marry the past and the future.

He had succeeded at last, however—he and Webster and the others who could not see the shape and the temper of the future. The climax had approached rapidly during the late summer of 1850, and all the compromise proposals had finally been shaped into an Omnibus Bill. The Texas bondholders were to realize on their securities by the adjustment of the Texas boundaries and by a large payment to be made by the government. The territories of Utah and New Mexico were to be organized on the basis of a rejection of the Wilmot Proviso, although without a guarantee of the extension of slavery, California was to be admitted with her free constitution, and the slave trade—not slavery—was to be banished from the District of Columbia. To be acted upon separately, and overshadowing all the rest in the popular mind because it came with such a ferocious impact, was the new Fugitive Slave Law.

The Omnibus Bill was passed, but the fight was carried up to the day the Fugitive Slave Law passed the Senate. It might even have failed in the House, for it had less than a two-thirds majority, had the opponents of both sides not been induced to see that a vote must be taken. Only three free state Senators voted for it. Restive, perplexed, uncertain, as the roll call droned on, the ominous implications of the law were heavy in the mind. Hale had pronounced a kind of doom over it for the antislavery Senators, declaring that the influence of slavery had never been more powerfully exerted in a Congress before, while in the House George Julian, pronounced the same obsequies. "The passage of the Fugitive Slave Act will open a fresh wound in the North, and it will continue to bleed as long as the law stands unrepealed."

From the twin days in September that the Senate passed the amendment and the President signed it, the consternation of the common people of the North grew as the words of the law expanded in meaning. The identification of a fugitive could be made on the affidavit of a slave catcher without effort to substantiate his word. The fugitive could offer no defense, could not testify for himself. He was not allowed a trial by jury. The fee of the commissioner who settled the case was to be ten dollars if he found for the master and only five dollars if he freed the fugitive. If a Federal agent hampered in any way the seizure of a fugitive he was to be fined a thousand dollars, and if a fugitive escaped, with or without his help, he would be held responsible for the entire value of the slave. Bystanders could be forced to lend a hand if a fugitive tried to escape. And friends, in the underground work, or casual humanitarians, were liable to a fine of a thousand dollars or imprisonment for six months, if they were convicted of passing him on.

It was said by some that the law was made deliberately barbaric so that Northerners of sensibility would be humiliated by its brutality and refuse to obey it, giving the slavocracy thereby, sufficient grounds for secession. What truth there was in this could only be measured by the next ten violent years.

## Chapter 6

## STOCKS RISING ON THE "RAILROAD"

THE gap that stretched between the Boston which fired a salute of one hundred guns when the amendment became law and the Boston of Theodore Parker who slapped a revolver on his desk and left it where anyone could read its message was the same gap which divided the sentiments of the country. Business men were frankly pleased at the success of hardheaded acumen. The fugitive and his friends were stricken by a calamity which had befallen not only themselves but the whole structure of justice and the law. All three moved swiftly.

On black men and women in the North the greatest burden fell. Since no identification was necessary, free Negroes everywhere were exposed to slavery. Frederick Douglass was in as much danger as Big Jim who could not read or write. James W. C. Pennington, with his Heidelberg degree, was as liable for seizure as any black man or woman who had just emerged from the underground line. William Wells Brown had gone abroad the year before as a delegate to the Peace Conference in Paris. He did not dare return home, for his freedom had not been purchased. Garnet soon joined him, and stayed three years in England and on the Continent, where his reputation as a "Negro Tom Paine" brought the crowds to his lectures.

More than fifty thousand fugitives were living in the North— $30,000,000's worth of property—and intermarried with them were free Negroes. Within the space of time it took the telegraph wires to carry the news of the law, terror had spread. The law would not become operative for eight days, but forty Negroes left Massachusetts for Canada within thirty-six hours, and the exodus continued until it had reached immense proportions. Columbia, Pennsylvania, lost nearly five hundred of the nine hundred and forty-two Negroes who lived within its limits, and those who remained were only prevented from burning this gathering place of slave catchers to the ground by William Whipper, a well-to-do colored "stationmaster" of the town. In the northern part of Pennsylvania, the settlement of Sandy Lake disappeared completely. From a small town in New York, eighty-two members of the Negro Methodist

Church, including its pastor, packed up and disappeared over night, and from Rochester all but two members of the Baptist Church went in the same manner. Throughout the East, wherever fugitives had settled, came the same reports, although Negro leaders were urging their people to stand firm.

Meanwhile, the slave catchers had not waited for the first day of the law to pass. New England, and especially Boston, had been regarded as a kennel of freedom-loving hounds, set to bay at the sight of a slave catcher, but now armed with the law slave catchers put aside their fear, and Bunker Hill, Faneuil Hall, Bowdoin Square around which the colored population lived, saw the slightly shabby men with the predatory look gather like hunters. Dark figures, scuttling down streets to do their marketing, dark figures hurrying to work, dark figures merely walking with their children, knew the look of a slave catcher, and shadows came and went instead of people. Many propped up a musket against their doors. Others allowed themselves to sink out of sight and reappear in one of the strong antislavery towns which made it a point of honor to see that a fugitive was safe.

This meant that friends must be strengthened, personal liberty laws held steady, opinions kept at a white heat. There was no danger that this would fail. Nothing within the memory of that generation had roused the country to such violent partisanship. Men were not silent. This was no time for discretion. Giddings shouted out his challenge in the House, Theodore Parker pounded out his challenge on the desk of his pulpit, Walt Whitman, brought up in the Democratic party, left it in a burst of rage and wrote his first poem, *Blood-money* in the heat of indignation. Young Susan B. Anthony, thrilling to the furious indignation of the militant Quakers among whom she lived, listened to the despair of her family's close friend, Frederick Douglass, and resolved to be an Abolitionist. Henry Ward Beecher rode till midnight through a snowy Maine night to his sister Harriet Stowe, and they sat together until dawn, wondering what protection his name could offer to the exposed and terrorized Negroes. Churchmen, startled into action, denounced the law as a crime against God. In Rochester, in Providence, in Philadelphia, in New York the voices of men who had been notoriously silent rang out in pulpits and in newspapers with a chorus that fell strangely on Abolition ears.

Their collective wrath fell against Webster. His Seventh of March speech was laid like an albatross about his neck. All the evil, all the degradation, all the inhumanity that was required of the North was his doing, and although men of property might call him the savior of the Union, men of the Higher Law had another name for him.

And finally, at the very hour that the bill became a law the excitement reached a climax. James Hamlet was seized in New York. What had been theoretical horror now became an actuality. Slaveowners did not intend to wait a moment. Slave catchers who had been watching, identifying, were now free to operate under the dignity of law. A certain irony lent itself to the fact that James Hamlet was a free Negro, not a fugitive. But a Miss Mary Brown of Baltimore swore that he was her escaped slave and the officers took him while he was at work. Uncertain of the peoples' temper, well aware of the militancy of New York Negroes, the commissioner's men hurried him into a private room, tried him within the hour, handcuffed him, pushed him into a carriage and shipped him off to Baltimore before he could see his family or communicate with friends.

The news of Hamlet's arrest spread like fire. The colored people of New York called a mass meeting, stirring up the popular indignation by handbills that littered the colored neighborhoods like early snow. Fifteen hundred black lovers of liberty crowded Zion Church. Speeches were not enough. Before the evening was over five hundred dollars had been raised, and within a fortnight James Hamlet came back to New York, to the singing and the dancing of his colored friends, a free man indeed.

Pressing beneath the excitement of his arrest, overshadowing the rejoicings in his freedom, was the deeply shocking realization of the secrecy with which he had been spirited into slavery. So this was the law, this proceeding which stripped every vestige of hope and redress from the victim, that built itself upon cupidity and violated every conception of Western justice? Disbelief flared into open horror, and those Abolitionists who had been preaching the ruthlessness of slavery in season and out, seized on this moment to rally friends and sympathizers as fast as they could reach them.

Conservative Americans were shocked out of their reticence. Some gave themselves to fulminations and denunciations, others to immediate action. On the day that James Hamlet was seized in New York, a call went out for a mass meeting in Syracuse, and on the 4th of October a large indignant crowd gathered in the City Hall. It was not an Abolition meeting, (this notable fact must be repeated again and again) for Democrats and Whigs were there as well as Free-Soil and Liberty party men and Negro leaders. To hear them crying out for the resolutions that were offered; to hear their vociferous recommendations for the Committee of Thirteen, the duty of which would be to make certain that no person was arrested without the full protection of his legal rights; to hear their shouts of "No! No!" when a Baptist clergyman of the city cried, "Shall a live man ever be taken out of our city by force of law?"; to hear the chairman of the meeting say with irresistible calmness, "The colored man must be protected; he must be secure among us, come what will of political organizations"; to hear a judge—and being a judge a man held responsible for this new law—to hear him explain, "I am an officer of the law yet I will tell my constituency that I will trample that law in the dust"; to hear and to be witness to all of this was to become convinced that the agitation of two decades—oh, it was longer than that since the laying of the first underground line—was indestructibly a part of themselves, like their right to vote, to marry or to build a home.

Boston was a little slower to take action, perhaps because Bostonians had not seen as many demonstrations of slave catchers or as many flying men as had Syracuse and New York. The first to call a meeting were the Negroes coming together in Belknap Church. They pledged themselves to armed defense and to deathly resistance to the kidnaper. Garrison was there prepared to do whatever was asked of him, unsurprised, no more deeply moved by these events than he had been by events of the past.

The white Abolitionists called their meeting for the 14th and filled Faneuil Hall. The men responsible for the meeting were among those who gave Boston her air of superiority. Charles Francis Adams was there, the son of the pride of Massachusetts, and Richard Henry Dana, the Whig, the proud man, the aristocrat. Theodore Parker and Wendell Phillips came to add their uncanny skill at raising both the emotions and the intellect to a fine fever, and on the platform, Frederick Douglass and Charles Lenox Remond sat as men in danger of their lives.

They called for instant repeal at the next session of Congress, they challenged the constitutionality of the law, and they made their promise of protection to the colored people, whom they urged most strongly to remain in Boston.

Without delay they showed how they proposed to protect them. A resolution provided "for a Committee of Vigilance to secure the fugitives and colored inhabitants of Boston and vicinity from any invasion of their rights by persons acting under the law," and the committee was organized then and there. Fifty good Bostonians, colored and white, were chosen for the executive committee, the finance, legal, and special vigilance and alarm committees. The list of members who pledged themselves to the aid of the fugitive grew with reassuring speed—Bronson Alcott and Henry Bowditch, Lewis Hayden, the fugitive who had been the cause of Fairbanks' arrest and was in due time to serve in the Massachusetts legislature, Garrison, Samuel Gridley Howe—Chevalier Howe who had known the poet Byron and fought for the rights of man in odd corners of the globe and had in addition the distinction of a beautiful wife, Julia Ward—Francis Jackson, Ellis Gray Loring and Edmund Quincy, traitors to conservatism, James Russell Lowell and Theodore Parker. All in all there were 209 dedicated to the protection of the colored citizens of Boston.

They settled to work quickly, issuing an immediate appeal to Bostonians, reminding them of the steady arrival of fugitives in Boston, destitute of clothing and unable to hold their freedom without employment. Another appeal was sent to the clergy of Massachusetts asking them in the name of Christianity to raise money as quickly as possible. Sixteen hundred dollars came swiftly back to them. A third notice was sent to all towns in Massachusetts, urging them to organize local vigilance committees and to protect the Canada-bound fugitive and the colored families who had settled among them.

At the same time, the Underground Railroad which had never been a very active department of Boston Abolition took a gigantic spurt. Stocks skyrocketed. Many Negroes arriving in Boston from stations farther South, or Negroes, whose homes were in Boston, were not impressed by the reassurances of the committee and preferred to push on to the known security of Canada. The Committee of Two Hundred and Nine had to teach itself the lightning decisions, the unerring diagnosis, which "railroad" men in the South and the West had perfected long ago, and the committee's ledger grew to be a touching record of courage and enterprise.

"To Samuel Clemens (sic) for passage from Missouri penitentiary to Boston, he having been imprisoned there two years for aiding fugitives to escape . . . To Palmer and Company, artificial leg for John H. Walker, a fugitive slave who, in his flight from slavery, had his foot crushed by the cars at the Railway station in Wilmington, Delaware. . . ." To a miscellany of friends and strangers for badly needed help.

The committee met regularly in Tremont Temple. Printed notices were delivered in person by Captain Bearse, a worthy seafarer whose underground exploits were soon to add a dashing flavor to the committee's work. These notices contained instructions how to enter the temple and what rooms to pass through. The meetings were held in secret and all minutes destroyed.

Vigilance committees spread rapidly in most of the large centers of the North. Philadelphia organized nothing new, but concentrated additional responsibility in the committee secretary. In Lowell the cry, "The

man-hunters are in the land. Defend your home at any cost, at any sacrifice!" was acted on with promptness. In New York and Brooklyn, groups
of the clergy met together and urged the immediate repeal of a law which
laid guilt and murder on the souls of citizens, while Arthur Tappan
spoke for the New York Vigilance Committee when he announced calmly,
"I will submit to the penalty if need be, but will not obey," a pro-
nouncement by no means idle for his underground work extended as far
as Pennsylvania where he owned "half-share" in a horse which made
frequent journeys with fugitives on his back. Rochester and Providence
gathered their cohorts and challenged the law in a manner which would
have roused a mob in the old days. Mass meetings were called in Pittsburgh by white and colored, and the political issue was raised for the
future. Congress need not think she had brought peace. War was declared
and the fight would take place within the walls which had heard Clay's
compromises and Webster's overreaching ambition.

Four huge mass meetings said the same things in Chicago. The Underground workers, Liberty party men and nonvoting Abolitionists of Illinois called a renovated antislavery organization into existence. Lecturers
were sent out; the work of educating public opinion was undertaken;
within three weeks, thirteen thousand copies of an anti-Fugitive Slave
Bill pamphlet had been sold at five cents a copy.

In Ashtabula the law was a dead letter, and antislavery men, who had
not met for years, came together solidly to say that they would not "aid
in catching the fugitive but will feed him, and protect him with all the
means in our power, and will pledge our sympathy and property for the
relief of any person in our midst who may suffer any penalties for an
honorable opposition to the requirements of this law." It was a dead
letter in Cleveland where "we deem it the duty of every good citizen to
oppose and resist [it] by all proper means," a dead letter in Highland
County where Chase and old underground men like Rankin and Crothers
called a meeting to resolve that "disobedience to the enactment is obedience to God," in counties all over Ohio, in Indiana, Michigan, Wisconsin, Iowa, Rhode Island, in "places too numerous to be even mentioned,"
as Samuel May said.

The friends of the bill had not expected the revolt that followed.
Popular support was essential to make the law of any value. All the
machines that molded popular opinion were wheeled into position, and
the barrage began.

The Democratic newspapers and politicians of the North fired the
first round, ably assisted by the doughface Whigs and the determined
lovers of the Union. The second round was deposited in the hands of

Northern traders with the South, the banks which controlled the financial transactions of the two halves of the country, and the manufacturers who did not want the outraged temper of their Southern clients to shake the fine industrial equilibrium that was maintained with such dexterity.

No one was surprised to find Daniel Webster moving with the majesty of an elder statesman at the head of the machines. He had his reputation, his ambition, and his statesmanship to vindicate. He had past utterances to repudiate and new friends to win to take the place of old. He did very well, although he observed rather ruefully that he could travel by the light of his burning effigies the length of Cape Cod. He worked hard during the two months after the passage of the law, travelling, talking, heading torchlight processions. He addressed Union meetings all over the East, wrote letters as in the old campaign days, urged vigorously that all Abolition heresies be ruthlessly removed from Whig policies.

New England began to swerve to his side After all he was their man, their creation, and hatred of Abolition had filled them longer than hatred of a Fugitive Slave Law. The "best people" of Boston were Whigs. A mild attenuated liberalism had allowed them to nod approval when Webster spoke thunderingly, if briefly, for the Wilmot Proviso, when he showed a discreet interest in the Free-Soil party, but when he went over, for all practical and moral purposes, to the slavocracy, they found where their own interests lay. Under the persuasions of "Union" and "Constitution," the society of Boston became in its conscience and inward parts, proslavery. Faneuil Hall echoed to the cry, "It is revolution or it is treason" to obstruct the law in Massachusetts. Slave catching found itself in the unfamiliar role of patriotism, and hysteria for the Union was stirred throughout the length and breadth of the East.

Union meetings were called in all the large cities, and assumed the blandishments of slavery. In New York a gigantic meeting was called in Castle Garden "by thousands of the mercantile and professional men of New York." The mayor presided. The luminaries of the bar, the finest speakers for the Union, put the Constitution and the Union above all other ties. Merchants who refused to sign the call of the meeting or who declined to subscribe to its resolutions were proscribed, and their names were put on a "black list." Confused and honest men everywhere were awash with the sanctity of law.

The words of the Southern politicians were not heard so clearly in the North. But, among their own constituents, they made everything superably plain. "A Southern triumph!" Clay exclaimed, his diplomacy no longer necessary. California, that Northern excuse for compromise, had been won by neither side, but in New Mexico and Utah "the wishes of the South had prevailed," while Texas was safely in the bag and the "pretended concession" abolishing slave traffic in the District of Columbia was called "a measure equally demanded by the honor, dignity and true interest of both the North and the South."

Some might say that Clay talked hurriedly to cover up the "compromises," a word well hated by the slavocrats. Perhaps the fire-eaters of the deep South—Toombs of Georgia, Rhett of South Carolina, Yancey of Alabama, Downs of Louisiana—became apostles of peace and union in order to still the fears of secession which they had raised among their own people. But the chances are good that they were well satisfied, and that their stirring love of a united country, which rang in the speeches these pre-election days, was ably explained by Mr. Clemens of Alabama when he said, "A majority in Congress has yielded more than any majority ever before yielded to a minority."

At last to a country torn by opinions, President Fillmore attempted to give the concluding palliative. The compromise measures, he claimed, were a "final adjustment," the Union was preserved, the Fugitive Slave Law was the solution of a grievous wrong, and his party and himself were pledged to its enforcement.

These were all fine words, stirring in the manner of 1850 oratory. They fastened many wavering minds, they brought a sensible preoccupation with the law to timid men, they answered the questions of those who might have doubted the innate wisdom of their Congress, they satisfied all who saw in strife, not differences of principle, but merely stubborn pleasure in the battle—but they did not stop the Underground Railroad.

And, if they did not stop the Underground Railroad, what was the good of the law?

Never had the "road" had such a boom. The "stockholders" were triumphant. The service was excellent, the accommodations, perhaps not all that could be desired, but adequate for the rush. "Passengers come at all hours of the day and night," Samuel May in Syracuse announced, "from Maryland, Virginia, Kentucky, Tennessee and Louisiana." The dangers of breaking the law had been pounded out on the palm of every doughface politician. Commissioners were signing up; ten dollars for the rendition of a black man was easy money. Yet fugitives came on foot, in disguise, by rail, by boat, by hired carriage, and never failed to find a friend. Josiah Henson—Uncle Tom—writing from Canada said, "Some have found their way to England, but the mass are flying to Canada where they feel themselves secure. Already several thousand have gone thither." *The Voice of the Fugitive* soon published from Canada the fact that Negro "men of capital, with good property, some of them worth thousands, are settling among us from the Northern states." In the Southwest, the long story of greed, treachery, murder, the loss of two thousand lives and the expenditure of $40,000,000 to bring the Seminoles and the Seminole-Negroes to quiescence with the government reached its bitterly ironic climax.

Nearly a hundred years of slave catchers' and soldiers' attacks on the deeply isolated havens of the Seminoles and Exiles in Florida, of men and women seized and taken to fictitious owners, of the bloody confusion of masters' claims which turned Florida rivers into replicas of Africa, of Indians made drunk and their Negro friends and families bought from them, of Indian chiefs and Negro leaders fighting side by side and refusing to consider treaties which did not include the other, had been brought to an exhausted end by the migration of Seminole peoples to the Oklahoma lands. Peace had been promised, land. They found no land, only refuge on Cherokee reserves. They found their old enemies, the Creeks, who joined with white kidnapers in forays. They found hunger and no tools with which to grow their food.

By 1850 they could no longer endure their situation. The government had promised them protection, and Wild Cat, the Seminole chief, went to Washington to redeem that promise. How bitterly ironical was the gift which he brought back—the Fugitive Slave Law. Negro blood filled too many Seminole veins to permit them the peace they had been promised. Wild Cat laid his plans with the Negroes, Abraham and Louis Pacheo. Their only hope lay in a further exodus, and Wild Cat told of Mexico which lay beyond the Texas border.

Several hundred strapped their possessions to their shoulders, put their women and children on their ponies, and in September, 1850, prepared for that country to the south which long ago, they had been told, turned away from slavery.

The Creeks, like the Egyptians, followed them, but the Comanches had attacked first and, gathering up the wounded, had loaded them on ponies and borne them off to the slave dealers. Those who were left continued across Texas like an army, at no time unprepared for battle.

Their way led across the steep banks of the Colorado River, across exposed plains where their progress was slow and cruel, through forests where wild animals were a constant danger, across rivers, rank with vegetation. As winter came on and they reached farther westward, they survived the northers, those gales of ice and sleet, when everything must take shelter or die under a white covering.

After the last of the westernmost settlements had been skirted and left behind, four days of desert lay between them and the Rio Grande. In stark and arid desolation, they reached the mountain passes, and saw the river flowing beneath them.

It was night, but Wild Cat and the men lost no time in searching for a fording place. On hastily built rafts, they pushed their people swiftly onto the river just as the dawn was breaking.

The Mexican government, smarting from the war with the United States, and secure in the moral superiority of a nonslaveholding country, observed the gifts they had to offer—hatred of slavery and bitterness against those people to the North who had hounded them from home to home—and offered them grants of land if they would guard the border.

Their going and their haven were watched with indignation by the Texas slaveholders. The newspapers presently said that slaves were escaping into Mexico. It is true that Wild Cat returned to Arkansas and told the story of their success and urged the advantages of flight. It is also true that small bands came from great distances in terrible danger and that some reached the settlements while others were cut down on the plains by the Comanches who killed them, as they quaintly said, because they were the slaves of the white men and they "were sorry for them."

However this may be, the Texas slaveholders attempted to raise a company of volunteers to visit the settlement with guns. But the adventurers had apparently learned something from the history of the Exiles, for no mention was made of their expedition till it was over, and then it was necessary to print it obscurely, for they returned with their "numbers somewhat diminished by their conflicts with the blacks." Twice again they made attempts to raid the border, but the conclusion of their forays was the capture of a little girl and the loss of a number of their men.

They did not make a fourth attempt, but they kept the refrain singing in their papers: terror on the frontier, plantations destroyed, buildings burned, people murdered, slaves carried away, Wild Cat leading a band of warriors to pillage in the name of freedom. Possibly all this happened in the way it was described. Certainly Mexicans and Seminoles helped fugitives in every way they could—by showing them the path across the Rio Grande, by proving to them once they arrived that both modest wealth and good family connections were available to those who applied themselves to self-improvement, by embodying in themselves a long history of tenacious courage, of articulate and unrelenting determination to possess freedom.

It was in November of this year that George Thompson returned from England to test again the temper of Americans. Would it be rotten eggs, a gallows, mobs at his heels and frenzy from Wisconsin to Maine? He had his answer as soon as he arrived. Georgia slave agents had reached Boston and were preparing to seize the Crafts. The city was alive with excitement.

The Vigilance Committee had swung into action. Ellis Gray Loring, learning that no commissioner had been found who would undertake to serve the warrants, slapped a warrant on the agents, the Messrs. Hughes and Knight, charging them with slander for saying that William Craft had stolen the clothes in which he had escaped from slavery, and asking $10,000 damages. This was a fine turnabout, and a good sized crowd went along to watch developments. Bail was set at $10,000. And was promptly paid. By whom? Garrison demanded but no one would say.

The Vigilance Committee called a meeting. Phillips, Sumner, Emerson were there, as well as Garrison, Hayden and Theodore Parker. William and Ellen must be hidden in a safe place. Ellen was at work in an upholsterer's shop. Mrs. Hilliard, a friend, instructed by the committee to appear very calm and ordered, called to see her and suggested that she come immediately and do some upholstering for her. Ellen, looking into her face, burst into tears.

But William would not allow her to stay with the Hilliards. "Mr. Hilliard is not only our friend," he explained, "but he is a United States Commissioner as well, and should Ellen be found in his house, he must resign his office, as well as incur the penalty of the law, and I will not subject a friend to such punishment." The committee apparently agreed with him. Theodore Parker drove her, in the dark and the silence of the early morning, to Loring's home in Brookline. William returned to his store, where he followed the trade of cabinetmaker, and put a loaded horsepistol on the bench beside him.

For a week they laid low, the Vigilance Committee bland and artless, missing nothing; the slave agents still searching for a commissioner. Then another alarm was flashed from member to member. Henry Bowditch hurried out to Brookline as fast as his horse could gallop, but along the way he met Parker, walking calmly by the roadside munching an apple. Everything had been seen to. Ellen was safe in the Parker home.

Garrison and George Thompson hurried to Lewis Hayden's house where William had been persuaded to go. They found the house barricaded with double locks on all doors. Hayden's sons had taken up a vigil within reach of a table where loaded weapons lay, and down in the basement was Lewis Hayden with two kegs of gunpowder, preparing to blow up the house if the marshal broke through the guard upstairs.

Loring hurriedly slapped on another warrant, charging Hughes and Knight with conspiracy to abduct a peaceable citizen of Massachusetts.

The same mysterious and wealthy source provided an additional $10,000 bail. It was now evident that if the Crafts were to be protected, the agents must be driven from the city. A Committee of Sixty headed by Parker, marched down to the United States Hotel where the agents were lodging. Parker and Loring established the fifty-eight members of their party on the staircase for guests to trip over until the Messrs. Hughes and Knight had been produced, while they themselves paced back and forth in the corridor with tireless energy. A harried and unhappy pair, the slave agents soon appeared. That afternoon they took the train for New York. There had been something profoundly disturbing in a city where crowds had followed them shouting, "Slave hunters—there go the slave hunters!" and where a man had broken the door of their carriage and threatened to finish them off.

There was no boisterous rejoicing, but the first round belonged without a doubt to the enemies of the Fugitive Slave Law. Still, they all knew that the Crafts would not be safe until they had left the United States.

Thompson insisted that England would receive them like heroes, and he made all the arrangements for their going. The only danger that might conceivably face them there was the doubtful legality of their marriage, contracted in the manner of slaves. So Parker married them, with the Vigilance Committee present to give its blessing.

That night he was howled down by a well-dressed crowd as he attempted to make a speech of welcome at a meeting for George Thompson, and he went home to meditate on the paradoxes of society. Old John Adams, a generation before, had found that men of property and men of organized religion were invariably on the side of oppression. Heartened by this, he wrote a letter to President Fillmore. He told him the Crafts had escaped, and he asked him how he intended to enforce his monstrous law.

When the by-elections came that fall nothing played so large a part as that "monstrous law." The friends of the law were perfectly aware that support of no indifferent kind must be brought to it, and the determinations of both camps shook the elections mightily. Compromises had become contagious. The Democrats of Massachusetts hoped to make their party "the great antislavery party of the state and through it the great antislavery party of the United States." But when the elections were over they found that they had accepted all the compromises, accepted the Fugitive Slave Law, and by 1853 ushered in a Presidential administration that was the most proslavery of all that had gone before.

The Whigs hoped to teeter dexterously between the duty of law enforcement and their attenuated antislavery doctrines. They were crushed all over the country. In Boston their defeat was complete, and his enemies looked toward Webster to see if he understood the significance of their collapse. Webster, it was said, understood.

Everywhere the Free Soilers were determined on increased representation. To do this meant compromises and coalition. Party lines began to disappear. Men who had represented militant Free Soilism two years before were finding their way back into the ranks of the Whigs or the Democrats. In some of the Northwestern states antislavery had infiltrated the major parties sufficiently to repeal "black laws" and elect a few antislavery legislators and Congressmen. It appeared more and more clear that there was no leader and no party in all the land strong enough to denounce slavery and create the militant party of the North. Political Abolition was broken and confused. The only accomplishments seemed to be "underground." Must there be a return to old ways? The organization of religious and nonpartisan antislavery agitation, reminiscent of the days when Garrison's voice was first powerful, was beginning once again.

The protests which had spread over the Northwest with the passage of the law were not likely to release their hold on the consciences of hard-bitten frontiersmen. Old work was taken up where it had been dropped a decade before. In Indianapolis, and in Illinois towns ardor was raised by thumping good meetings and old Abolition songs.

Politically it meant nothing. The leaders of the two parties sedulously claimed that the issue of slavery was no longer alive after the Compromises of 1850. Their greatest concern at the moment was to rid their parties of all Free-Soil taint and to sit firmly in the happy illusion of the compromises.

And yet the South was not pleased. Could the North be depended on to make the Fugitive Slave Law a success? President Fillmore made a point of speaking highly of the law and urging its patriotic enforcement when Congress reassembled in December, for he knew that something must be done to calm the fears of a South which had voted, through a Georgia convention, "that it is the deliberate opinion of this convention that upon the faithful execution of the Fugitive Slave Bill by the proper authorities depends the preservation of our much-loved Union."

The Union had a general and a particular meaning, and in the mouth of a Southern statesman it did not always carry the common interpretation. There was a union at home to be considered as well, and every politician knew that the unmistakable signs of unrest were all about him. De Bow, whose *Review* caught all the vibrations of the South, printed a letter from a South Carolinan named Taylor, and as far as De Bow was concerned it apparently needed no comment. ". . . the great mass of our poor white population begins to understand that they have rights and that they too are entitled to some of the sympathy which falls upon the suffering. . . . It is the great upheaving of the masses we have to fear as far as our institutions are concerned," and the *True Wesleyan* supplemented this with a letter from a citizen of Guilford, North Carolina. "You may discontinue my paper for the present, as I am inclined to go Westward, where I may enjoy religious liberty, and have my family in a free state. There is more moving this fall to the far West than was ever known in one year. People do not like to be made slaves."

Where there was white disaffection there was Negro disaffection, and where there was Negro there was white. The two operated one upon another, blindly and unpretentiously. The weakening of power, which the slavocracy dreaded sufficiently to threaten disunion, came not only from the North but also from its own people. To understand the frenzy of this next decade, the power of the Underground Railroad, the significance of the drama which ran from the Kansas-Nebraska Bill to the election of Abraham Lincoln, one must understand that a system, dying, has a supernatural strength, until like Actaeon at bay, it is torn by its own dogs.

During this winter of 1850 and 1851, slave conspiracies sprang up like a contagion in the South. Southern newspapers told of attempted or successful insurrections in Missouri, Virginia, Georgia, Louisiana, North Carolina. No slave, sharpened to freedom, failed to sense that his master's fear of the unenforceability of the Fugitive Slave Law meant that friends waited for him in the North. "Any great event having the slightest bearing upon the question of emancipation," ran the report of a traveler in the South, "is known to produce an unwholesome excitement among the slaves."

To divide and rule had been the policy of the slavocracy. Racial antipathy, as the old lawmakers of the South had discovered, was largely a cultivated thing. Their danger would come, they knew, if the landless and poverty-stricken blacks and whites ever came together.

In the winter of 1851 unrest flared in the western part of Virginia, flared as it had done many times before and as it would do again until this section ceased to be Virginia. The slaveless small landowners, joining with the artisans and mechanics of eastern Virginia, called for a constitutional convention, and won two great points that were bitter losses to the slavocracy. Legislative representation from the free-labor west was almost equalized in the slavery-dominated legislative hall of the state, and the right to vote was given to all free white males of twenty-one. No poll taxes, no property ownership, could now keep them from speaking their minds.

The same spirit was alive in North Carolina. Again the mountainous west, believing in free labor, made overtures to the free-labor east. The new governor was elected because he had championed universal manhood suffrage in the election of state legislators, a procedure that had previously been impossible since no one could vote for a senator unless he owned fifty acres of land. However, in spite of the electorate, the slavery-dominated legislature refused to pass the bill of manhood suffrage, and the issue was aggressively raised at each election until 1857 saw its success by a two-thirds triumph.

And what about South Carolina? Secessionists—that is to say, slavery politicians—were beaten all over the state and it was freely agreed that this could not have come about had not the farmers and the free laborers of the cities fought together. Bitter denunciations were flung by "free-men of the back country against the barons of the low country."

In 1847, Hammond, Senator from South Carolina, had prophesied that slavery's "only hope" was to keep "the actual slaveholders not only predominant, but paramount within its circles." How much longer could they do this? Would it be worth while to act on the advice of De Bow's Review which advocated industrialization of the South and the employment of non-slaveholding whites instead of Negroes, to keep them from the danger of becoming "Abolitionists"? Or would the threat of secession be more effective? Emancipation was now, for all practical purposes impossible; masters who wished to give freedom to their slaves were bound, without appeal, by the law. Slavery, dominant, had been maintained by the continuous reiterations of chauvinism. What reason was there for believing that what had succeeded in the past would not succeed in the future?

Yet the desire for freedom could not be legislated away, and certain Southern men made it their concern to see that freedom came to those who asked for it. Lewis Paine of Georgia, for instance, spent five and a half years in the penitentiary for assisting a runaway. Thomas Brown of Kentucky went to prison for three years although legal proof of aiding slaves was never established. And then there was the Virginian, John Fairfield. But he stood as far apart from these men as the artist does from the layman. Perhaps some would call him an adventurer with a little of Robin Hood, a little of Conrad the Corsair, but that would be going no deeper than the surface.

John Fairfield was an artist in the art of freedom. A Virginian, his relatives were all slaveholders. But he lived close to those western mountains where a traditional love of freedom was bred. He was, according to reports, a handsome, reckless and passionate young man. When the time came to make a living, he determined to leave slavery behind him and go to a free state. But before he did so, he wished to express his own opinion of slavery, and this he did in a practical way. As a child he had played with a young slave named Bill who was owned by his uncle. As he grew older his attachment for Bill increased, and they talked many times of ways by which Bill might escape. It was inconceivable to young Fairfield to leave him in slavery. So Bill escaped one day; they met by prearrangement and traveled on to Canada together.

Fairfield stayed in Canada a few weeks, and then returned to Ohio. But before settling down he felt an irresistible impulse to return to Virginia. There he learned that his uncle, convinced of his part in the escape of Bill, had sworn out a warrant for his arrest. Out of the state he must go, as inconspicuously as possible, but not before he had exchanged a word or two with other slaves.

He brought them safely to Canada, and his career began. The word of his success spread among the friends of his friend, Bill. Canadian settlers, with relatives in slavery brought him their savings and begged him to exert his magic for them. He had no settled income; why not allow his hatred of slavery to support him?

With full descriptions of masters and plantations, of habits and characteristics of relatives and neighborhood, he would set out. Arriving near his destination he always took a fictitious name, engaged lodgings under the pretense that he had business in the neighborhood—poultry and eggs became his specialty—and always he was enthusiastically proslavery in his manner and his words. He was so clearly a Southerner, by speech, by recklessness, by voluptuous pleasure in life, that the disappearance of slaves came as a disagreeable surprise. It took some time to associate Mr. Fairfield with their disappearance.

Sometimes he appeared in a neighborhood as a slave trader, and gained, in this way, the knowledge necessary to establish contacts with certain slaves. Sometimes he stayed six or twelve months at a time in the South, familiarizing himself with various neighborhoods, talking with slaves, laying plans. He did not always conduct his fugitives the entire way to Canada. More often than not, he brought them as far as Levi Coffin, and then returned to a spot across the river where he had not been seen before. The only similarity in his raids was the disappearance of human property. He seldom carried off one or two, preferring whole companies. He liked his fugitives to be strong and reckless, willing to fight if necessary.

When a number of free colored people begged him to bring off their relatives, he agreed although he knew that the difficulties would involve long and careful planning. He must round up close to twenty, make sure that they understood him perfectly, that there would be no obstacle to his success. The potential fugitives lived near salt works on the banks of the Kanawha River. To the salt works he promptly made his way, accompanied by two Negro assistants who could assume any number of roles at a moment's notice. He announced his intention of becoming a salt trader, ordered the building of two boats, and contracted for salt to load them. The building of the boats gave Fairfield's assistants time to locate the potential fugitives and arrange their escapes with them. On the night when the first boat was finished, one of Fairfield's assistants took half the fugitives with him, rowed down the river until the tide changed, and then floated as quickly as possible into the Ohio River. The escape took place on a Saturday night. Masters spent Sunday searching for their slaves. The boat was not missed until Monday, and then no master could have exceeded in rage the furious salt trader who turned on his one remaining "slave," and accused him, in the presence of the defrauded masters, of having a part in the escape. The masters set out in wild pursuit up the river, confident that no slaves could row fast enough to outstrip them. When they found the new boat, tugging gently at its rope, drifting happily with a gentle current at a point near the mouth of the Ohio, they did not know that it had lain there nearly twenty-four hours.

The histrionics of Fairfield and his "slave" were continued without a falter; one suspicious and surly, the other obsequious and resentful. The second boat was finished by the following Saturday night, and, before dawn, had disappeared with another load of fugitives. The outraged "salt trader" managed to simulate a Homeric fury and himself led the pursuers up the river, lashing his horse and cursing at the top of his voice whenever he recalled how completely he had been duped.

It was probably he who pulled in his horse violently and pointed—at what? At a trim new boat, gently tugging at its rope, drifting happily with a playful current. They ferried across, he and the fulminating Kentuckians, and Fairfield, whose fine rich oaths had given him unquestioned leadership, suggested that they divide into companies, taking routes which he designated, and meeting again at a selected spot. Probably some of them expected to meet him again, even after several days had gone by. Perhaps even one or two actually refused to believe what their outraged friends insisted. . . .

The genius of an artist lies in the use of all the tools of his profession.

It must have been a matter of great pleasure to Fairfield when he discovered that the "clients" in a subsequent enterprise were quadroons and mulattos. They lived in scattered sections of Maryland, the District of Columbia and Virginia and he spent some time traveling between these points, learning to know his clients well, judging his course according to the degree of their intelligence. At last he was satisfied. He took the train to Philadelphia and there he spent eighty dollars on wigs and make-up. The first scene of the small drama took place at Baltimore where his Maryland "passengers" had been gathered. In a closely locked room, with suppressed laughter and a grim appreciation of their friend's daring, the mulattos and quadroons selected wigs that fitted them, applied powder to their faces and waited their turn for Fairfield to add the deft touches that would carry them safely through the middle of a slave mart. When he was satisfied, he put them on a train for Harrisburg, Pennsylvania, where he had arranged a meeting with a fellow conductor who would see them to Cleveland and a Detroit-bound boat.

He went straight to Washington. His second group of passengers, wigged and powdered, well mannered and not given to ostentatious gestures, he himself accompanied in the white cars as far as Pittsburgh. At Harpers Ferry, the third company was waiting him. He looked at his empty pocketbook and went to Philadelphia as fast as he was able. But the Vigilance Committee had never heard of him. This did not mean, however, that his work might not be as secret as theirs, so they wired on his recommendation to Levi Coffin, and Coffin—who had tried often to bring a spiritual leaven to this voluptuous lover of life— wired back with a grim smile about his lips, "If John Fairfield needs money, give it to him."

The Virginia slaves were transformed into white ladies and gentlemen—all but one who was too dark and had to be left for another journey and another conductor—and Fairfield led them calmly, no backward looks, no apprehensive undertones in his voice, no anxious glances to see if wigs sat straight, to the white cars of a Pittsburgh express.

To tempt fate three times was preposterously godlike. This time his pursuers caught his scent. They made a gesture almost as dramatic as his by engaging an engine and a special car to catch the Pittsburgh express. Fast and unhampered, the road open before them, they caught sight of the express just as it was pulling into Pittsburgh, but Fairfield had been warned. Before the train had fully stopped, he and his fugitives, wigs askew and wigs straight, had spilled out of the car and were scattering in all directions to be swallowed up by the politely yawning city.

One of the more articulate of the fugitives whom he brought to Cincinnati said to Coffin, "I never saw such a man as Fairfield. He told us he would take us out of slavery or die in the attempt if we would do our part which we promised to do. We all agreed to fight until we died rather than be recaptured. Fairfield said he wanted no cowards in the company; if we were attacked and one of us showed cowardice or started to run, he would shoot him down."

The slaves he aided knew he did not speak idly. On one occasion they arrived at Coffin's home, dirty, ragged and exhausted, Fairfield looking more worn and beaten than any of them. "They were lying in ambush at the end of the bridge," he told Coffin as he dragged himself to bed, ". . . patrollers."

"Was anybody hurt?" Coffin asked.

Fairfield did not reply. He merely spread out his clothes and pointed to several bullet holes and a flesh wound on one arm, clumsily bandaged.

"You see we were in close quarters, but my men were plucky. We shot to kill, and we made the devils run."

Coffin was shaken by this man, distressed, as always, when near him. "It is better to suffer wrong than to do wrong, and we should love our enemies."

"Love the devil!" snorted Fairfield. "Slaveholders are all devils and it's no harm to kill the devil. I do not intend to hurt people if they keep out of the way, but if they step in between me and liberty, they must take the consequences. When I undertake to conduct slaves out of bondage, I feel that it is my duty to defend them, even to the last drop of my blood."

Twice he was betrayed and arrested, twice he escaped from jail, "being a Free Mason, high in the order." He gathered his fugitives from Louisiana, Alabama, Mississippi, and Georgia as well as from the border states. His health shattered, coughs racking him, he brushed aside all efforts to stop his work. His friends were the colored people; he lived with them and for them. His life was a cypher without them. He tried once to open a store in Indiana, but he soon gave it up and disappeared. When he reappeared it was by way of the Ohio River, mud-soaked, desperately knocking on the door of a colored friend, John Hatfield, the Negro who was a frequent transmission belt to Coffin. He told Hatfield that he had hidden twenty-eight fugitives in the hills about the city. How were twenty-eight fugitives to be smuggled into the city?

Coffin struck his fist against his palm and told Hatfield to hire two coaches from the German livery keeper, to borrow as many buggies as possible which were to go out slyly and inconspicuously, one by one, to the scattered hiding places and gather the fugitives into the vehicles. The carriages would then form a funeral procession and roll solemnly along the road to Cumminsville where lay a colored burying ground.

The funeral procession, black-draped, slowly moving, wrung the hearts of passers-by. Inside a carriage a woman was truly weeping, for her baby, exposed to the rain and the cold of the hills had died. Once safely beyond the burying ground they knew that they were safe. The fugitives poured out of the buggies and scattered to the Negro settlement. Fairfield, Coffin and Hatfield probably drank a cup of tea in celebration. To artists like these three there was a natural and not unseemly satisfaction in a creation so perfectly executed.

For Fairfield passivity was impossible. His work continued for twelve years. Then he disappeared. Had he gone to Canada? No one had seen him there. Then he must have returned to the South. He traveled in only two directions. Talk of war was chilling the nation. In Tennessee, an insurrection flamed in the ironworks on the Cumberland River, an insurrection which a South, preparing for war, could not endure. A small army of vigilantes went out to put down the insurrectionists. Reports filtered through that a white man, who the insurrectionists claimed as their friend and leader, had been killed with the slaves. The friends of John Fairfield believed and said that he was the white man.

By now the cruelty of the law's operation was increasingly evident. Everywhere fugitives were being seized and borne back to a slavery they had not, in some instances, ever known; white men and colored had been killed for defending them. Apathy watched, but even apathy was occasionally roused sufficiently to be outraged by the ruthlessness of the law. It was not American, they said, and even apathetic dismay can develop a cumulative impressiveness. By the end of that winter of 1851 it was becoming apparent that the Fugitive Slave Law, given a little time, would devour itself.

It was Giddings who lashed out at the restive framers of the law. "Freemen will never be metamorphosed into bloodhounds, to track [the fugitive] to his hiding-place, and seize and drag him out, and deliver him to his tormentors. Rely upon it—they will die first."

He was a realist; he allowed them to guess what lay behind his words; he allowed them to catch a brief and disturbing glimpse of a situation which they still hoped would never come to pass. He allowed them to finish his words and come gradually to the realization that, for certain Americans, it was now a point of honor to disobey the law.

These Americans presented, over a period of time, an impressive front. Thaddeus Stevens fought in the court and in Congress. Richard Henry Dana said a well-considered good-by to his rich clients, and for twelve years fought the battle of the underprivileged—the poor man, the fugitive, the sailor. Rutherford B. Hayes, when he was an elderly man, wrote that, "As a young lawyer, from the passage of the Fugitive Slave Law until the war, I was engaged in slave cases for the fugitives, having an understanding with Levi Coffin and other directors of the Underground Railroad that my services would be freely given." As celebrated cases invaded the court dockets in the next ten years, celebrated lawyers were invariably on hand to see that no loophole of escape was overlooked, no appeal to the humanity of a court unmade.

It was respectable men who arranged for escapes on the new steam railways which had only recently opened in Ohio. In time these railways became a favorite "surface line" to freedom, and trainmen were found to be as zealous Abolitionists as the farmer with a secret compartment in his wagon. Sometimes the fugitives traveled in the freight or baggage cars under the care of railway employees, sometimes openly in their best clothes, on tickets bought without dissimulation. It was a respectable man who set his horses to stamping on the hay in his barn in order to dispel suspicion from newly arrived fugitives, hidden under the floors; a respectable woman who seized a crying colored baby—the only member of the group who might betray them to the master pounding on the door—and saved all their liberties by the expedient of slipping into bed and pretending that she was a nursing mother. It was a justice of the peace who refused to allow slave catchers to search his farm until they had a warrant, although he knew perfectly well that he was the only man in the neighborhood authorized to issue the warrant and used the interval, before the outraged slave catchers' return, to scatter the fugitives he was aiding.

Any expedient became legitimate and respectable as long as it did not fail. An itinerant bookbinder of Troy, New York, especially constructed his large wagon with a concealed compartment for a fugitive, and Mr. Marks of upper New York state, being an undertaker, used his hearse for the transportation of live black bodies to freedom.

Underground Railroad stations were usually indistinguishable from any other house, but as the days increased in tension, as the fugitives poured up the lines, reaching their flood in this decade, many ardent Abolitionists gave their lives so completely to the work that even their houses assumed a new aspect. While Joseph Morris of Ohio, for instance, kept a slave agent busy in the front yard of his home, a fugitive might be crawling through one of the two tunnels which had been dug from the cellar to the barn and from the cellar to the corn crib, or an escaped slave or two might be hiding in his attic behind the complicated and ingenious network of false walls constructed solely for the purpose of deluding the slave catcher, or yet again, as many as a dozen refugees might be concealed in the cellar's secret chambers. Then there was J. M. Fitch of Oberlin who resolved to build his house with at least two extra rooms for the fugitives who frequently stopped with him on their way to Elyria and a boat on the Black River. If the slavecatchers were hot on their heels Fitch thought nothing of opening his house and allowing the law to search as much as it pleased, since he was perfectly confident that a certain inoffensive closet would never reveal the secret door to a chamber beyond.

False closets through trap doors in kitchens or parlors, false cupboards over brick ovens, sliding panels by fireplaces where wood was stowed, secret rooms without windows—these became "stations" on the underground route. Octagonal houses, a pride of the 1850's, provided unlimited scope for admirers of secret compartments. A row of white brick near the roofs of certain houses in Vermont flashed a code to the fugitive, "We are Underground Railroad stations!"

Since it was clearly impossible to disentangle one's life and one's emotions from the perpetual adventure of such a "road," it was only natural that the concern of some conductors for individual passengers should persist even after the passenger had gone out of sight—(a passenger such as the boy who came all the way from Alabama wearing an anklet and chain on one leg, or the two Virginia slaves who bribed a poor white man to dress as a gentleman, stole a carriage which they mounted as driver and footman, and drove thus into Canada, or the Negro shoemaker from Virginia who had lost both legs above the knee and yet managed to reach Ohio on the stumps—the slaveholders were desperate at not being able to catch *him*; James Birney's *Philanthropist* taunted them through several issues). Elizabeth Buffum Chace, when sending fugitives on from her home in Valley Falls, Rhode Island, gave them a stamped envelope to mail when they reached their destination; the postmark being all the information that she needed. A great number of the fugitives wrote back on their own initiative, or returned later with some memento or with money which they offered in payment for the help they had received.

Levi Coffin, who knew that escape into British lands was not the end of the journey, that rehabilitation and contentment were essential before the "railroad" had completed its work, made several trips into Canada to see his charges. In 1844 he and a colleague, William Beard, had made a tour through Canada West, visiting many fugitives whom he had set on the northward path, dining with them, praying with them, often resting in their homes overnight. Here they were allowed to vote, were elected to county offices, served as school directors, sat on juries. Everywhere throngs of settlers crowded to kiss Coffin's hand and cry, "Bress de Lawd, if it hadn't been for you, ah wouldn't be here." Forty-thousand fugitives had at that time, he said, settled in the cold friendly regions above the lakes. Not long after the passage of the law he returned again to Chatham, and everywhere he went like a Caesar, greeted, wept over, extolled, children brought to see him, successes told him, failures minimized in the joyful, bittersweet memories he conjured up.

These colonies were a source of perpetual interest to friends, north and south of the border. Here in an alien land the Negroes' capacities were being tested. Coffin found that committees of business men, clergymen, housewives, or mere advocates of reform were taking shape in St. Catharine's, Toronto, Hamilton, Niagara Falls, Salford, Windsor and other towns, as well as in the older Negro colonies where communities had struggled along since the days of the first refugee. The members of these committees had quickly established contacts with the antislavery workers of England and of the United States, and a formidable relief project was being undertaken by the women's auxiliaries. The influx had called for swift amelioratives. At least six thousand fugitives were reported to have gotten through into Canada within six months of that fateful day in October when the bill became law.

The disorganized, spontaneous acts of friendship which had been the Underground Railroad were passing out in deference to a more integrated organization of lawbreaking and humanitarianism. Routes were constantly being opened up in places that had been, only a short time before, a wilderness of suspicion and unfriendliness. In the East, well-run "tracks" lay from Washington to Rochester with branches or stops at New York, where a militant Vigilance Committee under the leadership of the colored clergyman, Charles Ray, was meeting the dangers of so exposed and important a city, and sending their "clients" by boat to New England or up the Hudson River valley to Albany, where Stephen Myers, the colored publisher of *The Elevator*, an Abolition sheet, was chief stationmaster. From there they went to Syracuse where J. W. Loguen, himself a fugitive, had been put in sole charge of all activities, and so on to Rochester where Frederick Douglass had established a terminal that looked across the lake to freedom.

Through Pennsylvania, east, west and north the lines stretched, through Philadelphia, Harrisburg, Pittsburgh, or east to Trenton and so on through New York state, to Albany, Schenectady, Utica; or up from Wilkes-Barre through the station kept by Gerrit Smith at Peterboro. All passed through the little towns, the isolated farms that were the strong links in the line. Up the western coast of New York other "tracks" lay, through Westfield, Fredonia, Buffalo, Niagara and across the bridge, a short quick palpitating distance, taken many times on the run. Mazes ran through Ohio, threading their way from nearly every town along the Ohio River, and explaining themselves as inevitably as a finished puzzle when the lake had been reached. Illinois lines reached from Cairo, Chester, Alton, Quincy, shooting straight as an arrow toward Chicago or mingling in Springfield to wander off into another foxy tangle, inextricable from the Iowa and Nebraska lines, that were putting out tentative feelers in the direction of Milwaukee and again Chicago. Indiana "tracks" crossed and recrossed as though no sureness, no plainness could ever be made of this gigantic fantasy, but they led somehow to Toledo, Detroit, Chicago and, occasionally around the cold peninsula of northern Michigan into Lake Huron and down to Sarnia, Windsor or Collingwood, in Canada.

The longer the route, the more complicated the system, the more hazardously balanced the chances between escape and the law, the more militant and prepared must be the men who had taken "employment" in this dangerous business. The Quakers still pursued their guileful course of embroidering the truth, of ruses and nonviolence, but more and more often, a pistol lay strapped to a man's hip, a rifle lay when he slept at night, within easy reach of his hand.

No supporter of the new law could be found, after the first six months, who did not maintain with restless stubbornness that authorities must soon pump a law-abiding spirit into the country. Indications were all about them of the flouting of the law, of respectable men who made themselves outlaws—wantonly, perversely, unpatriotically! All you needed to do was take a long unblinking look at the Boston Vigilance Committee—those fine gentlemanly brigands—to know what was being done to respect the integrity of the Union, the feelings of our Southern brethren. Something must happen very soon—in Boston, which in Southern eyes was the home of Garrison—something that would show how devoted Bostonians were to the law.

It happened one February morning, 1851. Men in their counting offices, their business offices, their shipyards, had opened their morning mail, considered the orders for the day, gone out for lunch. At lunch time they heard a rumor. A Virginia fugitive had been taken out of the coffee house where he was working and rushed to the courthouse. They looked at each other with bright eyes and thrust out their lower lips. So Boston is vindicating her respectability? They went back to their offices with a new buoyancy to their walk and ordered the first newspaper that would bring them the details. Bankers thought of their Southern clients that afternoon with an ease in their hearts; merchants felt how foolish their embarrassment had been. Clients knew their interests were being watched; shipowners wondered if perhaps a new vessel might not soon be needed for the Southern run.

It was evening before they discovered how futile were their best-laid plans. Was such devilment possible? They got the opinion of all their friends, and then they sank back into their horsehair rockers and gave themselves up to such blasphemous indignation that their women folk were driven to the upper reaches of the house.

A few words told the story. The renegade Dana's office was only a few steps across from the courthouse where the fugitive Shadrach had been taken. It took him—how long, five minutes?—to cross the street. Chief Justice Shaw did everything he could. He refused to read the petition of habeas corpus; when Dana persisted he raised technicalities that Dana claimed were not in the law. Dana hurried off to find another judge or to rephrase his petition. In less than half an hour he looked out of his office window. What he saw would have horrified a man whose feelings were not blunted by lawbreaking. There, down the courthouse steps came two large Negroes holding by either arm a swiftly moving, half-naked and stupified man whom Dana had seen as a prisoner less than an hour ago. Dana and his clerks rushed to the window. Their own exclamations were lost in the shouts and singing of the crowd of Negroes who were pushing out of the courthouse door. It did not seem possible that things could happen so quickly. A carriage drew up—so swiftly it must have been prearranged—Shadrach and his two guards got in, the horse was lashed and almost before the eye could adjust itself it had gone swaying and rattling down the street "like a black squall." The crowd of black men jumped into other carriages or ran toward the bridge over the Charles River. Dana and his clerks looked at each other. No arrests, no pursuit; the law must apparently know when it is beaten.

By the next morning nearly everyone knew what had taken place in the courtroom. Lewis Hayden, having heard of the arrest almost as soon as Shadrach himself, had hurried to his colored friends and by the time Dana had argued with Justice Shaw and left, these friends had gathered, strong by the scores, pushing their way quietly into the room. They had not known exactly what they intended to do until they saw the prisoner, a tall intelligent-looking fellow, standing in an empty court-room, with only a few constables about him. It was perfectly evident now that they had made signs to him. He had stood up, they had closed about him . . . and the first test of the law in Boston had ended. By nightfall conductors had him far along the road; they had passed Lexington, Concord, Leominster; they were in Vermont, and Canada lay ahead.

The storm broke quickly enough. By the end of the second day the rage of Washington had shaken Massachusetts. Webster cried "Treason!" Clay urged extraordinary powers for the President since this law seemed to demand more than ordinary law enforcement. The President himself issued a proclamation in which he called upon the army, the civilian authorities, and all good citizens to "aid in quelling this and similar combinations" and to assist in the seizure of the culprits. The Secretaries of the Army and the Navy telegraphed orders to be alert and ready for any emergency.

The trials which followed brought divisions in families, divisions among friends, divisions in the jury itself. The whole force of the government had been thrown against the "combination" which had rescued Shadrach. Conservatives everywhere had cried for the arrest of Lewis Hayden and James Scott, the leaders of the Negro rescuers, of Robert Morris and the ubiquitous Elizur Wright. Dana and John Hale had retaliated by arguing against the constitutionality of the law, while Parker had scornfully asserted that the jury was packed—"all that Boston influence and money could do, has been done." Yet, three weeks passed, and still the jury was unable to agree. The case was dismissed. Parker said the consciences of men had been touched. But two years later Dana met a sinewy blacksmith in a town in upper Massachusetts. From him he learned that the jury had stood eleven to one for conviction. The blacksmith alone had held out. He could not seem to forget that it was he who had driven Shadrach from Concord to Leominster on the night of his escape.

Yet the tension did not relax. In the mind of every man who stood close to the rising temper of the people—whether proslavery or anti-slavery—it was becoming clearly evident that there would be no rescue, no dramatic clattering off of carriages the next time. The next time the government would enforce the law if it took the army to see that it was done.

The next time came with a swiftness that cut through the slowly settling apprehension.

A Negro boy of seventeen named Thomas Sims was seized a few weeks later on an April night and rushed under cover of the darkness to the same courthouse which had, for a short time, held Shadrach. He was arrested on a charge of theft and held as a fugitive slave from Georgia. The word spread before the night was over. No dweller on "Nigger Hill," no member of the Vigilance Committee, no undeclared friend in Boston believed that Sims would be given up without a fight. But how was the fight to be waged? The lawyers, Dana, Sewall and Rantoul, prepared a writ and thrust it at Judge Shaw. He refused to have anything to do with it. They persisted. Nothing could persuade him to honor it. The committee, meeting hurriedly, wondered if all defense was to be suppressed. Perhaps Sims was to be spirited away—slipped through their fingers?

A messenger arrived breathlessly in Newburyport, urging that new convert and aristocratic firebrand, the Reverend Thomas Wentworth Higginson, to come immediately to Boston. Higginson, who only longed for an opportunity to double up his fists in such a cause, found the Vigilance Committee meeting in *The Liberator* office, Garrison composedly preparing an editorial, the others doubtful of the right procedure. Higginson was for action—let hell or high water break loose. These were not men, sitting here pondering ways and means. "Only the Negroes," he said sharply, "know how to handle these matters." Lewis Hayden nodded and said, "Of course, we will handle them easily." His face was solemn. Later he drew Higginson aside. "That was bluff," he said. "We do not wish anyone to know how weak we are. There are practically no colored men in Boston; the Shadrach trial has scattered them all. What is to be done must be done without them."

Higginson was dismayed. Later he went out and took a look at the courthouse. The crowd that filled Court Square was so immense and so uncertain in its temper that several shops, bordering on the square, had closed their doors for protection. Around the courthouse stretched the most sinister object of all, chains that ran from pillar to pillar and beneath which one must stoop to enter the courthouse. This was an indignity that Boston had never seen before. To the Abolitionists it was a symbol of the power of the slavocracy. Higginson, impetuous, hotheaded, the plumed knight, talked to everyone upon whom he could with discretion lay his hands. From one he learned that the courtroom was up two and a half flights of stairs, that six men were at the door of the courtroom, that the prisoner was guarded by two men on either side of him and five in a row behind him, that, in spite of the Massachusetts law, nearly all his guards were Boston policemen acting under the orders of the mayor. The trial was apparently closed before it had begun.

Words—words were too much for Higginson. What advantage was there to Sims in the handbills which the committee was circulating, calling for a mass meeting in front of the State House? True, a crowd was there, a crowd big enough—Higginson's eager eyes told him—to smash through the prison doors, but the authorities drove them to the head of the Common. True, Phillips and some of the others stirred them with fine speeches from steps on Beacon Street, but still what good was it? Sims was going back to Georgia. Higginson took another look at the courthouse. There were no gratings at Sims' window . . . He went musingly to a meeting at Tremont Temple that evening.

Sam Howe paid him the compliment of saying that his speech brought his listeners to the verge of revolution—and Howe, the friend of Byron and Lafayette, should know. He might have done something with this crowd, Higginson knew bitterly, for some of them were fighting men, but the moderates talked moderately, and men whose blood was water saw only the lines of soldiers that filled the streets, the chains about the courthouse.

When the moderates and the firebrands had gone home, when Parker had stumped off in a rage, and Phillips had wiped his fine brow with a cambric handkerchief and let his mind play with daring ideas, when Garrison had shrugged his shoulders—"there is no way but the immediate abolition of slavery"—and Horace Mann had wondered whether his constitutional oath as a Congressman was really the final word, Higginson beckoned to him six trusted men. Perhaps he had a crazy plan, but dangerous times reassort values. Leonard Grimes, the colored clergyman and "stationmaster," and Hayden, the most daring man in Boston, nodded their approval. The others looked at each other. Before they separated their plans were complete.

Grimes, the only man allowed to visit Sims, spoke to him the next day, told him to be at his ungrated window at a specified time without fail. Not looking back, not hesitating, he was to climb quickly onto the sill of the window and leap. Mattresses would have been dragged from an office across the street a moment before, a carriage would be standing a few feet away. Within an hour he would be on the road to Canada.

The following day . . . dusk . . . Higginson and a fellow conspirator strolled carelessly into Court Square. They stopped rigid. The carriage had already started, men were waiting in the office with the mattresses— and bars were being fitted across that third-story window!

They never knew what happened. Had they been betrayed or had the authorities merely been as smart as they? Higginson, unable to endure his helplessness, went back to Newburyport.

At three o'clock on the morning of April 13th, Henry Bowditch was awakened and sprang out of bed. The commissioner had ordered Sims returned to slavery, the messenger told him hurriedly, and in the dead of night he was being taken under heavy guard to the Georgia ship.

Dr. Bowditch, pale with sleepiness, found the faithful gathered on the spot on State Street where Crispus Attucks had fallen—Crispus Attucks, the Negro, the first victim of the Revolution. They had taken time to drape a coffin-shaped box in black and had drawn the word Liberty where flowers might have lain. Someone held a shrouded flag. They knew each other by their voices. As their eyes grew accustomed to the dark, they recognized individual forms, Parker, moving restlessly, his long coat flapping unopened, Grimes, very still, his hands clutched in front of him, his head bowed, Phillips, shifting from one foot to the other, talking softly to Garrison, Channing, reaching out his hand to the stragglers who came walking swiftly, maybe running, down the street. Presently there was close to a hundred of them, filling the street like black specters. They were terribly silent. Now and then a movement was seen through the windows of the courthouse, but the Death Watch did not shift its position.

At four o'clock it was evident that Sims would soon be led out. Three hundred soldiers and police had gathered in Court Square and the streets around, and some of them were forming a hollow before the courthouse. Only a few minutes later, Marshal Devan appeared in the door, and Sims was with him. They came down the steps hurriedly, and the marshal motioned Sims to take his place within the hollow. The signal of march was quickly given, and as silently as six hundred feet could move, they started down Court Street.

The quiet and ghostly group on State Street watched them pass and then fell in behind the soldiers, bearing the coffin and the shrouded flag. Down State Street they went, past Faneuil Hall where the company of militia had been drawn up, down as far as the Long Wharf where the Georgia ship lay tugging at its hawser. It was dawn now. Sims could be clearly seen. Someone said that his face was wet with tears. They watched him. He seemed to hesitate for a moment, then he stepped onto the deck. A shout went up from the boat. The hawser was released. In the cold dawn breeze the jibs fluttered slowly. Presently the boat began to move.

Above the flapping sails, the creaking ship, a voice from the Death Watch could be heard. The Reverend Mr. Foster was saying a prayer.

As his voice fell silent, other voices quickly rose, and across the soldiers' heads, across the still harbor, they sent their song to soar and linger.

> From many a Southern river
> And field of sugar cane,
> They call us to deliver,
> Their land from slavery's chain.

Thus Massachusetts was brought to justice. The owners of Sims publicly thanked, through the medium of a Boston newspaper, the merchants who had been "conspicuous in their efforts to serve us," and beat Sims publicly when he reached Savannah.

Yet Marshal Devans, who had also served them, could not sleep at night. Three times he tried to buy Sims back. He offered finally $1,800 for him. But Sims was not for sale. Sims was the slavocracy's triumph over the state of Garrison, the sinkhole of Abolition.

Antislavery was at a pitch of indignation. The outrage to Boston, the stealth with which Sims had been returned to slavery, the armed forces which protected the slavecatchers must be answered in a stinging and incontrovertible manner. It was not enough that bells had tolled on the morning when Sims sailed back to slavery. It was not enough that two days later Judge Loring who had returned him to slavery could find no one to accept his "blood money" when he went to market. There must be no mistake in anyone's mind that Massachusetts stood for freedom. If the slavocracy could understand one blow better than another, then Massachusetts would administer whatever that blow might be. If it must be repudiation of Daniel Webster, still Massachusetts would not hesitate.

Webster was unprepared for this. He expected Massachusetts to sustain his fight for the Union. Fight for the Union, indeed! Death and destruction, horrors untold, the clank of chains and the rattle of padlocks—was that the way to fight for the Union? When the bells of New England rang out the election of Charles Sumner to fill the seat of Daniel Webster in the Senate of the United States, Webster knew that he had his answer. "The papers are ringing with Sumner! Sumner! and guns are thundering out their triumph," Longfellow wrote, stirred out of his contemplative detachment.

They sized Sumner up the day he took his seat in the Senate, men turning to stare frankly at him as he eased his huge frame into the chair that had held Webster so comfortably. Some said he was the handsomest man in Congress, others talked about his naïveté, his ingenuousness, his lack of humor. Few of them came straight to the fact that antislavery was stronger because he was there.

The Washington to which he came was a sloppy, dusty, overgrown village, where slavery was dragged as a bargaining agent from Senator's office to Senator's office, a city of eccentrics, dupes and honest men, of scientific splendor—the Smithsonian lectures were unprecedented in the country—but of doubtful intellectual grandeur, of chicanery, drunkenness and brawling, of dazzling receptions and décolleté women, of swordsticks, leaded canes, and flashing cloaks, of blasted hopes, and ambitions still cherished, where the most brilliant salon was held by an Abolitionist and the most popular Senator was an antislavery man.

It was a strange world to Sumner, who had had sufficient money to avoid both the eccentric and the opportunistic. Brilliant men and exhibitionists he had known in Boston and in Europe; women he was afraid of; swordsticks and swinging capes were uncongenial to his temperament; men did not go often to the Gamaliel Baileys' salons, they sent their women instead, and Sumner had no woman to send. But he nodded when Hale said that their soirees were as witty and striking as any outside of Paris, and that they did an incalculable amount of good for the Abolition cause since the best doctrines can sometimes be most effectively administered under candlelight.

Sumner's colleague from Massachusetts was "Honest John" Davis, and he gave his opinion of this world into which Sumner had moved in five pithy words, "At Washington, slavery rules everything." Sumner had no party, for the coalition that had elected him was bound to split before the next election came around; he had no genuine following, for Abolitionists had seen too many failures to regard his inexperience with any premature enthusiasm. His enemies were prepared to blister him if he gave all his devotion to antislavery agitation or to call him a demagogue if he fought for other issues as well.

He made his first speech five weeks after he had taken office. He demanded the repeal of the Fugitive Slave Law. Webster stood in the Senate Chamber that day and listened with his dark eyes snapping under the massive dome of his forehead. When he turned away, he was never seen again in the Senate.

Within a year, Sumner was the most hated man in Washington. He was the very incarnation of the antislavery conscience.

There was no quiescence now in the antislavery ranks. A dismaying wakefulness was everywhere apparent. George Thompson—denounced as a "foreign agent"—was making a triumphant tour through the East, sitting on platforms with fugitive slaves, shaking the hands of large crowds. The old antislavery harmony and enthusiasm were blooming. Garrison, joining Thompson on his tour, found all the halls of New York and Brooklyn closed to him, but the upper counties of the state full of shouting enthusiasts. The same quality of enthusiasm spread straight across the country, ebbing and flowing in the cities, at full crest in the small towns, finding a peak in Iowa where many of the state's most respectable men were station keepers on the Underground Railroad.

It was hardly surprising then that a harried government should order out the marines and raise the cry of "treason!" after the Christiana riot, for to the unhappy lawmakers, nothing that had happened in the long story of the slavery fight was more alarming than this bloody defiance of the law. Christiana bound within itself the brutal despairs of the enslaved and the enslaving. Christiana lay within the very orbit of oppression, in the southern section of Pennsylvania, near the Maryland border where kidnapers kept an unsleeping watch and communities of Negroes never let their eyelids close.

For some days in September settlers had felt apprehension like geese walking over their graves. Strange peddlers had been passing back and forth, asking questions, smiling, full of gossip—*spies*. William Parker was a leader among the Negroes. He was valuable to the slavocracy. His sister-in-law begged him to escape. All he said was, "If a fight occurs I want the whites to keep away. They have a country and may obey the laws. We have no country."

One evening the Philadelphia Vigilance Committee sent word to be on guard. Federal agents were on their way with slaveholders to seize fugitives held by William Parker. William Parker was concealing no fugitives, but he and his neighbors propped guns against the door.

The slaveowners stole up on the house at dawn, and the Negro sentry raised the alarm. "Get out of my house," Parker advised Marshal Kline, but the marshal called instead for straw to set around the house. From an upstairs window, Parker's wife sent out across the misty fields a cry from a conch shell and colored neighbors, fastening their belts, their shoes untied, slipped into the house with guns across their shoulders.

Daylight brightened. The slaveowner, Gorsuch, and his son looked at the Negroes as they appeared one by one at the upper window, and agreed that none of them were their fugitives. But William Parker was, after all, more important than fugitives. Two Quakers passed by at this moment, Castner Hanaway and Elijah Lewis, and Kline called out to them to join his constabulary. They called back that blood would be shed if he attacked innocent men. He swore at them and at that moment Edward Gorsuch shouted out a warning. Parker and four friends appeared to be escaping. Kline drew his pistol and motioned his men to close in around the house.

When the morning was half over, Edward Gorsuch lay dead on the ground and Dickerson his son was dying close by. Kline had taken refuge in the field, and the Negroes, some with flesh wounds, some with holes in their sleeves or trousers, had scattered into hiding. The wounded white man was carried to a Quaker neighbor's, the wounded black men were not seen again.

The fight was a nine-day horror in Washington. Marines arrived to bring order to the deathly quiet of the battlefield; special constables beat the neighborhood far and wide for fugitives and armed settlers. The quiet neighborhood became the most conspicuous place in the United States that night. The Abolitionists were dumb in their dismay at bloodshed and their expectation of reprisals.

Around Christiana the excitement grew as the days passed and constabulary rounded up as many colored suspects as they could comfortably house, and arrested in addition Castner Hanaway and Elijah Lewis. If the law could not be made to fit the crime, then the crime would be adjusted in accordance.

At their trial and the trial of a score or more of Negroes, "treason" was the charge. "Treason," said Thaddeus Stevens, with high scorn, as he faced the district attorney, the attorney general of Lancaster County, the attorney general of Maryland and a civil attorney retained by the government. "Treason—levying war against the United States: Do the facts sustain the charge? That two non-resisting Quakers and thirty-eight wretched Negroes armed with corn-cutters, clubs and a few muskets, headed by a miller in a felt hat without coat or arms, levied war against the United States? Blessed be God, our Union had survived such a shock."

The tide began to turn. People frankly wondered how much justice was represented in the trial and how much retribution for the failure of slave catching. Friends began to trickle into the prison to shake the hands of the prisoners, to bring them comforts and advice. Roberts, one of the marshals set to guard the prisoners, made no effort to conceal his sympathies. When two Negro prisoners, who had been identified as among the fugitives sought by the Gorsuchs, were suddenly missing, no one said aloud that Roberts had put them on the Underground Railroad but no one took the trouble to speculate on other ways and means.

The trial was highly important. The slavocracy pinned much hope to it. If resistance to slave catchers could be established as treason against the government, the day of the fugitive slave might be at an end. The effort was sanguine, but without the chief culprits—Parker and his two neighbors—the case of the slavocracy was visibly weakened. And those three were unproducible for the simple reason that, some time before, they had passed through the hands of Frederick Douglass in Rochester who could have, had he been so minded, introduced the gun which killed Gorsuch. Since Parker's absence left so large a hole in the case, they should not have offered as their first defendant Castner Hanaway. The disintegration of the case against him took place before the eyes of all. When the evidence had been presented, there was very little for an honest judge to do but charge the jury in a manner that was hardly in keeping with the indictment. It took the jury twenty minutes to say "not guilty." Additional indictments of riot and murder were ignored by a later grand jury, and the district attorney declined the responsibility of putting the other prisoners on trial. They all went out of the prison unexpectedly, shakingly, free.

It was, without question, a defeat for the proponents of the law. They did not conceal their chagrin. And yet no antislavery success was ever a matter of blind rejoicing. It struck at the heart, and alarmed with the question of a next time.

The struggle was now identified in clear round terms. The Abolitionists said the slavocracy must be defeated. A year had passed since the law became effective, and the government had been flouted with humiliating regularity. When catcalls and hisses had shocked the ears of Webster at Syracuse, he had cried, "This law ought to be obeyed and it will be enforced—yes, it shall be enforced, and that too, in the midst of the next antislavery convention, if then there shall be any occasion to enforce it."

How simple to manufacture such an occasion! When was the next large antislavery gathering? In October the Liberty party held a convention; Gerrit Smith was there and Samuel J. May and all the stalwart lawbreakers of upper New York state.

Fillmore had made the same vow as Webster, and every Southern Congressman had determined that these Abolitionists must be crushed. How blindly they selected their course! Where Boston had its proslavery merchants and shipping men, Syracuse had its liberty-loving tradesmen, and the shocks of the last year had shaken them into a wariness and militancy that must have been evident enough even to blind government agents.

The convention came to order one morning, adjourned for the noon recess, and delegates went off to dinner. Just as they were rising from their tables, a bell rang. The bell of that particular Congregational

Church would ring at this strange hour for only one reason—a fugitive was in danger.

It must have been an interesting phenomenon to see how quickly the convention delegates arrived! Hats clapped to heads, skirts gathered about ankles, several thousand feet pounding up the street, they made for the commissioner's office.

How the word could have spread so quickly was a marvel to the commissioners. Before the first questions were asked of Jerry, the courthouse was surrounded. Free Negroes, fugitives, white men and their women-folk, children, were shouting, dogs were barking, the city was in an uproar. A native said that no such excitement had ever before been known in Syracuse. Reinforcements arrived by the moment, for Syracuse had her Abolition honor to defend.

The Vigilance Committee set to work immediately. The rumor spread that Jerry had put up a terrible fight when seized. They could apparently depend on him. Gerrit Smith, large and dignified, took the arm of Samuel Ringgold Ward and led the way to a conference room. The crowd outside the courthouse had not been overlooked; it would be used.

That evening, as dusk came down and the street lamps were lighted, the sound of many voices was still rising to the room where Jerry, bleeding from half staunched wounds, heard the automatic voice of the commissioner following the prescribed course of the law. The commissioner wondered if that crowd would never go away. He and the counsels left the courtroom. Jerry was safe on the second floor. Perhaps they did not notice that a number of buggies were standing along the curb, each drawn by a white horse. If they saw them they did not apparently look twice. Midnight came.

Packet's Landing was on the canal, but not near enough the courthouse to attract attention. Yet the quietness of two thousand men was remarkable. Charles Wheaton's store stood near Packet's Landing, and Wheaton had promised to provide arms to the extent of his stock of iron bars and axes. Jo Norton—our hero of the Washington Underground Railroad—was at their head when they began to filter into the street opposite the courthouse. He had a crowbar in his hand, and several of his colored friends walked as lightly as men could who bore a log twenty feet long. Jo gave the signal and the battering ram was thrust against the courthouse door. The door sprang open. Jo rushed first up the stairs and pounded with his crowbar against an inner door. He broke it down, but the marshal's bullet, which was fired at him the moment the door fell in, glazed his head. A moment later the marshal's broken arm hung at his side. Jo rushed on with his crowbar. The others, filling the stairs, caught the deputies before they could defend themselves. The marshal jumped some thirteen feet out of the window and escaped in the darkness up the towpath of the canal.

Jerry was found in chains on the floor of his cell. Thrust into one of the carriages drawn by white horses, he was driven off, zigzagging through the dark streets, while the other buggies and their white horses drove quickly out of the city in different directions so that the confused pursuers could only wish that the devil would explain the multiplicity of white horses. The silent army, which had gathered and was not needed, slipped away as quietly and as quickly as possible.

Jerry stayed in hiding until his wounds had healed and clothing been provided. Then, by relays of fast horses, he was taken by night to Oswego and again concealed. When a suitable ship's captain was found, he was taken across the lake to Kingston.

Twenty-four respectable citizens of Syracuse, including the Reverend Mr. Loguen, Samuel May and Charles Wheaton, not to mention Gerrit Smith, a visitor, were indicted for "constructive" treason. The charge of treason had not worked before, but the idea was still interesting. When the arrested men went to Auburn where the district attorney had ordered them for questioning, nearly a hundred well-mannered citizens of Syracuse, men and women, accompanied them. When bond was demanded for them, William Seward was the first to sign the note.

"I have seen that it was necessary to bring the people into direct conflict with the government," May wrote to Garrison, "that the government may be made to understand that it has transcended its limits . . . As far as I can learn, twenty-five persons have been indicted, twelve of them colored men, all but three of whom have escaped to Canada; and four of the white men have also gone thither . . ."

The case for treason, after a year, fell through, and a Jerry anniversary was celebrated in Syracuse until the Civil War. It was a sentimental occasion in the best tradition, but it was also a reaffirmation that "such abuses . . . the people could not, would not tolerate."

Faced by the guns of deputies and commissioners, Abolitionists were coming to believe that force alone would end slavery. The war was being carried into the enemy's country. It is our duty, they now said, to go into the South and negotiate the escape of the slaves.

How much Harriet Tubman was responsible for this change of attitude must always remain in the agreeable realms of speculation. One can say only that those who knew her—and by 1852 she was an eagerly watched figure in Abolition circles—never recovered from the spell of her heavy rolling voice, her sharp brilliant eyes, her continual iteration, "Mah people mus' go free."

She had escaped in the summer of 1849, and it took the Maryland slaveowners only a comparatively short time to realize that with her went a large measure of their peace of mind. She had begun to brood herself and her people out of slavery eighteen years before when, a spindly, stupid-looking little Negro girl, she had sat on a rail fence and nursed a head broken by a drunken white man and told herself over and over, "Mah people *are* goin' t' be free."

One night the cabins heard her singing—she was a woman now and her master set her price high—

> When dat ar ole chariot comes
> Ah'm gwine t' lebe ye,
> Ah'm boun' for de promised lan'.

They talked about that singing for a long time, for the next morning Harriet had disappeared.

They did not hear from her again; no secret message came back such as fugitives sometimes sent, no token that she was still alive, until a year had passed. Then one night a cabin door swung open and a Maryland slave started to his feet. "It's me," a familiar voice said from under a wide-brimmed man's hat, "Harriet. It's time to go No'th."

Within a few months, there was no cabin within the distance of walking that did not know of "Moses" who came at night and left before morning and took with her another bale of "black wool."

When the lights blazed in the plantation house and visitors relieved the long monotony of the days with a dance, or when the warm night lay over the fields and the master sat on the veranda and smoked his pipe, some of the slave cabins might be lying still as death, obeying "Moses'" message to "be ready." These messages came in many ways, some in letters to elderly slaves, signed in the name of a son or a daughter and worded so cryptically that even the master could make nothing from the mention of the "good ship Zion," soon to arrive, and the faithful who would board her; some by those spirituals which carried hidden meanings to the slaves. Some seemed to come by telepathy, for one night a slave would shiver and speak of "Moses" and make his preparations, and true as the coming of dusk, a knock would sound on his cabin door and there would be Harriet, hidden by the darkness.

Her own flight had set the pattern for the future, the long dangerous future that stretched through the Civil War and included nineteen raids over the border. It had led her, hungry, frightened, through swamps and thickets, and up to the doors of friendly houses, selected, it seemed, only by her profound intuition.

Her returns to Maryland were always made when she had saved enough of her wages to be able to sustain the deeply spiritual conviction of freedom that burned in her heart and soul. She never had time to coach her comrades in more than the bare essentials of escape—obedience, silence, promptness. She had the strength to lift a man in her arms and run with him if he did not move quickly enough to hide himself from danger, she had the sharp intelligence that met every emergency —and proof lay in the fact that in her nineteen raids over the border which brought over three hundred slaves to freedom she never lost a fugitive or allowed an enemy to lay a hand on her. She had the ruthless courage, too, that enabled her to carry a pistol wherever she went and threaten to use it if any of her friends showed timidity or a desire to escape from unfamiliar terrors to the terrors which they knew. A finger around the trigger and a calm, "Dead Negroes tell no tales" was all that was ever needed. The sound of a horse galloping in the dark meant a quick concealment by the side of the road, the cry of a slave baby meant an extra dose of paregoric so that it lay in a stupor in its mother's arms. Hiding in potato holes, in slave cabins when dangers seemed too close, fighting the painful and terrifying embraces of swamps, beyond everything dominating the feelings of those fugitives whom she had chosen, four times out of five, because of their tenderness and inability to cope with slavery, called for wits keener than a scythe.

She usually chose a Saturday night for the start of her "train," because a day would then intervene before a runaway advertisement could appear. Her routes varied. Sometimes she went west toward the mountains, again she struck off in the direction of Wilmington where her good friend Thomas Garrett was always waiting for her. Nothing was prearranged. She had to be prepared to make any adjustment. If food was not available, if danger called for scouting, she would hide her charges under a haystack, in a wood, by a swamp and do her reconnoitering.

Her wits never failed her. She acted by faith and intuition. On one occasion, riding north on a train, she heard her name spoken. Frozen with fear, she looked under the edge of her sunbonnet up the long body of the passenger who stood beside her and saw that his eyes were fixed on an advertisement which he was reading aloud. A runaway slave named Harriet Tubman was worth the incredible reward of $5,000. She did not raise her head again until she reached the next station.

There she took a train going south, knowing that a Negro woman going south as fast as the wheels could turn was above suspicion. She went to the town near her old home, bought a pair of live fowls, and crooking her back and bending her knees hobbled down the street, past—in the best tradition of stories—her old master who never saw in the bent, sunbonneted old woman, trying to control her struggling birds, the instrument of some perverse justice who had already run off with close to $50,000 worth of slaves. The old crone remained until the hue and cry blew over.

As far as she was concerned a single explanation took care of all such miracles. "I always tole God, I'm gwine to hole stiddy on to you, an' you've got to see me trou."

By 1852, her friends stretched up the long unseen line of the Underground Railroad. Seward knew her and "a nobler, higher spirit, or a truer, seldom dwells in human form." In the Emerson home, in the Alcott home, in the home of Horace Mann she was a welcome guest as often as she would come. On antislavery platforms she was irresistible, with her rolling words, colorful and biting.

It took her some time after the passing of the law to realize that her charges were no longer safe once she had delivered them to Wilmington or Philadelphia. All right then—Canada it would be. For herself she was utterly unafraid—but she felt no ease for her charges until she had set them on that bridge that ran from slavery across the Niagara River into freedom.

The reward for her capture mounted to $40,000. The wonder grew when people learned that because of the piece of iron which had hurt her head as a child, she would often lose consciousness at unexpected moments—in the middle of a sentence perhaps. She never knew where or when it would come upon her. Her head would nod for a minute or two, then up she would jerk it and resume her sentence where she had left it off or finish the action she had started. Why was she not lost at times like that? Maybe she was right. "Jes so long as He wants to use me, He'll take keer of me, and when He don't want me no longer, I'm ready to go."

By this time the Underground Railroad was one of the greatest powers in the country. It touched only a small per cent of the slaves in the South but it made slave property insecure and it allowed no slave master to relax. Nowhere did it function more effortlessly than in Philadelphia.

William Still, a free-born colored man, was secretary of an active committee, the work of which was as simple as it was unforeseen. It must be prepared at any time during the day or night to receive fugitives, passed on by station keepers farther to the south, it must be able to anticipate and to meet whatever the need of the fugitive—clothes, rest, food, disguises, or railway tickets. The closest possible contact was maintained with the underground lines of Harrisburg, Wilmington, and all other towns which stood at a converging point. The committee also subscribed to the Baltimore *Sun*, every issue of which was priceless to the cause of freedom, since its fugitive slave advertisements were the best of the upper South. In addition, it notified slaves, brought into the city by their owners, that they were by state-law free.

The ears of committee members were magnets for information from friends and enemies. When a letter, addressed to a Philadelphia slave catcher, was dropped by mistake into a slot in the *Philadelphia Ledger* office instead of into the United States mailbox, the newspaper clerk who came upon it opened it promptly, and without complicating fuss, delivered it to the Vigilance Committee. The letter was from a Maryland lady, then visiting in Philadelphia, who requested the well-known slave agent Mr. Alberti to call on her and discuss the reclamation of her fugitive slave. Strategy was obviously the answer. Without ado, Mr. Cyrus Whitson of the committee went, complete in his fine big whiskers, to call on the lady. He introduced himself as an associate of Mr. Alberti who had been sent to transact whatever business she might have. "But, madam, by no means must this matter leak out; if it does, the damned Abolitionists—pardon—may ruin me." She assured him that she wanted no publicity either, and gave him without delay the name, height, weight, age, and color of her runaway.

It took him five minutes to return to the committee rooms, and only a few minutes more to notify the fugitive, who was known to them and was employed not far away. James McKim, meanwhile, was composing a poster which, as soon as it came from the printer's hands, was plastered in many parts of the city, giving the name of the Maryland lady and her business in Philadelphia, as well as the names of two other slaveowners then in the city, and warning any interested parties to keep clear of these people.

Having made sure of the fugitive's safety in Philadelphia, the next task was to get him safely on the long road that eventually led to Canada. The most important route out of Philadelphia ran to Jersey City and New York. Once across the Camden River the fugitives were taken to a house in Burlington known as Station A; there they changed horses and pushed on to Station B at Bordentown. New Brunswick was their next destination, where they stopped to consult with Cornelius

Cornell, a station keeper, on the slave catching situation, since the Raritan River near which four roads came together, was a favorite spot for those enterprising business men. If the Raritan road was clear, they headed straight for Rahway, fresh horses, and a clear road to Jersey City. In Jersey City they were usually turned over to a Quaker named John Everett, who brought them as skillfully as possible through their next danger point, the ferry to New York, where more slave catchers loitered to watch for black faces. Sometimes the Jersey City ferry meant a narrow escape, but invariably Everett brought them safely to the Forty-second Street Station—now Grand Central—where tickets were bought for Syracuse.

In the records of the committee, written by William Still and kept locked in the loft of Lebanon Seminary, was included as detailed an account as possible of every fugitive who passed through their hands. The reasons for escape seldom varied—the death of kind masters and a fear of the future, a realization of their own value in terms of hire, excessive cruelty, separation of families.

When blond, white-complexioned fugitives appeared, they were aided as readily as any others. Perhaps they had some Negro blood, or perhaps they were examples of those thousands who were said to be held in bondage, although pure Anglo-Saxon. Occasionally one of the thousands would take his claim to court and win his freedom, as the celebrated Salome Muller of Louisiana did by proving that, as a Dutch emigrant child, she had been kidnaped and sold into slavery; or fail to win his freedom as happened with the red-haired Louisiana slave who spoke with an Irish brogue. These white fugitives had the easiest time of all, since their movements attracted little attention and their value to their masters, because of their disconcerting fairness, was too low to offer large rewards.

By 1852 much of the fire that had been set to blaze when the law first agitated the country had subsided and the tasks of the "railroad" increased. Only to the faithful was the agitation as fresh as ever. Dark days meant nothing. They had known them before. "I believe in the twenty million," Phillips said, "they will arrange this question which politicians have sought to keep out of sight. When the nation sees that the interests of a class only are subserved by human bondage, then the change will come. It is a great thing to keep alive a protest. The anti-slavery cause does not seem to move; but like the shadow on the dial it gets to twelve o'clock at last."

These were the days when liberty was being fulsomely praised by the anti-Abolitionists. Men like the Hungarian Kossuth made it fashionable. Garrison was enraged, and Abolitionists spoke in private and in public with stinging irony about the unspeakable, incomprehensible fact that their slavery-tainted government had offered a ship of the Mediterranean squadron to bring the fugitive Kossuth to the United States. How it loved liberty!

Kossuth, escaping from his own country, was the very symbol of oppressed manhood. At what point did Kossuth differ from their fugitives? How great a man was Kossuth? Was he "strictly local, territorial, national," as Garrison maintained? American, Scotch, English, Irish Abolitionists had given their share to the Hungarian Fund. Now who was going to tell Kossuth about American freedom? The slaveholders in Washington who had offered him the ship? "Save him," Henry Wright wrote to Haughton, the Irish Abolitionist in Dublin. "Tell him of American slavery." The British Abolitionists needed no prodding. They knew as well as the Americans the vast moral influence of so celebrated a fugitive, with his name ringing through Europe and on the lips of every workingman and liberal in the western world. They did everything they could. They sent him protestations to stay away from the United States and make public his reasons for doing so. They begged him, if he went, not to forfeit the respect of European lovers of liberty by ignoring the monstrosity of slavery. From all sides the bombardment continued.

Three weeks later Garrison wrote, "The die is cast. All speculation is now at an end as to the position Kossuth means to maintain on the slavery question. He means to be deaf, dumb and blind in regard to it. Oh, this is pitiable!"

Garrison's words were echoed in the dismay of American liberals. The noble Kossuth who had fought like a tiger for his own country's freedom had been caught in the murky trap of American politics. Through the eyes of Abolitionists, Kossuth's stature shrank to the level of the men who feted him. They quoted his politic speeches as he made a triumphant tour through Pennsylvania and Maryland where bills preventing the entrance of free Negroes were then before the legislature, through Kentucky where Calvin Fairbanks was being sentenced to his second prison term for underground activities (fifteen years this time), into Mississippi and Alabama where he pleaded again for support of national independence. Coming at last to Boston he spoke with some wit of his anomolous position, of his effort to balance himself to the satisfaction of all men for the sake of Hungary. But to the Abolitionists unless a man represented universal freedom, he represented nothing. And they were right. On the issue of slavery there was no "perhaps" or "maybe." The moral persuasion of Kossuth had failed, but his failure, they felt sure, would be seen as quickly by the revolutionists of Hungary, France and Italy, by the workingmen of England, Ireland and Scotland, by the insurrectionists of Germany and Russia as it was by the Abolitionists of the United States. And with these men of a larger world lay their moral strength.

After all they did not need Kossuth. Oh, how little did they need him! He was on a ship going down the Mississippi that day in March when their champion appeared, and from that moment Kossuth took a second place with the people of the United States. A small, shy, impractical woman with no experience outside her home, did what Kossuth had failed to do. Harriet Beecher Stowe took the antislavery fight into the homes of the lovers of freedom, of the poor and the oppressed, all over the world.

## Chapter 7

## "THE IRREPRESSIBLE CONFLICT"

MANY good Abolitionists could have told you about the serial which had been running in Gamaliel Bailey's *National Era* for almost a year after Garrison had rejected it for *The Liberator*. It had drawn many families about the lamps on the evening when the paper was delivered. Yet, in spite of its popularity, the book publisher, sharing no doubt the dubiety of many Abolitionists, agreed to issue it only if Mrs. Stowe would accept a cash settlement in advance.

Within twenty-four hours, three thousand copies had been sold. Within three weeks the figures mounted to twenty thousand. It spread across the country like a wave.

People knew of slavery, of course—south some place. Many towns had never seen a fugitive. Slavery was a moribund topic. The compromise had laid it to rest forever. But this— This book ——!

Men who had not read a book in years propped up their feet on their grocery counters and settled their spectacles. Women neglected their washing and the darning of stockings. Who was this Mrs. Stowe, they began to ask? Did she know what she was writing about? How do we know that our hearts are not being wantonly torn? They learned about her bit by bit. She had lived in Cincinnati. She had often visited the "Selby" plantation in Kentucky. She had friends among the slaveholders. She knew that many were kind and loved their slaves. People were reassured by this tolerance. But kind masters died—that was what Mrs. Stowe wished to say—or fell into debt. Of course—Eliza. Then there really had been an Eliza? And an Uncle Tom? And a Topsy? And a Simeon Halliday? Surely not a Simon Legree! Yes, little Eva, every woman knew there was a little Eva, and every young woman was sure of a St. Clair. Cassy was too dreadful; she of course was not real, and it was a little surprising that such a lady as Mrs. Stowe would conjure up such a person.

By the end of the eleventh week Mrs. Stowe knew she was a famous woman and must substantiate the heartbreak that one hundred thousand people in the United States had felt; that by the end of September, five hundred thousand people in England had felt. So she told how the Underground Railroad had run through her Cincinnati home, bearing some of her characters to her; she told about the other characters and how she had learned of them. The little boy "Harry" had lived in her home, and had been spirited away with his mother by that dreamy sweet man, Professor Stowe, when the slave catchers were close at hand. Like "Senator Bird," Professor Stowe and his brother-in-law, Charles, had driven painfully through the mud of a wet spring night to the home of that celebrated John Van Zandt whose subsequent conflict with the law made Abolition history. Mrs. Stowe described her meeting with "Uncle Tom." The great black slow-speaking Josiah Henson, in Boston on a mission from his institute in Canada, told her of his father who, with his ear nailed to a post, had been beaten into stupefaction, of his mother, sold to another master. He confirmed the story of Eliza and her husband—he knew them well in Canada. Eliza had died in Oberlin. Her husband, who might have passed for a white man, traveled and lectured with Henson.

As for Simeon Halliday—she did not need to go into that. Any Abolitionist in Ohio could have explained that if Simeon Halliday had not been called Levi Coffin in the book it was to spare the latter's Quaker modesty. Legree? Brother Charles had written her letters of Red River horrors when he was traveling through the Mississippi country. He had met that Yankee monster whose name became Legree. He had grown to know the people of the Red River neighborhood. What they told him he had taken down in shorthand and sent to Harriet. Any rich young man of New Orleans or Charleston could have been St. Clair, worn to a fine decadence by the refined savagery of the life around him, and that same young man would have been able to explain Cassy without the slightest wonderment. The Cassys were a part of New Orleans' fashionable life where the easy mingling of the races survived from the days of French rule, where quadroon mistresses were fashionable, and most unmarried young gentlemen had an establishment presided over by the voluptuous beauty of a quadroon or octoroon.

It was all true, Mrs. Stowe maintained, and every underground worker, every Abolitionist, every disillusioned Southern tongue agreed. She had written it because she knew that it was true, because she had taken her oath that she would write something to make the "whole nation feel what an accursed thing is slavery" as news filtered through to her Maine home of the horrors that came in the wake of the Fugitive Slave Law. She was an ingenuous woman. She believed that she could touch the hearts of slaveowners. Had she not shown that the evil lay at deeper levels than individual guilt? "Your book is going to be the great pacification; it will unite the North and South," a friend had written her, and she believed it. She had spoken the truth out of the mouth of her Southern friends.

For one hundred thousand copies she believed her dream was coming true. The South was accepting the book. Their bruised feelings were soothed by this generous acknowledgment of their kindlier natures. Then the storm descended. Into the chorus of praise, into the benign horror of the North and the waiting quiet of the South, two attacks appeared almost simultaneously The irony of their sources showed the nonterritorial aspects of proslavery sentiment. *The London Times*, admitting that the book was a skillful and moving work in spite of their personal dislike of Uncle Tom, dropped this heavy caution: "Its object is to abolish slavery. Its effect will be to render slavery more difficult than ever of abolishment. . . . Let us have no more *Uncle Tom's Cabins* engendering ill-will, keeping up bad blood and rendering well-disposed, humane but critically placed men their own enemies and the blocks to civilization and to the spread of the glad tidings from heaven." Three weeks later the *New York Observer*, equally concerned about "the glad tidings from heaven," shocked the Christ-loving Mrs. Stowe by accusations that must have opened her eyes to the extraordinary cynicism of these lovers of the status quo. "We have read the book and regard it as anti-Christian. . . . We have marked numerous passages in which religion is spoken of in terms of contempt. . . . Mrs. Stowe labors through all her book· to render ministers odious and contemptible by attributing to them sentiments unworthy of men or Christians." The imagination was not strained to see two sides of the same medal—the conservative who counseled moderation, the reactionary who magnified the non-essential to conceal the essential. They were the two hands of the slavocracy. Upon the heads of Mrs. Stowe and patient, trusting Uncle Tom the vials of wrath descended.

From Maryland to Mississippi these critiques were published. The ecstasy of the Southern press was unbounded. Their hands had been tied as long as the tolerance of the book was the object of general praise. But now with the endorsement of two nonslaveholding authorities, they were able to clear their records. The rage of all who were afraid of change, who were the exploiters and the oppressors in an age of world-wide struggle, built itself to a crescendo.

And meanwhile eight presses were running day and night to meet the demand for the book. For all practical purposes one may say that it appeared everywhere. To the friends of freedom it brought a painful joy, to the intellectuals and progressives, the revolutionists and the workingmen it spoke a universal tongue. So stirred were the Italian working classes by *Il Zio Tom* that the Vatican placed it upon its Index "as subversive of established authority." *Caban F' Ewythr Twm* appeared among the Welsh miners. In Hungary three translations were published within five years. In France, Sweden, Germany, England, it was praised by the intellectuals as a great work of art. In Poland, India, Bengal, Siam, Arabia, Armenia, Russia, Persia, Japan, China—twenty-two nations in all—it came as glad tidings to the poor and the oppressed.

Within the year, one and a half million copies had been sold in Great Britain and her colonies. Mrs. Stowe's arrival in England, where she had gone somewhat reluctantly to face her admirers, became a mammoth demonstration. Crowds met her at the boat, crowds lined the street when it was known she would appear, crowds choked the entrance to her lodgings. Everywhere the common people brought her their admiration— Scottish shepherds, millworkers, dock hands, clerks and housewives. Public men of England, still aglow with the social reforms that were slowly penetrating English life, acclaimed her book as a great document of human society. The Earl of Shaftesbury, Lord Carlisle, the Duchess of Sutherland gave vast receptions for the mild and slightly bewildered author who had sent them copies of her book for the purely altruistic purpose of exerting pressure on influential people at a time when there was danger that Canada would be closed against the fugitives. She had also sent a copy to Prince Albert, and Prince Albert had persuaded the Queen to read it, and the Queen expressed a desire to meet Mrs. Stowe. The continued sanctuary of Canada did not depend on the action of any single person, but the fact remains that no further discussion was heard barring the fugitive from his only haven.

Everything was going into the antislavery mill as it never had before. The years were full of changing values. Garrison, setting out on another Western tour, had his ears close to the hearts of the people. Not for him the world of money-making where the Astors and the Goelets were building huge fortunes from tracts of city land, where Samuel Colt was building a firearms fortune, and Nicholas Longworth, the richest man of the Middle West, was growing comfortably old; not for him the plutocrats of the iron foundries or the textile mills or the steam railways—although he spared them an occasional bitter word about wages and hours. No, his world ran straight and unswerving through the plain moral virtues of plain people. By these people, the cancer would be cut out, through them the second revolution would come. He freely called it revolution.

There seemed no other word strong enough to encompass the overturning that must come.

He saw and he heard everything that flew to roost on the Abolition perch: the growing influence of antislavery in local communities by the capturing of minor offices—school boards, town clerkships, magistracies; the widening, deeping struggle of the women suffragists, whose cause he had long ago espoused. Their fight was inextricably entangled with his own. Lucy Stone or Elizabeth Cady Stanton, lecturing wherever they could get a hearing, might talk nine times on Women's Rights, but the tenth time they would give to Abolition. Susan B. Anthony or Lucretia Mott, willing to convince audiences anywhere, might talk five times on Abolition and once on Women's Rights, but whatever the ratio both causes were strengthened. Dorothy Dix might be pleading up and down the country for the care of the insane, or Amelia Bloomer agitating against unhealthy petticoats; Emma Willard might be fighting for a freer education for women or Jane Swisshelm defying western mobs in order to gain an equal place for women journalists. Whatever it was, wherever they made their plea, every male Abolitionist knew that humiliation would be their meat, but most male Abolitionists also knew that human thought would be proportionately expanded and that all such expansion enlarged the hope of the slave.

Garrison encountered the full effect of this mental excitement when he reached the Middle West. The reviled Garrison was now a man received with evergreens twined to form his name. "A thousand people" came to his meetings in the larger towns.

What did he sense behind this? Certain things could hardly have escaped that persistent observation which sifted all things to the Abolition level. The unprecedented popularity of plays, for instance, which rang with proud words against Roman and Theban slavery, which made heroes of rebellious English serfs; the millions of voices raised to sing of the sad fate of "Darling Nelly Gray," whose beauty made her so desirable a slave; the hundreds of thousands of copies sold of all *Uncle Tom's* successors. Profits were the first sign of a change in public sentiment. Yet these intimations of freedom bore none of that living quality which caught and held men's admiration. Dr. Robert Mitchell of Indiana, Pennsylvania, had just paid $10,000 for the privilege of keeping fugitives on his farm. There was no play-acting about that. Negro lecturers were submitting to indignities and personal dangers. There was no extraneous drama here. Mrs. Frances Harper, the genteel and soft-voiced schoolteacher, and Sojourner Truth, the great gaunt sibyl who seemed the very soul of Africa were pleading for their race with profound effectiveness. Negro newspapers were exerting small but irrepressible voices amid a great din of hatred. Douglass and James McCune Smith were writing and lecturing at top speed, bearing most of the responsibilities that Garnet and Ward had left when they went abroad with the antislavery message. Negro Abolitionists had never been more persuasive. At the Convention which they called in Rochester in July, 1853, they flung out their protests with desperate urgency into a Northern world that was still enacting "black laws" against the colored population. Their protests were unequivocal against the Fugitive Slave Law—"the most cruel, unconstitutional and scandalous outrage of modern times"— against their disfranchisement, against the exclusion of their children from schools which they, as taxpayers, supported, against the social barriers which prevented them from learning trades. They missed no detail of segregation and prejudice and they offered full remedies for all of this, for "we are Americans, and as Americans we would speak to America."

When all these impulses of freedom-loving men and women came together, Garrison's work would be done. It was not hard to see portents of the end when the first blow of the Civil War was struck in Kansas.

Stephen Douglas was a tricky politician from the Middle West who understood all the sophistries and crudities of the game of politics and played them openly and without reluctance. The President's chair was the prize and the way to it lay with the man who could reckon most adroitly with the black issue of slavery. If, at the same time, he could sound a note which rang pleasantly in the North his work was done and all that remained were cheering crowds to greet the victor.

The air was still in 1854; slavery slept, manacled and bitter, dumb except for the whispers that came up the long line of underground routes, except for the flaming bursts of insurrection, quickly crushed. Yet slavery was essential to ambition. And Stephen Douglas found it a matter merely of bold aggression to do what Calhoun had only talked about, what Jefferson Davis had not dared.

Between the Missouri River and the Rocky Mountains lay land enough to form six states, land that was Indian territory, called Kansas and Nebraska. The man who gave that land to those most hungry for it would make his political fortune. There could be no hesitation, no caution, no reluctance to strike whatever blow was necessary. Men and their possessions were hungry for the land—immigrants pouring in from Europe, Yankees pushing out to the frontier, slaveowners sickening on the exhausted lands of the South.

A slaveowner's possessions were his Negroes. The significance of this penetrated slowly. Douglas spoke persuasively. Within those territories, essential to the expansion of two systems, the question of slavery would be decided by the settlers. The constitution it presented for statehood would decide the matter of freedom or slavery. Then such a question could be settled away from the end of a gun? Reasonable men were aghast. It passed their comprehension that a territory, shared by free-labor men and owners of slaves could ever be brought to statehood without a bloody struggle. Had they forgotten the Missouri Compromise? comforters inquired. Never! All that had stood between them and the aggressions of slavery had been the Missouri Compromise. Why then were they disturbed? These territories lay north of the line which, by the Constitution, divided freedom from slavery. Into the pregnant silence that fell, Douglas' answer came like a clap of doom. The Missouri Compromise must be repealed.

The North and the South were speechless. Where were they sleeping when this happened? The South regarded it first as a trick; only when the indignation of the North rose to a steady clamor did they accept the fact that the doughface Douglas had offered them a rich prize.

For four years the country had believed the professions of peace and unity which shaped the Compromises of 1850. The North came alive with public meetings. "Nebraska" was a louder cry than Texas had ever been— Nebraska and slavery. This time the antislavery leaders were not alone. With them were many of those conservatives who had fought for the Compromises. Slavery in the North! They were face to face with a monster which bore no relation to reality.

Memorials and protests beat in a torrent against Congress. Mrs. Stowe led eleven hundred women in protest, and the effigies of Douglas burned across the North. From New England came a petition signed by eighty per cent of the clergymen crying out against the proposed bill as a "great moral wrong, a measure full of danger to the peace and even the existence of our beloved Union."

Douglas and his colleagues were astonished. Moral indignation was an emotion for which they seldom took account. To Douglas, protests could only come from his enemies, from men who wished to curb his vaunting ambition. The petitions of the clergy, from New England, from the middle and the Western states, were received by him with the grossest language.

The fight wound itself out, taut and dangerous, through the early winter months. Party lines were broken. Opponents of the bill found strange friendships. But for Douglas there was no turning back. His own interests and investments, real estate, railroads—were brought too closely into his plans. And, moreover, the slavocracy was now roused to the great gift which lay so close at hand. Through the persuasions of the Secretary of War, Jefferson Davis, President Pierce was induced to throw the full measure of administration prestige and patronage behind the bill. In an age of brutal struggle, when politics were at their most sordid ebb, and fisticuffs were a popular device on the floor of Congress, the barroom manners of Mr. Douglas served him admirably.

The mass of Northern voters seemed to find no organized means of protest. So deeply had they been persuaded that the forensics and emotions of 1850 had settled the question of slavery extension, that beyond memorials and petitions they had no other weapons. They saw, as plainly as though it had dimensions, the great wedge that attempted to separate the free states of the East and West and give the Mississippi Valley to the slave power. They came by the hundreds to antislavery lectures for an answer. Garrison lecturing in New York, in New Jersey, in New England found himself in the role of spiritual adviser to those who had once called out the mobs against him.

But through it all ran a melancholy note. Richard Henry Dana, unpossessed by the prophetic fury of Garrison, seeing no issues larger than could be answered by a practical man of politics, wrote a three-quarter truth to John Jay. "All the Whigs express disapproval of the Nebraska Bill, but take no action. The Democrats differ and are paralyzed by the Executive. . . . We can have no effectual vent for opinion. This depresses and mortifies us to the extreme."

What was the remedy? Would there never be an answer more enduring than the guerrilla attacks of the antislavery men, the underground operators, the disciples of Garrison? In Boston a bitter and vociferous anti-Nebraska meeting was called at Faneuil Hall which the newspapers attempted to discredit. In New York, a workingman's mass meeting resolved that "capitalism and land speculation" had been well served by the bill and that their fight must now be directed against "both white and black slavery." In Milwaukee, Wisconsin, an honored and unmistakable method of protest was employed.

When two wagonloads of Federal officials seized a Negro fugitive named Joshua Glover in Racine, beat him into unconsciousness and rushed him off to Milwaukee, the courthouse bell rang with such insistence that a meeting larger than Racine had ever seen before gathered in the courthouse square. A single cry went with a beautiful ring through all the speeches and culminated in a resolution which declared that since the Senate had, through the Nebraska proposal, repealed all compromises, "we, as citizens of Wisconsin, are justified in declaring and *do declare, the slave-catching law of 1850 disgraceful and repealed!*" To suit their actions to their resolutions, one hundred citizens of Racine moved on to Milwaukee to officiate at this "repeal."

Milwaukians, equally aroused, had gathered, five thousand strong, to act upon their own resolutions, and the Racine delegation went with them to demand the delivery of Glover. When refused, they paused only long enough to appoint a Committee of Vigilance to see that Glover had a public trial if the large beam of wood which they planned to use did not serve its purpose.

But the beam, riding up to the jail door on the shoulders of the men, accomplished its purpose, and Glover, borne through the broken door, was flung into another wagon, and sent along the underground line to Waukesha and Racine.

The reactions to the Glover rescue were of more significance than the methods. The state sprang into life. Mass meetings in all the large towns voted thanks to the men of Racine and Milwaukee and denounced the Kansas-Nebraska machinations in Congress. Congratulations came from towns as far away as Syracuse, New York, and in many cities of the North the defiant words of the Racine resolution were caught up as their own. Mass meetings spun Wisconsin into violent activity when some of the rescuers were found guilty by the United States District Court after the state courts had refused to act, and solemn warnings were given that people of Wisconsin were willing to fight for their cause with guns. The Wisconsin courts defied all the thunderings of Chief Justice Taney and dared the Federal courts to prove the constitutionality of the Fugitive Slave Law, while the legislature passed resolutions in which "a positive defiance is urged as the 'rightful remedy'" against such Congressional wickedness as the Compromises of 1850.

The significance of the fight, the challenge to the Supreme Court and to all compromise measures, including that of Kansas and Nebraska, was not lost on an apathetic country, watching with unbelieving eyes the headlong course of Congress. The Missouri Compromise—it became a bulwark as sacred as the Constitution. If the Missouri Compromise could be set aside, then what assurance could one have that the slavocracy would ever stop its depredations? "Political action, political action," rose louder and clearer.

It is not surprising that the Abolitionists were cynical, but political action was the natural expression of Americans, and political action it became. At first it was sporadic. Wavering Free-Soilers, rebellious Whigs and anti-Nebraska Democrats attempted in one or two instances to come together long enough to capture local, off-year elections. But action—action so direct as to be unmistakable—came only from that same rebellious, unredeemed Wisconsin.

In Ripon, a meeting of rebels resolved that if the Kansas-Nebraska Bill were passed, old party organizations should be thrown to the winds and a new party organized on the sole issue of the nonextension of slavery. The name "Republican" was suggested. One of their organizers, writing to Horace Greeley, asked that mention be made of the meeting in the columns of the *Tribune,* for "the actors in this remote little eddy of politics thought at the time that they were making a bit of history by that solitary tallow candle in the little white school house on the prairie and whether ever recognized . . . they will think so still."

Petitions and memorials continued a steady assault. Douglas, swearing, sweating, was jamming his way through toward his ambitions. At five o'clock one morning, after seventeen hours of continuous debate, the Missouri Compromise was repealed and the Kansas-Nebraska territory was, for all practical purposes, thrown open to slavery.

To many Northerners the shock tore at the very roots of their national consciousness. The Compromises of 1850 were for all good purposes destroyed on the day that the Missouri Compromise was brought to an end. All the heartbreak, all the drama, all that the Abolitionists and the antislavery men had said again and again became, overnight, the watchword of a million men. The political excitement that was engendered on that day did not reach its climax until the swirling torchlights of triumphant Republicans proclaimed the election of Abraham Lincoln.

On May 22, "against the strongest popular remonstrances, against an unprecedented demonstration of religious sentiment—in subversion of plighted faith," the Nebraska Bill became law. Two days later, in Boston, the slavocracy was shown the temper of the North.

It was a normally quiet late afternoon and all over the city people were going homeward for their dinners. Anthony Burns, a Negro, who had only been in Boston for a month, locked his employer's store, and started up the street. Five minutes later a man across the way gave a signal to six men in a grog shop, and Anthony Burns was lifted off his feet, carried in their arms a few feet to the courthouse where a marshal with drawn sword motioned them hurriedly up the steps and closed the doors.

There had been no confusion; no one, apparently, had seen men running half a block. At nine o'clock the next morning Richard Dana, walking past the courthouse to his office heard his name called, and saw on the steps a gentleman of his acquaintance making urgent signs. "They've got a fugitive slave," he said. "The commissioner's starting now." Dana ran up the steps, and entering the commissioner's room made his way with difficulty to the side of the Negro on the prisoner's bench. He spoke to him swiftly. "I am a lawyer. I can help you." The eyes that were lifted to his face were dull. The words came so low he barely heard them. "It's no use. They'll swear to me and get me back, and I'll fare worse if I resist." Dana urged him, he showed him where there might be flaws; the commissioner standing by Dana's side told him his only chance lay in a defense. Burns sat there like a black statue, no life showing in his staring eyes. "He is paralyzed with fear," Dana said to the commissioner. "His master never takes his eyes from his face." "Delay of trial for two days," the commissioner announced. "Prisoner to decide on counsel."

Before Dana left the courthouse the word had spread. So the slave hounds were at it again! They wanted everything—they wanted Nebraska, they wanted the whole new North, they wanted a poor Negro who had turned the tables on them! Before nightfall, Anthony Burns' name was on its way across the country. As labor prisoners would become the rallying point for progressives of a later age, so Burns became a symbol for the free North.

Boston was ablaze, her indignation kindled by the handbills scattered with a prodigal hand by the Vigilance Committee. Committee members were hurrying into Boston on the heels of messengers. They met, sixty strong, to debate the course of action. The moderates advised caution until they heard the decision of the commissioner. The advocates of immediacy demanded that the courthouse be stormed. The committee split, adjourned to meet later. Thirty stayed behind to contemplate the way it could be done. Higginson was, as a foregone conclusion, elected chairman. Leadership was needed, they were reminded, action must be decisive. The rescue of Burns must have the momentum of a public meeting. The Faneuil Hall gathering which had been called for that night would provide the necessary impetus. But they must not wait till it was over—the marshals would be expecting something like that. They must move at the height of the meeting; someone with a good loud voice must rush into the gallery and yell that a mob of colored men were attacking the courthouse—come on, boys! Let's give them a hand! Phillips, previously warned, must jump to his feet and the whole meeting pour out of the doors and race the short distance to the courthouse. Three thousand strong, nothing could hold Burns after that.

It was one of the best plots, said Higginson later, that ever failed.

Only a short interval lay between the decision and the meeting. The committee was to come together in an anteroom before the larger meeting, and there Higginson would explain the plan, and the action, cry by cry, would be understood. But the success hung on the size of the crowd, and the crowd was too big! It pushed and jammed its way into the hall; committee members were seen, caught by an arm, instructed. Some approved, others shook their heads. Howe and Parker, hearing below the noise of the crowd, nodded hastily and afterwards admitted that they had only half understood their respective parts. Phillips' could not be found.

Every inch of the floor was covered; a solid mass filled the galleries, the stairways and the platform. Men who had taken great pains to be insulting, now stopped some of the more prominent Abolitionists to shake their hands and murmur something about the Nebraska Bill as though to make everything clear.

Meanwhile, in Court Square, Higginson, tall and powerful, had relaxed casually against the wall of the courthouse. The night was very still. He listened hard for the running feet, the wave of voices that should soon be heard coming from Faneuil Hall. Up there, on the third floor where a light was burning, lay Anthony Burns.

At length, down the street, out of sight, he heard that unearthly sound that is many voices, and the dull beat of many feet. He glanced hastily at the courthouse door. It stood slightly ajar. The noise grew louder; voices were clearly distinguishable now. Still he did not shift his position. Around the corner they swept, how many—hundreds—thousands? Where were the leaders? Where were the men who would magnetize this crowd into obedience and discipline? He found Martin Stowell, who told him hurriedly that some of their men were bringing a beam to the west door. The west door it would be then! Higginson pushed his way through the crowd. There was the beam; there were men to batter it against the door. He and a powerful Negro seized the front end. The dull roar of beam against wooden door could be heard above the aimlessly moving crowd. The door gave, was bolstered up, split and swung on a single hinge.

They saw the half-lighted hall; the steps that led to Burns' cell. Higginson glanced at his colored ally. The Negro sprang up the steps in a bound. Higginson followed. Six or eight policemen were awaiting them inside. Higginson and his friend put up their arms but clubs beat on their heads. They backed against the wall, and Higginson felt the blood running down his face. Helpless, they were driven toward the door where a deputy constable lay dying of a knife wound. Higginson, in rage and pain, stumbled onto the steps. "Cowards!" he shouted at the crowd.

Breathing hard, the blood falling on his coat, he looked back into the lighted hall and saw that the deputies had retreated to the stairs and had their pistols pointed toward the door. Where were the reinforcements, where was the coalescing force that would turn this crowd into a battering ram? A young lawyer flung himself up the steps but Higginson held him back. That was no place to venture alone. The day was lost; the plot had failed.

The soldiers had arrived by now. The police were making arrests. Parker and Channing were on the edge of the crowd, frustrated, unaware of what was going on until too late. Phillips had heard nothing and gone home. Higginson slipped away, seeing no advantage in arrest.

The crowds came in the morning to inspect the scene of the battle. The courthouse was like a beleaguered castle. Troops from Fort Warren, ordered out by President Pierce, a company of marines, two companies of artillery surrounded the building. Sentries guarded every entrance to the courthouse and filled the corridors. Two small fieldpieces were planted in the square.

The Committee of Vigilance had called a meeting to consider the next move. Explanations filled the air. Phillips must explain how he knew nothing of the plan last night, Howe must tell how he was caught in the crowd, Parker must urge caution now that the authorities were roused. Higginson merely sat holding his cloak against his wounded face, his hot bright eyes bitter. Burns would go back to Virginia, and the slave power would win again.

The first of the week the trial began. Dana had been asked by the Vigilance Committee to conduct the defense. The corridors of the courthouse were so lined with soldiers that it was almost impossible for the friends of Burns to move. The trial lasted for three days in an atmosphere of tense nerves and frayed tempers. Rumors filled Boston like the plague. More rescue attempts would be made: the owners of Burns would be driven out of town: Abolitionists had been selected for assassination. Sober men carried pistols in their pockets; the genteel and the stay-at-homes loitered in the streets and hissed the soldiers who filled the streets of Boston. Negro and white waiters refused to serve food to the troops on guard. Higginson, Stowell, Parker, Phillips and others conspicuous at Faneuil Hall and the courthouse were arrested. Visitors were pouring into the city all week—dangerous visitors, for a peculiar fate had designated that the annual meeting of the antislavery society, the state convention of the Free-Soil party, and sundry spring meetings of religious bodies should gather in Boston this week of all the year. In addition came six or seven hundred workers from Worcester's machine shops and factories.

By the end of the week the owner of Burns had taken heed of these portents, and had opened negotiations for the sale of Burns. For twenty-four hours, Leonard Grimes worked to raise the money, and he had it all—$1200—when the United States Attorney intervened. The United States Attorney had no legal concern in the case, but the telegraph wires had been humming from Washington. Burns must be convicted and returned to Virginia.

Dana's defense was eloquent. He hammered at the loopholes of the law, at the divergent testimony of witnesses. Crowds moved slowly about the courthouse. A double guard stood over Burns. The Vigilance Committee sat taut. The whole North was waiting. On Thursday the mayor ordered out the entire military force of the city, fifteen to eighteen hundred men. They filled the streets as far as the wharves where a new revenue cutter lay. Was this cutter to take Burns back to Virginia? Boston men and women stared at the soldiers as people in a vanquished country stare at the invaders.

On Friday morning a whisper went around. The marshal had given Burns a new suit of clothes. Were these the sacrificial garments? That morning they took Burns through passages where soldiers stood with fixed bayonets. Commissioner Loring entered the trial room hastily. He read his decision without clearing his throat, without looking at the prisoner. On the evidence of the prisoner's owner, he would have been obliged to dismiss the prisoner; but something else had interceded. On the night of Burns' arrest, his owner had, in the undisturbed quiet of the fourth floor of the courthouse, extracted a confession from this man Burns, and by this disposition, signed and sealed, he was bound to return Burns to his lawful master.

What a monstrosity! What a devilish jugglery with the law! Loring had done this—Loring who had also sent Sims into captivity. The mutterings rose. The strangers lingered. The mechanics and the factory workers from Worcester lingered. The slave whip had won again; it crackled over their free heads. Rescue was talked of freely. No one knew of what outraged tempers might be capable.

The authorities saw the moving, restless crowds, the faces that looked up at the courthouse. A battalion of Light Dragoons, twenty-two companies of artillery and infantry, and a corps of cadets were paraded on Boston Common the morning of June 2. A detachment of soldiers was sent down State Street to notify every merchant and business man that he must close his business for the day and leave an empty store. The crowd still gathered. The soldiers had orders to fire if the crowd became unruly.

At eleven o'clock that morning, the clearing of the streets began. Eleven rounds of powder had been allotted each soldier, and there in the street before the eyes of the crowd he was instructed to load his gun. In the empty square before the courthouse a cannon was wheeled, facing Court Street. The crowd driven into Court Street formed such a solid mass that a man might have walked on their heads and suffered no inconvenience. When a soldier moved across the square a long hiss followed him till he was out of sight.

It took three hours to clear the streets. Two o'clock came and went; Dana and Grimes waited inside the courthouse but were not allowed to see Burns. But they did see the preparations; they saw the cavalry drawn up, the battalion of artillery. They saw the company of marines, and then the marshal's special posse of Southern gentlemen and Boston "dregs" which formed a hollow square. They saw Burns move into this square, his hands unbound, his face expressionless. Behind him they saw two more platoons of marines, a fieldpiece and a regiment of artillery.

The soldiers, the horses, the guards, the prisoner, moved from Court into State Street, and a long rising moan greeted them. "Shame—shame —shame." The crowd pressed forward; twice soldiers charged with bayonets—a man held up a bloody hand, another was carried away with an open gash in his head. Above them fluttered a line of black, for nearly every merchant who had closed his shop had draped the front of it in mourning.

The roofs were dark with people. Above the sound of marching feet, the high sibilant hisses ran from one closely packed street to the next, and the rising unearthly moans of "Shame!" quickened the steps of the soldiers and set the cocks of their pistols. There was no music to pick up the dead sound of two thousand feet. As the soldiers passed, the people fell in silently and fifty thousand of them were marching when they reached the waters of the bay. The government steamer lay at the wharf. As Burns was taken hurriedly aboard and pushed into a cabin out of sight, the church bells began to toll, and other bells around the bay picked up the melancholy farewell.

Thus they returned Burns to Virginia, and it cost the government $40,000. "A few more such victories and the South is undone," said the Richmond *Enquirer*.

Was peace probable now? Bostonians had Burns by whom to measure time—"When Burns was taken back . . . When soldiers lined the streets . . . When the President of the United States sent a ship to take a man into captivity . . ." Even the Webster Whigs talked in this manner, and the Hunker Democrats. Nebraska and Burns—they had happened at the same time.

The indictments against the Faneuil Hall speakers and the courthouse besiegers were quashed on a technicality. What kind of case did the state have? No one knew how the deputy marshal had been killed. Why not try the fifty thousand people who had cried "Shame"? Would the authorities willingly give Parker another rostrum from which to praise freedom, or Phillips an opportunity to convince all who came within the range of his persuasiveness?

Over it all shone the bright fact that Burns was soon back. $1,300 had bought him. He paid his respects to all his Boston friends, he refused an offer of P. T. Barnum to exhibit himself in a Museum, he went to Oberlin for an education, he was at last ordained a Baptist clergyman and went to St. Catharine's as a missionary among the fugitives.

Yet in all this Phillips found little comfort. "The government has fallen into the hands of the slave power completely. So far as national politics are concerned, we are beaten—there's no hope. We shall have Cuba in a year or two, Mexico in five. Events hurry forward with amazing rapidity; we live fast here. The future seems to unfold a vast slave empire united with Brazil, and darkening the whole west. I hope I may be a false prophet, but the sky was never so dark. Our Union, all confess, must sever finally on this question. It is now only a question of time."

The Abolitionists celebrated the Fourth of July that year at a picnic in Framingham. Garrison burned a copy of the Constitution on that day, and cried as the flames caught the paper, "So perish all compromises with tyranny! And let all the people say Amen!" A great shout of "Amen!" went up from the three thousand gathered there and some of them looked at each other, wondering at their daring.

Yet how insignificant were such gestures in the light of the times. The Fugitive Slave Law was still on the statute books, Kansas and Nebraska had been given to the slavocracy, for the South had made it clear that it must take, at the point of a gun if necessary, those Western lands if it were to hold the wavering loyalties of Missouri, and after Missouri, Kentucky, Maryland, Virginia, which were essential to the economic stability of slavery throughout the entire South, as well as to its power in Congress. It was not love for the Negro that was infecting the North; it was the need to put an end to the stifling of free initiative, to make certain that the vast lands of the West would belong to the free-labor giant who was bursting his swaddling clothes. And indignation was not enough for that.

The seed had been planted in Wisconsin. *Republican.* . . . It had a fresh tang to it; it drove with an impact against the doubts and uncertainties of politically minded men.

Vermont, Michigan, Ohio, Indiana, New York, Connecticut, Massachusetts waited only for the signature of the President to the Kansas-Nebraska Bill to call their new Republicans together and set the match to their fuse. There seemed no way to halt this spontaneous uprising of free states against the abrogation of the Missouri Compromise.

Yet what a quixotic dream it must have seemed! Cotton was king in 1854 as it had been in 1850 and as it would continue to be for some six years. The country lay in its hand, lay so deeply and so comfortably that Emerson questioned bitterly whether it would be freedom or slavery that was eventually abolished. The cotton empire reached as far as the looms of England and the harbors of China. Nearly two billion pounds of cotton were produced a year. Prosperity lay like a dream over the country. Human values were of no importance. "The lords of the loom and the lords of the lash," as Sumner called the brothers North and South, were making more money than their wildest dreams had fancied. Westward the cotton empire was pushing, northward it was reaching, southward it was gazing at the rich fields of Cuba and South America.

Yet Cuba was a second potential Negro republic . . . Pierce instructed the ambassadors to England, France and Spain to meet together in some European city and determine how Cuba could be brought into the United States. The Ostend Manifesto was the answer.

If "after we have offered Spain a fair price for Cuba . . . and this shall have been refused . . . we shall be justified in wresting it from Spain if we possess the power."

The manifesto shocked many people. It was cold-blooded and audacious. It exposed the United States as a slaveholding nation, without restraint in its greed. What could a handful of antislavery men do?

Yet that fall of 1854, the Democratic party was so bludgeoned at the polls in the free states that the slavocracy was alarmed. The new territories must be taken quickly. Kansas was the battlefield of slavery and free labor. If free labor won, the defeat of the slavocracy would begin with the new representatives in Congress and spread as far as the Rio Grande.

The Missourians were there first—those "amateur emigrants who proposed to reside in Missouri but to vote and fight in Kansas." They nailed a few boards together to provide the necessary residence, posted a scrawled sign which claimed ownership of the plot, and retired across the line into Missouri. Antislavery men saw that freedom must be poured into the territory with plows and seed. Seven hundred and fifty men set out that summer under the auspices of the Massachusetts Emigrant Aid Society. They came in over the lonely trails, their wagons painted "Kansas" and "Nebraska." They sailed down the Missouri River, their farming implements fastened to the deck of the steamers. They were not Abolitionists; they were free-labor men whose future lay in the West.

That fall the territory had its first election. Proslavery instructions were explicit. "When you reside in one day's journey of the territory," David Atchison, Senator from Missouri, told a Missouri crowd, "and when your peace, your quiet and your property depend upon your action, you can without an exertion send five hundred of your young men into Kansas who will vote in favor of your institutions. Should each county in the state of Missouri only do its duty, the question will be decided quickly and peaceably at the ballot-box!" And General String-fellow of Missouri clarified the instructions. "Mark every scoundrel among you who is the least tainted with abolitionism or free-soilism, and exterminate him. I advise you, one and all, to enter every election district of Kansas and vote at the point of the bowie knife and revolver . . . It is enough that the slaveholding interest wills it, from which there is no appeal." The fury of the free-state men was Homeric. They had not come over a thousand miles to be driven from the polls. In the East and Middle West their rage was duplicated. More and more emigrants, filling the rumbling Kansas-bound wagons could be the only answer.

The free-state men thought they were prepared when March elections came round, but they were still young in frontier violence. The second invasion was monumental. One thousand proslavery men devoted themselves to Lawrence alone, where the Abolitionists had concentrated. The polling places were grim with musketry and bottled courage. This time the Congressional Investigating Committee reported that only one-sixth of the votes cast were valid.

The free-state representatives who managed to survive the balloting were promptly unseated by the territorial legislature, which without further delay adopted the Missouri slave code as the law of Kansas. The death penalty or ten years' imprisonment for aiding a fugitive was hung about the necks of Kansans, and two years' imprisonment for the possession of Abolition books, pamphlets, or newspapers.

Free-state men responded promptly. Within the next three years, three

hundred fugitives—mostly from Missouri—passed through the dangerous and exposed stations of the Kansas "railroad."

All through that deadly cold winter, Kansas lay like an armed camp,
and when the spring came no one knew where violence would next
strike. Old John Brown, restless with plans which now bore the name
of Harpers Ferry, could not endure the letters from his sons who were
fighting armed Missourians at their doors. Later—later he would strike
the blow that would weaken the money value of slavery; now Kansas
must be saved. A wagonload of guns and his own angry spirit set out
for the West in the spring of 1855.

Abolitionists were divided on Kansas. The seed of nonresistance was
still buried deep in most of them. The "Kansas troubles" seemed no
more pernicious than the invasion of a free state in search of fugitives.
Their own troubles lay too close at hand. To the Garrisonians, the
emigrants were not Abolitionists; they did not embrace the cause of the
Negro, they merely fought for the right of free white men.

Yet the interest was tightening for those who saw in every blood-
letting of the slavocracy the sign of its coming end. In Congress, the distrust of Pierce and his motives made an armistice out of the question
between the new Republicans, their older confreres, and the enemies
across the aisles.

The South, clamping the lid tighter, could only just conceal the unrest
that bubbled up seven times in insurrections in Louisiana, Mississippi,
Alabama, South Carolina, Maryland and Missouri, in incendiary fires in
Georgia and South Carolina where property damage was large and
"many persons were seriously injured" as the Milledgeville *Federal
Union* reported from Georgia. Slave unrest was growing. In 1851, Virginia, which provided compensation to masters for slaves executed for
crimes or banished out of the state, had found it necessary to appropriate
$12,000 in repayment to masters—an expenditure which was usually a
half or two-thirds less than this amount. By 1855 the appropriations
had grown to $19,000. And the Philadelphia Vigilance Committee re-
ported that for the first thirteen days of a single month, fugitives had
arrived each day, straining their budget, bringing sleepless nights to
conductors.

Congress, meeting in December, had heard the President attack the
free-state men of Kansas as lawless revolutionists, deprive them of all
support from the Federal government, and threaten them with the
penalty of "treasonable insurrection" if they went to "the length of
organized resistance to the authority of the general government." But
Congress was in rebellion, and Northern men showed their temper during

the two months that were necessary to elect a Speaker. The choice finally took the speakership from the hands of the slavocracy for the first time in Congressional history.

In Kansas, men were shooting from behind boulders, riding up to a squatter's shack and pumping lead through the door. Free-soil men were organized, their guns strapped to their shoulders, their women trained to spot an enemy before his head appeared over the brow of a hill.

Steady immigration was tugging at pro-slavery domination. Slavery men were sending out calls to the South for reinforcements. "Twelve months will not elapse before war, civil war of the fiercest kind will be upon us . . . We must have the support of the South. We are fighting the battles of the South . . . Let your young men come on in squads as fast as they can be raised and armed." Two governments now contested the Kansas territory, for free-state men had drafted their own constitution to fight the Black Laws.

It was becoming increasingly evident that only violence could hold the territory for slavery. The sack of the Abolition town of Lawrence confirmed that evidence.

Gutted, burning Lawrence sent a wave of anger across the country. In Washington, doughface looked at doughface, and free-state men looked at their enemies across the aisles. Abolition Congressmen had been watching the siege of Lawrence from the impotent distance of the capital. Sumner lifted his huge frame from his seat and with blazing eyes thundered out his denunciation of "a crime without example in the history of the past." He pounded out names with his fist—Douglas, Senator from Illinois, Butler, Senator from South Carolina—and held them up as the murderers of the men of Lawrence. The fires were still licking about the houses of Lawrence as he flung out his unvarnished shocking words.

His voice was bigger than most; he put into words the passions that had been smoldering in Congress since the beginning of the session. Two days later young Preston Brooks, a Representative from South Carolina and cousin of Senator Butler, found him writing in his seat, came behind him, and beat him over the head with a walking stick.

Sumner, lying in the aisle bleeding and unconscious, reduced the whole vast struggle to simple terms. Brooks symbolized slavery. Attacks against undefended men, midnight assassinations, and guerrilla warfare were a challenge to free men everywhere. Kansas must be delivered from the oppressor.

Kansas and Sumner—the news spread as fast as the telegraph could carry it. In Boston, Oliver Wendell Holmes raised his glass and drank a toast in terrible solemnity: "To the surgeons of Washington. God grant them wisdom, for they are dressing the wounds of a mighty empire of uncounted generations." In Washington a vote of censure but no expulsion from Congress and only a moderate fine from a municipal court awaited Brooks; Senators and Representatives of the North and South went nowhere unless fully armed. From the South came tokens of appreciation for Brooks; gold-headed canes inscribed, "Use knock-down arguments." Across the North spread a chain of indignation meetings, while Boston, grim-lipped, resolved to keep empty the seat of Sumner however long it took him to recover from the paralyzing effects of the assault. In Kansas, a man rode over a prairie to the Browns' with the news of Sumner hidden in his boot.

Two days later John Brown swooped down on Pottawatomie and avenged Lawrence—and Sumner. It was a bloody and ruthless revenge, a midnight raid, in which five proslavery settlers were dragged from their beds and cut to death with an old army cutlass. War was on with a vengeance. Guerrilla bands of Missourians stalked the territory by day and night, throwing their pickets across the borders of Iowa and Nebraska, shooting, turning back the emigrants from the East, finally blockading the Missouri River and sending down its current, tied to logs, those who attempted to pass into Kansas.

The political battle in the world outside took fire from the fight in Kansas. Bleeding Kansas lay on the lips of Abolitionists as a cry to rouse the sleeping. Rich antislavery men poured out money to send wagonloads of settlers rattling down the cold unfriendly trails to the West. When the Republicans called their convention in June, 1856, they did not fail to tell again the story of the horrors to which free-state settlers were subjected and they demanded a return to the "self-evident truths of the Declaration of Independence." They needed a hero to dramatize their cause, and they nominated John C. Frémont, the explorer, for President. The Democrats, maintaining with inspired monotony their support of all that had gone before—the Compromises of 1850, the end of the Missouri Compromise, the Kansas-Nebraska Bill—accepted the aged and obliging James Buchanan, Minister to England, as less disturbing to the voters than Stephen Douglas or Franklin Pierce who were too battered by the fight. The Whigs, broken and dismembered, settled on the ticket offered by the proslavery Know-Nothings who had set up Fillmore as their candidate.

Few campaigns in American history were as bare-toothed and momentous as this. All the bitterness of the past ten years had accumulated to breed excitement and dark forebodings. Portentous rumors of Southern secession if Frémont won battled with the heightened and sharpened work of the Abolitionists. Between lay the great mass of the people, tired of the unending struggle, loving, not Negroes, but freedom, and yet reluctant to become revolutionists.

Antagonisms within the antislavery ranks were swept away. Pleas for Kansas rang out from the pulpits of Henry Ward Beecher, Theodore Parker, James Freeman Clarke. Higginson, in Worcester, turned his church into a Kansas Aid Society, and finally went himself to Missouri to find some means of outflanking or breaking the river blockade. All through that summer, the news from Kansas fell into the hands of the friends of freedom: men murdered, women and children driven out of burning homes, duly elected free-state men shot from ambuscades, old John Brown like a grim specter riding with his six great sons toward Osawatomie and the first straight-on battle of guerrilla-ridden, sharp-shooting Kansas, Federal troops overriding the country like hawks at the instigation of Governor Woodson, two hundred lives and two million dollars' worth of property lost in a year of chaos. By election time, every phase of antislavery work was alive with an astonishing vitality. The Ohio "railroad" had increased its activities twenty-five per cent over any other year. The best men were now in the business of "passing on," and Democrats found new accusations to level against Republicans.

After Burns, no fugitives were ever captured in Boston. But Abolition "sinkholes" in other parts of the country were not so fortunate. Pennsylvania, New York, Ohio Underground Railroad men were all concerned with the single purpose of defeating a law which had already caught two hundred black men and women, free and fugitive, in spite of the necromancy which made the "railroad" one of the most irresistible forces in the country.

What help would the Republicans give them? None whatever, said the men who kept guns against their doors; the Republicans had deliberately failed to mention a word about the Fugitive Slave Law. And yet, some ruminator over a dry-goods counter, some prognosticator in a lawyer's office maintained that if the Republicans shook half a century of Democratic rule, they would shake the whole foundation of black slavery.

Never were lines more clearly drawn. To the Republicans it was a crusade; to the Democrats who, for the past four years, had been drawing in all the proslavery elements in politics, it was a supreme challenge to power. Crowds by the thousands—by the hundreds of thousands—pushed and jostled, hooted, brayed and cheered at campaign rallies. The great writers were, almost to a man, antislavery zealots and the

Republicans attempted to rally the working class, as well. The Democrats, on the other hand, did what they could to frighten the moneyed interests with threats of chaos and disunion. The electioneering in the deep South bent itself to two cries—disunion, or support of Buchanan who had always been "as reliable as Mr. Calhoun himself" in the interests of the South.

In the interests of the South . . .The interests of the three hundred thousand slaveholders, or the interests of ten and a half million non-slaveholders? Like a mesmeric chant, the politicians of slavery cried out the identity of interests to the slowly stirring masses of nonslaveowners.

Slavery, Senator Brown of Mississippi declared, was the "living, breathing exemplification of the beautiful sentiment that all men are equal" since men with white skins stood so high above the Negro. Yet a white man told Olmsted that "niggers" were worth too much to be risked in dangerous work and that if white hired workers were "knocked overboard or got their backs broken, nobody loses anything," and the Charleston *Mercury* glimpsed a direful future when white laborers would "question the rights of masters, invoke the aid of legislation, use the elective franchise to that end, and acquire the power to determine municipal elections," turning "the town of Charleston, at the very heart of slavery, into a fortress of democratic power against itself."

The mesmerism was certainly beginning to lose some of its potency. 1856 was a year of unprecedented restlessness. A correspondent writing from Kansas to Virginia, claimed that "the slaves are in a state of insurrection all over the country . . . The ball is moving and they have heard the sound, and intend to keep it moving." On the southern side of the Ohio River slaveowners' losses mounted so rapidly that many slaves were moved away from the river districts of Virginia and Kentucky, and guards were established along the shore, while all the junctions of the Underground Railroad were crowded beyond capacity. In central and western Texas, the loss from runaway slaves was so great as to call forth public meetings where proposals were made that slaveholders pay for the upkeep of one hundred rangers, stationed at the river to intercept the fugitives, and that all slaveholders west of Colorado organize a mutual insurance company to which a percentage of every Negro's value should be paid.

From Tennessee a correspondent revealed that "certain slaves are so imbued with the fable [that Frémont would bring them forcible assistance] that I have seen them smile when they were being whipped, and have heard them say, 'Frémont and his men can hear the blows they receive!' "

But these supporters of Frémont could not vote for him, and the threat of secession won for the country not only another proslavery President but the triumph of the squatter sovereignty which had been adopted by the Democrats in this election.

Buchanan was a merciless blow to those who had for the first time believed that slavery might be overthrown without fire and sword. Disillusionment ran through the North. For twenty-five years Abolitionists had appealed by tongue, by pen, by agitation in and out of season, to break the power of the slavocracy; for two years Kansas had been bleeding for the North; for months Republicans had been spending hundreds of thousands of dollars to expose the stranglehold of the slave power. But still the people had remained faithful to their old loyalties. Was there no hope?

To Boston John Brown had come to tell about the end of slavery. He brought a letter from Governor Salmon Chase of Ohio; he wished to raise $30,000 to arm the friends of freedom. All the Boston Abolitionists met him—Samuel Howe and Theodore Parker, Samuel Cabot, Wendell Phillips, Garrison. The meeting with Garrison produced as much conviviality as two pillars of fire sitting down for an evening's chat. Garrison hated "carnal weapons"; Brown hated men who talked and did not act. They met in Theodore Parker's parlor, Garrison tall, spare, his eyes like twin hawks, his words incisive and relentless; Brown, tall, square, his eyes like stalactites, his words homely and unsparing. They talked about peace and non-resistance; Brown measuring his quotations from the Old Testament against Garrison's from the New.

Brown's listeners grew as the weeks went on. Parker, for one, was willing to give this incredible old man all he asked for. Stearns, a successful merchant of Boston, did everything but hand him his purse. To Thoreau and to Emerson he was a "man to make friends wherever on earth courage and integrity are esteemed."

Several thousand dollars came to him, as well as rifles, provisions—part of what he wanted. In New Haven he received a thousand dollars, and here and there another thousand (Gerrit Smith's money was running out toward him like a mountain brook), and his plans were settling. If they led him westward for a time, they would lead him eastward and southward as sure as destiny carves out a place for a man. "I have no purpose but to serve the cause of liberty."

Words like these must be graven into the hardest tissues of a man's heart. Otherwise his spirit might become immeasurably despondent and his mind find only the continued repudiation of justice. There had been a hint that justice would be repudiated when Buchanan made his inaugural address and passed aside the importance of the extension of slavery by calling it a judicial question to be settled by the Supreme

Court. Many men looked at each other, wondering whether this complacent acquiescence meant that he already knew what the decision in the Dred Scott case would be—the case which had been pending for three years and which had raised the entire question of territorial freedom and black men's rights. But he knew nothing, he said; he was only prepared to obey whatever the Supreme Court decreed. Slavery had already been entrenched in the legislative branch of the government; it now held the administrative. All it needed was the judicial. Two days after the inauguration that need was filled.

No Supreme Court decision ever shook the country more ominously than did the words that Chief Justice Taney read in his black-robed splendor with his eight black-robed colleagues stretched out to right and left of him. He dealt at some length with the social aspects of what he wished to say, yet all but a few of his words might have been dispensed with: "the black man has no rights which the white man is bound to respect"; the inalienable "rights of the Declaration of Independence do not relate to the Negro for whom citizenship is impossible," and finally, "Congress has no power to abolish or prevent slavery in any of the territories."

We have now no seismograph to measure the shock that convulsed the country. The question had seemed so simple. Dred Scott had been taken by his master into Illinois and Minnesota, where by the Northwest Ordinance and the Missouri Compromise he was free. When he had been taken back by his master into Missouri he had claimed his freedom. Was he a slave or a free man? The answer could have been as simple as the slave laws of Missouri where his suit was filed. But the occasion was too badly needed by the slave power to pass by quietly. Seven proslavery justices chose to go beyond the sectional phenomenon of slavery, make it an organic part of the country, and settle, without appeal, the question that had torn Kansas in two and stung the entire country into political revolt.

The two dissenting justices, relying on a formidable array of precedents, wrote an impressive rebuke to the decision, recalling that Africans had at one time been voting citizens in nearly every state of the Union and declaring their rights to be as inviolate as any who "bears the impress of his Maker."

Very few people, even among the Democrats, doubted the political motives which lay behind the decision. The North, steadied after its first shock, denounced the usurpation of the Supreme Court in terms which that Sanhedrin had seldom heard before. The press flung at those seven justices the almost forgotten democracy of Jefferson who had himself attacked the court on more than one occasion, and they demanded to know if this was also the end of white men's freedom. Legislative bodies all over the North burst into revolt, and courts of Ohio and New York promptly declared the Negro free the moment he stopped across their borders.

In the Senate, Seward unloosed the most devastating attack of all and shocked even his rashest colleagues. A political trick it was indeed, he claimed, and a trick that Buchanan had been well aware of when he took his oath of office; a trick which he had arranged with the Supreme Court so that the stone of slavery would hang into eternity about the neck of the country.

What an accusation! Reckless, unfounded, libelous—how dared Seward so expose himself? even his colleagues demanded. For fifty-three years Seward's attack ricocheted against the impeccable character of Taney and the dull honesty of Buchanan. But when Buchanan's papers were at last published, two letters were discovered; one from Justice Catron of South Carolina: "The Dred Scott case has been before the judge several times since last Saturday, and I think you can safely say in your inaugural that the question involving the constitutionality of the Missouri Compromise line is presented to the appropriate tribunal to decide. Will you drop [Justice] Grier a line, saying how necessary it is and how good the opportunity is to settle the agitation by an affirmative decision of the Supreme Court, one way or the other?"—the other from Justice Grier: "Your letter came to hand this morning. I have taken the liberty to show it in confidence to our mutual friend, Judge Wayne and the Chief Justice. I will give out in confidence the history of the case before us with the probable result. There will be six if not seven who will decide the compromise law of 1820 to be of no effect."

From Frederick Douglass came the words with which the Abolitionists, black and white, intended to meet this new attack. "My hopes were never brighter than now. The Supreme Court of the United States is not the only power in this world. We, the abolitionists and colored people, should meet this decision, unlooked for and monstrous as it appears, in a cheerful spirit. This very attempt to blot out forever the hopes of an enslaved people may be one necessary link in the chain of events preparatory to the complete overthrow of the whole slave system."

Along the underground line the reaction was inevitable. When a deputy with nine assistants descended on Mechanicsburg, Ohio, in pursuit of Addison White, they were met by gunfire from the Negro concealed in the attic of Udney Hyde's home, and when they retreated before the gunfire, they ran into the arms of the "whole damn abolition town of Mechanicsburg"—young men with clubs, old men with pitchforks, women with dough still binding their hands together, all jeering, hooting, threatening. The officers left hastily. Returning twelve days later, they found that Addison White had left for Canada. But Udney Hyde, concealing himself in friends' houses, in swamps, was still a lawbreaker.

The only place for men like Udney Hyde was in prison, for he had already sent along close to his quota of 517 fugitives. They tried to catch him when he stole back to his home, covered with swamp mud, impersonating a mad man with bits of straw in his hat and a wild look on his normally sagacious face, but he escaped again. Instead they put other lawbreakers into a carriage and started where? To a slave state? They left at two o'clock in the morning, and a hundred men fell out of their beds, and with their guns and horses set out in pursuit. Villages from Catawba to Xenia and back again to Urbana were shaken out of their sleep by the pounding of a hundred horses riding after that carriage. They caught up with the marshal in due time and the marshal's posse scattered in all directions, even breaking into sleeping houses in their flight from these crazy lovers of the "nigger." But the angry citizens captured several of the marshal's posse, and bore them off to jail in Springfield, while the Mechanicsburg men returned under the hand of their own sheriff to Urbana. The district court, acting for the Federal authorities, released the marshal's men, claiming jurisdiction over the quarrel. Without a moment's hesitation, Ohio announced that this was a violation of her state's right, and the whole issue was catapulted onto a national stage.

Governor Chase and President Buchanan met and finally agreed to a bargain; the United States District Attorney at Cincinnati would drop all cases against the citizens of Mechanicsburg and the state would oblige by dropping all cases against the marshal. It appeared as though the Federal government had lost. The proslavery Cincinnati *Enquirer* declared it "a declaration of war on the part of Chase and his abolition crew against the United States Courts. Let war come, the sooner the better."

The cry for war was becoming a common phrase. A hypothetical war or a war between the states was not always distinguished clearly. But bloodletting was in the mind. The Mechanicsburg case profoundly stirred the people of Ohio. The day of overturning would surely come, and rebellion was not an abstract word when a law was despicable and unalterable save by the will of the people.

When Alexander Ross came down from Canada, driven by the effects of slavery which he had seen among the refugees, as well as by the impulsion of *Uncle Tom's Cabin*, and asked Gerrit Smith how he might most effectually aid in this overturning, Smith counseled the policy that lay closest to his heart—invasion. This merely confirmed Ross' own decision, reached after talks with refugees in Canada. He slapped his pockets where he already had the names, the addresses and the routes to freedom. Smith took him to Boston, New York, Philadelphia, and introduced him to distinguished radicals, Garrison, Phillips, Sumner, Parker, Emerson, Lucretia Mott, Lydia Child. He was acceptable on any number of grounds, as a distinguished physician, as an authority on ornithology, entomology, ichthyology, as the author of several books, as the recipient of many degrees. Later, when he was knighted by the Emperor of Russia, the kings of Italy, Portugal, Saxony and Greece for his scientific discoveries, decorated by the French Academy, offered and refused a barony by the King of Bavaria, and served as consul to Canada from Belgium and Denmark, they could say with laudable complacency that the best thing he ever did was invade the slaveland. He was a man of great physical daring as well as intellectual curiosity. In a small café in New York, he learned the practice of revolution from friends of Garibaldi; over innumerable cups of coffee he learned the theory of revolution from the German Communists who were bringing the doctrine of Karl Marx to a country which was already faced with bread lines and industrial crises. He was perfectly aware of the danger that awaited him in the South. He might be killed suddenly; he might be lynched slowly. But he was convinced that the only answer to slavery must come through the slaves themselves.

For the first few weeks he wandered about Richmond talking casually to people, watching. At last, at the home of a colored preacher he stood before forty-two slaves, selected for their intelligence and initiative. He explained to them why he had come to the South, what he wanted to do. He told them how the Underground Railroad operated and gave them the names of conductors in the border towns. This information he asked them to pass along as quickly and secretly as they could.

When nine young men presented themselves the next Sunday night, ready to take advantage of their information, Ross gave each a few dollars, a pocket compass, a knife, a pistol, as much food as they could conveniently carry, and the necessary directions.

The news of their safe arrival came to him many months later, after his activities had made such an impression on Virginia and neighboring states that the newspapers were beginning to urge a reward against the organized band of Abolitionists, functioning in the South, who were supplying the Negroes with information and materials of escape.

Ross took the hint and promptly left for Philadelphia until the excitement subsided. He remained there all the summer of 1857, collecting statistics, consulting the Vigilance Committee on the best means of circulating information among the slaves. He had already evolved his own code which, when the key was committed to memory and the instructions written on a slip of paper, led the slaves safely from station to station. Meadville, Pennsylvania was known by the number 10; Seville, Ohio, by 20; Medina, Ohio, by 27; Cleveland was called "Hope," Sandusky—"Sunrise," Detroit—"Midnight," and the ports of entry into Canada were bursts of praise: Windsor, "Glory to God"; Port Stanley, "God be Praised." Thus, "Helpers at work at midnight" was a poetic obscurity to all but the slave who held the key.

The word and ways of freedom were needed most by the slaves in the deep South, Ross decided, and on his next trip he set out for Georgia where he fitted eleven fugitives for the long journey to the North. His ornithological interests protected him, and equipped with shotgun and preservatives, he could wander carelessly into fields and woods with the distant expression of a scientific man, while establishing his contacts with black and white alike.

From Georgia he went to South Carolina, and from South Carolina to Vicksburg, Mississippi. In Vicksburg, the quiet, well-bred scientist lived with a private family, making frequent visits to a neighboring plantation and always returning with a fine botanical specimen which he eagerly displayed. That slaves disappeared was not related to him. They vanished from plantations some miles away.

Only once did he run into trouble. When seized by a mob he made the Masonic sign of distress and several men promptly intervened, insisting on the full protection of a trial. The missing slave who was the cause of his arrest was concealed in a hideaway provided by another slave when he heard of the capture of Ross. He came out, presented himself to his master with the explanation that he had hurt his ankle while visiting the next plantation where he had leave to go. Ross was released to continue his work.

To the slaveowners, men like Ross—and he was not alone in such dangerous work—must have seemed like the terrible genii of legends. Property given wings. Tangible objects made transparent. It is no wonder that the air of these days was electric. This 1857 was not a happy year to live in. Border warfare flared up again and again, with slave catchers making raids into free states only to be driven back by outraged Abolitionists. ("They gave us twenty minutes to leave," a distraught slaveowner testified about Painesville, Ohio, "and then wouldn't allow us that! There was a crowd of fifty or sixty, armed. Might as well hunt the devil there as to hunt a nigger!") In Congress the excited distrust of Buchanan and the men who surrounded him never allowed the battle to relax between the small body of antislavery men and the large body of those dedicated to slavery. Northern men were as nervous as Southern men. Radical Abolition was encountering the impatient resistance of many who were beginning to see the ultimate triumph of freedom in the Republican party. The country was prostrate under the terrible depression which had begun in August, and anxious flurries of social reform never reached beyond the tongues which uttered them. The efforts of white workers and Abolitionists to unite in a common fight were spasmodic and unassertive. Although the New England Workingmen's Association had put itself on record in 1845 as eager to promote better conditions for workers "without regard to party, sect, creed or color," not enough labor leaders were prepared to go beyond their contention that slavery was the result of the degraded state of society in general, a state which must be remedied in order to destroy slavery. Although Abolitionists had joined a National Industrial Congress in 1845 and *The Anti-Slavery Standard* tried to make clear the common fight of slaves and workingmen, most Abolitionists—unlike Phillips, Garrison, Douglass and Lysander Spooner—failed to relate the underpaid labor of the North to the unpaid labor of the South.

From England came the clearest exposures of black slavery and white exploitation—England which had been giving such unduplicated moral support to the Abolitionists. The Chartist movement, growing increasingly strong, continued its blasts against "the damning stain upon the American escutcheon" and all the intense and vigorous sympathy which had been stirred by Douglass, Remond, Wells Brown, Garnet, Ward, Pennington, Mrs. Stowe and a stream of lesser apostles of freedom was bearing strong and healthy fruit. The bitter struggles for freedom in Europe had long ago opened the eyes of English workers to the relation of slavery and white workingmen. They tried this year to rouse the white workers of the United States to the preposterous situation in which they lived, and an Antislavery address came to the United States signed by eighteen hundred English workmen, a blasting protest against the evil circle of American slavery, and cotton, English industrialists and British workers.

To the slaveowners all the sufferings of the North—unemployment riots, starvation, reproaches from abroad—merely gave an unholy truth to their gibes against the Northern "wage slaves" and allowed them a comfortable complacency from which to regard a system of chattel labor which tended "to neutralize the ruinous effects of universal suffrage and to limit the absolute quality of popular sovereignty." In fact the whole situation provided such a fine occasion to display the advantages of enforced labor that the eloquent William Gilmore Simms cried, "Pity it is that the lousy and languishing lazzaroni of Italy cannot be made to labor in the fields under the whip of a severe task-master!"

There was a frantic exaltation in all this, and apologists for slavery were now pouring out words like a river, as though they were all priests of a dying cult, exponents of a world that was already past. No statement was too monumental, no hate too devastating. "We have got to hating everything with the prefix free," a Southern journalist wrote bitterly, "from free Negro to free will, free thinking, free children, and free schools—all belonging to the same brood of damnable isms."

The South of these late 1850's was filled with old adages, freshened for a new generation. Why talk about black slavery when white men were the victims of lust, passion—wages? Here in the slaveland were no poverty, no almshouses, no jails—"the perfect equality of the superior race, and the legal subordination of the inferior are the foundations on which we have erected our republican system," said Toombs of Georgia. Of course it was not the republican system of Jefferson—that had been repudiated a generation ago because "taking the proposition literally" (that all men were created equal) one found that "there was not a word of truth in it." No, it was the hallowed republicanism of the slave empires, Greece and Rome, upon which they proposed to erect their "institution of divine appointment."

The preparation for this cult of race, religion and solid investments was intricate, of course. It led into many unexpected fields of political investigation, scientific inquiry, historical analysis, Biblical study and wishful thinking. It called upon an elaborate machine of propaganda, since the human mind was not by nature equipped to grasp the subtleties it propounded.

Dr. S. A. Cartwright of Mississippi was of inestimable value. Profiting handsomely from the popularity of scientific investigation he had come to several interesting conclusions. Running away was traced to a peculiar form of mental disease called drapetomania, common to Negroes and to cats. He also discovered that the Negro brain froze in a cold climate, inducing insanity, and he urged, out of kindness to the Negro, that he be kept in the South. In addition to this he was able to make the interesting confirmation that the Negro was identical with the serpent who had tempted Eve, the word "Nachash" having been wrongly translated "snake" when it should have read "Negro."

Although Dr. Cartwright was the scientific oracle of the South, a man of vast importance because of the essential necessity to condition the mind to a belief in physical and mental inferiority, yet George Fitzhugh provided a more dazzling impact on Northern minds. A young man of considerable brilliance, he had taken cognizance of the societies which Adam Smith, Karl Marx, and John Stuart Mill were offering to the world.

His advantage lay in the fact that he had a better one to offer, one which would be a repudiation of the free society—"the cannibalistic exploitation"—which he had seen in the North and in Europe. His new society was predicated on the enslavement of white as well as black. He extolled the virtues of socialism—of the Fitzhugh brand—since it would abolish competition, and bring about a community of property and unity of labor. This, he maintained, had been accomplished by slavery. But slavery had not gone far enough. It dealt only with one class and one race. In the true society of the future there would be no idleness since all would be compelled to work, and everyone, employer and employee, would be subordinate to the government which, in turn, would make employees of the employers, while the employers enslaved their former employees in exchange for care and work. In the West, the government would cease giving free land away in small parcels. Instead, vast acreage would be given to responsible individuals who would hold it for their sons and attach to themselves, as tenants for life, the workless and landless of the East.

In the South, however, there would be no white slavery. The South would remain as it was, the paradise of the white race. Gentlemen would be educated at the expense of the government, and women would be goddesses. Crime would end, for crime was bred by poverty, and everyone, even the Negro, would want for nothing.

Fitzhugh had many friends in the North—he was, indeed, a relative of Gerrit Smith. Moreover he had known and talked to many of the Abolitionists. He was no outsider when he issued his appeal to the North. "We warn the North that everyone of the leading abolitionists is agitating the negro slavery question merely as a means to attain ulterior ends . . ." ends that would be obtained by the revolutionary overthrow of slavery and would result in the Abolitionists' dreams, "a surrender to Socialism and to Communism—to no private property, no church, no law, to free love, free lands, free women and free children!"

How simply the agitation of the Cartwrights, the Fitzhughs, the Hammonds, the Dews could have been stated. We do not intend to lose $1,000,000,000's worth of property. The commercial conventions, which had begun to meet each year in Charleston, Savannah, Montgomery, Vicksburg, came like healthy blasts. Here were no shilly-shallyers, no slavery-intoxicated clergymen or politicians. Here were only the new, hard, tough, slavocrats—the successors to the gentlemen of half a generation before—with sleeves rolled up, cigars lighted, whisky bottles handy and no curbs on the real issue. The South was to survive *as it stood* with more markets and better prices, with an empire of railroads, mines, and great plantations to consolidate the power of slavery, with free schools for whites established, soil conserved, disfranchised whites and the rising class of mechanics and artisans kept pacified by renewed assurances of their social and economic identification with the slave system.

It was evident, by the end of 1857, that the crisis, heightened by the Dred Scott decision, was approaching. The stake in Kansas was incalculably high; the Lecompton Constitution, which proposed to settle the issue for the slavocracy, was denounced even by Stephen Douglas as legalizing a civil war instead of localizing a fight in Kansas. It was a masterpiece of trickery, whereby Kansas settlers were given slavery, with no opportunity to vote against it. Although the territorial governor resigned in protest against the Lecompton Constitution, Buchanan still sent it to Congress with a message, denouncing the free state Kansans as rebels, and claiming that "Kansas by virtue of the Constitution of the United States . . . is at this moment as much a slave state as Georgia or South Carolina."

Congress divided more sharply than ever, slave and free, and finally compromised with an amendment—or a bribe as the friends of free Kansas called it—offering the territory a land grant if it agreed to the Constitution and came in immediately with slavery. "The bribe was spurned" by more than ten thousand Kansans.

The slavocracy had built its future on Kansas and lost, in spite of Dred Scott. The commercial convention meeting in the spring of 1858 in Montgomery agreed that if a Black Republican was brought to Washington by the next election, the South would have no alternative but secession.

They were quite right in feeling that the Republicans had made their position unmistakably clear. The Dred Scott decision and the Lecompton Constitution had provided the Republicans with more syllogisms than they needed. Any further doubtful points were clarified that June, clarified—some party members believed—almost too precisely, by Mr. Abraham Lincoln, their nominee for the Senate. They were, in fact, frightened at his boldness, and many of his friends begged him, if he valued his political life, to tone down his radicalism. But he was an antislavery man—his public utterances for the last twenty years had made this intermittently clear—and most antislavery men could have told you how timid that speech was: "A house divided against itself cannot stand. I believe this government cannot endure permanently half slave and half free." Antislavery men had been saying that for nearly thirty years, and slave masters had been saying it, in effect, since the Constitution was first drafted. Yet Northern men did not make a political issue of it if they valued their future. Lincoln had done a rash, unequivocal thing—perhaps he had ruined the chances of his party. The Republicans stood only for the nonextension of slavery; although antislavery sentiment pinked their edges, to hint at interference was a desperate step.

In the light of torches in public squares, in the light of the sun in fair grounds, down a link of Illinois towns stretching from border to border, Douglas challenged Lincoln to say that he was not advocating sectional warfare, that he was not setting his radicalism against the law of the land. Douglas had a senatorship to hold and Lincoln had one to gain. People, coming in wagonloads over the dusty roads, in trains, by horseback, must decide between them.

More was at stake than a senatorship. Perhaps no one knew this— unless it were Lincoln. Changing times . . . old ways going . . . "the charter of the free man must not be broken by slavery" . . . Douglas— round, clever, brilliant little Douglas with the whisky breath—was a hero on the stump, he never failed to give the best show that circus politics could provide. He would make short work of the slow lean man who contested his Illinois power.

But the country was listening hard. It looked as though Abe Lincoln were getting the best of it. He talked the way you talked—no frills, no demagoguery; he said good things in simple words; plain men understood them. (Jefferson Davis, vacationing in Maine, wished they would eat each other up, but that was probably because Lincoln was bringing so many things into the open.) Politicians didn't altogether like his words, but we, the people, are the ones who cast the votes.

In Illinois, the people cast their votes, and Lincoln won by a popular majority, but Douglas won the control of the legislature, and the legislature in those days selected the winner. All Lincoln said was, "I am after larger game."

The Republicans won Pennsylvania that year, and they made gains East and West. To Northern industry they promised support and a protective tariff. The slavocracy needed nothing more to know that the

Republican party was its natural enemy. Against such a tariff, the South had fought for over thirty years. To legislate such a tariff would put the whole long chain of Southern credits, Southern loans, Southern buyers into a violent spin. Long statistics were meticulously gathered by "dough-faces" to show how Northern prosperity was dependent on the good will of the South; alarming information was broadcast that differed in no essentials from the alarums that were raised in the riotous days of the thirties.

The South was shocked, shocked as men are who discover they have been building their house on another man's property, that nearly every-thing from food to a university education was supplied by the North. This was servility, the South cried, and no Southern gentleman could endure it. The situation was by no means new to them, but the strong new body of extremists was crying loudly for the severance of all inter-course with the North, for the development of direct trade with English mills, for the building of a railroad to the Pacific, for the legalization of the flourishing illicit slave trade. Without the revival of this trade the plantation system was doomed, they claimed, for the breeding farms of Virginia and Maryland were unable to keep pace with the demand, and curtailment of slave labor meant the end of slavery expansion.

It was up to the Federal government. Would the Southern demands be recognized as necessities? Or must the fearful step be taken—a League of United Southerners; a Confederacy?

The slave power was perfectly aware of all the forces operating against it, both within and without. New laws were discussed to curb the rising evidences of arson and theft and "reckless destruction of life and prop-erty" by both blacks and whites. Maryland was merely imitating the action of Virginia, she was merely anticipating the action of Louisiana, North Carolina, Georgia, when she called conventions in two consecu-tive years to consider her plight, to offer some remedy for the extravagant losses of runaway slaves and to propose legislation that would enslave or drive away all free Negroes or compel them to sell themselves as slaves for the privilege of staying in their homes.

At the twenty-fifth anniversary of the New England antislavery society, Higginson's words were terrible and challenging. "Is slavery destined as it began in blood, so to end? Seriously and solemnly, I say, it seems as if it were." Was he using prophetic words when he spoke of a "new element coming to settle the question of slavery bye and bye on the soil where it exists?" Was he speaking of John Brown?

John Brown—now *there* lay a danger slaveowners could understand. But how many of them had heard of *John Brown!*

## Chapter 8

## FIRE AND SWORD

BACK and forth, a thin old flame was burning with an incredible heat. I tell you, Douglass, the time has almost come! Brown, we're waiting. Fifty men, Frederick Douglass—a hundred men—hidden in the Virginia mountains—slavery will be blown to hell.

The secret line of flaming loyalties; in Boston, Higginson meeting secretly in the back room of the Revere House, young, passionate, ecstatic over the call to action; Parker, his fine deep eyes never leaving the old man's face; in Peterboro, Gerrit Smith walking in the woods with Sanborn: "You see how it is, our dear old friend has made up his mind to this course. We cannot give him up to die alone"; in Syracuse, huge, dark-skinned Loguen, waiting to know how many men to gather; in Philadelphia, Douglass again, Henry Highland Garnet, William Still, dark faces showing no surprise: violence was to be met with violence, blood with blood, the Underground Railroad which ran through Still's hands in Philadelphia to provide the link which the old man needed when the insurrection had burned a path to the North; in New York, the Hoppers—Isaac Hopper's family—listening with prim lips and flashing eyes, the old man's friends.

The time was almost here to bore like a mole into the heart of slavery. The Alleghenies were stretching into the South like a long arm of freedom, ready to pluck out the wretched black man, to conceal him and his arms in a vast embrace of trees and hidden places. "Nat Turner, with fifty men held Virginia for five weeks. Give a slave a pike and you make him a man . . . (This was to be no wanton uprising, but the conferring of manhood on the slave) . . . Woods and mountain sides can be held by resolute men against ten times their force . . . Twenty men in the Alleghenies would break slavery to pieces in two years . . . Harpers Ferry may be seized; it has an arsenal."

Brown ordered one thousand pikes. "They'll do easily in the hands of free-state women," he explained. What he said in his heart was, "Slaves would need no training to handle them."

Finally Brown went to Canada, Loguen with him.

Seventy-five thousand fugitives were there, men and women, some strong and daring, most acute and intelligent; they knew the secrets that he wished to learn. How were you helped? What underground routes did you follow? What security lies along those paths? He held Harriet Tubman's hand for a long time. "General Tubman . . . What a man! What a man!" He told her what she could do for him and her people— describe her routes, pass about the word of his coming, prepare the field. He went from home to home, to doctors, clergymen, mechanics, trades-men, farmers—men enslaved once; he saw the Elgin Colony, a model haven for the fugitives. He read their newspapers and went into their schools and roughed with his gnarled hand in that absent tender way of his the dark little heads. Yes . . . the war would start in western Virginia, but the ceremonies of induction would begin here, among these freemen whose thoughts dwelt with such profound intensity on the whips and sorrows of the places they had come from. He was pleased. None of them had held back; none of them had believed that slavery would fall away without blood, each of them could tell of the weapons he had used.

The convention: thirty-three colored men and thirteen white drew up a constitution of freedom, division of land, treatment of prisoners, citi-zenship for Negroes, organization of schools and churches. Harpers Ferry lay across it like a deep shadow. Kagi was there, and Stevens, Anderson, Cook and Taylor, Tidd and Owen Brown. They had all, except Taylor, been fighting in Kansas and seeing slavery at first hand. William Lam-bert was there as well, but they did not ask very much of him. He had pretty well finished his work. In the thirty-one years of his devotion to freedom, he had passed thirty thousand fugitives from Detroit across the river, and now his hair lay curled and white against his black skull, and his voice was a thin reed. But Martin Delany was robust—he had been to Liberia and to Haiti looking for a home for his people—and they made him corresponding secretary.

Brown was pleased with the organization. He had its support now, and he had his white friends, and he had those young men, black like "Emperor" Green who had escaped from South Carolina, like Leary with the blood of an Irish grandfather giving swagger to his courage, like Newby, showing his Scotch blood plainly in his face, thinking with a relentless grief of his wife in slavery; white like the Coppocs, Edwin and Barclay, who had the remorselessness of Kansas written in their eyes, like Hazlett and the Thompsons, all waiting for the word. Very soon now arrogance would crumble; the eyes that saw the glory of the Kansas plains would see the end of Antichrist, the reign of the Great Whore. If this was madness then let us make what we can of it.

Eight months were to go by, smuggling arms into Kansas, stirring restlessly with delay, thinking only of the mountains of Virginia. Kansas need not trouble him very much. It would soon be won for freedom. On the heels of his return, free-state men had cast 11,300 votes to the 2700 of the proslavers. Yet he paid a last debt to Kansas. Free-state men had been massacred at Marais des Cygnes; the Browns and their followers moved down to the border, not "to seek or secure revenge" but to watch the movements of the Missourians. A slave, Jim Daniels, crossed over from Missouri, ostensibly with brooms to sell, in reality to find help for himself, his wife, and his babies who were to be sold apart. The smile that turned Brown's eyes into white fire came to rest on Daniels. "God had provided him a basis of action."

The next night they crossed the border, and separating into two bands, set about their work. Daniels knew the names of slaves who desired their freedom. A grim old man, sitting slightly crouched over his bridle, his young men behind him, came to the darkened cabins one by one, and at the point of a revolver held off the master while the slaves ran to the horses. He did something else as well; he took property "to the amount due the negroes" for services rendered, property that could be converted into funds with which to support the fugitives until they were self-supporting. He staunchly believed it theirs; when he learned that possessions had been taken from a boarder in a master's home he ordered them returned since they did not relate to the justice he was dealing. This midnight raid was terrible in its Old Testament justice and its implacable steadying of unbalanced scales. One man was killed. His hand had reached for his gun, and Stevens had shot him.

Before dawn the two bands, augmented now by eleven slaves and a white hostage, had ridden across the Kansas border once again. Before the sun was well up the border towns rang with the awful deed. Border ruffians forgot their midnight rides and murders, conservative free-state men forgot their kinsmen killed in bed, Administration men forgot that so well-directed an assault had killed only one man. The wires to Washington vibrated fiercely. The President, curiously silent when free-state settlers were killed, offered to add two hundred and fifty dollars to the three thousand reward posted by the governor of Missouri for the capture of the old man. How trifling such a thing was to Brown. He looked with his blazing blue eyes at the posted rewards and his knuckles showed whiter than ever against his bridle.

God only knew where freedom lay. Three women, six children, two men, dressed in cotton clothes and slave shoes, proposed to follow an old man, who lived and thought like a curling whip, across the guerrilla-

infested plains of Kansas, the wild empty lands of Nebraska, the cold
hills of Iowa, the frozen fields of Illinois—twenty-five hundred miles.
Later, some people called it the boldest exploit of the Underground
Railroad.

There was no time for rest or hesitation. The rewards had stirred the
greed of men. The Brown party paused long enough to add a new baby
to their crew, and pushed on, across the prairie, covered in December
snow, across the wild bleak hills where the little foxes ran and the wind
came down like piercing blades of steel. They beat off posses, fighting
the Battle of the Spurs with the objects which gave its name; they took
prisoners, they heard the dull quick thudding of Kagi and his forty men
riding as hard as horses could carry them to catch up with the old man
and drive off fresh pursuers, they crossed the ice of the Missouri River,
and pushed on toward their friends at the underground station in
Springdale, Iowa, where they distributed themselves among the Quakers.

Here they lay out in some sort of peace until word filtered in that the
deputy marshal had almost reached Springdale and the flight must be
resumed. Influential friends promised to have a freight car on a siding
at West Liberty. The fugitives came down at twilight, hid in a gristmill
and climbed aboard during the night. The freight was coupled to an
eastbound train. Rocking with the unaccustomed speed, peering out
through the wind-swept cracks at the flat cold plains of Illinois, they
came at length to Chicago. Allan Pinkerton met them there, and taking
them—fugitives, Brown, Stevens, Kagi—in charge, brought them to
Detroit and Brown ferried with them across the river.

The papers were full, this spring of 1859, of the trials of the Oberlin
and Wellington men. John Brown smiled. These Oberlin men—now
*they* were heroes!—men who had gone out with their fists to rescue a
Negro and set awry the whole machinery of the law.

He came down to Cleveland with Kagi, and he stood up in the Public
Square to tell monster crowds of Oberlin sympathizers about the law
which had trapped these Oberlin men, which had made necessary his
mighty trek to Detroit.

They cheered him ecstastically, these hero-worshipers of the Western
Reserve who had managed to make their opinions strong enough to turn
the tables on the Fugitive Slave Law in the same manner as the men of
Mechanicsburg had done. They passed resolutions for him, they allowed
him to appreciate the full political significance of the events that were
transpiring. Northern Ohioans had recognized these significances well
enough. Thousands had gathered in the courtyard of the prison, coming

on trains from other towns, to pay their respects to the white and colored law-breakers who had snatched one of their black townsmen from the slave catchers. Mr. Fitch, the Sunday-school superintendent of Oberlin, had, from his cell window, greeted his four hundred charges who bright with shining faces, sedate in Sunday best, gathered solemnly below his window and piped a suitable and heartening air to the accompaniment of the Oberlin band and then listened to his amiable counsel as he leaned against the bars.

These men were making the most of their political martyrdom, and *winning*. Two convictions out of thirty-seven indictments, and the government said it would be content if the state dismissed its suits against the slave catchers. The Oberlinians went home like heroes. A salute of a hundred guns was fired as they came out of the jail, and several hundred sedate but merry Clevelanders marched with them to the station.

The political effects were quickly seen. The Republican State Convention demanded the repeal of the Fugitive Slave Law; the first defense attorney, Albert G. Riddle, was sent to Congress the following year. Those were small fires but they were burning brightly in the general darkness.

Why was the darkness so deep, men, dazzled by John-Brown courage, by Wellington-Oberlin courage, asked? With the whole North—with the Republicans—why, the Legrees were almost licked. But old hands at this game knew when a temperature was genuine, when credulity must be stiffened. To them the days were truly dark; snares lay all around. The Republican party, with so notable an exception as the Ohio convention, was hardly sustaining the role of a party of liberation. Its sedulously calm assurances of nonaggression against the South caused many Abolitionists to cry out that the Republican party was the greatest obstacle to the freedom of the slave.

The antislavery fight seemed worn to a thin bone. There was not much more the colored and white Abolitionists could say. Through them the North had learned of the moral and physical horror of slavery; if the North did not now act willingly it must act through combustion, of that they were confident. Every James Hamlet, every Thomas Sims, every Anthony Burns, every Joshua Glover, turned little ripples into large swells, spreading into an enlarged moral consciousness, an enlarged political and economic consciousness. The issues, vibrating tense but undefined, related themselves to every man, but every man did not know it yet. He did not know that under an irresistible force an outworn economic system was giving way to the future. All he sensed perhaps was that in the changing values of the world there was no permanence in any system. The time was a period of awful waiting, of deep pregnant silences, of wondering.

Many of the old Abolitionists were dying. Five of the signers of the original Declaration of Sentiments had gone within the year, and they were men who were badly needed. Early in 1859 Parker, the irrepressible, the irreplacable, was caught by the tuberculosis which he had been ignoring. To the men with whom he had fought, this sickness was a catastrophe that could not be measured easily in words, and his empty place in Boston was a mute reminder of changing times. What would happen when the fight was won? Where would go Phillips' golden oratory and what would Sumner talk about—Sumner now back in the Senate after four years of painful invalidism? Would Garrison dissolve like a powder? Would emancipation see the end of slavery?

The cause of Abolition might be worn to a thin sharpness, but a hard core of white-Negro restlessness was forming about the very heart of the South. Could fire-eating consume it? Could demagoguery soften it? Was there any need to fear? Was the fearing all in the imagination? Maybe— maybe. But the mind was not at rest, and into the restlessness exploded the unnamable terror that came with the dawn of a day in October.

It was a midnight, full of misty vapors, when the train from the West, bound for Baltimore, slowed up at the little station before it went on across the Potomac River. Nothing happened in this town, lying between two rivers; passengers seldom came aboard at Harpers Ferry. The conductor looked down from his car with unbelief when a white face appeared out of the dark, and Patrick Higgins told him that men with rifles had seized the bridge. The absurdity of this announcement made him jump off his train with a recklessness not characteristic of a cautious man, and the dark night swallowed him up until he came into the light of the train again, his face as pale as Higgins. Shots had been fired at him; Hayward, the colored porter was lying on the bridge, dying from a gunshot!

Send out word! Defy the madman! This was a rising of the slaves, "the old man" had said. Send out word! The army—the militia! Then he found that the wires had been cut. Passengers, huddled in the waiting room, waited for the end of the world. Out there in the darkness was holocaust, the thing most greatly feared—slaves in revolt. Yet a strange silence persisted as the mists began to rise over the two rivers, and the dawn came. Close after six they pulled out across the bridge. The old man had himself walked across the bridge with the conductor, his face surprisingly calm for a conqueror, his answer ready when the authority for this terrible deed was demanded. "By the authority of God Almighty."

The passengers, safe now in Maryland, must spread the alarm. Tearing sheets of paper, they wrote their frightful warning and dropped them from the windows as the train shrieked on. It was seven o'clock before Phelps, the conductor, was able to send a frantic message by telegraph. . . . At nine o'clock the master of transportation had wired back his doubts. But the president of the railroad had seen the wire, and he lost no time. The President of the United States, the governor of Virginia, the commander of the First Light Division in Baltimore heard before noon that an insurrection had lighted the powder of western Virginia and that treason against the government was ablaze.

At that moment whatever hope Brown might have had was extinguished. By noon troops were converging on the river town, from Fort Monroe, from Washington, from Fredericksburg. By night, all but the deaf and the stupid had heard what Osawatomie Brown had done at Harpers Ferry.

Time and distance cannot change what he did there, nor can it blunt for more than a bare moment the excitement that tugs at the mind and the imagination. Slaves in revolt—a firebreak racing down the South, burning away slavery? It might have succeeded—there was a hundredth chance. Abolitionists held their breath over what might have been. Slave masters drew in their breath with great sucking sounds over what *might have been.*

What had prevented it? Was it Colonel Robert E. Lee and Jeb Stuart leading their marines from Sandy Hook? Was it the soldiers tumbling into the town and turning it into an armed city? Was it some inadequacy in the old man's plan? That was probable. He had opened his plans to defeat by refusing to retreat promptly to the mountains as he had planned and as Kagi's frantic pleading counseled him to do. Instead he lingered through the day at Harpers Ferry to protect his prisoners and to wait for the slaves who did not rise. And for the slaves who did not rise there was an explanation more convincing than their masters' claims of contentment. He had chosen a section of the state where slavery had never flourished and slaves were scattered. He had given the slaves little warning, he had offered no proof of his sincerity, and slave thiefs as famous as John Murrell had for generations enticed them with promises of freedom only to sell them into a deeper bondage.

Or had he perhaps, as some contended when the excitement had subsided, known that he would fail but that his failure and his execution would bind the antislavery North together as no success of his might do?

On the 16th and 17th of October there was no time to ask these questions. Every item of news that came out of Harpers Ferry snapped like the cock of a revolver at the nerves of the country. Eighteen men had moved in the cover of the night out of a Maryland farmhouse. A creaking wagon had rattled down the road to the junction of the two rivers. Surprise, assault, treason, the United States arsenal in rebellious hands. Was it true they had taken a man with such a name as Washington their prisoner? True. Was it true that Negroes with guns were everywhere? That colored men had been deployed to guard the bridge? True. Osborne Anderson, with Kagi, held the rifle works, looking out across the green misty hills about the river. . . . "I was safe in Canada, but I haven't much more time—lungs spitting blood—my people . . ." Copeland, pacing above the river, had been released from jail a bare few months before with the other Wellington-Oberlin men and had gone back to his studies. . . . "But some things left no room for books . . . the voice of the old man for one thing, the voice of black men in chains . . ." Leary, older than his kinsman, Copeland, thinking of the young baby at home in Oberlin, of security that was not security as long as black men could be slaves. Daingerfield Newby, born a slave, freed by his Scotch father, guarding with young Oliver Brown and William Thompson the shining rails where they stretched across the river and cut into the hills and thinking of the wife and child in slavery . . . "and the baby has just commenced to crawl. Oh, dear Daingerfield, come soon as possible for if you don't get me, someone else will . . ."

It was they who stopped the first bullets of the Jefferson Militia as it swung over the hill from Charlestown, sending Thompson and young Oliver Brown flying toward the arsenal and catching Daingerfield Newby with one shot as he was running up the street. Kagi tried to take his men to safety across the bridge but all that was left of him soon floated down the river, while Leary lay dying on the ground, Copeland had his arms raised in surrender, and Anderson was in flight.

The old man in the watchhouse of the arsenal knew that the trap had been sprung. He sent out William Thompson and a prisoner to negotiate for the end of firing. Thompson fell into the enemy's hands, and they shot him so that he tumbled to the rocks below the bridge, and then they shot him again as they saw him dragging himself out of the water.

The old man sent out Stevens and Watson Brown under a flag of truce. Watson crawled back and seized his father's hand and lay on the floor of the watchhouse until death came. Stevens, bleeding and unconscious in the gutter, was taken to a shelter by a compassionate prisoner of Brown.

When night came there was no peace. The saloon was thrown open, and the night quaked with the sound of soldiers' voices. In the engine house, four men were all that were left to Brown. During the night Colonel Lee arrived and at dawn he drew up his men before the engine house. "Brown was the coolest and firmest man I ever saw," Lewis Washington said later, "With one son dead by his side, and another shot through, he felt the pulse of his dying son with one hand and held his rifle with the other, and commanded his men with the utmost composure, encouraging them to be firm and to sell their lives as dearly as they could." But Dauphin Thompson and Jerry Anderson were soon dead on the bayonets of the marines, and old John Brown had been beaten to his knees by a sword held in the hand of a young soldier.

"They are themselves mistaken who take him to be a madman," said Governor Wise. "He is a bundle of the best nerves I ever saw, cut and thrust and bleeding and in bonds. He is a man of clear head, of courage, of fortitude and simple ingenuousness." Governor Wise had followed the crowds into Harpers Ferry late that day, and went at once with other questioners to talk to the old man. Then, by his words, one could say there had been dignity in this desperate blood-letting? Colonel Lee had given it dignity; he had been solicitous that his wounded prisoners, Brown and Stevens, should not tire themselves during the interview with the Governor; Governor Wise had never let his voice rise at the old man lying on a pallet, the blood still matted in his hair. Only Congressman Vallandigham of Ohio had attempted to make political capital out of his questions about Giddings, about support in Ohio.

The old man had never lost his calm; he explained what he had proposed to do. The New York *Herald* printed his words exactly; a reporter had been there to take down all that had been said. "I pity the poor in bondage that have none to help them; that is why I am here; not to gratify any personal animosity, revenge or vindictive spirit. It is my sympathy with the oppressed and wronged, that are as good as you and as precious in the sight of God . . . Whether my tenure here shall be fifteen months, or fifteen days or fifteen hours, I am equally prepared to go. There is an eternity behind and an eternity before, and the little speck in the center, however long, is but comparatively a minute . . . You all have a heavy responsibility, and it behooves you to prepare more than it does me . . . You may dispose of me easily, but this question is still to be settled—this negro question—the end of that is not yet."

Is it any wonder that such a purpose and such a belief should shake even the antislavery men? From his Cincinnati pulpit, Moncure Conway, the Virginian, cried, "I believe Brown to have been mad as the average view madness; but I thank God that in this selfish age, when everything is first weighed in its relations to bread and butter, one man is found who can go crazy for an idea." And Garrison declared solemnly, "When he says he aims to be guided by the Golden Rule, it is no cant from his lips, but a vital application of it to his own soul. He will not die ignobly but as a martyr to a suffering race." And then, with a long backward sweep of the eyes and the heart to that day, years before, when Abolition had first come into its own: "How marvelous has been the change in public opinion during thirty years of moral agitation . . . Ten years since there were thousands who could not endure the slightest word of rebuke of the South; now they can easily swallow John Brown whole and his rifle into the bargain. In firing his gun, he has merely told us what time of day it is. It is high noon, thank God!"

The rising tide of hero-worship startled men whose opinions were not yet crystallized. The old man a hero? The old man was crazy! The Republicans were at the bottom of it—the Republicans took their orders from the Abolitionists, and the Abolitionists were canonizing Brown. The Democrats found their hands full of unexpected gifts. Seward, Giddings, Greeley, Gerrit Smith became the archconspirators who should be hung in the place of Brown. The Republicans sprang quickly to their own defense by calling Brown a madman, by mocking at Southern fears. Seward, Lincoln denounced Brown. Anti-Brown meetings were held in all large cities.

Yet bit by bit, the deeper significance of Brown's actions began to penetrate the consciousness of Northern men and women. Each day the Abolitionists praised God that Brown had not been killed, a hasty martyr. Each day that he lived, each moment that the imaginations of Americans were fixed on that prison cell in Virginia, the dream that had possessed the old man would filter through and stir the deep levels of comprehension. Had it been merely Stevens and Green and Coppoc, lying there as prisoners, one could have dismissed them as outlaws and only a few would have disagreed. But this man—*this man*—with the letters he was writing, with the deep, calm, prophetic spirit which seemed a world removed from the Brown of Osawatomie, caught at something in the heart and moved men beyond their desires . . . "I do not feel in the least degraded by my imprisonment, my chains or the near prospect of the gallows. Men cannot imprison, or chain, or hang the soul." . . . "My dear devoted wife: The sacrifices *you* and *I* have been called to make in behalf of the cause we love, the cause of God, and of humanity, do not seem to be at all too great. You know that Christ once armed Peter. So also is my case." Here was a man who could become the conscience of the nation, who could lay before men the awful pattern of the future.

Men who had believed that slavery could be extinguished without bloodshed now saw in the raid the first battle of a terrible warfare. "I think the end of slavery is ten years nearer than it seemed a few weeks ago," wrote Horace Greeley, and other men, too, built new visions about the old man lying in the prison cell. Even the Republicans began to see in Brown the symbol of retribution for the repeal of the Missouri Compromise and the horrors of Kansas. His martyrdom would be made high politics. Higher and higher, wider and wider the implications spread. Brown was no longer a man; he was the symbol of outraged freedom. His words became the words of a prophet and like a prophet he burned with a zeal that consumed the forces of his enemies. By one blow he had shattered the complacency of a passive North.

The South, usually so well equipped to deal with such a circumstance, was the victim of its own fear. Eighteen men had attacked an arsenal; a handful of well-trained militia could have put them down. Yet Virginia tumbled over its own fear. The armed camp which the state became, enlarged the symbol and made John Brown the sword of vengeance, the voice of the Lord.

"A most terrible panic [has] seized every slave state in the Union," a newspaper correspondent wrote from this northwestern corner of Virginia. Rumors of insurrection came from every section. On the day that Lee captured John Brown, "a general stampede of slaves" was reported to have taken place in Virginia and Maryland. "There must have been an understanding of some nature among them in reference to this affair, for in numerous instances—as I have been informed by the slaveholders since this insurrection—they have found it almost impossible to control them. The slaves were in many instances insolent to their masters, and even refused to work. It is believed by the slaveholders, since this insurrection, that the slaves were aware of it, but were afraid to co-operate."

Is it strange that rumors of invasion spread, that "mysterious Roman candles [were] seen shooting up at night among the mountains," that there was no rest to the fear that blazed up with the barns that were set afire not far from Harpers Ferry? Five in one week. Two slaves were arrested, convicted. Slaveowners tried to save them, for the evidence against them was incomplete and "since we of the South have boasted that our slaves took no part in the raid upon Virginia and did not sympathize with Brown," the effect might be undesirable. But others urged the penalty as a good example.

From Hagerstown, Maryland, and Alexandria, Virginia, large numbers of Negroes were reported to have left—voluntarily; from Berea, Kentucky, John G. Fee, the Abolition son of a slaveholding father, and a large group of his coadjustors left—involuntarily—for Ohio.

From Rochester, Frederick Douglass fled to Canada—Maryland soldiers had found some four hundred letters in the abandoned farmhouse of John Brown, and no one knew whom those letters would implicate. F. B. Sanborn, who had known as much as Douglass about the raid, set out on the same journey the next day. George Stearns and Sam Howe were on their way before the week was out. Hallucinations seized Gerrit Smith, whose political career and advocacy of insurrection put him in a painfully exposed position, and within three weeks he was behind the doors of an asylum. Only Parker, dying in Italy, and Higginson, scornful and fearless in New England, admitted their friendship with Brown and their reluctant agreement that such "insurrections will continue as long as slavery lasts, and will increase . . . as the people become intelligent and moral." "But such is my confidence in democratic institutions," Parker wrote on, "that I do not fear the final result. There is a glorious future for America—the other side of the Red Sea."

Yet all these were merely effects of a cause; the cause was lying in a prison cell and must be wiped out.

They tried Brown, lying on his cot in the courtroom, one week after his capture. For six weeks the ears of the country listened to the reports of his courage, to the tender communications that came from the jail, to the words of friends who had journeyed to see him, to the messages that Copeland, Cook and Green sent to say that they regretted nothing, that their faith in him and their common cause was as great as ever, to the words with which he saluted his sentence, "Had I interfered in the manner which I admit . . . in behalf of the rich, the powerful, the intelligent, the so-called great, or in behalf of any of their friends, every man in this court would have deemed it an act worthy of reward. I say I am yet too young to understand that God is any respecter of persons. I admit that to have interfered as I have done—in behalf of His despised poor—I did no wrong but right. Now, if it is deemed necessary that I should forfeit my life for the furtherance of the ends of justice, and mingle my blood further with the blood of my children and with the blood of millions in this slave country whose rights are disregarded by wicked, cruel, and unjust enactments, I say, let it be done."

Why should he die? some people asked. Higginson asked it; James Redpath and Richard Hinton who had known him in Kansas asked it; others wondered and planned. Then we will rescue him! But Brown forbade it; he refused to see his wife who had come to plead with him. Would kidnaping Governor Wise have the same effect? Lysander Spooner wished to know. Held on the high seas, Wise could be a hostage for the freedom of Brown. "Wendell Phillips was in favor of it. W. I. (Bowditch) would contribute." These were nineteenth-century Boston business men. War must certainly be approaching.

Germans, refugees from European tyrannies, gathered together in New York and talked of storming the prison. Ohioans were said to be forming under John Brown, Jr. Fugitives in Canada, grief-stricken and wailing, were declaring their willingness to die in the place of "their liberator." Kansans were gathering, reluctant to leave their hero to his fate. In all cases men could be raised, but money failed them.

Guards around the prison were doubled. Governor Wise, reading letters that burned his fingers, learned of "9,000 desperate men," of groups crackling through the underbrush at night. President Garrett of the B. and O. called out the militia on his own initiative because he believed the rumor that parties were coming from New York and Pennsylvania. Guards were stationed on the line from Martinsburg to Harpers Ferry. Virginians were warned to arm themselves and establish patrols for several days before the execution, keeping their wives and children under cover. All local traffic on the railroads was shut off by the closing of ticket offices. Anyone traveling in the northwestern section of the state without a pass was arrested, and four Congressmen, come to see the execution, ended in jail.

They brought him out to die on the second of December. Two thousand troops stood about the scaffold and cannon pointed toward the roads. The telegraph wires were in the possession of the government. Not many citizens were on hand, having heeded the warning to stay at home and watch their slaves.

He stood for a moment in the clear December day and looked across the heads of the moving men, across beyond the gibbet to the dark Virginia hills. "This *is* a beautiful country. I never had the pleasure of seeing it before," he said half to himself, and then he sat upon his coffin, and two white horses drew the wagon across the field. He seemed not to notice the companies of infantry that fell in about the wagon, he took no one's hand when he stepped quickly down. He said nothing as he stood above the trap, but his eyes looked again toward the mountains where he had dreamed that a race's freedom might be found.

His dignity, his strange serenity and joy, were deeply moving. Stonewall Jackson, commanding a company of artillery, found himself shaken to the soul and "sent up a fervent petition" that this man not die.

They kept Brown waiting longer than they desired—he had prayed that they dispatch him quickly—but the sheriff's hatchet fell in time, the rope jerked, and a long thin body hung like a great exclamation point against the sky.

All over the North, at that moment, church bells were tolling, and prayers were going up from thousands who wept as they prayed. Around the scaffold no words were uttered; the only sound was the terrible solemnity of soldiers' feet moving, their duty done. In the North, cannon were booming one hundred salutes. In Boston, Longfellow was writing in his diary, "This will be a great day in our history: the date of a new Revolution," and Emerson was speaking of a gallows made glorious as a cross.

All through the journey of Mrs. Brown back to the North with her husband's body, the friends were gathering. In Philadelphia a reception committee of hundreds of Negroes greeted her, in New York Wendell Phillips and James McKim came aboard the train to stay with her till they reached North Elba; in Troy, Rutland, Westport, bells tolled as the train drew in; in Rochester, Syracuse, Fitchburg and a dozen other towns as far as Illinois, people met together at the call of tolling bells. In Cleveland they draped Melodeon Hall in mourning and fifteen hundred people called on the "law of brotherhood as inculcated by Jesus Christ and the law of freedom as taught by Thomas Jefferson" to condemn the caricature of freedom abroad that day in the nation. In Boston, Tremont Temple could not hold the crowds and above the head of the people stretched a placard with the words of Lafayette, "I never would have drawn my sword in the cause of America if I could have conceived that thereby I was helping to found a nation of slaves."

"Marvelous old man! He has abolished slavery in Virginia." Wendell Phillips was speaking beside a mountain grave as colored and white neighbors lowered the body into Adirondack soil. "You may say this is too much. Our neighbors are the last men we know. The hours that pass us are the ones we appreciate the least. Men walked Boston streets when night fell on Bunker's Hill, and pitied Warren, saying 'Foolish man! Thrown away his life! Why didn't he measure his means better?' Now we see him standing colossal on the blood-stained sod, and severing that day the tie which bound Boston to Great Britain. That night George III ceased to rule in New England. History will date Virginia Emancipation from Harpers Ferry. True, the slave is still there. So, when the tempest uproots a pine on your hills, it looks green for months —a year or two. Still, it is timber, not a tree. John Brown has loosened the roots of the slave system; it only breathes,—it does not live,—hereafter."

How reluctantly, though, it learned of its own death. When three days after the execution, Congress met again, the glory and the shame became hardheaded matters of expediency, although social life in Washington was shattered and extra-political friendships went down under the tension. The tentacles of a Democratic Congress were reaching out for political game that might make the fortunes of ambitious men. Those papers, found in the Maryland farm . . . Who were Brown's supporters? The Republican menace, might, by these revelations, be cut down. They reached out with their subpoenas, but only Higginson was there and they had not asked for Higginson who knew more of old Brown's affairs than even Sanborn or Smith. They did not want Phillips or him, he said with his ready scorn, because they didn't want "to have John Brown heartily defended before the committee and the country."

Yet Virginia could not relax, although her soldiers were on a partial wartime footing. The things that were happening in Washington concerned her. It was taking the House eight weeks of physical violence and violent epithets to elect a Speaker because the Republican candidate had been accused of indorsing an insurrectionary volume, *The Impending Crisis of the South* by one H. R. Helper who was, by an inexorable turn of fate, a nonslaveholding North Carolinian.

Helper's book they called a greater danger to the slavocracy than *Uncle Tom's Cabin. Uncle Tom's Cabin* was an emotional appeal to slaveowners' better nature; *The Impending Crisis* was a statistical appeal to the nonslaveholding whites' most immediate interests. Words that Helper used had been denounced as treason in every Southern state.

> The first and most sacred duty of every Southerner [he wrote], who has the honor and interest of his country at heart, is to declare himself an unqualified and uncompromising opponent of slavery. Nothing short of the complete abolition of slavery can save the South from falling into the vortex of utter ruin . . . For the last sixty-eight years slaveholders have been the sole and constant representatives of the South, and what have they accomplished? We can make neither a more truthful nor more emphatic reply than to point to our thinly inhabited states, to our fields, stripped of their virgin soil, to the despicable price of lands, to our unvisited cities and towns, to our vacant harbors and idle water power, to the dreary absence of shipping and manufactures, to the millions of living monuments of ignorance, to the squalid poverty of the whites,

and to the utter wretchedness of the blacks . . . Notwithstanding the fact that the white nonslaveholders of the South are in the majority six to one, they have never yet had an uncontrolled part in framing the laws under which they live. There is no legislation except for the benefit of slavery and slaveholders. As a general rule, poor white persons are regarded with less esteem and attention than Negroes, and though the condition of the latter is wretched beyond description, vast numbers of the former are infinitely worse off. To all intents and purposes they are disfranchised and outlawed, and the only privilege extended is a shallow and circumscribed participation in the political movements that usher slaveholders into office . . .

The bitterness of the slaveless white allowed him to overlook nothing: the legislation which suppressed freedom of speech and the press, and found "its parallel only in the meanest and bloodiest despotisms of the old world"; the "mobbings, lynchings, robberies, social and political proscription to which the men of the South were subjected, simply upon the suspicion that they were the enemies of slavery"; the scarcity of schools and libraries, the indifference to culture; the overwhelming domination by the slavocracy, the Federal government, from Presidents and Chief Justices to consular officials abroad. He wrote on and on with passionate accusations, spreading out a terrible picture of disfranchisement, poverty and ruthlessness.

That such a man should speak for the South was inconceivable; he had been driven out. That such a man's book should be read by an aspirant to the Speakership of the House made that aspirant a man "not only not fit to be Speaker, but not fit to live," as Millson of Virginia put it laconically.

Northern representatives tried to be conciliatory. John Sherman, the guilty endorser of Helper's book, explained how the endorsement had been made; Thaddeus Stevens explained carefully that the Republicans wished to see every law obeyed until legally repealed on popular demand. But an issue had been shaped by John Brown and given focus by Hinton Helper, and conciliation did not lie in words.

Conciliation did not lie anywhere within this slowly balancing Congress. For the first time it had divided evenly—the Senate for the slave power, the House for its opponents. Violence flared, more deadly than ever in the past. Bowie knives were drawn. Aisles were filled with shouting, passionate men and the sergeant-at-arms arrested Congressmen to keep the peace. Up in the galleries a crowd, armed to its teeth for both sides, shouted its sympathies.

"A saturnalia of words"—this session. But something tinged the words now, some new desperation. An awful recklessness ran through the words secession, secession . . . One by one—two at a time—men jumped to their feet—men of Georgia, Florida, Mississippi, Virginia, Alabama, North Carolina—and shouted their defiance.

The heat and fury seared the country, and fear tightened the heart. To the slavocracy, the North was no longer divided; every bell that had tolled for John Brown proclaimed "to the South the approbation of insurrection and servile war." Divided by Harpers Ferry, the "North and the South are standing in battle array." Travelers brought back word to the North of being stopped by patrols and forced to give an exact reason for their presence; agents of Northern business men sent word of threats and terrorizing; salesmen reported attacks not only on themselves but on all who professed antislavery sentiments.

Was this merely the old threat of secession or had the temper really changed? The slavocracy insisted that this was no idle talk. If the Republicans gained power, the republic would be shattered "from turret to foundation stone."

Men began to ask, was this Union worth fighting for? The question pulled at the mind, but if one answered he might speak the first words of war. Certainly between peace and war lay appeasements, compromises . . . What vigor those words would have pumped out a short time ago; now their magic was worn to a faint pulsation.

The Abolitionists were no war-lovers. That the economic structure which had risen out of slavery could only be destroyed by bloodshed was a fact they were prepared to face, but they found no pleasure in it. Blood and chaos and despair . . . reason did not demand that slavery end that way, but a billion-dollar investment did.

Along the Ohio River the tension lay deep and poignant. Rankin's light in his study window glowed undimmed, and yet his nine sons went about armed with a new caution. The "trains" coming up from the river carried their heavy loads with that tense expectancy that any trip might be the last, that somehow the end of slavery was near.

Farther west, in Kansas, where the first campaign of the civil war had not yet burned itself out, the antislavery zeal caught fresh fuel from John Brown. But here the conductors on the road to freedom were no longer men of conscience, skillful in guile, but men of daring, sharp on the trigger, and the "railroad" was coming to the surface, a challenge to open conflict.

Farther north, in all the old "stations," the well-known scenes were being multiplied a dozen times. Stephen Myers, the colored superintendent of the line in Albany, New York, announced that in January, twenty-six passengers had gone through his depot, and added with a touch of humor, that many people would be shocked if some of the regular contributors to the upkeep of the road were identified. Staunch Democrats, he offered tantalizingly, who swore in public by the name of James Buchanan!

Staunch Democrats! The phrase itself seemed split in two. It was staunch Democrats who had held the country for the oligarchy these many years. It was staunch Democrats—Douglas' men—who came from the Northwest. It was staunch Democrats—Yancey's and Davis' men— who came from the deep South. Could there suddenly, after all these years, be two meanings to the word "staunch?" The terrifying fifties had twisted many meanings. What would come out of the Democratic Convention? The end of the Union or the consolidation of the slave power?

Charleston was unbearably hot for April. The Democratic delegates hired a hall and slept in rows on cots. The delegates from the North had an opportunity for the first time to see in operation that system for which they had given their political lives. After ten o'clock at night, they were told, they could not play their military bands; the drums might be mistaken for the alarm signal of a slave uprising.

Each delegation had a barrel of whisky; it helped them to perspire the committee hours away while the fighting, the logrolling and the trading went on.

The issue was simplicity itself. But that very simplicity was ominous. Douglas controlled the majority of the delegates, but Douglas was the ghost of a man who had committed political suicide when he opposed the Lecompton settlement. Douglas must be defeated. Douglas, for all his years of faithfulness, had now become a renegade; on Douglas' shoulders lay the guilt of vast lands given to freedom, of tariff proposals which would aid and comfort Northern manufacturers and leave the Southern planters desolate in their hot cotton fields. If Douglas were given the nomination, the Southern delegates would split the party open! Two days or arguing, of eloquence, of Yancey's most impassioned words, and the vote was cast. The Northern platform won. The Northern platform agreed to abide by all that the Supreme Court decreed for slavery, and since the Dred Scott decision had thrown the territories open to slavery, this would have seemed to be all that the slavocracy could desire. But the North was unwilling to guarantee complete party sovereignty to the planters, and the split came with a mighty roar.

"Go your way!" Glenn of Mississippi shouted, his face gray as ashes, "we will go ours! The South leaves you, but not like Hagar, driven into the wilderness, friendless and alone! I tell Southern men here, and for them, I tell the North, that in less than sixty days you will find a united South, standing side by side with us!"

That night, outside the courthouse, before the blazing of torches and the spellbound eyes of the people, Yancey hailed the new revolution; and up into the dark sweet air went three mighty cheers for "the independent Southern republic."

So the end had come. In the stronghold of the slavocracy, close by the slavepens, in sight of the Battery where aristocracy walked in the cool of the evening, the end had come. Everyone knew it for the end. If the Democrats were divided, the Republicans would win, and the Republicans were Abolitionists made palatable for cautious men in the North. Seward men—Sumner men—Giddings men—hated men—spokesmen for a rising tide that found its ebb when the country had begun and might reach its flood at the turn of this new decade. Nearly fifty years of undisputed power—knocked from the hand by a renegade! Was any man more hated in the South than Douglas? Was any man as dangerous as the tousle-haired, cigar-smoking, dynamic little Seward with his profession of a "Higher Law"? Seward knew all the tricks. With Seward controlling the Republicans the machine of politics would be readjusted and devour its children.

Never before had such passion and such turbulence torn American politics. But never before had a system come face to face with its death in this manner before. Perhaps something could still be done! They adjourned, deciding to meet again in Baltimore after they knew exactly what the Republicans had plotted for them in convention at Chicago.

"I feel an 'irrepressible' desire to congratulate you all upon the triumphant progress of the 'irrepressible conflict' in all parts of our country," Garrison's spectacles shone with the effervescence of his eyes. "For at last even the invincible Democratic party has been reached; and by the power which has been brought to bear upon it through the antislavery agitation, thank God! that party is no longer a unit in behalf of slavery. The antislavery society might adjourn *sine die*, after we get through with our present meetings."

The Republicans met in convention on the 16th of May, 1860. Never had the sprawling, shiny-new metropolis of Chicago seen such a crowd. It was evident that the Republican party was no longer the mere instrument of men with antislavery ideals; as a party it was bound SOME PLACE! and the jobseekers were aboard. A huge wooden building called the Wigwam had been built for ten thousand people, and twenty thousand people pushed their way inside. Seward's men were there by the thousands, with bands, with ensigns, with money to throw away. Seward was the man of the hour. Brilliant, devoted and skillful, he had fought a good fight. What a President! In Washington that day he said good-by to Henry Wilson. He did not expect to return to the Senate. From the Higher Law to the White House was a straight and inevitable step on this day when a new political age was being ushered in.

What happened? There were many explanations; that Greeley, who hated Seward, had swung the convention away from him; that Seward's men were overly confident and had ceased to fight; that Seward was found to be a dangerous man whom the West would repudiate.

The truth lay clear in these changing times. Seward *was* a dangerous man. All his political life he had been an antislavery man. He was a radical. The country knew him as a Higher Law man. And slavery was no longer the solitary issue. Thirty thousand people would not have crowded into Chicago if slavery had been the only issue. Protective tariffs, free homesteads, railways, jostled with the resolutions against the extension of slavery. "Vote yourself a farm." Out in the West they understood things which the tight-fisted manufacturers of the East did not. A Higher Law man might be hard for the West to swallow—the West which had room first for free lands and then for antislavery.

Who was acceptable to the East and the West? The wind began to veer around the second night while Seward's men were sleeping. The men from the West had been shouting a name all day; they hired a man whose voice, it was claimed, could outcry any storm on Lake Michigan to shout the name so that all the delegates could hear. They had decked the city with the fence rails which their favored son had cut; and all night his name worked a new and personal magic. "Honest Abe! Honest Abe! *Honest Abe!*" A safe man, a brave man, a shrewd man, self-educated, of Southern birth; on tariff and homesteads sound, on slavery, outspoken but conservative. He hated slavery, but he was prepared to see that the law was enforced until repealed. Was there anything hidden about him? East, West, and a little to the South he should be acceptable.

The next morning when the delegates assembled, the air was electric. During the night Lincoln's managers had pocketed the delegations from Indiana and Pennsylvania. The roll was called. Seward 173½—Lincoln 102. The delegates were wild with excitement. "Call the roll! Call the roll!" A second call with the air vibrating. Vermont came over to Lincoln, Pennsylvania delivered her votes. Seward's men looked like ghosts. The air was heavy with silence and then the scratching of twenty thousand pencils recorded the count for every man who was not already making for the doors to spread the word. When the third roll was called, no official announcement was needed. The yell, shaking the walls, gave the signal to the man who stood upon the roof to fire a cannon and to the thousands who jammed the street outside.

So the next President of the United States was to be Abraham Lincoln. Who was he? His pictures, multiplying overnight, put no end to speculation. A homely man . . . well, yes, a homely man even though his eyes were fine. A railsplitter. A country lawyer. An inconspicuous legislator. A Congressman who had left little mark. Lincoln-Douglas . . . people eagerly remembered snatches from his speeches. But all in all an obscure man.

It fell to Wendell Phillips to explain Lincoln to the Abolitionists. Most of them had been dismayed at the loss of Seward. They had known him for a long time in all his weaknesses and strengths. Phillips, giving a cursory glance at Lincoln's Congressional record, set a violent stage. "Who is this huckster in politics?" he demanded, "this county-court advocate? Who is this who does not know whether he has any opinions about slavery? . . . Abraham Lincoln, the Slave Hound of Illinois!"

Garrison was not sure of his opinion. He did not like Phillips' words. Suddenly cautious—face to face with the dissolution of that Union which he hated—he could not be sure whether Lincoln deserved such condemnation.

Abolitionists were torn in their opinions. For thirty years they had borne attacks: who was this man to whom they were passing on their disrepute? Abolition defenders of Lincoln were vocal and articulate. After Phillips produced a transcript of the Congressional debate on slavery in which Lincoln had demanded the return of fugitives, other Abolitionists replied by his advocacy of abolition in the District of Columbia, the petition against slavery which he had presented to the Illinois legislature nearly twenty-five years before, his indignant attacks on mob rule. The balancing went on. The scandal Giddings had had to raise in order to incorporate the principles of equality from the Declaration of Independence into the Republican platform versus the Douglas Debates, Lincoln's southern antecedents against the radical Abolitionism of his partner, Billy Herndon. The arguments were healthy. Lincoln's stature grew.

The Democrats had already delivered their ultimatum. They were as aware as Gerrit Smith that the Republicans' refusal to see slavery extended would mean the ultimate death of slavery, the quick unbalancing of representation, the end of power. Their steps were bold and climactic. Their effort to annex Cuba in order to balance the free lands of the West was defeated, but Buchanan vetoed the Homestead Bill (the Homestead agitation represented to free labor of that day what unionism does to the working people of this day) with the sonorous explanation that the bill would have introduced "among us those pernicious social theories which have proved so disastrous to other countries." They kept tariffs high and defeated a national banking and currency system, as well as subsidized shipping—all measures which were essential to Northern industry. They committed the Democratic party to the doctrine that slavery was protected and extended by the Constitution. They demanded that on no "pretext whatever, political, moral or religious," should the institutions of any state be touched and that the Fugitive Slave Law be strictly observed. Of farmers and mechanics they demanded complete subservience to the interests of the slavocracy, and finally of Northern capital, complete capitulation. The Republicans said that power, slipping from Democratic hands, was driving them mad.

They all tried to call it madness. But it must have been a canny madness that was doubling and tripling orders to Northern manufacturers, that was inspiring Floyd, Secretary of War, to stock Southern forts at the expense of Northern arsenals, and Toucey, Secretary of the Navy, to scatter the fleet so that it could present no massed strength for the government.

Actions were obscured in the hysteria of Washington. Northern men refused to see what was going on. Only Southern leaders perceived their course with wonderful exactness. Audacity had given them their power in the past; audacity could be used again. Audacity could even take the form this time of a slaveowners' *coup d'état*.

The pattern was simplified when the Douglas Democrats assembled, gloomy and disheartened in Baltimore. In the interval since Charleston there had been no mending of the breach; there had been only the brilliant invectives of Davis and Douglas hurled at each other across the Senate floor, and the rising enigmatic figure of that lawyer from the West. In melancholy desperation, the Northern Democrats nominated Douglas, and gave him, as a final frantic measure, a Georgia running mate who had taken for his own slogan the motto of the slavocracy, "Capital should own labor."

To repudiate Douglas was dramatic and well planned. It passed for madness with the unperceptive. But to the necromancers of the South it was as clear as water. By this action the last tie with the industrial, free-labor North would be broken. The compulsion of the Democratic party into the currents of the age would be prevented and the inevitable exposure of slavery to a new philosophy prevented. For if that philosophy were elected at the polls it would automatically expose, by the new army of officeholders which would fill the South, the suppression of free speech and free press upon which much of the slavocratic strength had depended. The fall of the Democratic party meant little if the slave power could be made secure.

All through the summer the fight deepened, a fight losing none of its significance because waged on fields apart from politics. It had as its pivot a solitary figure, $150,000,000, the approximate value of the trading in this year when "Negro fever" reached its height, when slave coffles, stretching the length and breadth of the South, brought a precarious and illusory prosperity, when the illegal slave trade was sailing in a sea of Southern patriotism and slave ships were putting out from every harbor—New York not excepted.

Against this pivot swung the $1,000,000's worth of property which had been annually escaping for several years. Estimators called this a conservative figure, since all sources were not available. Both slaveowners and "railroad" men multiplied it without hesitation. Be that as it may, it dramatized the revolt within the South—the revolt of that desperately ignorant minority which felt the vibrations of these swiftly changing times. Insurrections had blazed in the South for two hundred years, but the climax was reached in this fateful year.

Not a slave state in the Union was spared the profound terror which came with even a small band of armed slaves. If with those armed slaves were united poverty-stricken whites, if in their planned uprisings was the recurring theme, "land, animals, tools for civilization," the terror might, with reason, root wide and deep. That was the tale of 1860.

Slaves and whites were arrested, beaten and hanged together from Texas to Virginia. Strikes were spreading, adding that subtle fear that came when beatings failed to bring discipline, when a plantation of field hands laid down its tools and refused to lift a hand until work was lessened or treatment improved. Slaves in groups were taking to the underground road more than ever before, and obeying, whether they knew it or not, the words of Gerrit Smith, who spoke before the Vigilance Association of New York this year but addressed himself to those who might relay his advice, "When you are escaping, take all along your route, in the free as well as the slave states, so long as it is absolutely essential to your escape; the horse, the boat, the food, the clothing which you require, and feel no more compunction for the justifiable appropriation than does the drowning man for possessing himself of the plank that floats in his way." White friends were waiting at both ends of the fugitives' route. Alexander Ross was still spreading his news of freedom from Virginia to Mississippi, and would continue to do so till the guns at Sumter sounded. Thomas Garrett, writing to Still from Wilmington, told of the continued visits of Harriet Tubman and allowed a sense of mounting danger to creep into his reports: "There is now much more risk on the road than there has been for several months past . . . yet, as it is Harriet, who seems to have a special angel to guide her on her journey of mercy, I have hope." James Montgomery, the old friend of Brown, was good-naturedly challenging a detachment of Kansas troops,who were attempting to break up his station, to post a regiment in every Kansas county and watch the conductors get their passengers through.

The records of the conductors were mounting to amazing figures. Obscure conductors, reaching from Wisconsin to New England, were rounding out their records which ran into the hundreds. In the larger stations—the Rankin's, the Coffin's, the students' at Oberlin, the Vigilance Committees' in Detroit, in Cleveland where assistance to over one hundred a month was reported, in Philadelphia, in New York, the figures were mounting in the thousands.

In this atmosphere of dismay and change, the Presidential campaign spun through the states. Lincoln, the unknown, Lincoln the man with no record, Lincoln the homespun wit, must bear the Republican party to victory and somehow silence the audible horror of many business men and financiers who had arrayed Northern capital against this revolutionist from the West and formed desperate coalitions to dam this fountainhead of danger.

Against their golden stream of money some of the most brilliant men in the country set themselves. But still the Abolitionists were unconvinced. The Republicans maintained that by denying the right of slavery to extend into the territories, they would bring it to a painless death, but would they be faithful, a party which, to get Massachusetts votes, had urged the repeal of the personal liberty law? The Garrisonians answered to their own satisfaction, and they not only refused to support the Republicans, either politically or morally, but they lost no opportunity to speak against them in print, or by voice. Only Frederick Douglass, returning from the security of England, saw the future as a black man, and gave to Lincoln the power of his eloquence.

Horace Greeley said later that the number of speeches equaled all that had been made in Presidential campaigns from 1789 to 1856. Nothing had been spared. Young Republicans, organizing themselves in marching clubs as "Wide-Awakes" tramped through city streets, twenty and thirty thousand strong in their caps and their great oilcloth cloaks. Torchlight processions fastened themselves once and for all onto American political life. The shouting, the crackling of bonfires, the singing could be heard in the remotest piny woods of the South.

Already blue-cockaded "minute men" were drilling and parading in the large towns of South Carolina. "The fanatical, diabolical Republican party," as a campaign poster read, was bound for the White House with the "Southern renegade," "the human baboon," "the man-ape," and his dark-complexioned Vice-President Hamlin who was, as everyone south of Washington knew, a mulatto.

(In Natchez, Mississippi, half-grown slave boys drilled with sticks for guns; patrols listened outside Negro cabins; near the city Negroes were hanged for spreading the word of Lincoln.)

"Lincoln will be elected," Alexander Stephens of Georgia freely said, and white men were beaten for saying that they hoped he would be. Across the South stretched the shadow of the polling places, heretofore secure in the hands of two parties dedicated to a concern for Southern rights, but now in deadly danger. Voices were raised, from classrooms, from church pulpits, from newspapers, wherever men met together or extended their influence. "To subject the slavocracy to popular plebiscites means revolution and the subversion of all law and order!" For Helper's men, for the poor whites, there was no place on the ballot, since the name of Abraham Lincoln would be found on no voting sheet the length and breadth of the South.

The white-faced conservatives of the North were thrown into a panic. The Republicans were not yet in, but the South was arming! Appeasements, concessions—Maine, Massachusetts, New York, Illinois, Rhode Island, Pennsylvania offered "the unconditional and early repeal of their personal liberty bills." Massachusetts called up her respectable mobs again and turned them loose against the Abolitionists to show that a change in party was no call for a change in society. They took possession of a meeting, which was memorializing John Brown's hanging and for three hours pandemonium rocked the hall. They fell on the colored church on Belknap Street, where the saving of Wendell Phillips' life was attributed to the companionship of Maria Chapman. When, from the pulpit of the dead Parker, Phillips taxed his eloquence in describing the reappearance of these ancient horrors, he was again attacked as he left the church and his homeward journey became a procession of street fights.

On that very day in Brooklyn, a police guard was thrown around Henry Ward Beecher in Plymouth Church, and in Philadelphia, the abstractions of a lyceum lecture on Honesty by George William Curtis roused the apprehensions of the mayor and the owners of the hall and the lecture was suppressed.

But it was too late now to turn time back by such methods. On the 6th of November, in an atmosphere of unbearable tension which the bonfires, the shouting and the singing did not conceal, Abraham Lincoln was elected President. "For the first time in our history, the slave has chosen a President of the United States," Wendell Phillips cried, putting aside his disillusionment. "Lincoln is in place, Garrison in power."

To the South there was no extravagance in his words. The Abolitionists and the slavocrats had always understood each other perfectly. To the Abolitionist, the next morning's news came with no surprise.

The governor of South Carolina had sent a message to his legislature urging secession and advocating a volunteer force of ten thousand men. All business had been suspended in Charleston, palmetto flags were everywhere, palmetto cockades on men's hats and women's dresses. The judge of the United States District Court and the United States District Attorney had resigned their offices. Newspapers, politicians, preachers were calling for arms and calling on God. Alabama and Mississippi were calling conventions. Georgia was shouting for a million dollars to arm the state. Toombs was crying, "I ask you to give me the sword; for if you do not give it to me as God lives I will take it myself!"

The North was stupefied. Stupefied almost as witlessly as the poor old man who sat in the White House. Northern trade with the South ended on that 6th of November. The stock exchange went crazy, all loans were called in by the banks. From two to three hundred million dollars' debt stood on the Northern books from the South.

Some in the North, it is true, raised the cry of treason against the South, invoked the ghost of Andrew Jackson who had threatened to hang the nullifiers of South Carolina some thirty years ago. But a ghost proved too insubstantial to handle their fears. The South had threatened before—how had she been appeased? in whatever way, let us appease her again! Banks closing, the country on the verge of ruin, business men and financiers pointed out that no concession was too great.

The Abolitionists were watching and waiting. Lincoln, his hands tied, could only reiterate the sanctity of the Union, order Republicans "to hold fast with chains of steel" and refuse to be drawn into hysterical compromises. No voice would tell unless it was the voice of *The Liberator*, or *The Anti-Slavery Standard* of the undertow, the dark surging of the South. In Texas men went about with pistols and knives, preparing to shoot, cut down or hang any man who had cast a vote for Lincoln. In Georgia, plans of Negroes and whites to raise a rebellion on election day led to the hanging of a white conspirator. Farther north a secret and widespread organization of slaves came to the surface, but not before the leader had prophesied the defeat of the South " 'cause you see dey'll fight wid only one hand. When dey fight de Norf wid de right hand, dey'll hev to hold de nigga wid de leff . . . Pass on de word. De slaves is wild for freedom. An' white men'll be free too wid de end of bondage."

As November drew to an end, every eye was fixed on the new Congress. What remedy would the new Republicans, the old Democrats, offer? What would old Buchanan say? When Buchanan, with shaking hands and a tired voice offered his remedy, he turned for the last time against the North and preached a sermon on the sinfulness and folly of free states. He blamed the North for all the country's difficulties. Finally, he chided the South for not abiding by the choice of the majority, while maintaining their right to "revolutionary resistance to the government" if their slave property were further endangered, and felt for his chair as he urged a spirit of conciliation.

Jefferson Davis had stood by Buchanan's hand as he wrote much of that speech, but it pleased neither the North nor the South. It was nothing—less than nothing—the vaporings of a faithful and now senile servant of the slavocracy who was at the mercy of the Southern members of his Cabinet.

Speeches, tumbling over each other, had the heat and fury of Congressional debates at a gunpoint. To Southern Senators the end was foregone. They need put no restraint on their words, and they cried out furiously the words which had once before been used when troops were moving against Mexico. "We will welcome you with bloody hands to hospitable graves." Cries to reason, urgent and temperate pleas from the border states—Kentucky, Delaware, Tennessee—prayers for the Union seemed like pebbles rolling off an armadillo's back. Committees, resolutions held back the tide as effectively as hands against a broken dam. No man was to forget the uncertainty of that Congress, the bewilderment, the frantic devices to chain catastrophe.

They passed resolutions—eleven resolutions one day, eighteen another day, twenty-four soon after—all to avert the storm, all to make human property satisfied with its lot. Everyone felt the coldness of desperation—even Sumner had lost some of his golden eloquence and Hale's jokes

fell awry. Only the border state representatives claimed to see both sides
of the question, perhaps because their interests were so evenly divided.
Crittenden of Kentucky—the Nestor of the Senate they called him—
offered his ultimate panacea—six amendments to the Constitution,
allowing slavery south of the line of the old Missouri Compromise, protecting slavery and slaveowners in the District of Columbia as long as
slavery existed in Virginia and Maryland, providing government compensation for owners who had been prevented by the Underground
Railroad from recovering their fugitives, giving assurance that never—
never in the future—would Congress interfere with slavery, and proclaim-
ing the personal liberty laws null and void. It gave, in other words,
more than had been given at any time before, and it was called by the
time-honored name of Compromise.

But it was rejected. The South voted it down, after the country had
let the Crittenden Compromises lie joyfully in its mind as an alternative
to bloodshed. And with that rejection ended for all time the long, weary-
ing, dishonorable equivocations with slavery that had disfigured the
statute books. The South could have had it and more—but the South
had other plans. "The truth is," Alexander Stephens wrote, "our leaders
and public men do not desire to continue [the Union] on any terms. They
do not wish to redress any wrongs, they are disunionists per se and
avail themselves of present circumstances to press their object."

Down in Charleston Harbor, Major Anderson, the commander of
Fort Moultrie, besieged with his sixty men by enemies drilling day by
day, with the new million-dollar fortress, Sumter, ungarrisoned, was
sending urgent pleas to Washington. But Floyd, Secretary of War, had
nothing to send to Sumter. South Carolina would break her chains
soon, and then Anderson would no longer need his kind of help.

It came at last like an evil dream. America—states bound together
by common lives and common language did not really do as South
Carolina did, did not break a common destiny as though men could
truly order their own lives irrespective of their heritage. And all for what?
What did the secession ordinance base itself upon? "The violation of
Constitutional rights by the passage of personal liberty laws" (it was
thirty years ago that Garrison had laid that groundwork!), the irresponsi-
bility of "those states [which] have encouraged and assisted thousands
of our slaves to leave their homes, and incited those who remain to servile
insurrection." Was this enough to break, so solemnly, one state from
the Union?

The bells of Charleston, the exultant shouts, "The Union is dis-
solved!" the cannon, the state flag which appeared from every window,

found it a good enough reason even though its roots lay deeper than its words implied. Buchanan and Buchanan's Attorney General could find no precedent to help them in this terrible event, and in Springfield, without authority, without power, Abraham Lincoln could only watch a house divided fall.

Who was to blame for all this? The Abolitionists? From Boston, Garrison's scorn was pouring out hotly. "At last 'the covenant with death' is annulled, and 'the agreement with hell' is broken—at least by the action of South Carolina and ere long by all the slaveholding states, for their doom is one." The North hated him and Wendell Phillips more now than they had for twenty-five years. The house was falling, and Phillips was "speeding the parting guests." Massachusetts called up her respectable mobs again and turned them loose once more.

In Albany, the Democratic mayor put his Republican colleagues to shame by sitting on the platform, a revolver on his knees, while Susan B. Anthony and her friends fought all over again the battle for free speech. Minnesota mobs stoned the buildings of Republican meetings, and burned in effigy "the mother of the Republican party," Jane Swisshelm, whose press they had destroyed. In Philadelphia, the men of the Vigilance Committee went about in groups. William Still made the very briefest notations of his underground passengers on sheets which could be hidden at a moment's notice. Abolition sympathizers whose families lived in the South went frankly into retirement to spare their kin.

Barricaded in Charleston Harbor, Major Anderson, a Southern man but determined to do his duty, heard the bands, the cheering crowds, knew that the newspapers were clamoring for the seizure of the forts. Fort Moultrie, exposed by a long line of defenseless ramparts, would be impossible to hold. Fort Sumter sat on an island in the channel. The night after Christmas, he transferred his command across that half-width of channel, and Charleston, waking in the morning, found she had been duped.

Her indignation was as extravagant as her secession enthusiasm. She promptly took possession of the other forts, manned them, and sent commissioners to Buchanan demanding that Anderson be recalled. Poor Buchanan. The delegation bullied him; he protested that they did not even allow him to say his prayers. He had no place to turn. His Northern Cabinet members were trembling vessels—all but his Secretary of State who threatened to resign if Buchanan agreed to the demands of the commissioners. He refused them: he ordered reinforcements sent to the tenacious Anderson.

War seemed on the doorstep when the unarmed merchant vessel bearing supplies and two hundred reinforcements appeared outside Charleston Harbor and the South Carolinians opened fire. Major Anderson, his signal flags tangled, could not communicate with the vessel which slowly sailed away.

They were going rapidly now, the seceding states. Mississippi, Florida, Alabama, although Alabama was so reluctant that Yancey turned in a rage on the Unionists, calling them traitors and rebels.

A battle was raging at the Georgia secession convention. Knights of the Golden Circle, "minute men," vigilance committees, terrorist groups, threatened, bullied the "co-operationists" as the stubborn delegates clinging to the Union were called; Toombs, from Washington, bombarded them with telegrams. But the co-operationists did not budge. Douglas and Crittenden told them to hold on for the Union. The co-operationists elected a majority to the convention. But slavery politicians had never before been balked by a popular vote. They renewed their threats and their coercion on the convention floor, and they won by thirty-five votes. An effort to bring secession to the state ballot boxes was defeated and Georgia went out of the Union. But those co-operationists remained in the state. They should not be forgotten.

Louisiana went—no stumbling blocks of popular ratification here!

What was Washington doing when Texas left the Union and took a United States general and his gift of more than a million dollars in military property? Why, they were listening to talk of secession in New York, quite open talk; to the governor of New Jersey who was also certain that the Southern Union was "permanent," and New Jersey, "I say emphatically, would go with the South from every wise, prudential and patriotic reason." Fighting "will not be along Mason and Dixon's line merely," ex-President Pierce wrote to Jefferson Davis. "It will be within our own borders, within our own streets, between the Northern abolitionists and the faithful Democrats."

No further effort was made to relieve Sumter for no one would send the order. When the Secretary of the Treasury, on his own account, sent a wire to the captain of a revenue cutter off Louisiana, "If any man attempts to haul down the American flag, shoot him on the spot!" the message was not delivered. Lincoln, they said, looked like an old man. To those who received his letters, his policy was clear. Yield nothing. The new Administration must not be saddled with the terrors of the old.

And all the while the battle within a battle was going on. Charleston, so grave, so gallant with sword unsheathed, found her courage wearing thin. Business was motionless, the price of slaves had been slashed in half, her army was draining her resources at the rate of twenty thousand dollars a day. Where was that glorious panacea that came with secession? Washington stalling—stalling—stalling. Southern leaders talking—talking—talking the border states into solidarity. The loyalty of Delaware, Maryland, Virginia, North Carolina, Kentucky, Tennessee, Missouri, Arkansas was all that was left for the Unionists. In Montgomery, Alabama, the secessionists were meeting and there they proceeded with a formidable relentlessness to band themselves together into a Confederacy. The delegates of the seceded states adopted a constitution, modeled on the one under which they had been born, but with the word slave introduced where it had been most conspicuously omitted by the Founding Fathers. To acknowledge public sentiment and conciliate the border states, they prohibited the African slave trade. The government would take the form of the old, and a flag, like the Stars and Stripes, would be adopted. And Jefferson Davis would be their president.

They cheered him wildly—a graceful, slender figure, handsome, with a high fine brow and deep eyes. "Certainly a very different looking man from Mr. Lincoln," the London *Times* correspondent observed, "he is like a gentleman." And gentleman he was, by the rules of the new South where low birth ceased to stand like a high wall between a man and his ambition.

On the surface everyone was happy but South Carolina. The South Carolinians were in a rage. To ban the African slave trade was to give them no better than the old Constitution. The Charleston *Mercury* prophesied a new secession, although they knew, deep in their hearts, that they could not strike out alone. Yet how long—how long! When would business get better, when would this fine new Confederacy begin to bring prosperity to South Carolina?

Davis wished to communicate his confidence to all the citizens of Secessia, that beautiful new union of states which had found that "the ideas of the old Union were fundamentally wrong [since] our new government is founded upon exactly the opposite ideas; its foundations laid, its corner-stone resting upon the great truth that the negro is not equal to the white man and subordination to the superior race his natural and normal condition. This, our new government, is the first in the history of the world, based on this great physical, philosophical and moral truth." Fifteen million dollars was borrowed and one hundred thousand volunteers were called to sustain the principles of this lofty dream.

But was it any more the expression of the majority than it had been when three hundred thousand slaveowners ruled the South through Washington? It was not in the least surprising that vigilante groups visited the whites and that home guards were organized in every city or town to take charge of slave unrest and rumors of incendiarism and rebellion.

To the North, the climax upon climax never reached an end. While Lincoln was still an ordinary citizen no climax could be the last. No man seemed to agree on that final climax. Shall the erring sisters be allowed to go in peace, as Greeley urged? Or shall anything, everything be given them, as the mass meetings in New York shouted? Would a shot be fired—could a shot be fired? Could the North live without the South? Where was the dream, the hope, the faith that had rocked the monarchies of Europe and made the United States the spiritual home of the world's democrats?

(Up from the South the fugitives came, along the dark roads at night, across the dark rivers, tapping at the window of an unlighted farmhouse, passing on, passing on, telling of a black man there, a mulatto woman here, who would not make the trip, who exultantly would not make the trip, "caise Massa Linkum gwine come!" . . . "All de niggras know, Marse Linco'm is a-comin' and all de slaves are free!")

Lincoln left his home in Springfield. . . . "No one, not in my situation can appreciate my feeling of sadness at this parting . . ." Down in Charleston Harbor, Major Anderson still waited with his sixty men, a terrible hesitation mark to the Confederacy which had been seizing larger forts than Sumter. But Sumter was no longer a fort. Sumter was a test of nerves; whoever stayed his hand the longest was master of his fate.

In that curve of hills and river where Washington lay, the talk rose louder and louder. If Washington could be seized, the Confederacy would win the war. Stephens used the theme like a chorus to his speeches, and General Duff Green, dedicated to the slavocracy, made no effort to conceal the fact that the secessionists intended "to take possession of the army and navy, and of the archives of the government; not to allow the electoral votes to be counted; to proclaim Buchanan provisional president if he will do as we wish, and if not, choose another; seize the Harper's Ferry arsenal and the Norfolk navy-yard simultaneously, and send armed men down from the former, and armed vessels up from the latter, to take possession of Washington and establish a new government."

By all counts, that man making his way across the country from Springfield, must not be inaugurated.

Old General Scott, a Virginian, so fat and old he could not move without assistance, still bound himself to his duty. "Say to Mr. Lincoln that I'll look after these Virginia and Maryland rangers myself: I'll plant cannon at both ends of Pennsylvania Avenue and if any of them show their heads, I'll blow them to hell."

Lincoln was being cheered whenever his train stopped. He was talking always about the Union as though no Confederacy had been formed. Danger? He did not believe in personal danger until he came to New York, arrived in Philadelphia . . . In Harrisburg, Seward's son caught up with him.

Lincoln was not a coward; it took them all night to convince him that Pinkerton had uncovered a plot in Baltimore, where sporting men were laying wagers that he would never pass alive through their city.

He spent four days in Washington before he became President, trying to gather up what he could of four months' disintegration. Virginia, Tennessee, North Carolina, Arkansas still trembled just outside the Confederacy. The 4th of March came with armed companies marching through the streets. Old Winfield Scott had done his duty well, and Colonel Robert Lee was trusted. All night the Senate had been debating an amendment to the Constitution, an amendment which would close all doors to the abolition of slavery by Congressional action. If it passed it would become the Thirteenth Amendment . . . It took four years to pass the Thirteenth Amendment and when it was signed, freedom came to the Negro.

Lincoln looked odd in his fine new whiskers, some of the gaunt strange beauty of his face obscured. His voice was high and unsure, because to him the life of a country lay in the conviction, the patience, the broadness of his words. Douglas had stepped close to him and was holding the hat which Lincoln had found no place to lay. Douglas wished to say that this man was his President, that behind him he had come to range the million voters who might yet hold the issues of war and peace.

Lincoln said he had no mental reservation about any parts of the Constitution, he declared that the Union could not be broken except by the express consent of the whole country. "In your hands, my dissatisfied fellow-countrymen, and not in mine is the momentous issue of civil war . . . We are not enemies, but friends. Though passion may have strained, it must not break our bonds of affection."

Through the North his words spread swiftly, and many hearts were lifted. Surely the South must accept the hand that was stretched out. Even Garrison was moved by the "manly courage" of Lincoln and agreed that the South had been permitted a wide avenue back into the Union— if one wanted the South back. But events were bound to move more swiftly than conciliation. To the Charleston *Mercury*, afraid of any tide that might turn, it meant war as soon as someone took his courage in his hands and fired the first shot. Who would do it? Would it be Major Anderson, his supplies dwindling in Charleston Harbor, the fires burning nearer and nearer his keg of dynamite, or would it be some obscure insurrectionist, driven wild with nerves and an inflamed sense of honor?

Along the vibrating line of the Confederacy, news crackled. New Orleans' regiments were wild with excitement, the squares of Mobile were filled by troops as if by magic, Charleston echoed to the beating of drums and the galloping of horses. "The gauge is thrown down!" the *Mercury* cried. In an unarmed vessel, convoyed by a battleship, Lincoln proposed to send food to Sumter, Sumter which lay in a steel ring of seven thousand men and one hundred and forty cannon.

Yet the battleship was detached on Seward's orders and the relief ship stood off the bar of Charleston Harbor, unguarded. The guns of Charleston were manned; along the Battery the bravest and the most beautiful crowded to look out to sea where the Yankee ship lay against the sky. Would Sumter surrender? The United States flag told no tales; no men could be seen on the ramparts. Quiet—awful quiet lay on Sumter. In Charleston, the night was wild with rumors, the streets were brightly lighted. Each horse that galloped by came—who knows?—from Davis, from Beauregard, on whose joint commands lay Southern honor. Midnight came; in every house the lights still burned, and men crowded in the streets.

Two o'clock, three o'clock—a man heard of a message from Anderson —four o'clock, and a faint dawn was beginning to give an incandescence to the night. Along the streets people were moving again toward the Battery to join the nightlong vigilants. Faint, in the dawn, dim in the mists, what flag was flying over Sumter? A thousand eyes strained across the harbor, and a low sound that was neither sigh nor praise indicated that the night had brought no change. Perhaps today . . . perhaps another night would let them sleep. No one expected it so soon . . . it was the dawn brightening the sky, it was thunder out of a cloudless sky, it was anything but the fire and the roar of a gun. They stood transfixed in their houses, in the streets, along the sea wall, and then like a second reverberation from the cannon, a long unearthly shout split the air.

And thus the war began. The cannonading lasted for two days, and crowds came in carriages to watch from the sea wall. The week passed, ten days passed; Virginia hung in the balance. Lying across the Potomac, a lover of the Union, her Union men were being terrorized, a political machine held her fast to the secession convention. Senator Mason had even warned the voters in an open letter, "If it be asked, What are those to do who cannot in their conscience vote to separate Virginia from the United States? They should not vote on the question; if they retain such opinions they must leave the state." Forty thousand troops filled the state; yet the pro-Union men were said to be holding strong. The hours were agonizing. Where was the army? It seemed for a terrible moment that every officer of merit was a Southerner who had resigned his commission. And Washington was unguarded, corrupt with traitors. Cassius Clay, the Abolitionist from Kentucky, and Jim Lane, the wild man from Kansas, were scouring the city for volunteers to shoulder a gun and patrol the streets, guard the White House, hold the fort until the Massachusetts boys, the boys from Pennsylvania got there. In Virginia, no one knew what the vote had been. Maybe secession had lost; the spunk of the West Virginians was strong enough. The convention never published the figures of the vote; they merely said that the state had gone for secession.

Lincoln's face was more drawn. The Massachusetts troops had been mobbed, passing through Baltimore. He had to hold onto Maryland or Washington would be surrounded. He did not care about anything but saving the Union, and the Union was slipping from his hands. Arkansas went, 69 to 1—that is what they said, although, before Sumter, secession had been defeated. Union—Union—maybe it would become a choice between holding the border states and losing the Abolitionists. The Abolitionists had elected him, beginning back twenty years ago when the old Liberty party set the pace, and some said that he was at heart an Abolitionist. But he could not show them his heart. All they could see was his fumbling, fumbling with the border states, cajoling, wheedling, persuading the war-hungry recruits that they were fighting not for slavery, but for the Union.

No move escaped Garrison, and Garrison saw something that made him friendly. Garrison puzzled his friends. Had he not always preached disunion? Why was he supporting Lincoln now in a fight to restore the Union? He answered that the right to secession was based only on the rightness of the cause, and around Lincoln, he prophesied, "all the elements of freedom will coalesce." He persuaded the executive committee of the American Antislavery Society to postpone the annual meeting indefinitely "in view of the cheering fact that there is at last a North as well as a South, and that the present tremendous conflict is in its tendencies strongly and irresistibly towards the goal of universal emancipation."

In this point of view he had the support of the New York and the Philadelphia societies who saw in the confusion and tension of the days the consummation of their hope, the long-concluding story of Lovejoy,

Fairbanks, John Brown, and all the others who had given lives and broken heads for the cause of human freedom.

And yet there were many like Higginson, who refused a commission in the army, who questioned the antislavery sincerity of the government, who saw in the policy of Lincoln and the declaration of war "the darkest hour for the slave in the history of American servitude," who, wary with thirty years' persecution, demanded that the basis of the war (for was not Lincoln to say that the only thing which had ever threatened the Union was slavery?) be made clear with a prompt statement of emancipation. Intentionally or not, this was the slaves' war, and black men, North and South, clamored for their share. Douglass and other Negro leaders kept up a tireless agitation for colored regiments.

The government was disturbed. It could not present this conflict to the country as an Abolition war. Uncertain how to deal with the situation it refused the Negro any part at all. The Negroes gave their answer. New York Negroes formed a military club, drilling regularly until the police intervened. Pennsylvania Negroes offered to go South and organize slave revolts. Washington Negroes presented themselves, three hundred strong, for enlistment in the Union Army. Slavery was already gone. Only the government did not know it.

Among the slaves excitement was deep and wide. Hardly had the guns of Sumter been quieted before the exodus began. By May, fugitives were coming through Ohio in carloads. The Fugitive Slave Law still stood on the statute books, but the Underground Railroad dared to come to the surface now, and it was not necessary to carry the lines to Canada. Even the negrophobes looked with an oblique interest at these enemies of their enemy. The road's employees doubled over night.

Within the South the alarm was deep and chilling. Travelers along Southern roads saw masses of Negroes being driven to the interior away from the threat of abolitionizing armies. Everywhere the laws were tightened as they had been in the days of Gabriel, Vesey, Turner. In the cabins, in the nights, it was for Abraham Lincoln and to Abraham Lincoln that the prayers went up.

> It won't be long
> Poor sinner suffer here.
> We'll soon be free
> De Lord will call us home.
> My brudders do sing
> De praises of de Lord
> We'll fight for liberty
> When de Lord will call us home.

They put Negroes in jail for singing that, because although it was an old spiritual, the fervor was new and the spell was contagious. "Dey tink de Lord mean for say de Yankees," a little colored boy told a Federal officer, his white teeth shining as he sat in the moonlight outside his tent.

The strange breed of Yankee who camped along the border of the Confederacy and seemed as bent on slave docility as the master, became a richer symbol of salvation than the hierarchy of heaven, even if they were behaving with an inexplicable strangeness, as though this were not a black man's war, and were turning back the fugitives who came with all their belongings to the camps.

But the fugitives would not be turned back. Freedom lay with "Massa Linkum." At Fortress Monroe, the Yankee General Butler was faced with a settlement of the problem in the person of three fugitives. This was not an Abolition war . . . but away from the army he was a smart enough lawyer to know that they presented their case appealingly. Their master had joined the Confederate Army and had already ordered them to North Carolina to help in the building of fortifications. General Butler was gruff, but he needed laborers and he set them to work. In a short time, an agent of the master came into camp looking for his Negroes. With them came a question of great delicacy. If slave property was not protected by the army, the border states might shoot out of the Union without further consideration. Yet General Butler was perfectly aware that Negro labor was a source of strength to the Confederacy, releasing white men for the army. The General refused to return the fugitives. "You're using Negroes on your batteries," he snapped. "I shall detain them as contraband of war."

"Contraband!" The word straddled the question with Yankee ingenuity, it tickled the humor. The escaping Negro did not care what he was called. The day after the three slaves became a part of the Union, eight more presented themselves, on the next day forty-seven—men, women and children. They came by twenties, thirties, forties. By July 30th, nine hundred had appeared, all earnestly declaring their eligibility.

Butler appealed to the War Department to sustain his decision. The War Department, by a masterfully ambiguous definition of a commander's duties, agreed that all such props to the Confederacy should be received within the Union lines. Before the next few weeks had passed, several thousand, responding to grapevine messages, had streamed to the meager hospitality of "freedom fort" and to the colored schoolteacher whom Lewis Tappan had sent to induct them into the mysteries of their new station.

Within the South, the war within a war went on. North Carolina, Tennessee, Arkansas, hovered close to the Union orbit. Where did their future lie? The Unionists within the states were vociferous. The Confederates were adamant. In May, the Confederates won, and in the mountains guerrillas formed to fight for the Union. Maryland, Kentucky, Missouri were bedded deep into the Union and could not be entirely dislodged.

In the Confederacy secession was patriotism, but many men were not moved by patriotism and preferred the swamps to the army of the South. Those who came to fight for Southern honor and the preservation of the past brought their guns with them and so helped equip an army. Women's spinning wheels turned homes into textile factories until millworkers were trained and machinists returned from the North to assume a share of the burden. If gentlemen's fowling sticks and plebs' squirrel guns proved inadequate weapons, then there were the rich stocks seized with the United States arsenals, there was the Tredegar Iron Works at Richmond, there was the beginning of blockade-running. And, since battles could not be fought on guns alone, fields were plowed under, grain and corn planted where the king of the South had ruled.

But the king of the South would still win the battle, the planters insisted. Maybe one could not eat cotton, but the mills of the North would lie idle, people would die of starvation, the North would be brought to her knees because the precious white bolls no longer flowed in a rich stream. And England, bound to Southern slavery by her textile mills, would give her comfort to the South and sustain the men and women who needed what England had to give. "For, dear sir," a Southern host told William Russel of the London *Times*, "we have only to shut off your supply of cotton for a few weeks and we can create a revolution in Great Britain. Four million of your people are dependent on us for their bread."

Hopes were very high. A slaveholders' *coup d'état* had worked with the precision of a machine.

The tales of Yankee demoralization, of failing enlistments, of questions mounting, "What is this war being fought for?" of the tall fool in the White House who could come to no definite action, of Union troops kicking up the dust to Manassas Junction, lay like effervescent wine on the tongues of Southerners. At Manassas, gentlemen gave the Northern "mechanics" hell, and when the battle was over, when the wounded had been picked up and the dead buried, the unquenchable power of gentlemen over tradesmen was undisputed.

Only one thing remained to certify the victory. Virginia slaveowners in person went to their slaves, and told them that the Confederacy had won. Many Negroes were prostrated, many became ill and only turned their faces from the wall when the news was whispered that the war was still going on.

The slaveowners were suffering none of the delusions of later romanticists. Spies in Yankee uniforms mingled with slaves, slave codes were revised, patrols were increased and given unlimited authority; to every twenty slaves a white overseer was appointed. Yet the "left hand" which the anonymous Scipio had prophesied was unremittingly busy with conspiracies, arson, and murder. "The news is suppressed as far as possible," a Charleston lady recorded, "and kept entirely from the papers, for the Negroes hear what is published if they do not read it, and such examples might produce disastrous effects."

A Southern historian, B. I. Wiley, writing in later years disposed succinctly of slave docility. "Instances of positive loyalty remained foremost in the minds of the Southern people and have become the chief cornerstone of the tradition of the conduct of the slaves during the war. But these acts of loyalty, in the light of contemporary evidence, must be considered as exceptional. They were usually performed by domestic servants, a class constituting a very small minority of the Negro population."

By the hundreds, half-starved, half-naked, they were coming into the Union camps only to be handed over to slaveowners' agents, who received every courtesy from Union officers. Union officers were, on the whole, conservative, constitutionally minded with regard to the Fugitive Slave Law.

Howe of Wisconsin made an effort in Congress to put an end to the horrid business. The House of Representatives, more sensitive to the public temper than the army officers, voted on a resolution offered by Lovejoy, and said that it was no part of the duty of the soldiers of the United States to capture and return fugitive slaves. To still the outcries of the border states, remuneration was promised to the master if this war were ever over.

Frémont had gone out to Missouri to hold the West for the Union. And how was he going to do it with proslavery men fighting him from behind trees? Confiscation seemed a logical and incisive weapon. Confiscation included slaves.

The news spread like a shock down the Mississippi. Slaves as far as Louisiana learned to pronounce the name of Frémont. From north and south and east and west they flocked into his camp. Frémont was astute; his blow had been accurate. Most men of the North nodded, and the antislavery societies saw "the beginning of the end." They were in no way prepared for Lincoln's answer.

There had been no public display of Lincoln's distress, no publication of the letters which passed between him and Frémont, in which he explained his fear that the border states—always the border states!—would take offense unless Frémont modified his order. All that became public was Lincoln, harassed and unhappy, announcing that freedom could only come from an act of Congress and that Congress was not prepared to act. The shock of his announcement filled the pages of the loyal newspapers.

Moral and military bleakness lay upon the North. Lincoln, driven by his caution, by his unquenchable concern for human values, by his fear of a disunited North, allowed the depression to deepen. Slow trickling armies, reaching like thin fingers into Confederate land, desultory fighting in the Southwest, skirmishes in Virginia, generals of doubtful loyalty —and a solitary man who could command no respect was responsible for it all.

The Abolitionists, black and white, were filled with indignant despair. They saw Frémont removed for refusing to modify his orders, they heard no rebuke when Halleck, who succeeded Frémont, forbade his officers to receive fugitives within the lines, when Sherman in Kentucky and Dix in Maryland took the same stand, or when a trainload of fugitives was stopped by Union officers in Baltimore and returned to slavery.

The Abolitionists recognized their duty, grimly, tenaciously. Why should they be surprised that the government had failed them? And yet one blow—*one blow*—would end the war! They were as sure of that as of the rebelliousness of slaves. Agitation must start again—the forming of opinion. Gerrit Smith wrote an unsparing open letter to the President; Phillips pounded relentlessly from every platform he could reach; Sumner was pouring out his scorn of this "vain masquerade" of battles without emancipation. Henry Ward Beecher and Octavius Forthingham, seeing a return of the days of Pierce and Buchanan, were rallying New York, Moncure Conway, at the instigation of Sumner and Chase, was carrying his message of immediate emancipation through Ohio. Garrison's unnatural peace fell away, and he drew up a fiery memorial for Congress. In November, Abolition hope came alive again.

Then the Sea Islands, off the coast of South Carolina, fell to the Union fleet after a hurried evacuation by the slaveowners, and the Abolitionists could say again, "You see; the slaves believe in the Union cause. They're fighting the war for us. We cannot abandon them." For there they were when the army arrived, pushing to the shore, leaving the plows they had seized from their masters, the land they had appropriated for themselves, free men greeting free men. The men in the blue uniforms were touched.

General Saxton set up schools, teachers hurried from the North. School was a game; school was a serious business. Men, women, and children came to the schoolhouse at any hour expecting to "catch a lesson." School was any place covered by a roof—churches where the littlest child could not be seen because of the height of the pews, lean-tos, cabins, barracks. Learning was administered with any bit of printing that lay at hand. The Bible, missionary tracts, Tennyson's poems, all taught the alphabet. Fugitives were arriving not daily but hourly. Books, teachers were needed. Missionary tracts were torn in two; "contrabands" came forward and said they had gotten an education clandestinely years ago, that they could teach.

Escape was irresistible now. Words acquired new meanings. One slave might say to another "Good mornin', Sam, yo look mighty greasy this mornin'." Sam would seek him out soon in private for "grease" meant fresh news about freedom. Deep in the interior only was slaveholding relatively safe.

Before the end of the year private benevolence took over the duties of the government. Freedmen's Aid Associations were founded, from New England to Indiana. Old antislavery workers found a new outlet opening up for them.

"It is assumed that labor is available only in connection with capital. . . ." Senators and Representatives stirred, for the high singsong voice had been saying nothing significant, in their opinion, nothing decisive. Congress, for all its vaporings, wanted decision after a year and more of war. "This assumed, it is next considered whether it is best that capital shall hire laborers, and thus induce them to work by their consent, or buy them and drive them to it without consent. . . . Now there is no such relation between capital and labor. . . . Labor is prior to and independent of capital. Capital is only the fruit of labor, and could never have existed if labor had not first existed."

Congressmen stumped off when it was over. "Wishy-washy," they said, "feeble and rambling." Old Abe never got down to the point. Neither Democrats nor Republicans were in the least pleased. *What are we going to do with the black fellows?* What are we going to do about England? Tory England had no natural affection for the democratic North. The American Ambassador was working hard, but he had no material to offset the scorn of the Confederate agents who were still using the battle of Manassas with deadly effectiveness. Garrison was ill but he was writing voluminously to England. George Thompson and other powerful friends must disseminate the Union point of view and try to explain Lincoln to the British people. The Union might, in the end, die without their support.

"Repeal the Fugitive Slave Law!" "Protect the fugitives!" Congressmen were feeling the pressure of constituents. Debates were violent. Antislavery members seemed possessed with the horror of slaves shot down by Union soldiers. "How slow this child of freedom is being born!" Sumner exclaimed in despair.

And now another cry was growing. "Let black men fight for their freedom." It would be a gesture of emancipation. Negro Abolitionists never stopped their fusillade. The social test embodied in emancipation must be made clear to authorities who were deeply tangled in negrophobia. Certain white men agreed. And then, in March, 1862, the hearts of antislavery men quickened almost unendurably. To the Southern States compensation was offered if they freed their slaves—their last opportunity before the government took action.

Yet, after they had examined it closely, and realized that no time limit had been included, Douglass and Garrison wanted to know what it offered. To his old colleague, Oliver Johnson, Garrison wrote, "I am afraid the President's message will prove a 'decoy duck' or a 'red herring.'" From many quarters there was cause for alarm. Why had Wendell Phillips been mobbed in Cincinnati for declaring that the right hand of Southern aristocracy was Negro slavery and the left the ignorant white man? Why were there continual revelations of cross-purposes among the men closest to Lincoln?

And yet as spring lengthened, Garrison felt his gloom lifting—and his gloom always lifted in public. Congress was sending out a small but steady flow of antislavery legislation. At the end of March, officers were forbidden on penalty of dismissal to use their soldiers as slave catchers. In April, a fight which had begun thirty years before, that had harried Congress after Congress and had sent many a calm man shouting to his seat, was finally brought to an end with the abolition of slavery in the District of Columbia. In June, after a stormy passage through Congress, Lincoln signed a bill "securing freedom to all persons within the territories of the United States." In July, freedom was given to those slaves, men, women and children of disloyal masters who came into the Union lines for safety, and five days later an additional order provided wages for contrabands.

These were the cold facts. But they were soon brought to life by the stampede of the slaves. When the word percolated through the patrols, through the tightening grip of the master, that fugitives were safe within the Union camps, the flights increased to great mass movements.

One million dollars' worth of slaves a week were saying good-by to

North Carolina, a Confederate general reported early in 1862, and eastern Georgia sent an elaborate and urgent plea to the Confederate authorities to halt in some way the flight of property worth from $12,000,000 to $15,000,000, representing not only a good round figure but demoralization of other slaves as well.

The Confederates built a large elaborate system of overseership for slaves laboring on army projects, detachments of cavalry in some cases forming a circle around them, locks and keys in other cases holding them at night. Yet General Johnson found that he had "never been able to keep the impressed Negroes with an army near the enemy. They desert!" and the governors of Virginia, the Carolinas, Tennessee and Georgia were never able to forget their fears of insurrection.

The Underground Railroad had never seen such days as these. A greater insurrection was going on among the slaves than had been dreamed of—an insurrection of rising bondmen, taking their masters' possessions and leaving the fields and granaries of the Confederacy, the labor battalions, the factories. And what good were laws, pleas to loyalty, night riders? Five hundred thousand men, women and children coming into Union camps, were to find the answer that suited them.

Emancipation was in the air. For the first time, Lincoln was talking about it to his Cabinet. Even the repudiation of General Hunter's orders (Lincoln was still clinging to the remnants of his hope that the offer of compensated emancipation would bear its doubtful fruit) did not offset the advance toward the necessities of freedom.

During July and the following August, agitation all over the North for emancipation increased irresistibly. Mild men, compromisers, were swept into actions which would have startled them at another time. Church delegations drew up memorials or went to Washington to plead with Lincoln face to face. It had become the issue of emancipation and a quick peace or slavery and a long war. Men did not know of a document which had already lain on the Cabinet table, over which Chase had pursed his lips and Blair had shaken his head and Seward had brought his fist down on the table. All summer the bombardment kept up. Lincoln listened to it and felt its impact. All summer he knew a thousand things, fugitives, fugitives and more fugitives, a dissatisfied and questioning country, a Congress restless with its border states representatives, its slaveholding Democrats, its indecisive Republicans. He heard the voices of Greeley, of Phillips, of Purvis, of Douglass, of Garrison, of Thad Stevens, of antislavery societies, of wavering men, suddenly resolute—"Arm the black men!"

In Louisiana, General Ben Butler sent out a call to the free colored people—"Defend the Union!" In South Carolina, Hunter had gone ahead again and enlisted a regiment of freed slaves. The tide was moving fast. Colored men like Douglass, Langston, Purvis, Hayden, William Wells Brown, Charles Lenox Remond redoubled their efforts. They exhorted, they challenged, they recruited their people all over the country. "Pay or no pay, let us volunteer!" . . . "Who would be free themselves must strike the blow."

The inevitable was pushing hard at time. Antislavery was growing respectable, antislavery was the dimly sensed philosophy of the North. All the obscure heroes of the past—the men of the Underground Rail-road, the Abolition lecturers, the readers of *The Anti-Slavery Standard* and *The Liberator* had sunk into the wide pliant mass of Americans and were indistinguishable from many of their neighbors. A minority they still were, a minority they would always be, but they were spreading out now like water on the sand.

In Congress the forensics of opposition grew more wordy, but anti-slavery beat them down. Tentative and faltering legislation, enlisting five thousand black men, was made. Black men flocked to the recruiting offices. Within a month the First Regiment of Louisiana Native Guards went onto the battlefield. The way was open. Black men came tramping down the dusty Southern roads, their possessions on their backs, their children clinging to their wives. Mast' Linkum's colonels—Abolition men —looked with sinking hearts at these tatterdemalion recruits, intoxicated with freedom.

Higginson, in South Carolina with a regiment of white volunteers, received an urgent message from General Saxton, who had taken over General Hunter's experiment in black enlistments. Colonel Higginson must help. Would he accept a commission?

Higginson made his way to Hilton Head, South Carolina, to look over the recruits. He knew the dangers and the moral responsibility. If these black soldiers were a failure, the proslavery forces in the North would be strengthened in their inward parts. But he liked what he saw. The re-cruits were all black as night. Not a mulatto in the group. That was what he wanted. Africans whose good qualities could not be explained away by their white blood. He spoke to a man who had just been wounded in an expedition. "Did you think that was more than you bargained for, my man?" White eyeballs rolled to look at Higginson. "I been a-tinking, Mas'r, *dat's jess what I went for.*"

Raw! They were more raw than a farm hand who might have drilled with a plow handle. Yet the First South Carolina Volunteers, colored, went into action within six weeks. Higginson said they were born soldiers.

A whip might have driven them in slavery, but as freemen, half a night's work after a day's setting up camp was "no work at all, Cunnel; dat only jess enough for stretch we."

Missouri, still a slave state within the Union, was troubled. The slaves were melting over the border into Iowa, Illinois, Kansas. When the third Negro regiment took to the field it was the First Kansas Colored, and most of the soldiers had been ticket holders on the Underground Railroad. Desperate Missouri, helplessly watching nearly half of her human property shaking the dust of Missouri from their feet, now dispatched a plaintive request to Washington for permission to include the Negroes in the state's quota of troops.

But when would it become impossible to talk of some men enslaved and other men free? Preachers asked it from the pulpits. Newspapers asked it in bold headlines. People began gathering in mass meetings and exclaiming, "What's happening? Why don't we lick those rebels with their own slaves?" In Chicago a huge meeting memorialized the growing Middle Western conviction that this must be an Abolition war. They sent two of their distinguished clergymen to read their memorial to Lincoln, and the clergymen pointed out to him on their own account that the country needed the support of Europe which emancipation would accomplish. He agreed that there was much wisdom in this—he was as well informed as they on the solidarity of British workers in their fight against the recognition of the Confederacy. But what could he do? he asked, who had an emancipation proclamation in the drawer of his desk. How could emancipation be enforced in the South? Who would free the slaves if they did not free themselves? Would Jeff Davis? Would Alex Stephens?

He wondered all these things aloud on September 3rd. The delegation took the train for Chicago, perplexed and troubled. They believed in Abe Lincoln, they knew he was a true and a kind man, but why did he fail to understand that it was the people who were beginning to speak through all these memorials, these meetings?

They had scarcely shaken their top hats free of the dust of the journey when the telegraph wires began to hum. The country shook itself. What did this mean? The Abolitionists held their breath. Had the day truly come after all these years? They read it again and then again. ". . . That on the first day of January, in the year of our Lord one thousand eight hundred and sixty-three, all persons held as slaves within any State . . . the people whereof shall then be in rebellion . . . shall be thenceforward and forever free. . . ."

They were unprepared for the shock. They had not seen in the inconspicuous Union victory at Antietam the moral justification for which he had been waiting.

The newspapers rallied first. Their editors wrote out of the heat of their prejudices. Lincoln had at last justified their faith . . . Lincoln was an unconstitutional monster. The little journals, the two-sheets published in small towns, which shaped the opinions of their localities, sustained him courageously; the Democratic papers saw him as the betrayer of the country. The bewilderment, the rage, the rejoicing mounted wherever friends met together. The Abolitionists moved with caution. A friend, calling to congratulate Garrison, found him curiously silent. He was disturbed, he admitted. Why had the President not included the border states in the emancipation? Why had he left the slaves in the hands of angry and vindictive masters for three months? Why did he still talk of compensation and colonization? Why did he leave the Confederacy time to take the same step and win foreign support? Other "radicals" asked the same question. Garrison tried to hearten them, steer their course smoothly, as his conscience had directed him since this war of inevitable freedom had begun. Yet privately he and Phillips spread their caution to inexperienced and jubilant colleagues who wished promptly to disband their societies and end their periodicals. "There has never been a time when Abolitionists should weigh their words more carefully," he wrote. And Phillips, now a great man, a man above party or creed, warned them that real freedom must yet be won for the Negro. "The Proclamation does not annihilate the system. In the gospel, the devils came back to the swept and garnished chambers." Yes, evil remained, Douglass agreed, but the war had been put on a different basis. Abolition would now reach as far as the Union Armies. He was always willing to be grateful for small gains.

Yet fear did not slip from their minds. What if the long warning to the slave masters left them time to sell their slaves to Cuba, to spirit them off to South America? What if Lincoln weakened under the bludgeonings of an hysterical Southern press, under the resignations of conservative Union officers? What if Greeley was right when he claimed that the majority of the Northerners did not want emancipation if they could have peace instead? What if McClellan was able to gather the class-haughty, Negro-hating officers about him, the Lincoln-hating voters, the men who saw the Union abandoned for an Abolition war, and offer a greater threat to the Presidency than rumor had put in his mind?

But the underground telegraph had already spread the news down the Mississippi across the Texas plains, up to the Carolina mountains, through Tennessee, into Virginia. The proclamation was waiting for nobody, nothing. The increasing mass flights showed its effectiveness, the Confederate detachments sent to fight rebellious slaves, the pickets which left their duty to attack marauding parties—even the increasing signs of white disloyalty, the open defiance to the Confederate government, the signed petitions for Union meetings and the open declaration of Union sentiments, which sprang up here—there—in the very heart of the Confederacy.

How alarmed then should one be by the sweeping Democratic victories —Indiana, Illinois, Ohio, Pennsylvania, New York—gone against Lincoln that autumn? By the stocks which continued to fall and the troops who continued to desert and to stay away from the recruiting stations? By a graceless Congress which listened to the December Presidential message in dour unfriendliness? By the message itself which talked still of compensation?

The Abolitionists worked harder than ever through days that increased in darkness. Would the first of January never come—and when it came, what would it bring? The Abolitionists knew that their English friends were working for them day and night, that the ammunition which could be put in their hands by the Emancipation Proclamation would be sufficient to swing the British government to the side of the North. "The heart of the people is sound," George Thompson wrote to Garrison in December. "It would be impossible to carry a proslavery resolution in any unpacked assembly in the kingdom. But the sentiments of our leading journals, of a portion of our public men, and of the aristocratic circles—are precisely similar to those which prevailed in the same quarters during the struggle for the emancipation of our own slaves. . . ."

Every post from England brought the evidences of solidarity—meetings in Sheffield, Manchester, London, and other cities to greet the September declaration and to denounce slavery; John Stuart Mill, John Bright, Cobden, Lord Houghton, Herbert Spencer, banding together into the Emancipation Society to agitate throughout the kingdom against British intervention, against the threatened intervention of Napoleon III, to counteract the propaganda of Mason and other Confederate agents, to prevent if possible the sailing of Confederate ships in British ports, to say again and again to the workingmen of England that the battle in America was their battle, and that upon the success of the North rested the success of free institutions all over the world.

As 1862 drew toward an end, the pressure against Lincoln increased, while the voice and the pen of the Abolitionists took on a new fervor and eloquence. The intellectuals—even men like Hawthorne and Oliver Wendell Holmes, who had kept themselves clear of the battle—found themselves curiously exhilarated as though they were moving in a pre-destined time and space. The Christmas holidays tightened the excite-ment until it became almost a religious ecstasy.

New Year's Eve, the eve of Emancipation, assumed a Pentecostal fervor. Meetings were arranged, for Lincoln had remained steadfast, and a mil-lion hopes and a million desires would need the first of January for re-joicing. In London several thousand workingmen set aside this New Year's Eve as a watch night, a night in which to denounce slavery. In the North, New Year's Eve was watch night in the colored churches. In all the colored neighborhoods lights spread through the windows to show that the vigil had begun. Tomorrow—would tomorrow never come—tomorrow that carried the end of shackles, the end of slave whips, the end of bartering and selling human flesh? White friends were holding the vigil with them; in every city of the North they met together, a thousand memories closing their ears to the sounds about them, covering their eyes from all but the long struggle, the heroic dream, the bright consummation. A man with stumps for legs had hidden in the swamps by day, dragged himself along by night, *but he had won freedom!* An old woman had gathered her ball and chain together and fled through the woods to freedom. Eliza and her thousand brothers and sisters had taken the long road back into the slavelands and brought their families out to freedom. Coffin and Rankin had maintained their watches along the Ohio River, and all the named and unnamed heroes had hurried their black passengers along a road which no one ever saw, which ran beyond the reach of human greed into a strange brightness called free-dom. Harriet Tubman had grinned her wide white smile and Thomas Garrett had written in a calm fine hand to William Still, "Look for twelve more of God's poor tomorrow night." Garrison had stumbled through the broadcloth mob and smiled because he saw something they did not see—he saw this night, and these vigils, and black and white holding hands like brothers.

In the Boston church where Moncure Conway and two young Garri-sons, Fanny and William, sat pressed shoulder against shoulder, they heard the black preacher—"Brethren and sisters, tomorrow will be de day for der oppressed. But we all know dat evil is 'round de President. While we set here dey is tryin' to make him break his word. But we have come dis Watch Night ter see dat he does not break his word. Der ole serpent is abroad tonight wid all his emissaries, in great power. His wrat' is great, 'cause he knows his hour is near. *He will be in dis church dis evening!* As midnight comes on we'll hear his *rage!* But brethren and sisters, don't be skeered. We'll pray. He'll go ragin' back to hell, and God Almighty's *New Year will make de United States der lan' of freedom!*"

They cried and moaned, they sank to their knees. The nerves of their white friends tingled. They felt prayers rising in their throats. Suddenly like a long breath from hell they heard a curdling hiss. "He's here—*he's here!*" and from all parts of the churches the hisses rose, hisses so like a giant serpent that the flesh rose on the scalp. Above it could be heard the preacher's prayer, louder, more ecstatic, mounting higher and higher until above his voice, above the terrifying hisses, could be heard the strokes of a clock, marking off the midnight hour. As the twelve strokes died, the hissing died with them, and the voice of the preacher fell silent. Into that silence swelled the sound of a jubilee hymn, and hands joined together, tears ran down the faces, and all sang till their voices broke.

To Abolitionists this New Year's Day was to be a mighty celebration. From Kansas to Massachusetts the rejoicings would ring. In Boston, the night watches were to be carried through the day at Tremont Temple until the Proclamation came over the wires and they knew that the battle had at last been won. Everyone looked for the message to come by noon; a concert had been arranged in the Music Hall that afternoon as a fitting celebration for so great a day.

But the day went by, noon came, the afternoon wore on. In the Music Hall the crowds were ebullient with their own joy and expectation. Mendelssohn's *Hymn of Praise*, Beethoven's *Fifth Symphony*, Handel's *Hallelujah Chorus* kept their spirits free of wonderment and questioning.

In Tremont Temple, Douglass was waiting, William Wells Brown, the Reverend Mr. Grimes, Anna Dickinson—who represented the other outcasts, women voters. They had established messengers between the telegraph office and the platform of the temple.

Darkness fell. People began to stir questioningly. Friends tried not to look at friends for fear their own courage would fail. What was happening in Washington? Soon they would have to go home, and what would fill up this silence when their hymns and their music were still? In the Music Hall they started again to sing, swelling their voices more mightily than ever. At that moment a man ran down the aisles. First they heard his voice indistinctly, and then they heard it clearly. "Over the wires— *it's coming over the wires—now!*" he was shouting, and ran back up the aisles again. Even the orchestra dropped their instruments. The shout that rose should have lifted the walls of the building. People were weeping, singing, their hands pounding applause. Lincoln was a great man— Lincoln was the savior of the slaves! All their fears and suspicions went roaring to the roof as they cheered nine mighty times for him, and then looked about for their own great man to cheer. Garrison—*where was Garrison?* There he was, up in the gallery, and they called out his name, and as he rose, they hurled three more tremendous cheers to him. And then someone pointed again to the gallery, and another name ran from throat to throat. "Mrs. Stowe—*Mrs. Stowe!*" She stood there a moment, a shabby little figures, her bonnet slightly askew, her eyes filled with tears, but smiling, bowing- -"the little woman who started this great war" Lincoln had called her—and the whole audience was on its feet.

In Tremont Temple the vigil did not end till midnight. They were waiting for the words of the Proclamation. Ten o'clock, eleven o'clock, nearly twelve, and then a messenger ran in and laid a slip of paper on the chairman's desk. ". . . henceforward and forever free . . ." the Reverend Charles Ray lifted up his voice, and the thousand other voices joined him.

> Sound the loud timbrel of Egypt's dark sea,
> Jehovah hath triumphed, his people are free!

The Abolitionists might warn against the incomplete nature of this emancipation, point to the eight hundred and thirty thousand slaves of the border states left in slavery, and show again and again that it was a moral statement only with no power of implementation behind it; but to the average Northerner, freedom for the slave had come.

To the average Negro there were no qualms, no doubts. Douglass might question, Purvis might doubt, Still might fold up his books in the Vigilance office, and wonder, but to those who heard the news from the Union soldiers, the rejoicing was spontaneous and uncomplicated.

On that 1st of January the Confederacy ended. Jeff Davis might write angrily to the Confederate Congress ordering that Union officers, taken captive, were to be treated as inciters to insurrection, but nothing could offset the fact that the slavocracy was ended, and that the slaves, acting on the underground messages, came into the Federal camps by twenties, thirties, fifties, to see if this word were true.

In the border states, exempted by the Proclamation, Negroes simply packed up and left. Kentucky within the year lost thirty thousand in flight or to the army. Missouri complained that wagonloads of Negroes were rumbling to Union camps through every town in the state.

In the North, the last reluctance to do soldiering had died away. Free men could now fight, without humiliation, for a flag which belonged to them. Lincoln officially authorized the raising of Negro troops. They were desperately needed. The famous Fifty-fourt Massachusetts swung on its way in February, and the Fifty-fifth followed soon on its heels, some of those two hundred thousand Negro troops who were, by Lincoln's testimony, to turn the tide for the Union.

Garrison stood with tears in his eyes, on the very corner of Wilson's Lane over which he had been dragged on that memorable day in 1835, and watched the Fifty-fourth march past, the fair-haired young Robert Shaw at their head, and listened to the song that the rich Negro voices were rolling back, rank upon rank:

> John Brown's body lies a-mouldering in the grave
> But his soul is marching on.

So much had been accomplished. The Abolitionists could notch it on their yardsticks. But a week—a few days—had not gone by before they saw the need to keep their lines in order, combat the dissolution of the antislavery societies, keep their tongues and their pens sharp until something more constitutional than a wartime proclamation set their minds at rest.

In Louisiana they were afraid of General Banks who had been sent to curb the generous hand of Butler who might have freed the slaves in the exempted parishes where loyal people still held their property. In North Carolina they were alarmed by the appointment as military governor of an old-line politician named Stanly, who hated the Abolitionists and made it his business to fight the group of North Carolinians who had banded together to see that emancipation was an actuality. Although emancipation was only three weeks old, the Boston Abolitionists decided they had better see the President.

Lincoln listened to them carefully and argued, "Suppose I should put in the South these antislavery generals and governors, what could they do with the slaves that would come to them?"

Was this his only answer? With white laborers at a premium, black laborers should be welcomed any place. One month's cost of war would set up homes in Haiti or South America for every fugitive who came within the lines. Lincoln then intended to appoint only generals who would resist the freeing of the slaves? "All that I can say now," Lincoln was saying, "is that I believe the proclamation has knocked the bottom out of slavery, though at no times have I expected any sudden results from it." They were dismayed. Who was this man? They came back to Boston questioning. The word passed from Abolitionist to Abolitionist. Don't give way. The fight may not be over.

All that they allowed to sink into disuse was the northern branch of the Underground Railroad. If it were ever needed again the service would be as good as ever, but now the tracks ended in the Union lines, and workers like Coffin and Sojourner Truth and Laura Haviland transferred their sphere of duties.

Trained by the Underground Railroad their work led them inevitably to the points where the fugitives were now congregating along the Mississippi, to the camps, the settlements and the schools set up behind the Union lines, to the horrors that could be found in a country over which army after army had swept, wiping the lands clean. Owners in this rich plantation valley had escaped before the Unionists and left behind only those slaves who were valueless. They poured into the camps day after day, Coffin said, "an army of slaves and fugitives, pushing its way irresistibly toward an army of fighting men, perpetually on the defensive and perpetually ready to attack. The arrival of those hordes was like the oncoming of cities. There was no plan in this exodus, no Moses to lead it. Often the slaves met prejudices against their color more bitter than any they had left behind. But their own interests were identical, they felt, with the objects of the armies. Their condition was appalling. There were men, women and children in every stage of disease or decrepitude, often nearly naked, with flesh torn by the awful experiences of their escapes." He thought about many things. Maybe this was suffering and pain, he thought, but it was a different suffering and pain than the sick and trembling fugitives had felt who had clambered out of a wagon at his front door and scurried to the attic or to the spare room under the eaves. Maybe these, lying in the tents, working in the fields, were also fugitives, but they were at the same time free men, and from free men one could make a new race.

The morale of the contrabands was high; they had flocked into the deserted fields of the Confederacy and gathered in the corn and the cotton on a negotiated basis—a basis that was subject at any time to the repudiation of the Federal government. Around the field they had set guards of colored men, for raiders often swooped down in the night to kidnap slaves or to harry the colonists. In the spring they had plowed and planted. The policy of Grant had been to cultivate self-respect, to establish families together and to protect them. Each man was made responsible for his own family, a word which had carried little meaning in the lexicon of slavery.

Although the Union camps were chaotic and demoralized by fugitives, Grant refused to allow them to be driven away or maltreated. To John Eaton, the young chaplain of an Ohio volunteer regiment, he gave the task of shaping order out of this vast formlessness, combating disease, protecting the freedmen, of organizing some hope out of this despair. Grant assumed the responsibility for hiring the fugitives as teamsters, cotton pickers, road builders, cooks, seamstresses, providing them with soldiers' equipment. Some fugitives were distributed to points along the river, and Coffin saw these wretched, lonely creatures standing on the Cincinnati docks without food or shelter.

The colored people of Cincinnati came to him. "Help us with them. We've taken them in, we'll keep them as long as we can, but there's more coming all the time." He raised money again, he talked to friends again; their problems were inextricably his.

He knew that several thousand contrabands had been settled in Cairo, Illinois, and that they were destitute. He and two Quaker friends traveled to Cairo to see how they could help. The authorities welcomed them touchingly. Good Abolition officers, their despair was unmanning. What could they do against the smallpox, against the cold weather, against the lack of food and clothing? And it was women, children and old people for whom they were responsible. Coffin said he would go straight back to Cincinnati and raise more money. His Quaker friends said they would stay and start a school—young and old expected automatically to "ketch a learnin'" if they had men in blue uniforms about them.

Coffin used all his eloquence in Cincinnati. Money and supplies began a slow and steady trickle down to Cairo. The Western Freedmen's Aid Committee came into existence at the hands of the Quakers to distribute the supplies which went farther West. It was dangerous work traveling along the rivers, with guerrilla detachments and sharpshooters firing at the ships, but Abolitionists had long ago accustomed themselves to the possibilities of gunfire. The work spread to Nashville, to other points, spread like an inundating river, creeping up as close behind the moving armies as possible. Supplies were inadequate, volunteers insufficient. Coffin and his friends must make more trips into the Ohio and the Indiana country, must attend all kinds of meetings, must somehow show the way to money. But colonies were springing up. The Cairo refugees had been transferred to Island 10 where they were cultivating the land. Memphis could now boast of three large colonies surrounded by farrowed land, for Chaplain Eaton had been sent to follow the line of escaping contrabands.

To Island 10, Laura Haviland brought her thin little body and her prim little face, and set to work without a wasted word, just as she had set to work in the days when she crossed a river to fetch out slaves from slavery. Wasn't she doing the same thing? Wasn't she merely a modernized "conductor," prepared to show the way to a steady life and stable habits? The great work of the Abolitionists was by no means done. The front had merely widened. It stretched now into the South and it stretched across the Atlantic to England.

The friends in England had promised good news if Lincoln declared himself against slavery. Now it came in the shape of great mass meetings held in London and other parts of the country. Three thousand "noble sons of labor," many of them suffering terrible privations from the cotton famine caused by the blockade of the South, adopted by acclamation an address to Lincoln, sympathizing with his proclamation, and many vowed then and there that they would rather remain unemployed for twenty years than to get cotton at the expense of slaves.

Hundreds of thousands of fervent antislavery laborers were being created by Karl Marx, Greeley's London correspondent, through his International Workingmen's Association, by George Thompson, Bishop Noel, John Bright, John Stuart Mill, who seemed everywhere at once, exhorting, arguing, withering the slavocracy with their eloquence. Thompson was sending off happy letters to his friends in America. He was reminded of the days when antislavery was first victorious in England. The battle had been won for Britain and her colonies. The battle would be won for America too. He urged Garrison to come to England. The sight of him might work a magic and fasten the devious policies of Lord Russell, the foreign minister, offset the inevitable effect of Democratic political victories and put an end to the feverish efforts of the Confederate agents and their faithful ally, the London *Times*. But Garrison could not go; thirty years of fighting had weakened his health. He urged Gerrit Smith to make the trip, or Phillips who could turn a stone to water. Phillips hesitated, and then he visited Mrs. Moncure Conway and persuaded her that her husband, with his wit and his impeccable Southern background, was the ideal emissary. Conway debated for awhile, and finally sailed, his portmanteau filled with letters from Emerson and Garrison, the corner of his stateroom brought to startled life by the newly completed bust of John Brown which the George Stearns were sending to Victor Hugo.

He was a sensation in London—he and William Andrew Jackson, Jefferson Davis' late coachman, who could not materialize himself in all the places at which he was invited to speak. Conway found that two-thirds of the British authors were championing the Northern cause, Swinburne, Huxley, Cairns, Leslie Stephens, the Rossettis; that the common people of France, Sweden, Russia, Spain had set themselves against the aristocracy, that in Berlin so many presented themselves for enlistment in the Northern armies that the United States Minister was forced to put a sign outside the legation: "This is not a recruiting office." He quoted the extemporaneous reply of a Leeds mechanic to the argument that the South had as much right to fight for its independence as the American colonies, "I have no doubt that the Southerners are plucky fellows, but when they are willing to give to their laboring people the liberty they wish for themselves, they may justly come here and ask us laboring people for our sympathy—not before."

But the fact still remained that doubt sat everywhere. The vacillations of the American government, magnified a hundred times by the English failure to understand the constitutional restrictions of Lincoln, compounded with the crystal-clear hatred of all that the democratic North represented, had produced the evasive actions of the Palmerston Cabinet. They had had occasion for many years to fear the republican institutions of America, for the eyes of many Englishmen found them an irresistible attraction, and an "Americanized" England would mean the end of Tory rule. Their fear was great enough to tempt them to intervene for the South in spite of their belief that the South was, militarily, impregnable. When the South won, democratic institutions would cease to haunt them and the rising merchant marine threat of the North would be dissipated. Although tenseness in Europe tied their hands, war with the North seemed very imminent this summer.

Henry Ward Beecher, traveling on the continent for his health, found himself in the disconcerting position of cajoling the United States Minister to Belgium into a hopeful frame of mind. The Minister, understandably impressed, begged him to jolt King Leopold into the same state of mind, since King Leopold had such influence over Queen Victoria. From King Leopold to the British people was an inevitable step for Beecher, and he crossed the Channel, adding the weight of his prestige and oratory to the growing ranks of Union agitators. Toughs armed with knives and guns arrived to break up his meetings, threats against his life filled every mail, but the answer he desired came from the crowds which filled the halls to hear him speak, crowds so huge that when he spoke in Edinburgh he could only reach his platform by being handed over the heads of the people, hoisted into the gallery, and then lowered onto the platform.

To Robert E. Lee was attributed the opinion that the Beechers between them spoiled all chances for recognition of the Confederacy— Harriet with her book, and Henry Ward with his tour of Great Britain. Without them, Robert E. Lee claimed, France and England would have sent the moral and the material aid that would have meant victory for the South. However simplified the explanation may have been (and Beecher said two names only were magic to the British people—the humble printer, Garrison, and the aristocratic lawyer, Phillips), yet the summer of 1863 saw the danger pass. A bill to recognize the Confederacy was offered, argued and repudiated in Parliament, and although the full support of the government never came to the Union, the people of Great Britain had won their own particular battle.

At home the enemies of Lincoln were busier than ever. With their voices they called on him unremittingly to wage real war, win some battles, justify himself, while with their hands they dealt what blows they could to weaken his power, discredit him, strip him of the extra-legal authority that war had forced him to assume. Probably no man suffered so greatly at the hands of his contemporaries as did this man of vast heart and brave ideals, who might have gained immortality in his lifetime had he, in the midst of revolution, possessed the temper of a revolutionist.

Traitors were everywhere. Emancipation had not increased them but it had sharpened their weapons, multiplied the murders in alleys and recruiting offices, given impetus to talks of peace on Southern terms. In March, a crisis threatened when Lincoln signed a Draft Law, and the anti-war feeling, fanned, exploded in race riots in Detroit. Fifty houses were burned. Black men and women died. By May the crisis was mounting. The Confederate Army was moving northward, bloody defeats had been suffered at Fredericksburg and Chancellorsville, Grant was held at Vicksburg. By June, Lee had crossed into Maryland. Any day he might appear in Philadelphia and New York. A terrible darkness closed down on Union people.

Conscription was moving slowly. Men did not go willingly to recruiting offices when their minds were troubled. Now was the time to talk of peace, of concessions. Franklin Pierce, who had been President, and Horatio Seymour, who was now governor of New York, were telling their hearers that the crime of the North against the South could only be wiped out by a peace which left the South with all the constitutional prerogatives of her days of slave power. Men had to be strong and confident not to find the words unwholesomely sweet. Peace and concessions, and drafts—"what are you fighting for anyway!" Poor men, drafted, had to fight—hungry men with no money to buy their release in the manner of rich men. "And all for the niggers?" Resentment was skillfully directed. "That wasn't the way it began, was it? There were fine words at first—all about the Union, and fighting for the Constitution. Men, the niggers are responsible, the Abolitionists! Kill them, *kill them, kill them!*"

Those could not be men, sweeping down from the side streets, with suffused faces, open mouths filled with hoarse shoutings. Yet it was men's hands which turned New York into a city of terror. The police were powerless against the thousands who rushed like bats through the streets, exorcising the devil with a can of turpentine and a match. Burning buildings made mighty flares even in the daylight, and the nights were hideous. Flying Negroes, men, women, children whose fright held back their screams, made terrifying pictures and men drew their curtains rather than see the carnival of sadism which waited those who were caught. Police stations and arsenals, flung open as sanctuaries to those escaping burning houses, to those who dared not return to houses which had been spared, still could offer no firebreak against the mighty spectacle that lighted up the skies when the Colored Orphan Asylum went up in flames.

From killing and terrorizing Negroes to killing and terrorizing whites was a short step. An Abolitionist lived in this house—*fire it!* A Black Republican lived there—*fire it!* A solitary soldier in a blue uniform—string him up to the post! Draft officials—*kill them!*

Refugees streamed across the Hudson, the East River, hiding in the swamps and woods near Bergen, New Jersey, in the barns and outhouses on Long Island and Morrisiana. By the second day, soldiers had been mustered from forts in the harbor, militia had been gathered in the city, and casualties began to mount among the rioters. But riots, well organized though on a smaller scale, broke out in Boston, sending the Garrisons out of the city, in Jersey City, in Troy, and finally, across the river in Brooklyn.

In four days an undetermined number of lives had been lost and $1,500,000's worth of property destroyed. Soldiers were driving the mob slowly back into the tenement districts from which they had come. Victory at Gettysburg had a quieting effect, as well as the news that Grant had subdued Vicksburg and that Banks had captured Port Hudson. Sporadic killings of ambushed Negroes, a battle at 21st Street and Third Avenue between rioters and soldiers—the backfires kindling and dying out—meant the end of terror.

The inevitable reaction came on a wave of friendliness to the Negroes. White men and women were ashamed even if they had taken no part in the terror. The Negro was a part of the war. Abolition ways of talking and of thinking had sifted through prejudice and indifference. In a few months, a regiment of Negro troops, recruited and equipped by the Union League Club, was escorted down Broadway to its southbound ship by some of the leading citizens of the city, and thousands cheered from the sidewalks where solid lines had formed.

The Negro leaders, dignified by the use of colored troops, recruiting them zealously, fought persistently for an end of discrimination. White soldiers received thirteen dollars a month, Negro soldiers, seven. There was, moreover, no opportunity for advancement out of the noncommissioned ranks. The 54th and the 55th Massachusetts regiments served for a year without pay, rather than accept the discrimination. The fight was a hard one, and white Abolitionists joined in the protests and the agitation, which bore no fruit until July, 1864.

The hatred against the Negro as a soldier was never as inflexible again after the first confirmation of their bravery at Fort Wagner and the massacre at Pillow. "Nobody knows about the blacks," said a Union colonel, "who has not seen them in battle. Their fiery courage is above everything I have ever seen or read—except French Zouaves."

The Negro and his cause were strengthened when the Confederate orders were heard—Negro captives were to be regarded as insurrectionists. To the Negro soldier there was no alternative to courage; he must be valorous in a manner that white soldiers could not understand, for on the success of the army with which he was fighting depended his re-enslavement or his freedom, and the freedom of four million of his race.

The Negro soldier spread the word of emancipation along the swampy ways, by the underground telegraph, as zealously as any partisan of the old "railroad." To the majority of the slaves, shuffled about from place to place as masters desperately tried to keep falling prices from sinking lower and the Confederate Army acted as a gigantic overseer, freedom was a greater chimera than in the days of the Underground Railroad; the road to freedom was filled with magnified dangers and the path to it still ran over the mountains and through the swamps. Yet to that freedom came more fugitives in four years than ever rode the Underground Railroad, old and young, sick and dying, and everything movable came with them—pots, pans, hoes, rakes, cattle, horses—gifts for the Union Army which the Union Army could not afford to refuse. Those who came were numbered by the tens of thousands. Those who failed were not numbered. How did the slaves know when a Federal regiment moved from one point to another, when friendly generals had been transferred to another sector? How had they always known so well what concerned themselves? (At the dinner table of William Henry Trescott, a former Assistant Secretary of State, only French was spoken for "we know that the black waiters are all ears now, and we want to keep what we have to say dark.") White men still forged passes for them and, in Richmond and Savannah, organized bootleg rings to smuggle slaves to freedom. White deserters, returning to their patches of cotton, told them things they wished to know, showed them ways of escape and received the aid of slaves in exchange. Literate slaves could pass on newspaper information to other slaves. In October, 1862, a slave crossed the Union lines in Virginia, bringing word of important military plans. He had known not only what would be of immediate use to his friends, but he knew all the details of the first emancipation proclamation which he had read in a newspaper. He had read the autobiography of Frederick Douglass and the story of John Brown. ("I've read it to heaps of the colored folks. Lord, they think John Brown was almost a God!")

This was freedom, realized and held in the hand, this was the Land of Canaan, this was singing and rejoicing. What if some of them walked about idly—had they ever been allowed to do that before? Some were searching for their families, going from town to town, trying to find those wives and husbands and children who had been sold away from them; some were merely wandering. Why, when this war was over, nobody would raise a voice at them, nobody would swing a lash again, nobody would deny them the right to land, to homes, to security, to self-respect! If Massa Linkum was not fighting to free the slaves, the slaves did not know it.

Only men like Douglass, like John Langston, like Remond and Wells Brown, like Lewis Hayden, women like Frances Harper, Mary Shadd, saw the future tautly, wondering how the fight would shape itself. In Washington the black Minister from Haiti sat with white men at dinner tables; in Philadelphia black men were driven off streetcars. In which mental climate would the freedom of the future grow?

Government agencies were clumsy with Negro prejudice. Filth and disease, sufficient to raise a plague, were more evident than food and water in the contraband communities of New York, Philadelphia, Pittsburgh, Washington. Without resources of any kind they had been set to shift for themselves. "Be clean," cried Sojourner Truth, that tall gaunt old figure with her head wrapped in a white turban, as she went from one wretched hovel to another. "Cleanliness is godliness." And then, because cleanliness could not come until the rank tenements had been abandoned, she set herself to find a place for her people in the sprawling ruthlessness of America. "America owes my people some of the dividends," she shouted from pulpits. "I shall make them understand that there is a debt to the Negro people which they can never repay. At least they must make amends." The public lands in the West—that was what she saw—waiting for free men to cultivate. Let the government share with the Negro, let them erect buildings for the old and sick, give help to the young and hearty. Terribly old—some said she was ninety, others seventy—she started off to agitate, to make Congress feel her pressure.

Lincoln was thinking about the Negro. He asked Sam Howe, Robert Dale Owen and James McKaye to investigate the Negroes' capacity for looking after themselves. Everything was spread out in perfect array in the refugee colonies in Canada, and there they took themselves. Through the country the Abolition sentiment was mounting with every fresh victory of the Union Armies. The antislavery societies were circulating *The Anti-Slavery Standard* and *The Liberator* with a fresh zest, and watching, with unflagging concentration the ups and downs of this new sentiment. They were old students of human behavior. They were not sure how far it could be trusted.

When Vicksburg fell to the Union, and the Mississippi was opened to the sea, the largest center of Negro population in the South fell to the North, and thousands of slaves, in immediate and painful want, poured into the Federal camps. The Federals had nothing for them; they had neither medicine nor supplies. They watched many die in the streets. The country heard about *that*. When, in turn, the Confederates gained victories around Helena, Arkansas, and made bonfires of the refugee camps, and re-enslaved those who had not escaped, the country also heard about *that*.

Freedmen's agents journeyed to Washington to tell about the abuses of the lessee system—the best the army could devise—the suffering of the Negroes at the hands of the employers who had once been masters, the difficulty of protecting the Negroes on plantations where the slavery-warped mind made it dangerous for the agents to visit or make inquiries although they often knew that their charges had been sold back into slavery. They told about the Negro fear of employment contracts, believing them ruses of enslavement. They told of the profit gained by the government through the road-building, crop-gathering, miscellaneous labor of the contrabands. And they asked persistently how these freedmen could be redeemed for the future on the government wages of ten dollars a month for men and seven for women, on which they must clothe and feed and educate themselves and their families? The government was apparently the only employer upon whom the Negro could with any trust depend, and it was now up to the government to show its faith.

On Lincoln's desk, on the desks of Cabinet members and Senators, detailed reports were laid, and they all rang the same theme: land cultivations showed a profit when handled and owned by Negroes. Eaton pointed to the spectacular success of those freedmen—mostly Jefferson Davis' slaves—who had been leased tracts of land on the ten-thousand-acre plantation of Davis in Mississippi. Self-government, in the form of Negro sheriffs and judges appointed to have jurisdictions over certain districts, had been established, Negro troops had been appointed to protect the colony, and much of the land was worked on a co-operative basis. He wrote in very plain and distinct figures that out of the 113,650 contrabands under his care the previous year, 62,300 were now entirely self-supporting, having made good deals for their crops in the face of a world closed against them, or having established themselves in business enterprises with exceptional success. And the Reverend Joseph Warren, general superintendent of colored schools, described the Negroes' surprise at their own capacity. "They become ambitious in speech; and their high-sounding phrases are in strange contrast with their rustic and imperfect dialect. Their courtliness and gravity of manner are oddly mixed with childishness. The spectacle they present excites fear and hope, laughter and tears in succession. On the whole, hope predominates. They will make mistakes; and they will learn caution and shrewdness by them. They who are cheated and abused last year will hardly be so this year. They who make contracts desire to learn to read them. They who have once been cheated in changing money desire to be able to calculate. We can see the wants, desires and hopes of civilized life struggling within them. In some, these feelings are well formed; in others dim and uncertain."

It was a fight that must have perfect articulation. Negrophobia must be conquered in the North. Congress must aid the Negro, end the carnival of sarcasm and ponderous wit into which border-state representatives or the followers of Pendleton of Ohio turned the sessions. The Howe Commission, full of the success of the Canadian colonies, never let its agitation flag. Garrisonians, led by the resurgent Garrison himself and by Phillips, were beating down resistance, lecturing, exhorting; the antislavery societies were fighting not only the battle of the emancipated slave, but the battle of the Northern free Negro; the Quakers, adept at persistent bombardment, were harrying Congress through Henry Wilson; petitions were pouring in from a war-weary North.

Lincoln agreed. Help must be given. But he wanted the country to speak first. Send delegations to Congress, he advised, send strong delegations, buttonhole Congressmen. Delegations swept in, staid, dignified, from Boston, New York, Philadelphia, Cincinnati, Chicago. They saw

Stanton and Chase and found that they were their men. They talked with Lincoln, and Lincoln promised a message to Congress.

One could not say that the end of the war was near, but the obligations of the end of the war were more and more asserting themselves in the minds of thoughtful men. The end of the war . . . since Gettysburg and the opening of the Mississippi the North could talk more confidently of the end of the war, and the building up. What shape would the building up take? What place would the former slaveowners have in it? What position would the Negro be allowed? What about the land which the Federal government had been so reluctant to confiscate and yet which represented the very marrow of the slavocracy? Would the Negroes share in the land which would provide for their independence?

The questions were not popular ones for debate. Only the radicals, Thaddeus Stevens, Charles Sumner, seemed willing to bring them into the open and shake them in front of the government's eyes. How far did the reconstruction that Lincoln proposed reach to the heart of the matter? In his message in December, 1863, he included what he called a Proclamation of Amnesty, giving a full pardon to all but a few classes who would take an oath supporting those laws and proclamations "made during the existing rebellion." In Louisiana and in Arkansas he promptly directed that an effort at reconstruction and the writing of an antislavery constitution be attempted if ten per cent of the 1860 electorate could be found qualified to vote. Stevens hotly challenged the constitutionality of a move which put the majority of a state—however disloyal it might be—under the rule of a minority. But Lincoln believed in the constitutionality of his voting plan. Ten per cent of the voters in the two states were found to be loyal. In Louisiana they elected two Congressmen to Washington, in Arkansas a loyal governor and two Senators. Congress hated these actions; the Abolitionists were profoundly disturbed. The Abolitionists wanted to know if this war were really the revolution desired by them or merely a reshifting of control from a dying class in the South to a rising class in the North which had no more compassion and no more place for the Negro and the poor white than the age which had passed? What were the signs of a new economy in the South? Could the leasing of confiscated plantations to private contractors (whose failure to pay wages to the freedmen was already raising an unpleasant smell), be called the end of land domination? What solution was offered for the deep-lying plight of the poor whites, driven by the slave power years ago to small rocky acres, when any Northern man with money could buy up vast tracts and run them as he chose? Northern capitalists were fastening themselves on the rich lands of the Mississippi Valley. Was Northern capitalism assuming the place of Southern slavocracy? Land was what the poor whites and the empty-handed Negro needed, for they were agrarians, and land they were determined to have. Why, after the Confiscation Act of 1862, some were asking, was the land not given to those natural enemies of the slavocracy—the poverty-stricken whites and the landless blacks? They were the friends of the Union in the South as the whites showed by their guerrilla warfare and the blacks by their flights.

To the average Negro the end of slavery would only come when his empty hands were full. The government had promised . . . and when Federal soldiers, coming into Jackson, Mississippi, gave guns to the slaves on the Big Black Plantation with which to hold their freedom, the slaves laid aside the guns and without delay measured the land with a plowline, dividing it equally among themselves and apportioning the cotton and farming tools. An indignant Confederate told of "insolent Negroes, actually passing over their former masters' lands, measuring with old ropes and setting pegs to mark the favorite tracts they designed taking possession of as soon as the word was given."

They squatted along the coasts of North Carolina, where the Union Army had not yet gained a strong foothold, and grew cotton and corn and made turpentine on the land they had appropriated. They moved onto deserted plantations in southern Virginia, built cabins, and cultivated the land until they were driven off.

When the Negroes worked on the land assigned to them they did not possess it (the Sea Islands were the only grants made the freedmen). They worked for wages, for no wages and for share-tenancy. Those who were able to buy small tracts were in a minority so small as to make them exceptional. Those who had been assured that the government would confirm their rights looked for fulfillment of the promises until they were driven off the land.

And what about the voting strength when the war was over? To maintain it on the basis of the elections in Louisiana—ten per cent of the 1860 electorate—would confine it automatically to those men who though pro-Union were still antidemocratic and proslavery—and would, by the same token, exclude the great mass of whites and Negroes whose disfranchisement under poll laws and color lines had been complete.

Lincoln thought about this. When he wrote his congratulations to the new free-state governor of Louisiana, he offered the first indication of the evolutionary process he desired to see. "Now you are about to have a convention which among other things will probably define the elective franchise. I barely suggest for your private consideration whether some of the colored people may not be let in, as for instance the very intelligent and especially those who have fought gallantly in our ranks. They would probably help in some trying time in the future to keep the jewel of Liberty in the family of Freedom."

But in South Carolina, in that southeastern section which the Federal troops had occupied, the disfranchised acted without unnecessary talking. In April, 1864, a convention was called to elect delegates to the Presidential convention, and the call invited all Union men to come without regard for color. Two hundred and fifty people assembled, riding over the hot roads, piercing the heart of that state which had been the center of slavocracy—and one hundred and fifty of them were Negroes. When the electing had been finished, sixteen delegates had been selected, and four of them were Negroes. Perhaps their ignorance was horrifying—perhaps they had just come in from the fields. A democracy allows for that.

Demands began to filter through the mail of Congressmen. Negro suffrage . . . protection of civil rights in the South . . . Congress answered obliquely by refusing to seat the representative chosen by the ten per cent loyalists of Arkansas. Lincoln might claim that no state could secede, that the Union was only waiting for the erring sisters to return, but many felt that the bloodiest war in history could not be wiped out so easily. Many remembered the arrogance, the shouting, the bowie knives of prewar Congressmen. Were these same people to be put again in power? What guarantee was offered that the slavocratic mind had been done away with and that the old rulers would not return, able to juggle emancipation as skillfully as they had juggled slavery?

To Wendell Phillips, among the Abolitionists, the dangers lay crude and inescapable. Sensitized by nearly thirty years of anticipating, of analyzing the temper of the slavocracy, he knew that a war and a Proclamation could not end the evils of slavery. The Abolitionists, celebrating their thirtieth anniversary with tears of joy and tender remembrances of a long, gallant and conclusive fight, dwelt too much in the past for him and not enough in the future. His alarm bred suspicion, his suspicion struck at the long shadows of approaching events. He was a creature of tingling nerves and uncanny prescience. The gentleman, the barrister, the dandy with the golden voice was the only revolutionist among them, the only one who saw the shape of the future in terms of a new life, unrelated to the old. He spoke harshly at the annual meeting of the antislavery society in January, 1864. The shape of things was resolving; a new election was coming that would tend to consolidate the mold. Antislavery was somnolent in the enervating delusion that the end was being reached. *Therefore*—and his voice rose to the pitch that had heretofore sounded death to the enemy—therefore, he wished to offer a resolution: "That in our opinion, the Government, in its haste, is ready to sacrifice the interests and honor of the North to secure a sham peace, thereby risking the introduction into Congress of a strong Confederate minority to embarrass legislation, and leaving the freedmen and the Southern States under the control of the late slaveholders, embittered by their defeat in war, and entailing on the country intestine feuds for another dozen years."

Garrison was there, ill, weary in mind and body, but now dedicated to Lincoln. It was all very well—a conviction well established—that the crude and hazardous forms of reconstruction in the Union-held South, which omitted all concern for equal rights of black and white, must be recognized and attacked, but he could not stomach "excessive condemnation" at this time, he could not believe that traitors to human rights lingered in the orbit of Lincoln. He offered an amendment: let the resolution read, "That, in our opinion, the government in its haste, is in danger of sacrificing . . ."

Perhaps he was right, perhaps the loss of his amendment by a small vote laid a hand on the dignity of Abolition; perhaps, as Sam May wrote to Garrison, as McKim wrote to him, Phillips had at one and the same time expressed the deeper convictions of old Abolitionists and laid a blot upon them. Perhaps it was true that Lincoln was the best that any antislavery man could hope for and that he would give them what they desired when his evil counselors had been shaken off.

But Phillips and the majority of the Abolitionists cried that moderation was no more their weapon now than when Garrison had hurled out his immoderate challenge thirty-two years before.

The nominating conventions promised issues as important as those of four years earlier; Phillips was prickly with his vision of the future. He did what he had never done before in his life, he sought and accepted political support and went as a delegate to the State Convention which was electing representatives for the National Convention in Baltimore. There he made a fighting but unsuccessful effort to swing the convention away from Lincoln. He tried again in Vermont and again he failed. He swore that he himself would leave no stone unturned to bring about the defeat of the man whose only desire for re-election, he claimed, was to "conciliate the disloyal white man." He carried his fight to the New York meeting of the American and Massachusetts antislavery societies, and he made his views even more explicit. "My charge against the Administration as an Abolitionist," he cried, "is that it seeks to adjourn the battle from cannon shot to the forum; from Grant to the Senate-house; and to leave the poisoned remnants of the slave system for a quarter of a century to come . . ."

Stephen Foster, who had never spared his words, and Parker Pillsbury, who was most proud of the days when he had driven rioters out of meeting halls, wanted to say that they agreed with Phillips, and with them temperate words were not characteristic. They swung the voting on Phillips' resolution: "As abolitionists, we feel bound to declare that we see no evidence of [the Administration's] purpose to put the freedom of the negro on such a basis as will secure it against every peril," and it passed by a close margin. They voted unanimously for the other resolution; that the Emancipation Proclamation become the Thirteenth Amendment and be thus protected by the law.

But Phillips was not placated, and Douglass joined him now. To the new schismatic party of "radical" Republicans, meeting in Cleveland a week before the Republican Convention, Phillips wrote a letter to be read on the opening day, urging them to a radicalism that their subsequent platform failed to adopt, although Frémont was nominated, and with Frémont both Phillips and Douglass felt a bond close enough to permit wholehearted support. A week later, in Baltimore, an ungracious Republican Union Convention, prodded by the evident enthusiasm of the people and by their own complicated loyalties, nominated Lincoln without waste of time and gave him a Tennessean, Andrew Johnson, for Vice President.

Garrison sat in the gallery. His hair was gray now and fell in a little fringe about his ears. The lines of his face were deeper, but his eyes behind his small spectacles were still sharp and restless. Down below on the floor men were springing to their feet crying "Aye!" to a resolution for the Thirteenth Amendment. The Thirteenth Amendment—one word of it would wipe the country clean of slavery. After all these years . . . the joy was unendurable. Thirty years of persecution seemed now only a day of joyful living.

The day and the hour and the man had come together. That Phillips might be right in saying that this was not enough may occasionally have crossed his mind—Phillips and he had been too close to have their nerve centers and their reflexes entirely cut apart. Yet now, caught up in the noisy cheering and the crude jubilation of his first political gathering, he saw the grand end of a dream.

There was honor here for him as well. The monster man with a price upon his head had come below Mason and Dixon's line and people crowded to shake his hand. In Washington they urged speeches from him, but the flaying tongue was silent. What did he have to say? He had only to see, to feel, to know. Henry Wilson had written him that Stanton had declared "there was one person whom he wished to see before he died"—the man Garrison. Now Stanton pressed him into a chair—hard tough Stanton who had been the only unfailing Cabinet friend to the Abolitionists in the last three years—and told him eagerly about *his* Abolition antecedents, how his father had supported Benjamin Lundy and how he himself had sat many times on the great little man's lap.

Later he stood on the floor of the Senate with Sumner and Wilson on either side of him. Here Benton, with his breast exposed, had challenged Foote, here Sumner had fallen with a bleeding head, here slavery had ruled the land. Tears sprang into his eyes. Senators were crowding about him, men younger than he, men to whom William Lloyd Garrison was a part of their moral life for good or bad.

And finally he sat facing the man in the White House with the lean face and the beautiful eyes, and the old Garrison reasserted himself. For an hour he told him flatly how he had disapproved of the early conduct of the war. He was unsparing and Lincoln was amiable. But in the end he put out his hand. "Now you have my hearty support and confidence."

"There are no hundred men in the country," said Phillips bitterly, "whose united voices would be of equal importance . . . A million dollars would have been a cheap purchase" for Garrison's approval.

And yet—in spite of cheers and salvos, resolutions and handshakings —the Fugitive Slave Law still stood on the statute books.

Henry Wilson had tried to weaken it with amendments in 1862, and Stevens tried again for outright repeal. Five bills pounded against Congressmen in the session of 1863-1864. The members of the border states called them an "insult and an outrage," yet the pressure against Congress was beginning to say clearly, "You cannot draft black men into the field while your marshals are chasing black women and children to send them back into slavery."

In January, 1864, Sumner tried again. Opponents, tangled now in their own politics, unsure of themselves without popular support, argued automatically against the unconstitutionality of repeal, but there seemed no argument against the fact that slavery was doomed. In the House they gave in abruptly. On June 13th repeal went through on a vote of 82 to 57. In the Senate was more sophistry. If it could be pigeonholed . . . if it could be swamped by the urgency of other matters . . . Sumner refused to listen even to the caution of his friend Hale. For three days he argued, cajoled, and threatened, and finally forced a vote—27 to 12. Two days later Lincoln's signature put an end to the law.

The first step had been taken to supplement the Emancipation Proclamation, but the key had not yet been turned in the lock. The Proclamation was a military measure. Its constitutionality was in question. A political overturn, a new Congress could restore slavery more swiftly than the Proclamation had extinguished it. A Thirteenth Amendment was obligatory to the consciences of antislavery men. The Congress "radicals" set the wheels to spinning slowly.

That summer of 1864 would be long remembered, for talk of peace was in the air. Secret talks to be sure—clandestine agents sent at the request of the Confederates to Canada, where the Confederacy was well represented, and to Richmond. They returned empty-handed, but this carried only a surface significance. The truth lay deeper, as deep as the North Carolina gubernatorial elections, where the editor of the Raleigh *Standard* offered himself as a violent anti-Davis candidate whose election would deliver a terrible blow to the Confederacy, as deep as the incipient revolt of the governor of Georgia, or the reception Grant received from Tennesseans, who began to come into his lines for protection and advice.

Jefferson Davis, sending a message to his Congress, felt obliged to direct attention to "secret leagues and associations," to "the disloyalty and hostility to our cause," which were being shown with increasing boldness. The Order of Heroes of America had been uncovered to join the other pro-Union societies of the South, and it was the most powerful of all. Its influence spread through North Carolina, southwestern Virginia, and eastern Tennessee. It had evolved its own elaborate signs and countersigns, and its members infiltrated the Army of the Confederacy.

The upsurge of its power was easily traceable. In March, 1864, the Confederacy had felt itself obliged to increase the guardship over the slaves. Mass flights (twelve hundred blacks had escaped from Mobile in February and gone over to the Union Army as laborers to escape the new impressment laws that would have drafted them into the Confederate Army), the upflamings of slave rebellions and the hanging of leaders, black and white, the burning of the courthouse and fourteen homes in Yazoo City, Mississippi, by the slaves, and the firing of Jefferson Davis' home in Richmond, the uncovering of large maroon camps and the continuous skirmishes against guerrilla bands of fugitive slaves who were wandering in the back countries, were danger signals that could not be ignored. Instead of one overseer to twenty slaves, one to every fifteen was now required. Since the South was desperately in need of fighting men, it was the slaveless whites who were forced to fill out the conscriptions. Their resentment at a "poor man's fight and a rich man's war" deepened in bitterness. Who were they fighting for? The slaveholder and his slaves? To leave their homes for a slaveholders' army meant to leave bare acres untended and families unprotected. Poor men found more satisfaction in forming guerrilla bands, operating in the back lands, in the mountains and the swamps. Deserters from the army joined them. Runaway Negroes came to them. In Florida Governor Milton said that a proportion if not a majority of the west Floridians were threatening to raise the Union flag and were agitating for reconstruction, and that "depredatory bands have even threatened the cities of Tallahassee, Madison and Marianna." The Confederacy said that one hundred and ten thousand men were deserters.

From their hideaways guerrillas kept up communications with the Union troops, supplying spies and pilots, black and white, raiders of plantations and emancipators of slaves. In exchange they received food and ammunition from Federal troops and from blockading vessels. The Confederates sent bloodhounds against them and burned down their homes above their families. Renewed activity was the answer, and a long tightly woven net stretched through the South in the manner of the Underground Railroad and was, in fact, an Underground Railroad of surprising dimensions—not to carry off the fugitive slave but the fugitive Union soldier.

From the prison stockades of the Confederacy, starved and scurvy-tainted men found escape a not impossible accomplishment if they were able to fall into the hands of a Negro.

No disuse had impaired the "underground" system of the South, and no Negro was known to have betrayed a Union soldier. The first stop on this line was a slave's cabin where, the word having spread by grapevine, donations of food and clothing were silently handed in. Negro cobblers took over shoes and mended them; once an old Negro woman took the stockings off her feet for a barefoot officer, and on another occasion a slave gave a hundred Confederate dollars to a destitute prisoner, the accumulated gifts from more prosperous fugitives. Guides were provided around Confederate picket lines, and not infrequently, slaves picketed their own masters to keep the lines clear. The work of one conductor was laid down only when another was prepared to pick it up, and a night's lodgings might be found in corn-fodder houses, cabins, and swamps.

In the pro-Union sections of the Confederacy, prisoners were frequently guided by their black pilots to the local Union men, who, often slaveholders, gave them protection, food and clothing, and delegated one of their own slaves to act as guide. In the mountains, where the Negro population decreased, the pro-Union men took up the underground work. In the mountains of east Tennessee and western North Carolina lived the Union outlaws, the men who had blown up bridges and attempted to wreck transportation in the early days of the war, or who had been drafted into the army and escaped. Their wild exile was dedicated to the assistance of Union prisoners and Confederate deserters. Their eagerness to help, as soon as they had assured themselves that the fugitive was not a spy, was guaranteed by every Northern man who passed through their hands. They assured the fugitives that their organization was well and faultlessly run, that their underground lines moved without a hitch, that their grapevine method was in the best tradition, and that in North Carolina alone they had seventy-five thousand station keepers. So formidable a number would naturally include the unexpected. An escaping prisoner was momentarily dismayed when he found himself in the hands of a local sheriff. But the sheriff only intended to find him a guide across the mountains, and sent him off with a provision of food.

To the escaping Union man, whose background might not necessarily have included any antislavery sentiments, the friendliness of the whites was a fine but not a baffling experience, whereas the devotion of the Negroes was a sudden revelation which gave deeper meanings to this war and taught him what a year of rhetoric would fail to do.

In the North, during the summer of 1864, the popular excitement was divided between the rocking course of the war, the Democratic Convention with its peace-at-any-price candidate, General McClellan, and the stirring campaign for Lincoln, waged at the crossroad stores and the church sociables.

Men as widely separated as Greeley and Thad Stevens said Lincoln could not win. Abolitionists—all but Gerrit Smith—said he could not win. A dark thread of fear ran through the turbulent raciness of the campaign. Nothing was happening as it should. Northern armies were showing unimpressive victories. McClellan was an inspired choice for the Democrats, for since his dismissal by Lincoln he had moved in an ambiguous mist which led many to regard him as an abused hero. Since his nomination came so late, he was able to catch the weary and confused fancy of more voters than the supporters of Lincoln could afford to lose. But events worked for Lincoln. Farragut had already broken the defenses of Mobile, Sheridan was driving through the Shenandoah Valley. On September 1st, Sherman's troops marched into Atlanta. The backbone of the Confederacy had been broken.

Lincoln ordered thanksgiving in all the churches and a hundred guns' salute in every naval base and military headquarters, and McClellan attempted hurriedly to repair the evil done by his defeatist platform. The Lincoln camp promptly flung into the campaign all its resources, its best speakers, its most ardent young men. In the best traditions of those libelous times, no epithets were spared on either side, and night and day, from street corners and the backs of carts, in halls and churches, the oratory, the shouting, the vilifying and the exhortations went on, until the day arrived, and Lincoln by a popular majority of 411,428 votes was confirmed in the Presidency.

It came like a long breath, and on that breath the shouting rose: Pass the Thirteenth Amendment! *The Liberator* threw all its weight into the fight. A National Convention of Colored Men met in Syracuse in October under the leadership of Douglass and Langston to form an Equal Rights League and to discuss, for four days, their prospects of freedom and the vote. Men of all classes were there, printers, carpenters, blacksmiths, engineers, dentists, editors, farmers, physicians, merchants, college students, livery-stable keepers. To them Douglass emphasized again the uncertainty of their status as long as freedom was dependent on the doubtful validity of a war proclamation. Pass the Thirteenth Amendment!

Pass it, Lincoln pleaded in his December message to Congress. You must do it some time. Do it now—Sumner, Wilson, Hale, Fessenden, Lane, Hendricks urged. The time has come to cut ourselves clean from the past, to say why we have sent our young men to death and drenched the country in blood.

On the 28th of January it was evident that a vote would be called. On the 29th the galleries of the House were thronged with spectators, the floor of the House was crowded with visiting Senators, judges, Cabinet officers. A heavy dread hung over the antislavery men. What would the roll call reveal?

Name after name—yea, nay—how many? Had two-thirds said yea? Unofficial counters allowed their excitement to rise, and when the Speaker announced that two-thirds of the House had voted to abolish slavery now and forever, here and everywhere, pandemonium broke loose. Celebrations shattered the dignity of the House, celebrations up and down the staircases, on the floor, in the galleries. Adjournment was carried with shouts, the celebrants pushing off into the wider spaces of the building.

The shoutings spread over the North as the telegraph wires carried the news . . . Kansas City ablaze with lights, houses lighted from cellar to roof, cannon booming; Chicago, Philadelphia, crowds, flags, speeches; Washington, a serenade to the President; New Orleans, Negroes crowding the streets, speaking from platforms in the public square, dancing, singing.

In Boston one hundred guns were fired by the triumphant Governor Andrew and all church bells rang. Garrison went out on the Common to listen, so sweet a sound loosening the tight smile on his face, releasing a joy in him that lay against the long remembrance of the past, the death that must so often have possessed his soul. An end . . . an end . . . the thunder had rumbled away, the sword was sheathed. Garrison's work was done.

The radicals now had fresh fuel for their fight. The struggle over reconstruction lifted itself again in February when a bill was offered, recognizing the Louisiana ten per cent government. It appeared as though Congress might agree with Lincoln this time. But Sumner was in the Senate, and determined that color should not bar a man from citizenship, he fought it with every parliamentary trick he knew. Ben Wade came to his assistance, denouncing this Louisiana constitution as no better than the Lecompton Constitution. Five days of the session remained. By the fifth day Sumner had won, and the bill was not put to a vote.

Events were now to move as swiftly as the lifting of a hand. Maryland and Missouri abolished slavery within their borders, with no day of grace to slaveholders and no compensation. Illinois swept the Black Laws from her law books. Across the Potomac, Lee's estate at Arlington was turned into a freedmen's village with its Garrison and its Lovejoy Streets, while the homes of John Tyler and Henry Wise, who had fought the battles of the slavocracy so faithfully, became schools for colored children, and in the Wise home, the only surviving son of John Brown taught his black charges with a portrait of his father hanging on the wall. In Maryland, where Douglass had been a slave, his son was now teaching a freedmen's school, and on the Mississippi, a new village had sprung up on the land which Jefferson Davis' slaves had bought for their own use.

James McCune Smith was urging a national convention in Washington to create the machinery for Negro suffrage, and on Lincoln's birthday, that other disfranchised scholar, Henry Highland Garnet, delivered an address on the Thirteenth Amendment in the House of Representatives, while not far away, Chief Justice Chase, during a symbolic ceremony designed "to dig the grave for the Dred Scott decision," administered the oath to John S. Rock, the first Negro to be admitted into practice before the bar of the court. In March, Gerrit Smith took his still vigorous personality to Boston to give what assistance he could to the Impartial Suffrage Association which colored leaders had organized to obtain "the full enjoyment of equal civil and political rights, without regard to race or color," and Garrison was mounting the steps of an auction block which had been taken from a slave mart and sent North to be exhibited at meetings in behalf of the freed slave. In Washington, the Freedmen's Bureau after two years' wrangling was given legislative power to protect the Negro.

Lincoln had the Abolitionists behind him now, as never in the past. And from the hearts and hands of the colored people came processions of gifts, and words of devotion which rose like prayers. To his second inaugural address they gave their tears and their fervor, for the man who spoke so briefly seemed to lay bare his heart. "Fondly do we hope, fervently do we pray, that this mighty scourge of war may speedily pass away. Yet if God wills that it continue until all the wealth piled by the bondman's two hundred and fifty years of unrequited toil shall be sunk, and until every drop of blood drawn with the lash shall be paid by another drawn with the sword, so, still it must be said that the judgments of the Lord are true and righteous altogether."

With such words ringing in his ears, Garrison proposed to end the labors of *The Liberator*. For thirty-five years it had justified itself. Now the end had come.

The war was drawing to a close. Fort Sumter and Charleston had fallen to the Union Army in February, and three days later the 55th Massachusetts, weighed with honors and fame, swung into the town, the black soldiers singing of John Brown's body. With these calamities, the Confederacy had been driven to a measure that spelled its own defeat. "The proposition to make soldiers of our slaves is the most pernicious idea that has been suggested since the war began," General Cobb was thundering up from Florida. "If slaves make good soldiers our whole theory of slavery is wrong."

But there was apparently no choice. The white army was being bled dry by loss and desertions; the Negro soldier had proven himself an excellent ally of the North. Slaves must be pushed into the ranks to fill up its wounds. Yet to enlist a quarter of a million slaves would mean, as an Alabama legislator said, the loss of "250,000 slaves—for not one would ever return." To enlist them at all they must be enlisted as free men, and by such an action the Confederacy would repudiate the patriots and the heroes who had given their lives to perpetuate the ideals of slavery.

Thus the Confederacy announced its end. Enlistment would begin immediately, and freedom waited for those slaves who answered the call. But none of these slaves ever struck a blow for slavery, for the Confederacy was on its knees, and the end came before a Southern colored regiment could move into the field. Richmond fell on the 3rd of April, and Jefferson Davis fled from church to escape the moving tides. Into that battered city at two o'clock the next afternoon, came the touching unexpected figure of Lincoln and his little son. Shabby, gaunt and tender-eyed, he came without announcement, unguarded except for the sailors who rowed him from the boat.

He chose to walk to the new Union headquarters, with Tad's hand in his. Down the streets he went, matching his steps to the little boy's, his deeply lined, deeply sad face lifted to the ravages of war and to the few trees that were showing their spring leaves. No one knew he was in Richmond, yet they came—came from all the bystreets, hallooing, shouting, dancing, forming a cloud behind him and running about him on both sides, tripping as they ran backwards to see him—and they were all black.

Men flung up their hats, women waved their bonnets and their hand-kerchiefs, and "Glory! Glory! Glory!" rose in the air. Thoughts must have failed, only a deep profound emotion remained, as the shouts made the air ring, and the black crowds closed the streets until soldiers came to clear a way. But the tall man smiled and bowed and the little boy jiggled on one foot, and neither wished one shout less or one less tear.

The walk to headquarters was a long one, and when the President grew weary, he halted for a few moments' rest. As he stood there an old colored man with tears rolling down his cheeks, bowed. "May de good Lord bless you, President Linkum." And there, on a warm Virginia street, the man who had, willy-nilly, fought the war against slavery, drove a final golden nail into its casket. He turned toward the old colored man, and releasing Tad's hand, took off his hat and bowed.

The end came swiftly within the next few days. Lee's army, reduced to thirty-five thousand men, was hungry and abandoned. Jefferson Davis and his Cabinet were in flight. At Appomattox, on April 9th, Lee sat in Grant's tent and Union soldiers shared their provisions with the men in gray who had ceased on that instant to be their enemy.

Bonfires spread across the North and the intoxication of war, ended and won, seized the people. Killing was finished, a Union restored, a nation's honor freed of slavery. Flags waved from every building, and men found it impossible to express their joy except in shouting and singing, in parading and raising the bonfires higher.

Lincoln, pale, like a man waking from a terrible sleep, spoke to Congress. He spoke hastily of victory, and then he settled to a defense of reconstruction as he had conceived it in Louisiana and Arkansas. Congress had rejected those proposals, but he still believed that reconstruction depended on receiving the wayward as though they had never strayed, and in receiving as voters the "very intelligent" Negroes as well as those who had served as soldiers. "If we recognize and sustain the new government of Louisiana . . . we encourage the heart and nerve the arms of twelve thousand [Union men] to adhere to their work, and argue for it, and proselyte for it, and fight for it, and feed it, and grow it and ripen it to a complete success. The colored man, too, in seeing all united for him, is inspired with vigilance, and energy, and daring to the same end. Grant that he desires the elective franchise, will he not attain it by saving the already advanced steps towards it, than by running backward over them?"

It was evidently preoccupying him to the exclusion of everything else. This was the great work. War had ended two days ago, and two days had been wasted toward the rebuilding. He talked about reconstruction endlessly, he called his Cabinet together on the 14th to discuss his plans for the South. Building up—building up, became his obsession.

That was why he sent Garrison and Beecher to Charleston for the raising of the flag over Fort Sumter. The same flag was to go up, the same Anderson was to raise it—so much of time was to be nullified. It was a significant omen too. Garrison, whose head had been demanded by South Carolina, was now to walk the streets unmolested.

Lincoln did not hear about that trip—about the three thousand Negroes who marched shouting with Garrison through the streets, of the two thousand colored school children who came with garlands and flowers, of the three thousand freedmen who welcomed them to the village of Mitchellville, where the first self-governing community of freedmen made this a gala day. He did not hear about the meeting with Captain Robert Smalls, the former slave who now piloted the *Planter*, his stolen gift to the Union, back again into Charleston Harbor loaded with two thousand freedmen, nor of the speeches that Samuel Dickerson, a new free man, and Major Delany, the colored member of General Saxton's staff, and Garrison and Beecher and George Thompson exchanged, nor of the touching meeting with Lieutenant Garrison who had just returned to camp with twelve hundred ragged contrabands, nor of the triumphant procession back to the boat where flowers were flung into the water and piled into their arms, and packages of cakes, still warm from a free woman's oven, pushed into their pockets. He did not hear about these things, for he was dead.

The flag had been raised, the tears had been exchanged, the singing had filled the air, the flowers had lain on the water the night that the President's head had slumped forward and the deep, dreaming eyes had closed. The triumphant Abolitionists, bound for Florida and further jubilation, received the word when the boat came into Beaufort. They could only stare at each other—Garrison and Beecher and Henry Wilson, who were Lincoln's men, and Thompson who loved him better than many Americans—but they found no words. A sickness, that ran beyond grief, fell upon them. All the light had gone out. The flowers had faded. Black faces no longer smiled.

They ordered the ship to return to the North. "The heavens seemed dark," said Beecher sitting against the rail and looking off across the water. "Nothing was left for the hour but God, and his immutable providence, and his decrees. But oh, the sadness of that company, and our nights' and our days' journey back. We knew nothing but this: the President had been assassinated."

## Chapter 9

## BUT WE HAVEN'T FOUND PEACE

IT WAS a stunned North to which they returned, a North that could not think clearly for a little while, terribly unsure until a swelling rage took possession of it. The South had done this, the South that had already drenched the country in four years of blood. And Grant had let them go free, Grant had talked to Lee like a gentleman, Grant had helped Confederate soldiers return to the rebuilding of the South! The North, in a blind, unreasoning way became Abolitionized as it had never been before. Now the slavocracy must be destroyed once and for all. It had raised its head for the last time.

They did not hear the lamentations from the South, which realized that a man who was prepared to be their friend had gone. They did not hear the tolling bells nor see the mourning bands in the border states. And they did not hear the wailing of the Negroes, for the brief period of Northern concern for the Negro had not yet come about.

In the horror of white Southerners was mingled the fear of insurrection. To them Lincoln had been the restraining hand on those same Negroes who saw in him the Emancipator. Many families sent terrified messages to the Union officers in Tennessee and Arkansas telling of their fear that the blacks would rise against those who were known as Confederate sympathizers and therefore murderers of Lincoln. To John Eaton on the Sunday after the assassination, three messages came from the commanding officer within as many hours, each reproducing the mounting terror of the whites and saying that Eaton would be held responsible for any massacre. Eaton, who had assured him there would be no danger, hurried to that traditional gathering place of insurrections, the colored church, and found only huddled groups of weeping and lamenting people, crying out their fear, praying aloud for protection. Then he made his way to the colored quarter of the town and there his horse was engulfed in a sea of anguished blacks, begging him to say that the death of their "protector" would not send them back to slavery. Here only the dark swinging sword of slavery, hanging by a whisper's breath, occupied their minds, only concern for that "little bit o' black to pit around de tails o' my coat to mourn for Papa Sam."

In the North, the poor white Tennessean, Andrew Johnson had taken the oath of office, and the "radicals" in Congress were outspoken in their faith in him. They were demanding no policy of ruthless revenge—only a policy that would make clear to the slavocracy that their power had ended once and for all, and to the conciliators in the North, who professed to see in the war merely a white insurrection, led by unruly malcontents, that state privileges could not be returned promptly to men who had, of their own volition, repudiated them. Beyond this, every assurance must be given that, when education had done its work, the Negro would be admitted into the full rights of citizenship and that, in the interval, he would be protected from all efforts to exploit his undetermined status. In spite of later claims of the South, vengeance was not the desire of the North, but the utter crushing of the predatory power which had kept the country in an uproar for twenty years.

Johnson promised to be their man more than the slow-moving Lincoln, although Wade, judging him from his antecedents and his speeches, was afraid he would be bloody in his vengeance. A dour man, hard-bitten, unspectacular, he had none of that warmth of Lincoln which might lead him to soft decisions, misplaced confidences, leniencies. "Where the colored people know me best they have confidence in me," he said to a Negro delegation which came asking assurance of "complete emancipation" and "full equality before the law." He was prepared to follow the heart of Lincoln's reconstruction plans—education for the Negro and eventually the vote, the absorption of the rebellious states back into the Union in proportion to the strength of their Union sentiments. "I am charmed with his sympathy," Sumner wrote, "which is entirely different from his predecessor's." It seemed as though the end of the war had indeed come, that democracy would penetrate even the resistant bailiwicks of the old slave power.

They were lighthearted that spring. The only point of disagreement was the question of confiscation of the great plantations, the step necessary to make democracy workable for the landless Negro who was holding the dream of land before him like a banner and refusing to sign new contracts, so confident was he that the government's promises would be met. Perhaps Johnson was demurring on this point, but with his loyalty to emancipation, he would be sure to include those forty acres and a mule in the final program.

And then he betrayed them. They found no gentler word to use. In the hands of a Congress, democratized by the success of the North, the power must lie, not in the hands of the President. And Johnson, by his North Carolina Proclamation, had taken the power to himself.

So the war was not over! That the Proclamation and the amnesty resembled Lincoln's plan did not relax the indignation of the Republican leaders, for Congress had already told Lincoln what it felt about his proposals. The unwilling, repudiated, unmistakable cause of the war, the Negro, had been excluded from all consideration in the new constitution, and from the tone of Johnson's advice to the seceded states, the rigid exclusion of the Negro from the new constitutions was to be complete.

Sumner, Stevens, the leaders of the emancipationists, were wild with indignation, and Henry Winter Davis, in Maryland, was gathering his dying strength together to hurl a broadside at the man who had betrayed them. He demanded the immediate franchise for the Negro and recalled bitterly that "we remember his declaration that traitors should be punished, yet none are punished; that only loyal men should control the States, yet he has delivered them to the disloyal; that the aristocracy should be pulled down, yet he has put them in power again; that its possessions should be divided among Northern laborers of all colors, yet the negroes are still a landless homeless class." The whole course of reaction lay clearly before them. As far as Johnson was concerned, no practical effort was to be made to keep from office the old slaveholders (in spite of pleasant high-sounding words, their oath was confined to a defense of the Constitution and nothing more), and his lavish use of the Presidential pardon, which included the restoration of plantations, was opening another gate to the reconstruction of slavery.

Carl Schurz who had given his devotion to Lincoln—and did not Johnson claim to be following in a martyr's footsteps?—came to Johnson in dismay, and Johnson committed what one of his fondest admirers called a "serious tactical blunder" by sending Schurz on an inspection tour of the South. Sumner was attempting to rouse the East; he was talking wherever he could find an ear. Mass meetings in Boston were calling for Negro suffrage, for the antislavery fight would not be over till citizenship came to the Negro, and all over the North the new conception of democracy which had been slowly growing in the minds of people was stirring into ambiguous response. The Union League Clubs, powerful North and South by the end of the war, had made this suffrage the heart of their agitation, and as the summer came they saw that the only way to stem the resurgent slavocrats of the South was by the unremitting education into citizenship of the Negro.

Chase reported on this, for he had begun a tour of Southern states before the North Carolina proclamation, and he was out to observe what he could of the whole problem of Negro capacity for citizenship and white chauvinism. To Johnson he wrote that "everywhere throughout the country colored citizens are organizing Union Leagues" and to him it appeared that they "must exert a great influence on the future of the class they represent and not a little bit on the character of the states in which they exist"; he advised Johnson that they were "a power which no wise statesmen will despise."

He had had plenty of opportunity to observe them, for at nearly every town, white and Negro delegations came to see him, and to talk about themselves. Everywhere he addressed mass meetings of former slaves who were perfectly aware of what they needed to protect them from the returning signs of slavery. What were these signs, rising so quickly out of the shambles of the war? Chase could see them as well as any; Schurz had much to say in his report. Schurz traced the course of black and white relations from the day of the Emancipation Proclamation; he spoke of those slaves, living on remote plantations who had not been told of their freedom, or, learning of it, were terrorized into submission, and he explained the inevitable reaction which came with the end of the war. "The white people were afraid of the Negroes, and the Negroes did not trust the white people; the military power of the national government stood there, and was looked up to as the protector of both."

Was freedom then so violent and undisciplined a thing? Indignant landowners said that their new employees laid down their tools at any hour to sing, to make speeches. For two hundred and fifty years no slave had been allowed to lift his back without the tacit approval of the overseer. Why should freedom not be an intoxicating thing? Former slaves who now owned land were self-sufficient. They were not deceived into believing that laziness meant freedom. Those who worked on other men's land wanted to know why they should work for wages, which five times out of six were not paid, when they had been promised land for themselves? Some of them congregated in shacks, hungry, badly clothed, stealing sometimes, or waiting stolidly for the land that was to make men and women of them. Thousands of them were wandering, homeless and dependent, through the country. Some were wandering because they had never been able to move outside the orbit of a pass before, and freedom could not be appreciated without stretching the legs and going as far as the fancy called; others were searching for families, sold away from them, five, ten, even twenty-five years ago, believing that by a miracle old faces would be young again and families in some way magnetized together. Still others were the victims of a society without industries to absorb the workless, of a vast agrarianism whose huge plantations were the lodestars of these land-hungry peasants.

A social and economic system with roots in the centuries, had been overthrown and it was not in the nature of such overturnings to wait on long adjustments. No body of people was ever watched with such remorseless eyes as those freed Negroes of 1865. Slaves—chattels—men and women bound by every law in the statute books to perpetual enslavement had suddenly declared that freedom belonged to them, and that freedom was no trivial affair. "If you want anything call for Sambo—I mean call for Mr. Samuel, dat my name now." "I worked massa's lan' for fo'ty years. Ah wan' dat lan' now . . ." "Mamie wan's a red dress, Ah wanna get drunk. Why not. White folks does."

No people were watched with such unblinking eyes as the whites. The blacks remembered the degradation of the free Negro in the slavery days. Were they not all free Negroes now? What was it going to mean? In Gates County, North Carolina, Negroes who had remained in the country without work were being seized and sold. A Mr. Parker of that state, assured the military commander of the district that his old Negroes had willingly agreed to stay and work for him for board and two suits of clothes; the Negroes testified secretly that the agreement had been reached only when they had been kicked and beaten; that now they were guarded day and night, and that Bob, one of their men, was chained as soon as he came off the fields. "Springing naturally out of this disordered state of affairs," the implacably anti-Negro newspaper, the New York *Herald*, said, "is an organization of 'regulators' so-called. Their number include many ex-Confederate cavaliers, and their mission is to visit summary justice upon any offenders against the public peace. It is needless to say that their attention is largely directed to maintaining quiet and submission among the blacks. The shooting or stringing up of some obstreperous 'nigger' by the 'regulators' is so common an occurrence as to excite little remark. Nor is the work of proscription confined to the freedmen only. The 'regulators' go to the bottom of the matter, and strive to make it uncomfortably warm for any new settler with demoralizing innovations of wages for 'niggers.'" An Alabamian, sending an urgent testimony to Congress, warned that armed insurrection would follow the goading and the murders that are "particularly flagrant in the states of Alabama and Mississippi," and a Mississippian sent a solemn warning, "If matters are permitted to continue as they now seem likely to be, it needs no prophet to predict a rising on the part of the colored population and a terrible scene of bloodshed and desolation. Nor can anyone blame the Negroes if this proves to be the result . . . It is sufficient to state that the old overseers are in power again."

It was only outside agitation that made the reconciliation between former master and slave impossible. If they were left to work out an adjustment together . . . How painfully familiar this answer of the planters rang in antislavery ears. "Some of the planters with whom I have had occasion to converse," Carl Schurz reported, "have expressed their determination to adopt the course which best accords with the spirit of free labor, to make the Negro work by offering him fair inducements, to stimulate his ambition, and to extend to him those means of intellectual and moral improvement which are best calculated to make him an intelligent, reliable citizen . . . I regret to say that views and intentions so reasonable I found confined to a small majority . . . At last I was forced to the conclusion that, aside from a small number of honorable exceptions, the popular prejudice is almost as bitterly set against the Negro's having the advantage of education as it was when the Negro was a slave. Hundreds of times I heard the old assertion repeated, that 'learning will spoil the nigger for work,' and that 'Negro education will be the ruin of the South.' Wherever I go—the street, the shop, the house, the hotel, or the steamboat—I hear the people talk in such a way as to indicate that they are yet unable to conceive of the Negro as possessing any rights at all. The people boast that when they get freedmen's affairs in their own hands, to use their own expression, 'the niggers will catch hell.' "

It was an old Negro, talking to Chase, who summed it up most poignantly. "I tell you, sah, we ain't noways safe 'long as dem people make de laws. We's got to hab a voice in de 'pinting ob de law makers. Den we know our frens and whose hans we's safe in."

The men in the North who were fighting the battle of emancipation were not doing so only to keep the Republican party in power. Stevens was an old man, burning out, but the flame that ate at his body ate also at his terrible fury. Of all the Radicals, this grim old man from Pennsylvania with the devastating and Voltairian humor was the true revolutionist. And these were days of revolution. The friends of Johnson were glib with phrases of the French Revolution, hanging them about the necks of the Abolitionists like badges of shame. But Stevens was not ashamed. He saw the requirements clearly. To lift a beaten and despised class to a level of democracy, that class must be given its manhood. In the midst of an agrarian society, land alone would give the Negroes the right to demand the ballot and education alone the right to use it. With these convictions, and by his unerring political skill, he was prepared to pull Johnson from his high place if necessity demanded it.

The Radicals listened to the fateful calling off of states by Johnson as though they were warning bells in the night, Mississippi, Georgia, Texas, South Carolina, Florida, hastily gathered into his reconstruction plan, and emerging clear of all taint of secession.

All through the summer they attempted to build up, through popular opinion, a halt to this course of reconstruction. Congress must be stronger than the President. Through the eyes and the ears of freedmen's agents or Southern loyalists, they saw and heard the constitutional conventions called by the reconstructed states that autumn, and they saw and heard dismaying things.

A series of Black Codes were enacted in all the reconstructed states, and with their publication went the last hope that within the old slavocracy could be found that attitude of mind which would allow the democratic unfolding of a new way of living where two races might find an equal citizenship within the framework of their common country. Had it been done, had such a leadership, such a state of mind been manifested, had there been any concerted protest against the legalized exploitation, condoned by the legislatures, the whole wretched, moving, hapless story of reconstruction might have told itself with a different set of words.

But the facts were incontrovertible. All the Black Codes allowed the Negro in his new way of life were legalized marriage, the right to hold property, the right to sue or be sued. For the rest: he could rent property or houses only in restricted areas; he must never be without his contract of labor or his license from the police; if he quit his work he could be arrested and sent to the house of correction for a year, or if he were captured and brought back, his captor would be paid a reward of five dollars, and ten cents a mile for travel. Over him his employer held a control as inflexible as the slave master's, while his children were re-enslaved by apprenticeship laws. To restrict the movements of the freedmen were vagrancy laws, carrying penalties of hard labor or long imprisonment. Several times colored soldiers who, having been mustered out only a few hours and therefore technically without employment were arrested. Itinerant preachers were called vagrants, for itinerant preachers had carried dangerous messages in the past and it was to be assumed that they would talk of freedom again. Freedom was a very live word in the colored South. A four years' insurrection could hardly make it otherwise. Against Union Leagues and Republican meetings a Mississippi law was aimed, which declared that those who were "found unlawfully assembling themselves together, either in the day or night time" were vagrants, and it leveled the same law against the teachers and agents of the freedmen by declaring as vagrants "white people usually associating with freedmen, free people or mulattos."

Fines were established for misdemeanors, for absence from work for any cause, for "rioting, affrays, trespasses . . . seditious speeches, insulting gestures or acts." A system of taxation for propertyless Negroes foreshadowed the peonage and share cropping that was to become the residue of these years. In some states, any white man, whether authorized or not, might arrest a Negro, and in all states no Negro, unless he were a soldier, could own or carry firearms. Curfew laws were established, making a Negro liable to arrest if he were on the streets without a pass from his employer.

The sum of it all was clarified when certain states merely substituted "Negro" for "slave" and adopted their old slave codes.

When the freedmen's commissioners, reporting to Congress, declared that these Black Codes "actually served to secure to the former slaveholding class the unpaid labor which they been accustomed to enjoy before the war," the issues of the struggle were clear. A broken Confederacy found no better solution for its poverty and its rehabilitation than to look backwards. Even when one made allowances for the bitterness of war and defeat, the destruction of a system, the military occupation, it was still a fact that when the first opportunity came—and how quickly, with Johnson's guidance, did it come!—the South broke the freedom of a new and rising class. The terrible stultification of slavery had made the mind unable to grasp a new way of living, an evolved society. The terrible black stain that had been laid on the conscience, on the moral sense, on the social conditions, by the economics of slavery could not, apparently, be wiped away by war. Had anything changed? Only one thing: Freedom need no longer be whispered in secret, be sung under the breath. Gabriels and Veseys and Nat Turners could not be hanged for wanting freedom. The problem of the Negroes lay in seeing that they were not now hanged under another name for wanting freedom.

The Negro conventions which came together simultaneously with the constitutional conventions knew all about these things. The first convention, meeting in Nashville, Tennessee, in August with a local Negro barber as its chairman, passed resolutions that Congress must recognize Negro citizenship and must prove its good faith by disbarring all Tennessee representatives in Congress until the state had recognized the rights of its own colored people. In North Carolina they met in September. These were their first efforts toward political action, and they felt the danger that went with such daring.

The second one was, in the words of a newspaper reporter, "really a convention of colored men, not a colored men's convention, engineered by white men," and the one hundred and twenty delegates, coming from all sections of the state, were mostly former slaves, plantation hands, who were able to attend only by leaving their work secretly, after nightfall, and returning under the darkness of the next night. Their chairman was a former slave named Harris, "in the true sense self-educated; an upholsterer by trade, and latterly, a teacher by profession." The delegates were not all illiterate men; some had stolen an education, most could read and write a little, but whatever their past or present status, they knew what they wanted—cash for labor, education for their children, the repeal of legislation that discriminated against them. They voted to support certain men whose names they knew to be friendly, Sumner, Stevens, Wade.

In South Carolina and in Georgia they also gathered, reasserting that freedmen would not accept the Black Codes, urging, as the South Carolina convention did, that free education should be provided for white children and black children, that "every citizen, without regard to race, descent or color" should have "equal political rights," and they reaffirmed a vigorous and well-known sentiment when they voted against "taxation without representation."

Ignorance manifests itself in strange ways, and this was black ignorance. If they were protected by the military, if commissioners were known to smooth out the phraseology of memorials, the Negroes themselves dictated the objects of these meetings. The memorial that went to Congress from the South Carolina convention was written in fine, Shakespearian English, but the delegates had known exactly what they wanted if someone else provided the words. They wanted a law that would allow them security to "sell their labor as the merchant sells his goods," they wanted equal suffrage, and the assurance that colored men would not always be tried by white juries nor colored men always excluded from jury service, they wanted the right to know that they could discuss politics, go into business, protect their families, without hostility all about them. And finally they wanted the government to redeem their land pledges.

This was included because the former owners of the Sea Islands were coming back with their Johnson pardons and claiming their plantations. But the new owners of the Sea Islands were not prepared to give them up.

The Sea Island fight was a lonely one, and the friendly army officers, the freedmen's most powerful champions, were advising them to give up their pleas for land. But the new owners of the Sea Islands, repeating their belief that landed security was the only guarantee of freedom and the only protection from sharpsters, North and South, met the old proprietors with every weapon they could hold. One old Negro, who made himself their leader, put their thoughts into words of heavy scorn. "You'd better go back ter Charleston and go ter work dere and ef you cain't do nothin' else, you kin pick oysters and earn your living as de loyal people hab done—by de sweat ob der brows."

There was nothing to do but "go back ter Charleston" and the Freedmen's Bureau stood by the Negroes, and begged Congress to confirm the promises of this land that had been given through Sherman. Washington answered by sending General Howard, who was head of the Freedmen's Bureau, with compromise inducements to return the land to the old slaveholders. The Sea Islanders were angry. The government had deceived them again. White men could not be trusted. "See de gubbermint, and ax him if he wouldn't sell de land," they appealed to one of the officers, "and leff um to pay sum udder time, an ef we don't pay in two years, den he can take um back."

Give us land—land—land, the only thing that will convince us we are citizens.

In Washington, the smoldering hostility between the President and Congress was turning into fire. The "Radicals" distrusted his professions of friendliness toward the freedmen, his conciliation toward those who had compromised the old South; the liberals found their distress, not in conciliation, but in the usurpation of power which they feared more than they did the Black Codes. Only the conservatives, many of whom still showed proslavery leanings, were Johnson men.

As for Johnson, he stood between two implacable forces, the rising oligarchy in the North and his own temperamental inclination toward the old rulers of the South, an unquenchable characteristic of the Southern middleclass man. To an interviewer he said in something like despair, "The aristocracy based on $3,000,000,000 of property in slaves south of Mason's and Dixon's line has disappeared, but an aristocracy, based on over $2,500,000,000 of national securities, has arisen in the Northern States to assume that political control which the consolidation of great financial and political interests formerly gave the slave oligarchy . . . The aristocracy based on Negro property disappears at the Southern end of the line only to reappear in an oligarchy of bonds and national securities in the states which repressed the rebellion."

And this financial and industrial oligarchy, of which he was the willing or unwilling servant, was concerned only with the pacification of that huge treasure house in the South, where Northern capital was already making vast inroads and where complete domination might only be a matter of time. To this oligarchy, the Negro and his place in society was of no more concern that the poverty-stricken white laborers of the North had been to the old slavocracy. His demand for land struck at their concept of the sanctity of property. If Negro elevation was to be accomplished at the expense of a delay in Northern dividends, then the Negro must look out.

"Now is the critical time," Wendell Phillips sent out his warning, "the rebellion has not ceased, it has only changed its weapons."

"Hold the antislavery societies together," came the cry from Sumner. "The crisis is grave."

Congress, reassembled in December, saw the Vice President of the Confederacy, four Confederate generals, six Confederate Cabinet members and fifty-eight Confederate Congressmen, present themselves as Representatives, invoking the Constitution which they had repudiated as sufficient reason for them to be seated. Their assumptions were based on Johnson's reconstruction plans and the fine support which conservative newspapers in the North were giving to them both. But Congress, however confused, however unsettled on any specific policy, refused to be pushed headlong into Johnson's plans. They wasted very little time in making clear that reconstruction must be the work of Congress, not of the President. Stevens, remorseless, irresistible, incorruptible, proposed on the first day that a joint committee of fifteen members "be appointed from the House and the Senate to consider the suitability of receiving representatives from the seceded states." The committee was appointed by a heavy vote, and Johnson suffered his first defeat. Congress had won the right to dictate on all reconstruction proposals. The industrial North stirred uneasily. "Lack of business confidence" was the gloomy prediction. What if Stevens' confiscation program went through? Northern capital was determined that no confiscation program would be allowed. The Northern oligarchy must be permitted to expand without interference. No equalization in the South must hinder the march of industry.

That session was noisy, blasphemous and undignified. A fight was waged over every period and comma of resolutions. Congress, of as many minds as the country, was unanimous—to all practical purposes—on one thing only, that the future of the new South should not be determined by the men who ruled the old South; that Southern politicians, only waiting to repudiate the democratization of the South, should not be permitted to upset whatever gains could be plucked from the war. Beyond this, they were determined that Negroes without votes should not be counted into Congressional representation, a blow that would have far-reaching effects in that minority-dominated section of the country and wipe out the three-fifths strength that had given the slavocracy such power.

In the galleries, with strained and wondering faces, were the black and brown countenances of those who might take no part in the fight that was being waged for them. The Negroes filled the galleries this session; they could be seen in all the corridors, well dressed, badly dressed, articulate, dumb, but drawn by an irresistible magnetism to this alien world which held their fate.

To give to the Washington Negroes the right to vote seemed to the "Northern intellectuals and literati" as well as to the Sumners and Stevenses an example that should not be overlooked, a lesson for the states, North and South, who had yet to deliver an unrestricted franchise. The House fought desperately, noisily, and at last—for those brown faces—triumphantly. When the successful roll call was announced, the galleries and the floor went wild, black men and white men embracing and shouting together. But the vote was not yet in their hands. The Senate had not acted—and the Senate buried the bill as the session came to a close.

The fight, rocking back and forth, only making headway at the price of great bitterness, intensified the struggle between Congress and the President. Driven hard by the continual pressure from the Southern Negroes for the confirmation of their land, Trumbull of Illinois introduced a bill, extending the power of the Freedmen's Bureau, authorizing the distribution for forty-acre lots of unoccupied land to the Negroes, and increasing the bureau's judicial powers, as well as providing for a settlement of the Sea Islands and confirming early sales and early leases in land around Port Royal. Johnson, listening to the cries of impending insurrections raised by the old masters, vetoed the bill and ordered the recall of certain Negro regiments which were presumed to be giving revolutionary advice to the freedmen.

Well, Congress would wait, grim old Stevens decreed, and gather its strength. Johnson would hang himself with his own rope. Garrison heard the speech made by Johnson in front of the White House on Washington's Birthday, a violent speech that swelled in the flare of the torchlights and was fed by the excitement of his admirers. He claimed the people for himself, he turned violently against those men whom he knew were hostile to his policies, and he called out their names to the

shouting crowd. "Thaddeus Stevens of Pennsylvania . . . Charles Sumner of Massachusetts . . . Wendell Phillips of Massachusetts . . . Do
they want more blood? I am not afraid of assassins!"

This was bloodletting of a fine kind. It made the head swirl, the pulse
pound. Washington was a Southern city. Old Stevens, the whip, merely
drew his lips together in a hard line and Sumner tossed his leonine head
and beat harder than ever against the wall of opposition.

In battling for the Civil Rights Bill, which attempted to give protection to the freedmen's lives and property, Sumner argued for its enforcement with bayonets if necessary, by recalling the experiences of the
British government who found emancipation did not come through
"the arrant trifling of the former masters," and by repeating the words
of the Emperor of Russia who had found that the efforts of his ancestors
toward the emancipation of serfs had always failed "because they had
been left to 'the spontaneous initiative of the proprietors.' " But the
Civil Rights Bill was lost because Northern business was afraid of anything that might delay the reopening of trade with the South and
because Republicans were afraid that such radicalism would go against
them at the next election. The Freedmen's Bureau bill looked safer.

Round and round the violent carrousel went . . . a white man's
government . . . equality for all . . . the Constitution, the Constitution,
like some incantation that was presumed to heal problems of 1866 which
had not been dreamed of in 1791 . . . new defenses of the old way of
life . . . Johnson saying in his heart, "Damn the Negro; let's get business
started again," or Blaine and Conkling saying, "Property and industry
are all that is important; hold the South tight with Negro votes until we
can sew it up with Northern investments."

Stevens, the strongest man in the country, struck the only sharp
unequivocal note of pure democracy. "Governor Perry of South Carolina
and other provisional governors proclaim that 'this is the white man's
government.' Demagogues of all parties, even some high in authority,
gravely shout, 'This is the white man's government.' . . . Our fathers
repudiated the whole doctrine of the legal superiority of families or
races, and proclaimed the equality of men before the law. Upon that
they created a revolution and built a Republic . . . This is not a white
man's government . . . this is Man's Government, the Government of
all men alike."

But where was the great Southern leader, who repudiating the Yanceys,
the Toombs, the Davises, could see an unfettered vision of the future,
where education was free and minorities were under the protection of a
democracy; who would shake the former slaves from the ignorance, the

apathy, the poverty that had been nurtured by slavery? He could have been any of the slave masters who had recognized the capacity for learning in his slaves, who had seen free Negroes in the slave South build up their own professions and raise their children in dignity. He might have been one of those visitors to the zeal-stricken North of the 1850's who heard Douglass bringing an exhilaration to the mind or Garnet a religious surge to the heart.

But he was apparently to remain only a hope and a dream. The Negroes did not look for him, now that "Uncle Sam" was dead, but they were prepared to follow whatever leadership, black or white, offered them a guarantee of freedom. The Negro Equal Rights conventions of the North, the conventions in the South, were all articulate. They were, in spite of all their enemies, no one's dupes when it came to their own demands. They presented an impressive force that would have sustained and made possible whatever progressive legislation Congress had seen fit to pass. Yet they were still pariahs.

Garrison found no surprise in these events. He had put great hope in Johnson, but he was coming to put a greater and more bitter hope in the defense offered by Grant's officers and men in the old slavelands and in the growing opposition of the country to the readmission of any of the old Confederacy. He spread his alarm and quickened his doubt wherever he gained an audience. From antislavery societies, warnings were sent in a steady stream. There would be no rest until the black man was secure. But the ramifications of his citizenship were becoming more devious. If Southern representation was increased by the additional four million black citizens, the Northern balances would be threatened. Stevens, as head of the Committee of Fifteen, tried to answer all these arguments, and in doing so, accepted a first draft of the Fourteenth Amendment as a compromise. But Sumner was not compromising, even to keep the Republican party steady. It left a loophole for the disfranchisement of the Negro, and Sumner, deserted by friends and party, fought as tenaciously as he had ever done to defeat what his friend Stevens had with such pain wrenched through a timid House. Was Sumner right? the country wanted to know. Or had he overplayed his conscientiousness? Garrison said no and regarded his logic as unassailable. Phillips was his man also. Even the vacillating Beecher exclaimed that he covered "a ground which will abide after all contemporary questions of special legislation have passed away."

Stevens mastered his disappointment. When the debates on the Civil Rights Bill were revived in March, 1866, he was there with his remorseless whip, and it passed without too much acrimony through both houses.

But Johnson was there as well, with his veto and his logic. Chinese, Indians, gypsies as well as Negroes could become citizens if this bill became law, and when his peroration was over, he had concluded that the bill could only be regarded as a discrimination against the white race.

A second veto stirred that deep uneasiness which the country had been feeling ever since the guns ceased firing. Men in Washington looked in dismay. He had promised not to veto this bill—Trumbull had publicly promised that it would not be vetoed. Congress was indignant as it had not been heretofore. This usurpation was too much! Promptly the veto was overridden, and Congress in a militant frame of mind, was prepared to challenge any further movements of Johnson.

When the Freedmen Bureau's bill was presented again, it went rapidly through House and Senate, and rapidly to the President's veto. Congress did not flinch. Johnson was taking the rope that would hang him. Without debate, they passed it over his veto. It was now June, 1866. The committee had its eight-hundred-page report on conditions in the South. It was given a wide distribution, for state conventions were meeting and suffrage was to be decided in them all. In a part of the country where even white schooling had never been a pressing concern, acres of land had been bought, schoolhouses raised, teachers paid out of the desperately thin pockets of the Negroes. In Arkansas, Georgia, Florida, Kentucky, North Carolina, schools were kept open even when the Negroes were forced to seek credit on their next year's crops. When Louisiana military authorities put a stop to a general tax for colored schools, petitions poured in from colored parents—ten thousand of them signed, with their names or their marks, a document thirty feet long.

Against the popularly believed background of drunken and insolent Negroes shouting disrespect at whites, the Negro with a little land was making himself sufficient, was breaking through—bit by bit, painfully, despairingly—the hard mortar that slavery had called his life, his hope, his aspirations. He was going with the plantation hands to political meetings to learn more of civil rights and was listening as intently as possible to the old passengers of the Underground Railroad who were now beginning to return home in increasing numbers, bringing their more cultivated sense of minority rights.

In the old days the Underground Railroad had been the safety valve for the South, running off the natural leaders who might have raised a vast insurrection against the slavocracy. Now the leaders were returning, and some were opening schools and others were working with the relief agencies and still others were searching for broken families or spreading the news of political rights. 'And white freedmen's agents, like Levi Coffin, were meeting their old charges again, who on dark and danger-filled nights had once asked for shelter and a ticket on the "road."

This education, these rights, could have assumed a natural and well-ordered course. All the ingredients were here but the vision was lacking. Those who might have provided that vision, those who had, now and then in the past, met with the Negro on a common basis of outrage and revolt, those who had suffered as painfully from slavery as the slave, were now caught up in a more blind, unreasoning, inarticulate fear than they had ever known before. Where was the poor white's ideal now, where was his future, where was his hope? His condition had in no way im-proved. Sitting on his arid acre, he saw the black man move toward his own orbit, toward his own cotton land, toward his own job, into that inchoate and terrible fringe of living where starvation kept them on a common level of wonderment and unrequited hope. A common level? No, the white man still had his white skin, and if fear and humiliation made him forget it, a gun in his hand, and a lynching rope over his arm restored his self-respect.

It was not the great landowning planters who had suffered most in the war, it was not they who made up the terrible mortality rate in the white South when the first months of peace came; it was these men on the fringe. It was not the Negroes about whom one should ask, what is to be done with them, for they were prepared and eager for life? It was these whose lives had been stunted when the implacable weight of slavery had driven them from their lands, fastened their free-labor hands with the skilled labor of slaves, and were now removing from them the only drug that had brought them sustaining visions—the slaveholding aristocracy which, in their miasma, they might aspire to enter.

The friends of the Negro in the South knew that combustion must come from this economic desperation, from the well-nurtured passions of race. They sent warnings to Washington that there could be no settle-ment, North or South, no genuine peace, until a Fourteenth Amend-ment had established the status of the Negro, and brought some order out of the political and economic chaos of the South.

When, in the first part of June, 1866, a new draft of the Fourteenth Amendment passed through the House and the Senate, and was sent to the states for ratification, everyone but Sumner and Stevens, and those who had voted against it seemed pleased. Sumner and Stevens had voted for it, but they were depressed and dissatisfied. The Negro was declared a citizen, but no mention had been made of his right as a voter; no clarification was offered of the ambiguous phrase which made his life, liberty, and property subject to the "due process of law." Stevens, who knew that he was dying, made one final and urgent plea for full citizenship.

Congress was prepared now, he believed, to force the issue with the President. But Johnson also had prepared himself. They understood him now. They were not altogether taken by surprise when they learned that he had, with the moral blessings of the Democrats, sent out a call for a national convention. It seemed his desire to be the first to prepare for a showdown.

The Radicals promptly called a Loyal Union Convention at Philadelphia and set their policies on record by inviting delegates from the South to bring petitions for Negro suffrage. But expediency held back their hands. Although they sat in the cloud of the New Orleans' riot, in which dead and wounded Negro soldiers and white citizens had been carried off in drays, they took no action on the question which public horror was pushing, most pressingly, before them. Times were not right . . . Would times ever be right? . . . Education and the vote must come hand in hand.

Johnson was busy attempting to rally the country to himself by a tour through the Northern states, and the Loyal Union Convention heard the repercussions—the black-draped towns hanging with signs, "No welcome to traitors," the bands playing the death march, the polite crowds which turned into shrieking mobs, the governors who refused to meet him, and Johnson's defiant cries, "Hang Sumner, Stevens, Phillips—all of Congress!"

All this and much more stiffened public opinion which had shown itself, time and again, on the side of Congress. Northern capital began to see the advantage of Negro suffrage. Perhaps through the Negro the South could be grasped . . . The perpetual reiteration of the Abolitionists, exerting their magic again, the inducements of Negro lecturers, hammering their cause as they had hammered the fight for emancipation, the slowly growing support of newspapers and journals, all counted up to a changing point of view. American democracy became a tender phrase again . . . the world must not be mistaken in American democracy.

But it was a Yankee editor who found the conclusive argument. Since the North sold to the South "all sorts of Yankee notions amounting in the year to many hundreds of thousands of dollars, and destined soon to amount to many millions," and since "England at great cost to treasure and life, compasses land and sea with her navies to establish a colony that will buy its goods of Manchester and Birmingham," why forget that "we, at a cost not worth mentioning, and with a light brigade of school mistresses, can organize at our own doors a colony—so to speak—that will be worth more to us than any of England's most flourishing dependencies?"

Why not indeed?

The Negro had been first a beast, then a slave, finally an anachronism. Now suddenly he became a man.

The Fourteenth Amendment, expressing this change of heart, was ratified in nearly half the Northern states before the new Congress—defiantly anti-Johnson—had assembled. In all the Southern states it had been as abruptly rejected. Yet it was for the admission of these Southern states that Johnson was pressing so earnestly. He called attention to their Representatives and Senators merely waiting for the word to begin their journeys to Washington. They had, he assured Congress, ratified the Thirteenth Amendment—abolishing slavery—in every Southern state but Mississippi, and were doing everything they could for the comfort of the Negro. Occasional disorders were merely an indication of the unrest of a land recovering from war.

But Congress was not convinced. To reject the Fourteenth Amendment meant that the slavery spirit was still alive. After eight months, they admitted Tennessee. The rest could wait . . . Meanwhile, there was Johnson.

Wendell Phillips was calling for his impeachment. Hannibal Hamlin, Johnson's predecessor, had taken up the cry. Rumor, blowing itself up into fact, had a thousand lips repeating that Johnson and the South were planning a *coup d'état*. The sweep back toward civil war was evident even to the clumsiest politician, and the appalling chaos of the country made the vacillating days of the war seem steady and sure-footed. His self-assumed power must be stripped from Johnson before it was too late. The Abolitionists, nurtured in a philosophy of freedom which rejected such a thing as military occupation, had hesitated before the remedies offered by the Radicals, but now they saw their work to be done again. It was evident that only under military protection could the people be free to draw up constitutions that would be affirmations of democracy.

Congress hurried into action. A movement was made for impeachment. A movement was simultaneously made to put a stop to Johnson's reconstruction and substitute something that more closely resembled their plans. All the cloakrooms, all the barroom meeting places, all the offices were alive with facts and fancies, accusations, rebuttals and the strong hands of Stevens and Sumner, whipping direction out of the excitement. Stevens had always urged education first, suffrage second, but there was apparently no time now for anything but the confirmation of free-dom. From the South the word was coming fast. Georgia, Alabama, Louisiana, North Carolina, Virginia, Negroes were drilling in anticipa-tion of the next blow of the new, white-robed order that called itself the Ku Klux Klan and rode a terrorizing route at night in the name of white chauvinism. South Carolina Negroes, armed and refusing to leave plantations where their crops were growing and where they had built their houses, were saying "they would die where they stood before they would surrender their claims to the land." Five hundred Tennessee Negroes had attempted to seize plantations near Memphis and some had died in the attempt. Northern troops had subdued another five hundred near Richmond, Virginia, for refusing to pay rents on the land which they claimed as their own. The rumors of insurrection—the old fear and the only actuality—were raised now in the name of free land. And Johnson was hampering all legal means of relief.

Stevens' body was dying, but his mind was fiercely alive. He was shouting louder than ever that "More than $2,000,000,000 of property belonging to the United States, confiscated not as rebel but as enemy property, had been given back to enrich traitors." Small landowners, he claimed, should hold their land, but the great landowners, the "lead-ing rebels" should lose their property in forty-acre tracts to the freedmen. The rest should be sold to pay the debts of the war. Thus the former slaves would be cared for, the leaders of the rebellion would pay for the war, and the national debt would be taken from about the necks of the people; "yet nine-tenths of the Southern people would remain untouched." Stevens knew that the strength of a new South lay with landowning, small farmers, independent freedmen. But so did the old South. "With-out confiscation," wrote an Alabama editor, "the result of Negro suf-frage will slip through their fingers."

Why should confiscation be prevented? Land was being taken from the farmers of the West for railroad and mining companies. Small farmers who had staked their homes under the Homestead Act were being dispossessed, and public land, by the million acres, was being handed to the railroads.

But railroad companies and freed slaves were apparently unrelated fish. Defeated, Stevens turned urgently to other means. He proposed a bill of Congressional Reconstruction based on the conviction that life and property were not safe in the torn and dissident South, that order must be enforced until loyal governments could be legally established, that the old Confederate states must be divided into military zones with control in the hands of generals rather than the President, that special tribunals must be set up for the dispensation of justice, and the writ of habeas corpus suspended.

These proposals threw Congress into a furor. A Republican caucus was necessary before any clear point of view could emerge. Sumner was unwilling to support the bill without some guarantee of equal suffrage, and when it emerged from the violent debates of the House and the Senate and came to Johnson, it was a radical document indeed. No delegate was to be banned from the constitutional conventions because of race, color or previous condition; state conventions must provide for universal male suffrage; the constitutions drawn up must be accepted by a majority of the voters and must be acceptable to Congress before the state could again be admitted to the Union.

Surely the broadcloth revolutionists were not in the least surprised by Johnson's veto! They repassed the bill on the last day of Congress, and reassembled immediately so that the President could not interfere with the enforcement of the new law. Moving quickly, they passed three more laws, aimed at curtailing his power and consolidating their gains. The Tenure of Office Bill was designed to prevent him from removing officeholders without the consent of the Senate, and was within the year used to bring him to his impeachment trial. A measure against his lavish use of pardons was pushed through to hold the stage for Congressional Reconstruction. An act preventing him from issuing military orders except through the general of the army, was passed to give strong jaws to their legislation. Grant was the general, and Grant was working with the Radicals.

Again Johnson used his veto. Again Congress overrode him. Congressional Reconstruction became the law. Thus, into the South came that decade which has fathered such vituperation, such violence of opinion, such storms of indignation.

But what did it really represent?

Like a fire which burns too brightly for eyes too close, the brief blaze of reconstruction proved unendurable to a society faultily prepared for so radical a democracy.

Out of sorrow and poverty, out of ignorance and tears, black men and white men, who had been the disinherited and cast-off, struggled to find their citizenship, and instead of a crude saturnalia of corruption, a bitter revenge of slaves against masters and clay eaters against aristocrats, was a slow painful effort to establish a new and untried way of life, a government which represented the majority and not the tight oligarchy which had heretofore voted in the name of five million disfranchised men. In the end, the slander fell, not against the white Southerners who stood as a majority in the reconstructed governments; not, eventually, against the white friends and white sycophants who came from the North, but against the Negroes.

But was it deserved? Did any legislature of which Negroes were a component part pass laws of disfranchisement or laws of revenge? On the contrary they secured legal rights for whites and blacks, they argued for equal protection for all classes. Were they ignorant and vicious? Some of them had no education, some of them trusted to the advice of friends who misled them, some of them accepted bribes or sold their votes, but all of them demanded the first public school system which the South had ever known, demanded protection for the insane, the deaf, the dumb, the sick, the poor. Were they lazy? By the end of the Reconstruction period, the agricultural life of the South had been restored beyond the prewar level. Why then has Reconstruction been told in terms of almost unrelieved mockery and slander?

Perhaps the old Abolitionists could have answered it—those who survived the bad eggs, the bricks and the mobs. Perhaps the invisible, underground trains could have answered it, or the minds which accepted the Fugitive Slave Law—for nothing component had changed.

Bitterness lay in the fact that Reconstruction was forced to justify itself at a period when national corruption and high-placed thievery indicated that everything from a man's goods to a man's conscience could be bought or stolen; it was forced to justify itself in a section of the country which was torn by the bitterness of war and hardened by two hundred and fifty years of a cultivated and remorseless philosophy of racial inferiority.

A new country came into existence at the end of the war and removed the dam which had held back the chaotic expansion of industry, railroads and finance. A wild, undisciplined race for new fortunes, new aggrandizements on a scale unprecedented, cut through class and political lines, cut through moral values and everything which might stand between a man and his money.

Such power lay in the hands of the Reconstruction legislators, and such evidence of a new and advanced theory of democracy was unfolded by them that, had reaction, greed, and the power of the slavocracy been curbed, the whole social structure of the country would have undergone such a change as to make actual the hypothetical assumption of equal opportunities.

In the North the news of the Congressional action came with startling gratification. Northern capitalism had made the new experiment possible for its own purposes, but the Negroes and the friends of the Negroes and the voters who were prepared to disown Johnson were concerned only with the far-reaching and gigantic action which had taken place. That Northern Negroes could not vote seemed for the moment unimportant. If the impregnable defenses of the old slavocracy could be broken, every future step would be swifter. The fight in the South had, they knew, only entered the first stages. The consolidation of each new move was immeasurably important. The center of Negro activities was no longer in the North. A vast exodus began.

Many of the Negroes who turned back toward the South had received their training in the Abolition struggle, many were agents of the Freedmen's Bureau. Within the South, the Emancipation Proclamation had brought the educated free Negro to the top and catapulted secretly educated slaves into an unexpected prominence. The average were men and women no different than any others, some idealists, some opportunists, many profoundly ignorant, most reflecting the prevailing philosophy of success which went with these times, but all agreeing on the purpose of universal suffrage and the right to work in freedom.

White teachers, freedman's agents, preachers, politicians hurriedly put their belongings into carpetbags and joined the rush toward this new day. Within the South, articulate, slowly organizing whites who had prepared themselves for such a day and were willing to bear the epithet of scalawag had already begun to work. That among them were unscrupulous, vicious and greedy men no one at that period denied. It was equally undeniable that many of the poor whites joined themselves to the Negroes, not because they loved the Negroes but because they feared the power of the planters over the black vote, feared the possibility that a powerful oligarchy would strengthen itself politically by black representation as it had by the three-fifths clause which gave the slaveowners such disproportionate power. But that carpetbagger and scalawag deserved such unqualified disrepute is not sustained by their history.

Within the hands of these men and women lay the immense task of preparing a vast, fluid, yet surprisingly cognizant, new mass of voters.

Their enemies soon showed themselves. Johnson barely waited to let Congress act upon his veto before he extended a full pardon to the Confederates, claiming that disfranchisement for rebellion could only be established by the law courts. In this way he hoped to release a large body of voters who would take control of the new conventions. He advised some of his Southern friends to hurry enjoinment suits as fast as possible, so that Congressional Reconstruction could be halted. But the courts refused to act. Only one alternative remained: intimidation.

In Tennessee the year before, the white-robed Klan had begun its midnight calls and now it was spreading rapidly throughout the South, assuming many different names but always operating by the same means, with the same objective—Union men—Negroes. And against the Union Leagues where the two came together, the violence was direct and ferocious.

No single element presented such a challenge to the chauvinists nor such positive action to the Negroes as these Union Leagues. Their work of organizing and directing action along the lines of radical Republicanism made them concentrated and powerful. All Negro leaders were members; branches and women's auxiliaries had appeared in all Negro communities. Although white men belonged to the Leagues, freedmen regarded them as a special dispensation of their own, for they were perfectly aware that without the strong unifying effect of the Leagues, without the rifle clubs, the drilling, and the Negro militia which supplemented their meetings, the very hope of voting would have been bludgeoned out of them by their hooded enemies. League meetings were frequently well-armed affairs, with pickets surrounding the building, prepared to give the alarm if enemies arrived.

During that summer before the meeting of the constitutional conventions, the Leagues organized meetings wherever their influence was felt. Co-operation between blacks and whites was the basis of the appeal. They met together, they paraded together, they shouted the same slogans, Bread, Wages, and Schools. That it was all a powerful agitation for the Republican party no one denied, but the Negroes had accepted the party of Lincoln as their own, and were more than anxious to support it in return for its beneficent legislation, however painfully extracted.

The first registrations took place in September, 1867, under the eyes of the army. The importance was overlooked by no one, conservative or radical. The Reconstruction Acts had made it clear that no conventions could be called unless the majority of the registered electorate acted on the matter. Southern Conservatives were divided on their course. Some felt that they should register heavily, and then remain away from the voting, hoping thus to destroy the conventions before they came into being. Others felt that it would be safer to attempt to gain control.

Fiery crosses, hooded riders, intimidation by employers were used to keep the Negroes from the registration halls. But the leagues had organized them well, and although in some cases they marched under arms, they came by the thousands strong, perfectly aware what they wanted, equally determined to have it, bringing with them, on the wave of free electing, white men whose property disqualifications had never allowed them to enter a polling place before.

That Negroes outnumbered the whites was never true. Their proportion of registration represented a fair ratio. In South Carolina, Mississippi, Louisiana, Alabama, where the Black Belt was the darkest, they registered in the heaviest numbers. In Florida they represented a majority, in Georgia they were somewhat less than half, in Virginia, North Carolina, Arkansas and Texas they were in the minority. Certain conservative Southerners agreed that the elections were fair, and added that "criticism and denunciation were bitter and continuous; but no very profound research is necessary to discover that the animus of these attacks was chiefly political."

In every state the voting had been heavy enough to assure the constitutional conventions, and to these conventions there now came men whose presence could warm the hearts only of those who believed that a democracy embraced the poor and the despised. In South Carolina where the first convention met, seventy-six delegates were Negroes and forty-eight were whites. Political wires, pulled outside the convention, were attempting to bring the Negro votes under the control of the planting interests, but the South Carolina Negroes, who had always represented a larger percentage of educated freemen and a smaller ratio of brutalized slaves than the remorseless plantation world of the southwest, were unimpressed by the doubtful offers made them, and settled down promptly to legislate. "Beyond all question," the Charleston *Daily News* announced, "the best men in the convention are the colored members. Considering the influences under which they were called together, and their imperfect acquaintance with parliamentary law, they have displayed for the most part, remarkable moderation and dignity . . . They have assembled neither to pull wires like some, nor to make money like others; but to legislate for the welfare of the race to which they belong."

But it isn't only for our own race, Beverly Nash, a former slave and a delegate declared in a speech. "In these public affairs we must unite with our white fellow-citizens. They tell us that they have been disfranchised, yet we tell the North that we shall never let the halls of Congress be silent until we remove that disability."

Land distribution, the plight of the wandering worker, the breaking up of large plantations into small tracts to provide for the freedmen, increase the tax revenue and destroy one of the greatest bulwarks of slavery were all debated and acted upon. Racial and color discrimination were outlawed, which meant that legislation for the whites was pushed as hard as for the blacks, land and buildings valued below $1,000 were protected from forced sale, and the rights of women were amplified to a point where the polls were opened to them in several districts. And for the first time in the South a free common school system was established. Of all the acts of the convention this roused the greatest antagonism among those eyes and ears outside the convention halls. As a woman said to a Northern teacher, "You might as well try to teach your horse or mule to read as to teach these niggers." But a colored delegate, urging that a compulsory amendment be added, found himself in disagreement with her, "I contend that in proportion to the education of the people so is their progress in civilization."

Whipper, a Pennsylvania Negro, urged a petition to Congress to return the vote to the disfranchised white, and that motion was also carried. The judicial system was to be enlarged and made more flexible, judges to be elected instead of appointed, and mixed juries provided. Imprisonment for debt was abolished, dueling was made illegal, and property qualifications were no longer allowed to interfere with voting or holding office.

That this constitution, when it was finally adopted by the state, embodied necessary and progressive legislation the white conservatives themselves made clear. When they regained power, they lived under it for eighteen years. Nor were the wildly circulated stories true of Negro domination in the state. The first governor of South Carolina, under the constitution, was an honest but weak Northerner named Scott. The second governor was Franklin Moses, Jr., a well-born South Carolinian, whose father had been a Senator, whose connections were eminently conservative—who had, in fact, helped to pull down the flag at Sumter. Congressmen and Senators were Southern-born and Confederate-nurtured.

Among the Negro leaders was Francis Cardozo, free-born, of Negro, Jewish and Indian heritage, a Presbyterian minister, educated at the University of Glasgow and in London. He became secretary of state and treasurer for eight years. Of those Negroes who went on into the Senate and the House, Robert Elliot was educated at Eton, Richard Cain was a bishop in the Methodist church and editor of the most influential Negro paper in South Carolina, Robert Smalls had presented the Union with the gunboat which he piloted out of Charleston Harbor under the nose of Confederate guns.

But a convention of conservative whites, meeting promptly, found that the constitution was "the work of sixty-odd Negroes, many of them ignorant and depraved, together with fifty white men, outcasts of Northern society, and Southern renegades, betrayers of their race and country." They dropped their boycott for political action, and organized all their strength to work against the constitution at the polls.

Attending the Negro-dominated convention of South Carolina, James Pike, a conservative Republican, was not unshocked, but he was able to peer beyond his first prim reaction, and his picture can stand for any reconstructed state:

> About three-quarters of the crowd belong to the African race. They were of every hue, from the octoroon to the deep black. They were such a looking body of men as might pour out of a market house or a courthouse at random in any Southern state. Every type and physiognomy was here to be seen, from the genteel serving man to the rough-hewn customer from rice or cotton field. Their dress was as varied as their countenances. There was the secondhand frock coat of infirm gentility, glossy and threadbare. There was the stovepipe hat of many ironings and departed styles. There was also to be seen a total disregard of the proprieties of costume in the coarse and dirty garments of the field; the stub-jackets and slouch hats of toiling labor. In some instances rough woolen comforters embraced the neck and hid the absence of linen. Heavy brogans and short torn trousers it was impossible to hide.
>
> The leading topics of discussion are all well understood by the members, as they are of a practical character, and appeal directly to the personal interests of every legislature as well as those of his constituents. When an appropriation bill is up to raise money to catch and punish the KKK, they know exactly what it means . . . So, too, with educational measures. The free school comes right home to them; then the business of arming and drilling the militia.
>
> The laughing propensity of the sable crowd is a great cause of disorder . . . But underneath all this shocking burlesque upon legislative proceedings, we must not forget that there is something real to this uncouth and untutored multitude . . . They have a genuine interest and a genuine earnestness in the business of the assembly which we are bound to recognize and respect . . . They have an earnest purpose born of a conviction that their position and condition are not fully assured, which lends a sort of dignity to their proceedings.

Mississippi, a state which had been dedicated to the business of cotton raising, was raw and commercial, a state in which the Negroes outnumbered the whites, a state of planter domination, desperately poor whites and a degraded class of slaves. Every step of registration, convention-assembling and voting was bitterly fought by the planters. Of the hundred delegates, seventeen were Negroes, twenty-odd Northerners, and the majority middle-class Southerners. Their demands for land, their commission to investigate white and colored destitution in the state, their efforts to acquire part of the public fund to send slaves, sold into Mississippi, back to their homes, were basic demands that reflected their immediate concerns. The constitution, when it was finally submitted, provided a public school system, forbade property qualifications for voters, outlawed racial distinction in the holding and inheriting of property. Universal male suffrage, however, was only accomplished after a bitter fight and the resignation of twelve white delegates.

Louisiana presented a highly individual picture with its mixture of races penetrating into the most exclusive society, its system of common-law mulatto wives, the exceptional concern of white fathers for their colored children and the consequent high degree of education for many mulattos and quadroons, the wealth and education which had been acquired by many free colored people, all overshadowed by the large number of overworked field hands on the upland plantations. When the convention was called, the state had already gone through a period of lawlessness and murder, carpetbag depredations and conservative terrorism culminating in the New Orleans riot which General Sheridan described as "a massacre." When Congressional Reconstruction came to exert some jurisdiction over a desperate situation, many prominent Southerners, like Longstreet and Beauregard, urged that Negro suffrage be accepted, for if it were "properly handled and directed, we shall defeat our adversaries with their own weapons." But the implacable hatred of the average white made any such compromise out of the question, and the friends of the Negro strenuously urged that the colored delegates to the convention be of the highest and most educated type, in order to refute the arguments for a "white man's government."

Forty-nine Negroes attended and forty-nine whites. Many of the Negroes were men of property and education. The constitutional committee was made up of five whites and four Negroes, and their differences in outlook were incorporated in the majority and minority reports which they submitted. The majority report, which was the work of the white members, urged that all leaders of the Confederacy be prevented from voting or holding office; the minority report urged that everyone be allowed to vote. The majority wanted free education, but the minority insisted that provisions be specific and provide for a school in every parish as well as a state university. The Constitution finally absorbed some of both—the white men's determination to keep out the Confederate leaders, the Negroes' determination to provide schools and a university.

When the state government was finally set up, over the protests of the conservatives, a Negro lieutenant governor, Oscar Dunn, and a Negro state treasurer, Antoine Dubuclet, took office. Oscar Dunn was an ex-slave who had bought his own freedom and his own education, a man whom even the Democrats called "incorruptible"; Antoine Dubuclet was a free man, who remained treasurer for eighteen years, and under the attacks of enemies and the investigation of expert accountants was found to have been scrupulously honest. Yet the Louisiana battle was the most dramatic and complex of any in Reconstruction history because of the unpredictable elements that comprised it—Negroes, who had so little black blood that they might pass for white men, born free, respectable and well off, whose interests and inclinations, led them to the planters; Negroes whose freedom had come only with emancipation and whose education had come in contraband camps or fugitives' schools; dishonest carpetbaggers who were out to snatch what they could get under the benign eye of Henry Clay Warmoth, the carpetbag governor; and the unregenerate planters who resorted to cajolery and violence.

For the rest of the Southern states, the fight was only incidentally for the Negro. It became a struggle between the poor white, the planters and the carpetbaggers, with the Negroes in a minority, fighting without well-trained leadership, for the old demands. In Alabama, among the eighteen Negro delegates were sixteen former slaves, but it was they who demanded free schools and universal suffrage. In Georgia where the convention was dominated by the Southerners, suffrage, a liberal constitution, and relief for the destitute were the principal demands, and the thirty-seven Negro delegates made it their business to press for their acceptance. In Florida the convention was seized by rival factions of conservatives and carpetbaggers and for some time the acceptance of the constitution hung precariously because of the intimidation of the Negroes. In North Carolina, the Negro leadership was well organized and progressive, as many of the Negroes were abolitionized fugitives. A strenuous effort was made to divide the Negro vote between the radicalism of former Governor Holden, and the conservatism of the present governor, Worth, but without success, and the convention, representing the native Southerners overwhelmingly, wrote much the same constitution as the other reconstructed states. Yet the wrath of the planters fell against it and bombarded it with every weapon they possessed. In Virginia, the leadership of the Negroes had been assumed by a white South Carolinian named James Hunnicutt, and the convention made a strong effort to unite the whites and the Negroes with a sense of their interdependence in order to combat the violent opposition which had brought about the arrest of Hunnicutt and the loss of jobs to the one hundred and fifty Negro miners who had voted for the radical ticket.

Altogether, it was a history composed of every ingredient of human nature, and politics were, for most, the essence of the struggle, since corruption and graft were not the mainstays. Yet by a singular distortion of logic, the attacks of the enemy, virulent as the attacks of the slavocracy would be against such a miraculous combination of whites and blacks, were accepted as the truth.

In a day when graft was riding roughshod over political gatherings in the North, when bosses ruled the Northern cities, when stealing of public funds and public lands was considered shrewd politics, when Northern capitalism was spilling through the South as fast as lands could be gobbled up, the Reconstruction governments were shadowed by the philosophy of their time. Yet, had it been possible to enforce fully their legislation, a society which had, heretofore, existed only in the minds of political idealists, would have been brought into existence.

But the conservative whites never gave up their fight. Their outrage ran too deep. Their temperaments and mental conditioning were not prepared for such an overturning of a civilization. When public funds were dispensed with a careless zeal, they raised the cry of thievery; when former slaves stood up in the legislative halls and stumbled through a resolution to the encouraging shouts and songs of their friends, they exhausted themselves with scorn and epithets. The conservatives' capitulation, here and there, to Negro suffrage was frankly for political expediency. Such a change of heart did not come to men by going to bed under the sanctity of white men's governments and waking in the morning to universal suffrage. When, as in Alabama, the Negroes were invited to a Democratic convention and assured that their future lay side by side with the planters, the Negroes were not deceived, for generations of practice had caused them to inspect, doubt and usually reject what the master class had to offer. It would have been as natural for the Negro to agree verbally and repudiate in action a conservative white as it would have been for him to trust those whose friendship had been tried and found secure. When it became evident that the Negroes were not a formless mass, blindly following whatever leadership was offered, the conservatives turned their attention to the poor whites, and began the deep undermining which cut out the branches and the stalks of this revolution, leaving only the roots to struggle against the hard, drying crust which lay unyielding and remorseless over the land.

But nearly ten years passed before the reaction accomplished its purpose. And in those ten years the freedom, which had been desired since the first slave set off on his underground track, seemed almost within sight.

In the chaotic politics of these years, only a few things were affirmative —that the march onward of Northern industrialism must be unhampered; that rugged individualism and skyrocketing fortunes must be accepted as the moral principles of the day; that unimpeded enterprise must be allowed to swarm over the country south, west, east, and that the released dynamos which peace had set into motion must turn the wheels of the country at a speed and a recklessness undreamed of heretofore.

Johnson represented the old order, therefore Johnson was in disgrace. The contest between Congress and President represented, in a manner which neither Stevens nor Sumner desired, the uncontrollable will to power of the people themselves, and when Johnson put his implacable veto on all legislation that was intended to clarify the situation in the reconstructed South, when his appointees were men of strong Confederate leanings, and when finally he set an example for the country by his veto of the bill which offered suffrage to the Negroes of the District of Columbia, it was evidently time to act.

Johnson laid the necessary material in his enemies' hands when, in defiance of the Tenure of Office Bill, he ordered Stanton to surrender his Cabinet post to Grant. Impeachment was demanded.

By one vote he escaped impeachment, but his power was broken. Although Johnson had never professed Republicanism, he stood as a Republican President, and the party suffered. To the bankers and the industrialists, the success of the Democratic party would mean that the iron gates of the South would be slammed shut once again. A strong Republican must be nominated to turn the rising Democratic tide. Grant, the hero, the darling, was selected.

Neither party made conclusive statements on Negro suffrage, but the Democrats, anti-Negro, dared not push against the rising tide of liberalism, and both platforms evaded the question with as much skill as they were able.

Within the South a wave of terrorism was loosed, for the Democrats were determined to seize power. Toombs, returning from an exile in Europe declared, "I regret nothing in the past but the dead and the failure; I am ready today to use the best means I can command to establish the principles for which I fought." In the North bribery and fraud found an admirable example in the Philadelphia Supreme Court Justice who ground out five thousand naturalization papers within two weeks of election day. Grant was elected by fifty-three per cent of the voters, and Negro suffrage was defeated in Missouri and carried in Minnesota and Nevada, as it had been earlier in Iowa and the Dakotas.

When Congress reassembled, its first action was to pass the necessary resolutions for the Fifteenth Amendment which gave to all citizens, irrespective of race, color or previous condition of servitude, the right to vote. Stevens was not there to direct the fight, for he had died during the summer, two Negro clergymen saying the prayers for the dying. Now he lay in a Negro burying ground with the inscription he had written above his head: "I repose in this quiet and secluded spot, not from any natural preference for solitude, but finding other cemeteries limited as to race by charter rules, I have chosen this, that I might illustrate in my death the principles which I advocated through a long life, the Equality of Man before his Creator." But Sumner was on hand and before galleries tense and strained with colored and white listeners, an amendment was shouted through the House and Senate, and at length in February, 1869, speeded to the states for ratification.

Here was the triumph of Abolition, here the end of that immemorial story. In March, 1870, the Fifteenth Amendment became a law, and the Negro stood up, a citizen before the world.

With celebrations and tears of joy, the antislavery societies declared that their work had ended. The tears, the shoutings, the speeches swept over the North and the South. Garrison was in demand from Vicksburg to Boston to set the seal on this great triumph of democracy. In Cincinnati, a meeting was called, and before the white and colored friends who crowded every inch of the hall, Levi Coffin announced that the stock of the Underground Railroad had collapsed, the business ruined, the road closed. To wild and joyful applause, he offered his resignation as President.

In Delaware, old Thomas Garrett died, as though to say that his work, too, had ended. Negro pallbearers bore him to his grave and a vast funeral procession of whites and blacks followed to the burying ground the body of a man who had with courage and unquenchable faith released three thousand black men into freedom.

How could anyone believe that by every law and process of democratic procedure—inviolate, the admirers of democracy maintained—the rights of the black men and women had not been protected for as long as two races lived together? Such golden days . . . Such clouds gathering on the horizon. This victory, at its crest, was already beginning to fold in upon itself.

In the North, the Negroes listened to the words of white labor unionists—William Sylvis speaking in 1868—"Whatever our opinions may be as to the immediate causes of the war, we can all agree that human slavery was the first great cause; and from the day that the first gun was fired, it was my earnest hope that the war might not end until slavery ended it . . . But when the shackles fell from the limbs of those four millions of blacks, it did not make them *free* men; it simply transferred them from one condition of slavery to another; it placed them upon the platform of the white working man, and made all slaves together. The center of the slave power has been transferred to Wall Street . . . This movement we are now engaged in is the great antislavery movement, and we must push on the work of emancipation until slavery is abolished in every corner of our country. Then will come such a social revolution as the world has never witnessed."

George Downing, Isaac Myers, the Negro labor leaders of the North, knew with an experience intensified beyond Sylvis', that a ballot in the hand was merely the legal assurance of an unpredictable fact. The white labor unions, seeing in the Negro an employer's strike-breaking weapon, seeing also a new pro-labor voting power, had made halting and ungracious overtures. They were not prepared to accept the Negro within their own ranks (rioting whites sweeping down on Abolitionists, burning Negro houses, lay within the memory of this generation), but they were prepared to offer him separate unions within the framework of the labor movement. And Negroes, accepting an experimental invitation, had sent nine delegates to the 1869 meeting of the National Labor Union, where they sat in peace with two white Southern delegates, a former Confederate general and an Alabama gentleman, and discussed with a unanimity of action, a new kind of future.

In January, 1869, they had come together in their own convention—colored leaders traveling from the reconstructed states to meet Northern leaders whose struggle was their own, as they saw with increasing clearness. Douglass was elected permanent chairman, and they voted for the Freedmen's Bureau, for suffrage, for school taxes. In December a convention of artisans was called in Washington, representing twenty-three states. Politics and economics were now the twin sisters of emancipation. The *American Workingman*, a white journal published in Boston, communicated the impression made by the convention. "It was in some respects the most remarkable one we ever attended. We had always had full faith in the capacity of the Negro for self-improvement, but were not prepared to see, fresh from slavery, a body of two hundred men, so thoroughly conversant with public affairs, so independent in spirit, and so anxious apparently to improve their social condition, as the men who represented the South, in that convention." A weekly paper was established, and a resolution was passed, authorizing an agent to be sent into the South to organize colored labor. Isaac Myers was selected and set to work immediately, calling a first meeting in Norfolk, Virginia, and urgently pleading that white and colored workers come together within the same union.

Security, held fast by the ownership of land; wages, assured by legislative or concerted action; political power . . . the themes were beaten deep into the Negroes' consciousness. Even the most ignorant freedman could speak of what he knew, and his former master could answer all the questions, which this new independence roused, with equal spontaneity. Was it not posible to come to some agreement? The hope rose during these days. With a ballot in the hand, anything seemed possible!

But soon the deep division that lay across the morals of the time, the deep division which had already set capital and labor to deathly grips in the white world, darkened and strengthened the inexorable, the implacable antagonisms which shut the Negro world from the white.

The course of reaction became quickly evident. On the fringe of political power stood the planters thinking only in terms of past possessions, singularly untouched by the industrial mania of the North. Land was the key to Southern power. Both planters and reconstructionists knew this. Only the military occupation of the South stood between the planters and their return to power, to vaster lands, to greater plantations. On this tenet of land, the reconstructionists met one of their most serious defeats. Land confiscation was essential in order to strengthen the poor whites and Negroes. To acquire this land, a series of taxes were introduced.

In South Carolina, they provided a different form of assessment on property, a diametrically opposite system to that which had prevailed before the war when low taxation operated for landowners and slaveholders, and heavy taxation for merchants, professional men and bankers, the merchant paying five or six times the rate of the planter although the landowners dominated the state. These new taxes were, of course, bitterly opposed, and the collecting of them was one of the first problems of the government, which had to encounter not only the unquestioned poverty of some of the planters but the deliberate obstruction offered by other property owners.

The combination of irresistible forces weakened the reconstructionists to the point of endangering their whole social program. Congressional reconstructionists had seen the need of education before the vote was given. But the wave of terror which came with Johnson's Southern plans left no alternative. The franchise could not wait for education. Honest men were not strong enough to combat the looseness and graft which, in imitation of the Northern brothers, laid hands upon the South. In this dislocated and war-ravished land the pickings were inexhaustible, as Northern men and Southern men found to their profit.

The Negroes' plight was a bitter one. Those with no education often trusted people whom they believed to be their friends and were unintentionally or deliberately misled. The violent epithets, which were a part of the political manners of that day, were accepted as factual and documented evidence of rascality, stupidity and "gibbering buffoonery." Graft, however, was not a contemporary charge against the Negroes. That came with retrospection.

In all the states where the Negro vote was heaviest, reform movements were undertaken.

In South Carolina, the Negro leaders, De Large, Nash, Smalls, Elliott and Cardozo set themselves against Governor Moses, the aristocratic scalawag, and helped to sustain the charges of his corruptibility. In Louisiana, as in Mississippi, the Negroes searched about for a leadership that would carry them out of the muck of state corruptibility, a party to which they could attach their own leaders. But there was little choice between the Democrats and the Republicans in Louisiana. If ever the epithets, carpetbagger and scalawag, carried any clear meaning they did so here. Against the background of struggling and inarticulate laborers, white and black, the machine of Warmoth plowed merrily along. A group of Negroes, led by Lieutenant Governor Dunn, attempted a revolt within the Republican Convention of 1870, but Warmoth adroitly weathered the storm.

In Florida, they struggled under the ruthless activities of the planters, who were attempting to gain control through their old system of dividing the poor whites and the Negroes, and of the Northern capitalists, who were lobbying for advantageous bills. The Negroes, under Jonathan Gibbs, an energetic colored man who had graduated from Dartmouth, were struggling toward some form of labor legislation which would work for the benefit of both white and colored; and schools and construction work were somehow emerging out of the violence and bewilderment. But Gibbs slept in a room which had been converted into an arsenal against the Klan and died suddenly to the rumor of poisoning.

The course of reaction shifted frequently, but the strategy never varied. The purpose of the conservatives was to split the coalition of Radical Republicans within the South—Negroes, scalawags and carpetbaggers. The first attempt was made when the planters held out to the scalawags and to the Negroes the promise of universal suffrage if they would come into the Democratic party. The Negroes, perfectly willing to believe that they had much to gain from an alliance with white classes, would have been willing to submerge their strength in a political unity if they could be assured of land, education and full political freedom. But no conservative leader in the South would make such a promise.

In the North vast corporations and monopolies were bringing some order out of the cutthroat chaos, and were being supported, on the basis of "reform," by a disillusioned middle class. But neither property owner nor monopolist, North or South, had a place for the demands of laborers—laborers who represented the power necessary for the profits of the future. All over the expanding and industrialized globe, workers were finding the truth of this—Englishmen in factory towns, Africans in the Belgian Congo, in the outposts of the new British Empire, Chinese and Malaysians in the vast chaotic new labor markets of the Orient— wherever the philosophy, bred of quick money and expanding markets, was bludgeoning its way.

Since it was impossible to split the Negroes or more than a few scalawags from their Northern loyalties, the next strategy was to concentrate upon the whites and resort to the familiar device: divide and rule. "Awake! Awake!" the *Independent Monitor* of Tuscaloosa cried, "Let every man at the South, through whose veins the unalloyed Caucasian blood courses, who is not a vile adventurer or carpetbagger, forthwith align himself in the rapidly increasing ranks of his species, so that we may the sooner overwhelmingly crush, with one mighty blow, the preposterous wicked dogma of Negro equality! . . . We must render this either a white man's government or convert the land into a Negro man's cemetery." Many of the poor whites, who hated the Negro with the hatred of men who saw their scanty wages reduced by Negro competition, were inflamed by all the demagoguery that long experience had put into the mouths of the planters, and saw now the opportunity of joining, shoulder to shoulder, that class toward which they had always aspired. Under the white hoods of secret brotherhoods their differences could be forgotten.

When the Congressional investigation of Klan outrages was published, it embraced a long list of assorted violence, of outrages that went the distance from intimidations and whippings to torturings too offensive to be considered with any calm. With them came also the Klansmen's testimonies of provocation. The victims had been Republicans, or they had talked too much. They had carried arms, or they had insisted on being landowners. They had tried to hold elections or they had withheld information necessary to the conservatives. Sometimes because they had been "niggers" and sometimes because they had been "damn niggers." In Texas, where the army could maintain only a skeleton discipline, General Sheridan summed up the situation with bitter brevity: If he owned both hell and Texas, he would rent Texas and live in hell.

The Negroes struggled to consolidate their power and to defend themselves against the wave of terror. In order to enforce the new legislation huge state debts were necessary to build public schoolhouses, asylums, poorhouses and other phenomena largely unknown to the prewar South. This swelled the charges of money spent like water. Paper inflation also helped this charge, but paper inflation was necessary because the credit for certain reconstructed states was held by New York bankers whose association with the planters gave them unresponsive ears. Against the terror President Grant appealed for laws that would put down the Klan and destroy the attacks against the Fourteenth and Fifteenth Amendments. By the Enforcement Law of 1871, Congress gave him extraordinary powers to deal with the situation, but the will was stronger than a corrupt and inadequate military force in the South, and the outrages continued with scarcely a break, those arrested being freed, and a Republican governor impeached because he had called out militia against the Klan. Within a year the Enforcement Law expired, and Congress did not extend it. Other considerations had intervened.

Scandals were rocking the Republican party, voters were growing restless under the repeated blows against their credulity. Sumner, Greeley, Schurz, Adams, Julian had bolted and called a separate convention of "Liberal Republicans" and a wave of well-calculated reform was spinning through the election year of 1872. "Reformed" big business was offering to the West new land values, lower rates for railroads, greater markets, it was offering to the East investment securities and assurances that business men would run the government, it was offering to the South a return of leadership to the men of property.

The Republican party had gained what it was after in the South. It had provided for the unimpeded development of Northern capital by destroying the slave power which had received such a rebirth under Johnson. Peace was now the prime essential for party strength and industrial development.

The Southern planters had played an astute game. By denouncing carpetbag rule as responsible for all the ills of the South, they had put the burden firmly on the shoulders of the North. Either you must play the game with us or you must leave the South. The alternative was an agreeable one to the North. If they withdrew the army of occupation, the planters would know that their will had been re-established, and their friendliness would fall on those who had been most friendly. The Reconstruction legislators, although they still controlled the administration of the South, were naïve men, armed in no effective way against a coalition of such experts as the old ruling class of the South and the new ruling class of the North. From the moment that friendliness passed between these two, their defeat was settled. Big business would dominate politics in a North where no trouble was taken to conceal a philosophy of vote buying; property would dominate politics in the South as it always had except for these brief years. The end of a dream was surely a very small price to pay.

Amnesty bills were the first signs of the end. On Sumner rested nearly the entire burden of defending the dream. He was a humanitarian before he was a Senator, and he, along with other Abolitionists, failed to understand that certain systems of economics cannot be destroyed by laws. Stevens had recognized this when he attempted to build a mine of confiscation bills, but Sumner recognized it by attempting to eradicate the animosities within the South, a task of the noblest kind, but one that was bound to fail as long as the democratic ideal had no roots within the old slaveland. He was fighting now a desperate and courageous battle for civil rights, a fight he had carried with him since the Fourteenth Amendment had failed to encompass his whole concept of the rights of men. He talked of civil rights in season and out of season, the rights that prevented discrimination in railroads, in schools, in churches, in amusement places, on juries, even in cemeteries. The colored people in the North helped in every way they could, by mass meetings when his bills were up, by agitation and petitions, by filling the galleries of Congress whenever he was scheduled to speak. He held out to the Senate a ream of documented evidence to show that the bill must be passed, he read through letters and newspaper articles until his voice was hoarse, he used every ruse and strategy he knew, seeking to attach his bill to other bills and failing, sometimes only by a single vote. And finally he was worn out.

The fight had been a long one, stretching back to the dark days when the Fugitive Slave Law was casting such a deep shadow on the country and the Civil War had begun in Kansas. He had fought the vacillations that obscured the main issue of the Civil War, and he had seen the Emancipation Proclamation half complete his dream. And now, the waves were closing in once more, the enemies were stronger than he could battle, and the friends were few. Three colored men stood with Congressional friends around his bed as he lay dying, Frederick Douglass, George Downing and Sumner Wormley, and they heard his last hoarse plea, "You must take care of the civil rights bill—my bill, the civil rights bill—don't let it fail!"

But all such things were set for failure now. When the Republican party split in 1872, and the Democrats gained their first Congressional majority in twenty years, the gates were down. Reform was a great word, and reform cloaked a multitude of swift and doubtful movements. The trade-unions, where a diffident but integral struggle for Negroes and aliens was going on, came up against the implacable wall of the 1873 panic and Reform sweeping in on its heels had no place for such impediments to American Destiny. Reform had no place either for a military rule in the South, but without the small garrison—twenty thousand officers and men policed the reconstructed states—the Negro was unprotected from the enemies who were converging from all sides. The Democrats were winning in county after county of the South, and the ousted Republicans were refusing to give up their seats, appealing to Washington, and claiming they had been defeated with the dead bodies of Negro and white voters. As elections spread through the South, Negro militia armed. In Texas, government buildings were held by armed forces; in Arkansas dual governments were set up. In Mississippi, Grant objected to the "violent revolution" which made a travesty of election, but Congress upheld the Democratic claimants, while the White League patrolled the streets of Vicksburg and kept down the Negro vote. In Louisiana, a "butchery of citizens which in barbarity is hardly surpassed by any acts of savage warfare" brought a desultory punishment. Everywhere the Republican split left the Negroes standing alone, while their white allies took refuge in the Democratic camps. In the North, ears were deaf when the calls for help went out.

The 1875 elections were a reign of terror. In Clinton, Mississippi, fifteen hundred Negroes and one hundred whites, gathered at a Republican barbecue, were fired upon by mobs brought down on special trains, and fifty Negroes were killed. The governor called for Presidential interference but Grant refused to act. Peace must be bought at some price for the state was smoldering into flames. A "Peace Agreement" was signed, the Negro militias were disarmed on the understanding that the

Democrats would allow the Negroes to vote, and Mississippi went over to the enemy.

For what else could the "Mississippi plan for the restoration of home rule" be called? Negroes were shot down in the streets, they were dragged from their homes and terrorized; when the next election day came, they were kept from the polls, and being now legally disarmed, had no means of fighting back. The Republican governor and lieutenant governor were made to resign and were then driven from the state. "Mississippi is governed today by officials chosen through fraud and violence such as would scarcely be accredited to savages," Grant observed bitterly, but he did nothing about it. The new governor, choice of the planters, soon defaulted to the tune of $316,000.

The same design was worked out in Louisiana and South Carolina. A split, the riding of hooded terrorists, dual governments, and then, under the compliant shudders of the North, the full triumph of reaction.

"Every Democrat must feel honor bound to control the vote of at least one Negro, by intimidation, purchase, keeping him away, or as each individual may determine how he may best accomplish it. Never threaten a man individually. If he deserves to be threatened, the necessities of the time require that he should die." Wade Hampton, who gave these instructions, won his way to the governorship of South Carolina by combining these methods with counterfeit ballots at the polls, and consolidated his power by driving out seventeen Republican legislators when the administration was in his hands. A white Carolinian who made no pretense of his partisanship as Hampton's man, made no pretense either as to the winning of this election. "It is not now denied but admitted and claimed by the successful party that the canvass was systematically conducted with a view to find occasions to apply force and violence. The occasions came, and the methods adopted had their perfect work. By a system of violence and coercion, ranging through all possible grades, from urgent persuasion to mob violence, the election was won by the Democrats."

All through the South, that bloody fall of 1876, the Negroes were delivered up as a sacrificial offering, and Hayes and Tilden, contesting the Presidency, were merely the effects and not the cause. Tilden's electoral votes stood at 184, Hayes' at 166. Four states, South Carolina, Louisiana, Florida and Oregon were in doubt, but Hayes claimed them as his own. The electors of the doubtful states met in an atmosphere of fraud and violence, and the emotions of civil war spread again across the country.

But Hayes would win, conservatives of the doubtful states saw clearly.

Republican fraud was less brazen than Democratic fraud. If we cannot win the nation then we will make sure that we win the state.

While the Senate Commission weighed the counter claims, and the old days of violence brought the House to blasphemous life again, the deal took place behind the scenes. A written promise was made by Hayes' advisers, that if Florida, South Carolina and Louisiana assured him the Presidency, complete domestic control would be returned to those states, and no laws be binding except the laws of the Constitution. All troops would be withdrawn, men of property put in control again, and the right of black and white labor to vote be subject to the desires and expediences of those who would now have control.

The Southern Democrats were faithful to Hayes, and Hayes in turn was faithful. In January, 1877, the Supreme Court gave Florida to the Democrats. On April 10th, South Carolina was handed to Wade Hampton and all troops were withdrawn. On April 20th, the State House in New Orleans was taken from the Reconstruction government by the withdrawal of troops and handed to the rival government which the planters had set up.

Northern capital had betrayed an experiment for which it found no further use; Southern reaction had provided the knife; the poor whites had administered the blow. It was a story, brutal and characteristic of the times, for Reconstruction could not be separated from the economic or moral life of the country.

What was there to go back to? Submission, of course; docility. Negro Congressmen, for a time, came up the long road to Washington, but jobs did not wait for humble men along that route. "Safe" must be the word. "Safe . . ." and records were examined carefully. If one wanted to eat, politics were not a nourishing fare.

Northwards, they excused themselves with scientific phrases. The Negro was a weaker race, therefore he had not survived his opportunity to govern. It would only take a little time to build up the conviction that the Negro had had his opportunity and failed; that he was by nature inferior. The lights were going out for the Negro people everywhere. For some the struggle bound itself by food and clothes and inconspicuous security. Others turned their minds again toward flight.

When men, who had felt the lash of the slave driver, felt the lash of the Klansman, the "lily-white" politician, they thought naturally of escape, but escape meant a different thing now, for these men had for a few years believed that they too might share in a government, might own land, and see their children respected. Escape now meant that citizens of the United States were looking for a freedom which belonged to them.

From Tennessee came "Moses" Singleton, and from Louisiana Henry Adams. Free land still lay to the west. Land was still the Negroes' dream. Up and down the country the agents of Singleton and Adams worked, so quietly, so underground, that little sound came to the larger world. Word was brought, now by an itinerant preacher, now by a railway porter, again by the colored steward on a boat. A circular was thrust into a black hand, a picture was pointed to which showed a house on a wide plain with the sun setting in the distance— "Your home . . . you free man!"

A man would see his brother beaten to death for going to the polls, a woman would hear the cries of her husband as a whip curled around his back, and Singleton or Adams had a new passenger on the underground train that was soon to start. Scarcely a ripple showed on the surface; working in secret was an intuition; it did not need to be taught. And then, one morning in 1879, certain parishes in Louisiana, certain counties across the river in Mississippi, wakened to discover that Sam and Jake and Ben had gone, that Hiram and Joe and Bill had disappeared, that Betsy and Jane and all their families had vanished over night, and with them a large share of the colored community. Where . . . what . . . ! And then more went, and still more, and more again. A thousand, fifteen hundred, three thousand, five thousand. Close to ten thousand had packed up their belongings and set out for the Kansas and Nebraska lands before the full weight of consternation fell on the South and on the North.

Influential people, horrified by this loss of labor, attempted to stem the tide. By May, they had gathered a convention at Vicksburg, and urged the blacks to tell their tale. The Negroes presented a resolution of grievances. "The low price of cotton, and the partial failure of the crop. Fear for civil rights. Rumors of land and mules and money in the West." The whites were magnanimous. The men in charge of the convention were sympathetic and tactful. They had been wrong. The Negro had his rights. Were they not all citizens of one great country? Should not their interests be identical? Should they not have perfect equality under the law and elections free of intimidation? "Aye!" the convention shouted. Well, so they should. A new day had dawned.

But the migration continued—hundreds, thousands went. Nothing had been seen like it since the contrabands broke from the plantations and ran toward the Union camps. The whites were still interceding. They tried compulsion. Steamship companies were induced not to accept payment for passage. Writs were sworn out to detain some on false charges. But nothing could stop the exodus.

All over the North they were talking about it. In Washington they were debating the best course of action. In Kansas, where the fugitives were arriving, destitute and empty-handed, the Quakers were setting up relief agencies, and many of those who had served on the Underground Railroad were taking charge. Laura Haviland was there, taking down the statements of the new arrivals—"I saw one hundred men killed by shooting and hanging during the two years, 1878 and 1879, and my brother was one of them. I can point to their graves today in the two parishes I worked in. Their crime was their persistence in voting the Republican ticket." . . . "They gave me (a colored preacher) two hundred lashes because I preached that God had given us freedom of body and soul and spirit."

Laura Haviland helped to distribute food, clothing, seed and farming implements. Calls went out for volunteer help, for there seemed no end to this gigantic exodus, and many of those who had thought their work finished with the celebrations of the Fifteenth Amendment came to lend a hand; many who had reached maturity when the Emancipation Proclamation had been signed, joined the Kansas Freedmen's Relief Association or helped to raise the $40,000 that was required in that first year or the five hundred thousand pounds of clothes and bedding that were so desperately needed. From England came fifty thousand pounds of clothing and several thousand dollars.

And still they came. The Negro leaders were exhorting, protesting, according to their view of the matter. Richard Greener, graduate of Harvard, rising high in the Negro firmament, was urging them to come —more and more. The land belonged to them as much as to any citizen. Let them take it before the bars against immigration were lifted and the rush began. They had no future in the South. Let them go to the West! Douglass protested as loudly as his powerful voice could carry. The move was ill-timed. The Negroes should fight for their rights where they stood. They should not run away from intimidation. By going to the West, they were falling into the same trap that Liberia offered.

Sixty thousand had now come. Kansas did not want them. She sent word they would not be welcome, but she did not drive them away once they had arrived. Forty thousand owned only the clothes they wore on their backs. Twenty thousand acres were taken up, and the relief agencies gave them corn and cotton seeds and farming implements. Within the year most of those forty thousand were self-supporting and giving aid to their families and friends as they too ended their journey up the river and across the plains. Few ever came to the relief agency more than twice. They were jubilant over their success, and they believed that they could foretell their own future now.

Entreaties came from the South. Come back. Things won't be as they were. Some returned, and white planters sighed in relief. But by spring they had gone again. They had not said, when they returned, that they had merely come back to make better preparations for their new homes. They had omitted to say that they were, in fact, messengers from the Northern settlers, recruiting new passengers for the trip north.

Some spread to Nebraska, during the two years of the exodus, others settled with their old allies in the Indian territory.

Behind them they left the terrorizing, the chain gangs, the share cropping, the "grandfather clauses" which held them from the polls, the curfew laws, all the dark paraphernalia of oppression.

Behind them too were names that in another civilization would have become the names of heroes. The unknown first fugitive, the softly stepping men and women following their Indian guides through swamps and thickets, the woman with a brand on her forehead hiding in cornfields, the man with the lashed back listening to the bay of hounds as he crouched by the weeds in a river, the children in unmarked graves who died on the flight to the North, the cries, the ropes, and the end of a journey as the gap between capture and freedom was closed. They had all that behind them, and they had Gabriel as well, and Vesey who saw no strangeness in a black Messiah, and Turner who had heard the weeping in Egypt. They had Douglass, too, clasping the hand of Garrison, and the friends who sprang up like Jason's teeth from the ground; the disguises, the closed carriages, the gunshots along the border and the long resolute train which chugged so silently and sent up such invisible smoke. They had those unnamed heroes who decided in the darkness of a Southern night where the train would stop, and the sweet brief songs that rose in the twilight, in the darkness, in the morning to send a message that freedom was a living hope. They had those unnamed heroes who made the journeys back from freedom because they loved freedom so well, and those who went from door to door, from town to town, imploring, demanding the money that would buy their wives, their children and their friends. They had all the free men and the freedmen who tried to make democracy work within the limits of the old slavelands, who had given their lives before and would give them again.

In America, a minority had not found freedom. Oppression was strengthened over the world. But this was not the end. The seeds lay deep. The fruit would grow.

# BIBLIOGRAPHY

The value of the books consulted cannot be indicated, but a word must be said for the irreplaceable material in Dr. Wilbur H. Siebert's collection on the Underground Railroad; the *Reminiscences* of Levi Coffin; the four-volume life of William Lloyd Garrison by his children; the monumental work of Helen T. Catterall, *Judicial Cases Concerning American Slavery;* Henry Wilson's *The Rise and Fall of the Slave Power in America;* the extensive publications of Dr. Carter G. Woodson, whose pioneering in the study of Negro life and history deserves the unstinting praise of all students of American life; the excellent and exhaustive collection in the American History Room of the New York Public Library, and finally the books and pamphlets which make the Schomburg Collection of the same library such an invaluable repository for a study of the accomplishments and history of the Negro.

## SLAVERY

ANDREWS, E. A. *Slavery and the Domestic Slave Trade in the United States.* Boston: Light and Stearns, 1836.

BANCROFT, FREDERIC. *Slave Trading in the Old South.* Baltimore: J. H. Hurst, 1931.

BRAWLEY, BENJAMIN G. *A Short History of the American Negro.* New York: The Macmillan Company, 1927.

CAIRNS, J. E. *The Slave Power.* London: Parker, son and Bourn, 1862.

CATTERALL, HELEN T. *Judicial Cases Concerning American Slavery.* Washington: Carnegie Institution, 1929.

CHAMBERS, WILLIAM. *American Slavery and Color.* New York: Dix and Edwards, 1857.

DuBois, W. E. B. *Suppression of the African Slave Trade.* New York: Longmans, Green and Co., 1896.

FLANDERS, RALPH BETTS. *Plantation Slavery in Georgia.* Chapel Hill: The University of North Carolina Press, 1933.

GRAY, L. C. *History of Agriculture in the Southern United States.* Washington: Carnegie Institution, 1933.

HARRIS, N. D. *Slavery in Illinois.* Chicago: A. C. McClurg & Co., 1906.

KEMBLE, FRANCES ANNE. *Journal of a Residence on a Georgian Plantation.* New York: Harper & Brothers, 1863.

MALLARD, R. Q. *Plantation Life Before Emancipation.* Richmond, Va.: Whittet & Shepperson, 1892.

MORGAN, EDWIN V. *Slavery in New York: Status of Slaves under the English Colonial Government.* New York: G. P. Putnam's Sons, 1898.

NORTHUP, SOLOMON. *Twelve Years a Slave*. New York: Miller, Orton and Mulligan, 1855.

OLMSTED, FREDERICK LAW. *The Cotton Kingdom*. New York: Mason Brothers, 1861.

PHILLIPS, U. B. *American Negro Slavery*. New York: D. Appleton & Company, 1918.

———. *Life and Labor in the Old South*. Boston: Little, Brown & Company, 1929.

POLLARD, EDWARD. *Black Diamonds*. New York: Pudney and Russell, 1859.

REUTER, E. B. *The American Race Problem*. New York: The Thomas Y. Crowell Company, 1938.

SKAGGS, W. H. *Southern Oligarchy*. New York: Devin-Adair Company, 1924.

SMEDES, S. D. *Memoirs of a Southern Planter*. Baltimore: Cushings & Bailey, 1887.

STOWE, HARRIET BEECHER. *The Key to Uncle Tom's Cabin*. London: Clarke, Beeton and Co., 1853.

STROUD, GEORGE MCDOWELL. *A Sketch of the Laws Relating to Slavery*. Philadelphia: Kimber and Sharpless, 1827.

SYDNER, CHARLES S. *Slavery in Mississippi*. New York: D. Appleton-Century Company, 1933.

TREXLER, HARRISON ANTHONY. *Slavery in Missouri (1804-1865)*. Baltimore: Johns Hopkins Press, 1914.

WELD, THEODORE. *American Slavery As It Is*. New York: American Anti-Slavery Society, 1839.

WESTON, G. M. *Progress of Slavery in the United States*. Washington, D. C.: the author, 1857.

WOODSON, CARTER G. *Education of the Negro Prior to 1861*. Washington: Association for the Study of Negro Life and History, 1915.

NEGRO REVOLTS

APTHEKER, HERBERT. *Negro Slave Revolts in the United States (1526-1860)*. New York: International Publishers Co., Inc., 1939.

———. "American Slave Revolts," *Science and Society*, I, no. 4; II, no. 3.

———. "Nat Turner's Revolt. The Environment, the Event, the Effect." Thesis, Columbia University, 1937.

CARROLL, JOSEPH C. *Slave Insurrections in the United States (1800-1865)*. Boston: Chapman & Grimes, Inc., 1938.

COFFIN, JOSHUA. *Account of Some of the Principal Slave Insurrections*. New York: American Anti-Slavery Society, 1860.

DREWRY, W. S. *Slave Insurrections in Virginia*. Baltimore: Johns Hopkins Press, 1900.

HIGGINSON, THOMAS WENTWORTH. *Travellers and Outlaws*. Boston: Lee & Shepard, 1889.

JAMES, C. L. R. "A History of Negro Revolt," *Fact* Magazine. London, 1938.

VESEY, DENMARK. *Official Report of Trial of Sundry Negroes*. Charleston: Kennedy and Parker, 1821.

WISH, HARVEY. "Slave Revolts," Washington: *Journal of Negro History*, vol. 22.

FUGITIVE SLAVES

APTHEKER, HERBERT. "Maroons Within the Present Limits of the United States," Washington: *Journal of Negro History*, vol. 24.

FOREMAN, GRANT. *Five Civilized Tribes.* Norman, Okla.: University of Oklahoma Press, 1934.

FOSTER, LAURENCE. "Negro and Indian Relations in the Southwest." Thesis, University of Pennsylvania, 1935.

GIDDINGS, JOSHUA R. *Exiles of Florida.* Columbus: Follett, Foster and Co., 1858.

MCDOUGALL, M. G. *Fugitive Slaves (1619-1865).* Boston: Ginn and Company, 1891.

OLMSTED, FREDERICK LAW. *Journey Through Texas.* New York: Dix, Edwards and Co., 1857.

PORTER, KENNETH W. "Relations Between Indians and Negroes," Washington: *Journal of Negro History,* vol. 17.

WATSON, HENRY. *Narrative of Henry Watson, a Fugitive Slave.* Boston: B. Marsh, 1848.

WILLSON, MINNIE MOORE. *The Seminoles of Florida.* Philadelphia: American Printing House, 1896.

### UNDERGROUND RAILROAD

BAUGHMAN, A. J. "Underground Railroad," Columbus: *Ohio Archaeological and Historical Society Quarterly,* vol. 15, 1908.

BEARSE, AUSTIN. *Remembrances of Fugitive Slave Days.* Boston: W. Richardson, 1880.

BRADFORD, SARAH H. *Harriet, the Moses of Her People.* New York: G. R. Lockwood, 1886.

BROWN, WILLIAM WELLS. *Narrative of William Wells Brown.* London: Charles Gilpin, 1849.

BRUBAKER, MARIANNA G. "The Underground Railroad," *Lancaster, Pa. Historical Society,* vol. 15, 1911.

CABLE, GEORGE W. *Strange True Tales of Louisiana.* New York: Charles Scribner's Sons, 1889.

CHACE and LOVELL. *Two Quaker Sisters: Diaries of Elizabeth Buffum Chace and Lucy B. Lovell.* New York: Liveright Publishing Corporation, 1937.

CHAMBERLAIN, ALLEN. "Old Passages of Boston's Underground Railroad," *Magazine of History,* vol. 31, Tarrytown, New York: 1926.

CHILD, LYDIA MARIA. *Isaac Tatum Hopper.* Boston: J. P. Jewett Co., 1853.

COFFIN, LEVI. *Reminiscences.* Cincinnati: Western Tract Society, 1876.

DAVIDSON, JOHN NELSON. *Negro Slavery and the Underground Railroad in Wisconsin.* Milwaukee: Parkman Publishing Co., 1891.

DRAYTON, DANIEL. *Personal Memoirs.* Boston: B. Marsh, 1855.

FAIRBANKS, REV. CALVIN. *During Slavery Times.* Chicago: R. R. McCabe, 1890.

FAIRCHILD, JAMES HARRIS. *The Underground Railroad.* Cleveland: Western Reserve Historical Society Publications, 1895.

FESSENDEN, DANIEL N. *Underground Railroad in Portland, Maine.* (Siebert Collection)

GALBREATH, CHARLES B. *History of Ohio.* Chicago and New York American Historical Society, Inc., 1925.

"Thomas Garrett of Delaware," Detroit *Post,* 1871.

GRIM, PAUL R. "The Reverend John Rankin, Early Abolitionist," Columbus: *Ohio Archaeological & Historical Society Quarterly,* vol. 46.

HARRIS, N. D. *Slavery in Illinois.* Chicago: A. C. McClurg & Company, 1906.

HAVILAND, LAURA S. *A Woman's Life Work.* Chicago: Publishing Association of Friends, 1889.

HAYES, RUTHERFORD B. Letter to W. H. Siebert, written August 5, 1892, from Fremont, Ohio. (Siebert Collection, Columbus, Ohio)

HENSON, JOSIAH. *The Life of Josiah Henson.* Boston: A. D. Phelps, 1849.

HILLARD, ROBERT H. *Underground Railroad in Massachusetts.* (Siebert Collection)

HISE, DANIEL HOWELL. *Diary of Daniel Howell Hise, Underground Railroad Conductor.* Extracts in possession of Salem, Ohio, Public Library.

HOWE, HENRY. *Historical Collection of Ohio.* Columbus: Henry Howe and Son, 1891.

HUFTELENS, ELIJAH. *Underground Railroad.* (Siebert Collection)

HYPES, DOUGLAS. "Underground Railroad in Clarke County, Ohio," Columbus: *Ohio Archaeological and Historical Society Quarterly,* vol. 15, 1908.

JOHNSON, JAMES WELDON. *Black Manhattan.* New York: Alfred A. Knopf, 1930.

KNABENSHUE, S. S. "Underground Railroad," Columbus: *Ohio Archaeological and Historical Society Quarterly,* vol. 14.

LANDON, FRED. "Canada's Part in Freeing the Slave," *Ontario Historical Society Papers,* vol. 17, 1919.

LOGUEN, J. W. *Reverend J. W. Loguen as a Slave and a Freeman.* Syracuse: J. G. K. Truair Co., 1851.

MARTIN, THELMA F. "The Underground Railroad in New York," Thesis, Ohio State University.

MASON, E. G. *Early Chicago and Illinois.* Chicago: Fergus Printing Co., 1890.

MEAD, ELWELL O. "The Underground Railroad in Ohio," Oberlin, Ohio: *Church Historical Society Papers,* vol. 10, 1899.

MITCHELL, ROBERT, M.D. (typescript, Indiana, Pennsylvania), 1916.

MITCHELL, W. M. *The Underground Railroad.* London: William Tweedie, 1860.

OLMSTED, FREDERICK LAW. *Journey Through the Back Country.* Originally issued 1860. Later issued G. P. Putnam Sons, 1907.

PADEN, H. F. "Underground Railroad Reminiscences: an address before Firelands Historical Society," *Firelands Pioneer,* July, 1888.

PETTIT, E. M. *Sketches in the History of the Underground Railroad.* Fredonia, N. Y.: W. McKinstry and Son, 1879.

PRESTON, E. DELORUS, JR. "Genesis of the Underground Railroad," Washington: *Journal of Negro History,* vol. 13.

PURDEE, EDWARD O'CONNOR. "Underground Railroad from Southwestern Ohio to Lake Erie." Thesis, Ohio State University, 1935.

RAY, F. F. *Sketch of the Life of the Reverend Charles B. Ray.* New York: J. J. Little and Co., 1887.

RITCHIE, ANDREW. *The Soldier, the Battle, and the Victory.* Rev. John Rankin, Cincinnati: Western Tract and Book Society, 1870.

ROSS, ALEXANDER M. *Recollections and Experiences of an Abolitionist.* Toronto: Roswell and Hitchinson, 1875.

SCOTT, EMMA. "The Underground Railroad," *Woodford Co., Pennsylvania Historical Society,* 1934.

SEVERANCE, FRANK H. *Old Trails of the Niagara Frontier.* Buffalo, N. Y.: The Matthews-Northrup Co., 1899.

SHAFTER, SARA A. "On the Underground Railroad," *The Outlook,* vol. 78, 1904.

SIEBERT, WILBUR H. *The Underground Railroad from Slavery to Freedom.* New York: The Macmillan Company, 1898.

Dr. Siebert's Collection: 43 volumes of letters, clippings, photographs, miscellany, relating to the Underground Railroad, gathered over a period of forty years. In Dr. Siebert's possession at Ohio State University, Columbus, Ohio, and also, in practical duplicate, in the Widener Library, Harvard University, Cambridge, Mass., the gift of Dr. Siebert. (Invaluable.)

SIEBERT, WILBUR H. "A Quaker Section of the Underground Railroad in Northern Ohio," Columbus: *Ohio Archaeological and Historical Society Quarterly*, vol. 39, 1930.

———. "Underground Railroad in Massachusetts," Worcester, Mass.: *American Antiquarian Society Proceedings*, vol. 45, 1935.

SLOANE, RUSH R. "The Underground Railroad in the Firelands," Cleveland: *Magazine of Western History*, vol. 8, 1888.

SMEDLEY, R. G. "History of the Underground Railroad in Chester and the neighboring counties of Pennsylvania," Lancaster, Pa. Office of the *Journal*, 1883.

SMITH, W. H. "First Fugitive Slave Case in Ohio," Washington: *American Historical Association Annual Report for 1894*.

STILL, WILLIAM. *Underground Railroad Records*. Philadelphia: Porter & Coates, 1872.

STOWE, C. E. and L. B. "How Mrs. Stowe Wrote *Uncle Tom's Cabin*," *McClure's Magazine*, 1911.

SYNDER, CHARLES S. "Pursuing Fugitive Slaves," Durham, N. C.: *South Atlantic Quarterly*, vol. 28, 1929.

THOMPSON, GEORGE. *Prison Life and Reflections*. Hartford, Conn.: A. Work, 1853.

TURTON, CECIL. "The Underground Railroad in Kansas, Nebraska and Iowa." Thesis, Ohio State University, 1935.

WARD, SAMUEL RINGGOLD. *Autobiography of a Fugitive Negro*. London: John Snow, 1855.

WATTS, RALPH M. "Underground Railroad in Mechanicsburg, Ohio," Columbus: *Ohio Archaeological and Historical Society Quarterly*, vol. 43.

WILLIAMS, HELEN. "Underground Railroad in Iowa." Thesis, Ohio State University.

WILLIAMS, IRENE W. "Operation of the Fugitive Slave Law in Western Pennsylvania from 1850 to 1860," Pittsburgh: *Western Pennsylvania Historical Magazine*, vol. 4, 1921.

WITHROW, W. H. "Underground Railway," *Transactions of the Royal Society of Canada*, Sec. II, 1902.

WIXOM, ELBERT COOK. "Underground Railroad of the Lake Country of Western New York." Thesis, Cornell University, 1903.

"Fugitive Slave Law and Its Victims," *Anti-Slavery Tracts*, no. 15, 1861.

"Men Who Worked on the Underground Railroad," *Commercial Tribune*, Feb., 1900.

## THE SOUTH: SLAVERY AND ABOLITION

BASSETT, J. S. *Anti-Slavery Leaders of North Carolina*. Baltimore: Johns Hopkins Press, 1898.

BIEL, HERBERT. "Class Conflicts in the South." New York: 1939.

BROWN, THOMAS. *Three Years in the Kentucky Prisons.* Indianapolis: Courier Company Printing, 1857.

CUTLER, JAMES ELBERT. *Lynch Law.* New York: Longmans, Green and Co., 1905.

DODD, WILLIAM E. *The Cotton Kingdom.* New Haven: Yale University Press, 1919.

DUBOSE, J. W. *Life and Times of William Lowndes Yancey.* Birmingham, Ala.: Roberts and Son, 1892.

FITZHUGH, GEORGE. *Cannibals All!* Richmond: A. Morris, 1857.

FLEMING, W. L. "Jefferson Davis, the Negro, and the Negro Problem," *Louisiana State University Bulletin,* series 6, no. 4, 1903.

GARRISON, WILLIAM LLOYD. "The New Reign of Terror," *New York Anti-Slavery Society Publication,* no. 4, 1860.

GRAY, L. C. *History of Agriculture in the Southern United States.* Washington: Carnegie Institution, 1933.

GRIMM, A. G. "Anti-Slavery Movement in North Carolina and Tennessee." Thesis, Ohio State University.

HELPER, H. R. *The Impending Crisis in the South.* New York: A. B. Burdick, 1857.

HESSELTINE, WILLIAM BEST. *A History of the South.* New York: Prentice-Hall, 1936.

JENKINS, W. S. *Pro-Slavery Thoughts in the Old South.* Chapel Hill: the University of North Carolina Press, 1935.

MARTIN, ASA EARL. *Anti-Slavery in Kentucky Prior to 1850.* Louisville, Ky.: Standard Printing Co., 1918.

OLMSTED, FREDERICK LAW. *The Cotton Kingdom.* New York; Mason Brothers, 1861.

REDPATH, JAMES. *The Roving Editor.* New York: A. B. Burdick, 1859.

SHUGG, ROGER W. *Origins of Class Struggle in Louisiana.* University of Louisiana Press, 1939.

WALLACE, D. D. *History of South Carolina,* vol. 3. New York: The American Historical Society, Inc., 1934.

WEEKS, S. B. *Southern Quakers and Slavery.* Baltimore: Johns Hopkins Press, 1896.

WHITE, WALTER. *Rope and Faggot.* New York: Alfred A. Knopf, 1929.

WISE, JOHN S. *The End of an Era.* Boston: Houghton Mifflin Co., 1900.

WISH, HARVEY. "George H. Fitzhugh," *Southern Sketches.* Charlottesville, Va.: Green Bookman, Inc., 1938.

## THE NEGRO

APTHEKER, HERBERT. *The Negro in the American Revolution.* New York: International Publishers Co., Inc., 1940.

——. *The Negro in the Civil War.* New York: International Publishers Co., Inc., 1938.

BRAWLEY, BENJAMIN G. *A Short History of the American Negro.* New York: The Macmillan Company, 1927.

DETWEILER, F. G. *The Negro Press in the United States.* Chicago: The University of Chicago Press, 1922.

DOUGLASS, FREDERICK. *My Life and Times.* Boston: DeWolfe Fiske & Co., 1892.

DUBOIS, W. E. B. *The Negro.* New York: Henry Holt and Company, 1915.

DuBois, W. E. B. *Economic Cooperation among the Negro Americans.* Atlanta: University of Atlanta Press, 1907.

Hickok, Charles T. *The Negro in Ohio, 1802-1870.* Cleveland: n.p., 1896.

Higginson, Thomas Wentworth. *Life in a Black Regiment.* Boston: Fields, Osgood & Co., 1870.

Loggins, Vernon. *The Negro Author.* New York: Columbia University Press, 1931.

Odum, H. W. *Social and Mental Traits of the Negro.* New York: Columbia University Press, 1910.

Turner, Edward Raymond. *The Negro in Pennsylvania: Slavery, Servitude, Freedom (1639-1861).* Washington: American Historical Association, 1911.

Wesley, Charles H. *Negro Labor in the United States.* New York: The Vanguard Press, 1927.

Williams, G. W. *History of the Negro Troops in the War of the Rebellion.* New York: Harper & Brothers, 1888.

Wilson, Joseph T. *The Black Phalanx.* Hartford, Conn.: American Publishing Co., 1888.

Woodson, Carter G. *The Negro in Our History.* Washington: Association for the Study of Negro Life and History, 1928.

————. *Free Negro Heads of Families in the United States in 1830.* Washington: Association for the Study of Negro Life and History, 1925.

ABOLITION AND ABOLITIONISTS

Adams, Alice Dana. *The Neglected Period of Anti-Slavery in America (1808-1831).* Boston: Ginn and Company, 1908.

Adams, Charles Francis. *Richard Henry Dana.* Boston: Houghton Mifflin Company, 1890.

Aptheker, Herbert. "Quakers and Negro Slavery," Washington: *Journal of Negro History,* vol. 25, 1940.

Barnes, Gilbert Hobbs. *The Anti-Slavery Impulse.* New York: D. Appleton-Century Company, Inc., 1933.

Birney, William. *James G. Birney and His Times.* New York: D. Appleton & Company, 1890.

Dumond, Dwight L. (editor). *Letters of James G. Birney.* New York: D. Appleton-Century Company, 1938.

Boardman, Helen. "Behind Garrison Stood the Negro Abolitionists." New York: unpublished MS.

Bowditch, Vincent Y. *Life and Correspondence, Henry I. Bowditch.* Boston: Houghton Mifflin Company, 1902.

Brannum, Ruth G. "Frederick Douglass, the Abolitionist." Thesis, Howard University, 1937.

Brown, William Wells. *Narrative.* London: Charles Gilpin, 1849.

Buell, Walter. *Joshua R. Giddings.* Cleveland: W. W. Williams, 1882.

Chapman, John Jay. *William Lloyd Garrison.* New York: Moffatt, Yard & Co., 1913.

Chase, Nelka S. "Attitude of the Negro towards Slavery (1828-1850)," Thesis, Howard University, 1936.

Cochran, W. C. "The Western Reserve and the Fugitive Slave Law," *Western Reserve Historical Society,* no. 101, 1920.

COLMAN, LUCY M. *Reminiscences*. Buffalo, N. Y.: H. L. Green, 1891.

COMMAGER, HENRY STEELE. *Theodore Parker*. Boston: Little, Brown & Company, 1936.

CONWAY, MONCURE D. *Autobiography*. Boston: Houghton Mifflin Company, 1904.

DE FONTAINE, F. G. *History of American Abolitionism*. New York: D. Appleton and Company, 1861.

DETWEILER, F. G. *The Negro Press in the United States*. Chicago: The University of Chicago Press, 1922.

DUMOND, DWIGHT L. *Anti-Slavery Origins of the Civil War*. Ann Arbor: The University of Michigan Press, 1939.

FAUSET, ARTHUR HUFF. *Sojourner Truth*. Chapel Hill: The University of North Carolina Press, 1938.

FUESS, CLAUDE MOORE. "Daniel Webster and the Abolitionists," *Massachusetts Historical Society Proceedings*, vol. 64.

GAINES, FRANCIS PENDLETON. *The Southern Plantation*. New York: Columbia University Press, 1924.

GARRISON, W. P. and F. J. *William Lloyd Garrison*. Boston: Houghton Mifflin Company, 1894.

GARRISON, WILLIAM LLOYD, JR. "Boston Anti-Slavery Days," *Boston Society Publications*, vol. 2, 1905.

GRIMKÉ, A. E. "Anti-Slavery Boston," *New England Magazine*, December, 1890.

HALLOWELL, ANNA D. *James and Lucretia Mott*. Boston: Houghton Mifflin Company, 1884.

HANMER-CROUGHTON, AMY. "Anti-Slavery Days in Rochester," *Rochester Historical Society*, vol. 14, 1936.

HARLOW, RALPH VOLNEY. "Gerrit Smith and the John Brown Raid," *American Historical Review*, vol. 38, 1932.

———. *Gerrit Smith*. New York: Henry Holt and Company, 1939.

HARPER, IDA M. *Susan B. Anthony*. Indianapolis: The Bobbs-Merrill Co., 1899.

HART, A. B. *Slavery and Abolition*. New York: Harper & Brothers, 1906.

HELM, T. G. "Wendell Phillips and the Abolition Movement," *Reformed Church Review*, vol. 20, 1916.

HIGGINSON, THOMAS WENTWORTH. *Contemporaries*. Boston: Houghton Mifflin Company, 1899.

———. *Cheerful Yesterdays*. Boston: Houghton Mifflin Company, 1898.

HINTON, RICHARD. *John Brown and His Men*. New York: Funk and Wagnalls Company, 1894.

HOUSE, T. O. "Anti-Slavery Activities of Negroes in New York." Thesis, Howard University, 1906.

HUME, JOHN. *The Abolitionists*. New York: G. P. Putnam Sons, 1905.

JAY, JOHN. *America Free or America Slave?* (a pamphlet) New York: office of the New York *Tribune*, 1856.

JOHNSON, OLIVER. *William Lloyd Garrison*. Boston: Houghton Mifflin Company, 1881.

LANDON, FRED. "Benjamin Lundy, Abolitionist," Toronto: *Delhousie Review*, 1927.

LAWRENCE, GEORGE A. *A Pioneer of Freedom*. Galesburg, Ill.: The Wagoner Printing Co., 1913.

LEE, LUTHER. *Autobiography*. New York: Phillips and Hunt, 1882.

*The Liberator* files (used in New York Public Library).

LOVEJOY, JOSEPH C. and OWEN. *Memoirs of Rev. Elijah P. Lovejoy.* New York: J. S. Taylor, 1838.

LUDLUM, ROBERT P. "Joshua R. Giddings: Radical," *Mississippi Valley Historical Review,* vol. 23, 1936.

MACY, JESSE. *Anti-Slavery Crusade.* New Haven: Yale University Press, 1919.

MAY, SAMUEL J. *Some Recollections of Our Anti-Slavery Conflict.* Boston: Fields, Osgood and Co., 1869.

PARKER, THEODORE. Theodore Parker's Scrapbook (Boston Public Library).

PAYNE, DANIEL A. *Recollections of Seventy Years.* Nashville, Tenn.: A.M.E. Sunday School, 1888.

PIERCE, EDWARD L. *Memoirs and Letters of Charles Sumner.* Boston: Roberts Bros., 1893.

PRICE, ROBERT. "The Ohio Anti-Slavery Conventions of 1836," Columbus: *Ohio Archaeological and Historical Society Quarterly,* vol. 44, 1936.

PUTNAM, GEORGE W. "Rendition of Fugitive Slave Sims to Slavery." (Siebert Collection.)

QUARLES, BENJAMIN. "Frederick Douglass and the Women's Rights Movement," Washington: *Journal of Negro History,* vol. 25, 1940.

REDPATH, JAMES. *Public Life of Captain John Brown.* Boston: Thayer and Eldredge, 1860.

RICHMAN, IRVING B. *John Brown Among the Quakers and Other Sketches.* Des Moines: The Historical Department of Iowa, 1894.

SANBORN, F. B. *Life and Letters of John Brown.* Boston: Roberts Bros., 1891.

SAVAGE, W. SHERMAN. *Controversy Over Distribution of Abolition Literature.* Washington: Association for the Study of Negro Life and History, 1938.

SHARPLESS, ISAAC. *Quakerism and Politics.* Philadelphia: Ferris & Leach, 1905.

SHOTWELL, WALTER G. *Life of Charles Sumner.* New York: The Thomas Y. Crowell Company, 1910.

SHUMWAY, A. L. and BROWER, C. DEW. *Oberliniana.* Cleveland: Home Publishing Co., 1883.

SNODGRASS, JOSEPH EVANS. "Benjamin Lundy," New York: *Northern Monthly,* vol. 2, no. 5.

SPERRY, E. E. "The Jerry Rescue," *Rochester Historical Society,* vol. 1.

STEVENS, CHARLES EMERY. *Anthony Burns.* Boston: J. P. Jewett & Co., 1856.

STOWE, LYMAN BEECHER. *Saints, Sinners, and Beechers.* Indianapolis: The Bobbs-Merrill Co., 1934.

SWISSHELM, JANE. *Half a Century.* Chicago: Jansen, McClurg & Co., 1880.

TAPPAN, LEWIS. *Life of Arthur Tappan.* New York: Hurd and Haughton, 1871.

VILLARD, OSWALD GARRISON. *John Brown,* Boston: Houghton Mifflin Company, 1910.

WARD, SAMUEL RINGGOLD WARD. *The Autobiography of a Fugitive Negro.* London: John Snow, 1855.

WELD, RALPH FOSTER. *Slavery in Connecticut.* New Haven: Yale University Press, 1835.

WELD. *Letters of Theodore D. Weld, Angelina Grimké Weld, and Sarah Grimké,* edited by Dwight L. Dumond and Gilbert H. Barnes. New York: D. Appleton-Century Company, 1934.

WESLEY, CHARLES. "Negroes of New York in the Emancipation Movement," Washington: *Journal of Negro History*, vol. 24.

WHITMAN, WALT. *Gathering of the Forces: editorials, essays, reviews by Walt Whitman*, edited by Cleveland Rogers and John Black. New York: G. P. Putnam's Sons, 1920.

WHITTAKER, HELEN BEATRICE. "Negroes in the Abolition Movement (1830-1850)." Thesis, Howard University, 1935.

WOODSON, C. G. (editor) *The Mind of the Negro in Letters*. Washington: Association for the Study of Negro Life and History, 1926.

"Proceedings of Anti-Slavery Society Meeting on Anniversary of 1835 Mob," 1855.

"Narrative of Late Riotous Proceedings against the Liberty of the Press in Cincinnati," 1836.

## MANNERS AND POLITICS OF THE UNITED STATES
### (1830-1861)

BEARD, CHARLES A. and MARY R. *Rise of American Civilization*. New York: The Macmillan Company, 1929-39.

BUCHANAN, PRESIDENT. Messages of President Buchanan compiled by J. B. Henry. New York: n. p., 1888.

BUELL, WALTER. *Joshua R. Giddings*. Cleveland: W. W. Williams, 1882.

CHANNING, EDWARD. *History of the United States*. New York: The Macmillan Company, 1921-26.

CLAY, HENRY. *Works of Henry Clay, comprising his Life, Correspondence, Speeches*, edited by Calvin Colton. New York: Henry Clay Publishing Co., 1897.

COLE, A. C. *The Era of the Civil War 1848-1870*. Springfield, Ill.: Centennial Commission, 1919.

———. *The Irrepressible Conflict*. New York: The Macmillan Company, 1934.

———. Address. "Lincoln's House Divided Speech: Did it Reflect a Doctrine of Class Struggle?" Given before Chicago Historical Society. The University of Chicago Press, 1923.

DuBois, W. E. B. *Black Reconstruction*. New York: Harcourt, Brace & Co., 1935.

DUMOND, DWIGHT L. *Anti-Slavery Origins of the Civil War*. Ann Arbor: the University of Michigan Press, 1939.

GRIFFIS, WILLIAM ELLIOT. *Millard Fillmore*. Ithaca, N. Y.: Andrus & Church, 1905.

HART, A. B. *Salmon P. Chase*. Boston: Houghton Mifflin Company, 1899.

HERTZ, EMANUEL. *Abraham Lincoln, A New Portrait*. New York: Liveright Publishing Corp., 1931.

HUNT, GAILLARD. John C. Calhoun. Philadelphia: G. W. Jacobs & Co., 1907.

LUDLUM, ROBERT T. "Joshua R. Giddings: Radical," *Mississippi Valley Historical Review*, vol. 23, 1936.

MARTINEAU, HARRIET. *The Martyr Age of the United States*. Newcastle-on-Tyne, England: Finlay and Charlton, 1840.

———. *Society in America*. New York: Saunders and Otler, 1837.

McMASTER, J. B. *History of the People of the United States from the Revolution to the Civil War*. New York: D. Appleton & Company, 1885-1913.

MILLER, ALPHONSE B. *Thaddeus Stevens*. New York: Harper & Brothers, 1939.

MILTON, GEORGE F. *The Eve of Conflict.* Boston: Houghton Mifflin Company, 1934.

NEVINS, ALLAN. *The Evening Post: A Century of Journalism.* New York: Boni & Liveright, 1922.

OGG, FREDERICK AUSTIN. *Daniel Webster.* Philadelphia: G. W. Jacobs & Co., 1914.

RHODES, JAMES FORD. *History of the United States from the Compromise of 1850.* New York: The Macmillan Company, 1902-1907.

ROGERS, JOSEPH M. *Thomas H. Benton.* Philadelphia: G. W. Jacobs & Co., 1905.

SANDBURG, CARL. *Abraham Lincoln: The Prairie Years.* New York: Harcourt, Brace & Co., 1926.

SHEPARD, E. M. *Martin Van Buren.* Boston: Houghton Mifflin Company, 1888.

SHERMAN, JOHN. *Recollections of Forty Years in the House.* Chicago: The Werner Co., 1895.

SINCLAIR, UPTON. *Manassas.* New York: The Macmillan Company, 1904. (This is fiction but so impeccably authentic that it must be included.)

SMITH, JUSTIN. *The War With Mexico.* New York: The Macmillan Company, 1919.

———. *The Annexation of Texas.* New York: Baker & Taylor Co., 1911.

SMITH, THEODORE CLARKE. *The Liberty and Free Soil Parties in the Northwest.* New York: Longmans, Green and Co., 1897.

SMITH, T. C. *Parties and Slavery (1850-1859).* New York: Harper & Brothers, 1906.

SUCHAMPAUGH, PHILIP. "James Buchanan, the Court, and the Dred Scott Case," *Tennessee Historical Magazine,* January, 1926.

WILSON, HENRY. *History of the Rise and Fall of the Slave Power in America.* Boston: J. R. Osgood & Co., 1872.

THE YEARS 1861 TO 1865

APTHEKER, HERBERT. *The Negro in the Civil War.* New York: International Publishers Co., Inc., 1938.

BOTUME, ELIZABETH HYDE. *First Days Among the Contrabands.* Boston: Lee & Shepard, 1893.

BREWSTER, JAMES M. *Sketches of Southern Mystery, Treason and Murder.* 1903.

CONWAY, M. D. *Testimonies Concerning Slavery.* 1865.

COULTER, E. M. *The Civil War and Readjustment in Kentucky.* Chapel Hill: The University of North Carolina Press, 1926.

CROMWELL, JOHN W. "The Early Negro Conventions," *Occasional Papers, no. 9.* Washington: American Negro Academy, 1904.

DAVIS, W. W. *Civil War and Reconstruction in Florida.* New York: Columbia University Press, 1913.

DUBOIS, W. E. B. *Economic Cooperation Among the Negro-Americans.* Atlanta: University of Atlanta Press, 1906.

DUMOND, D. L. *The Secession Movement.* New York: The Macmillan Company, 1931.

EATON, JOHN. *Grant, Lincoln and the Freedmen.* New York: Longmans, Green and Co., 1907.

FRENCH, A. M. *Slavery in North Carolina and the ex-Slaves.* New York: W. M. French, 1862.

GREELEY, HORACE. *The American Conflict.* Hartford, Conn.: O. D. Chase & Co., 1866.

HAWKINS, WILLIAM G. *Lunsford Lane.* Boston: Crosby and Nichols, 1864.

HEADLEY, J. T. *The Great Riots of New York, 1712-1873.* New York: E. B. Treat, 1873.

HESSELTINE, W. B. *Underground Railroad from Confederate Prisons to East Tennessee.* East Tennessee Historical Society Publications, no. 2.

HIGGINSON, THOMAS WENTWORTH. *Life in a Black Regiment.* Boston: Fields, Osgood & Co., 1870.

HOWE, SAMUEL GRIDLEY. *The Refugees from Slavery in Canada West. Report to the Freedmen's Inquiry Commission.* Boston: Wright and Potter Ptg. Co., 1864.

JORDAN, DONALDSON and PRATT, E. J. *Europe and the American Civil War.* Boston: Houghton Mifflin Company, 1931.

LILLY, WILLIAM E. *Set My People Free.* New York: Farrar and Rinehart, Inc., 1932.

LONN, ELLA. *Desertions During the Civil War.* New York: The Century Co., 1928.

MITCHELL, STEWART. *Horatio Seymour of New York.* Cambridge: Harvard University Press, 1938.

NELSON, EARL J. "Missouri Slavery 1861-1865," *Missouri Historical Review,* vol. 28.

PECK, WILLIAM F. *History of the Police Department, Rochester, N. Y.* Rochester Police Benevolent Association, 1903.

PETIGRU, JAMES LOUIS. *Life, Letters and Speeches of James Louis Petigru, The Union Man of South Carolina,* edited by James Petigru Carson. Washington: W. H. Lowdermilk and Co., 1920.

RAYMOND, HENRY J. *Life and Public Services of Abraham Lincoln, Together with his State Papers.* New York: Derby & Miller, 1865.

SANDBURG, CARL. *The War Years.* New York: Harcourt, Brace and Co., 1939.

SHOTWELL, RANDOLPH ABBOT. *The Papers of Randolph Abbot Shotwell,* edited by J. G. deRoulhac Hamilton. Raleigh, N. C.: The North Carolina Historical Commission, 1931.

TATUM, GEORGIA LEE. *Disloyalty in the Confederacy.* Chapel Hill: The University of North Carolina Press, 1934.

WESLEY, CHARLES H. *Collapse of the Confederacy.* Washington: Association for the Study of Negro Life and History, 1937.

WILBUR, HENRY W. *President Lincoln's Attitude towards Slavery and Emancipation.* Philadelphia: W. R. Jenkins Co., 1914.

WILEY, B. I. *Southern Negroes: 1861-1865.* New Haven: Yale University Press, 1938.

WILLIAMS, G. W. *History of the Negro Troops in the War of the Rebellion.* New York: Harper & Brothers, 1888.

WILSON, CHARLES R. "Cincinnati's Reputation During the Civil War," *Journal of Southern History,* vol. 2, 1936.

WOODSON, CARTER G. *A Century of Negro Migration.* Washington: Association for the Study of Negro Life and History, 1918.

### RECONSTRUCTION

ALLEN, JAMES S. *Reconstruction: A Study in Democracy.* New York: International Publishers Co., Inc., 1937.

BOWERS, CLAUDE. *The Tragic Era.* Boston: Houghton Mifflin Company, 1929.

BURGESS, JOHN W. *Reconstruction and the Constitution.* New York: Charles Scribner's, 1902.

CONWAY, MONCURE D. *Autobiography.* Boston: Houghton Mifflin Company, 1894.

COULTER, E. M. *The Civil War and Readjustment in Kentucky.* Chapel Hill: The University of North Carolina Press, 1926.

DAVIS, W. W. *The Civil War and Reconstruction in Florida.* New York: Columbia University Press, 1913.

DuBois, W. E. B. *Black Reconstruction.* New York: Harcourt, Brace and Company, 1935.

DUNNING, W. A. *Essays on Civil War and Reconstruction.* New York: The Macmillan Company, 1894.

EATON, JOHN. *Grant, Lincoln and the Freedmen.* New York: Longmans, Green and Co., 1907.

ECKENRODE, H. J. *Rutherford B. Hayes.* New York: Dodd, Mead & Company, 1930.

FLEMING, WALTER L. *Civil War and Reconstruction in Alabama.* New York: Columbia University Press, 1905.

HAVILAND, LAURA S. *A Woman's Life Work.* Chicago: Publication Association of Friends, 1889.

HAWORTH, PAUL LELAND. *The Hayes-Tilden Disputed Presidential Election of 1876.* Cleveland: Burrows Brothers Co., 1916.

LYNCH, JOHN R. "Some Historical Errors of James Ford Rhodes," Washington: *Journal of Negro His' ry,* vol. 2.

MILLER, ALPHONSE B. *Thaddeus Stevens.* New York: Harper & Brothers, 1939.

Files of *The Nation,* 1865-1877.

PHILLIPS, U. B. *American Negro Slavery.* New York: D. Appleton & Company, 1918.

PIERCE, E. L. *Memoirs and Letters of Charles Sumner.* Boston: Roberts Bros., 1893.

PIKE, JAMES S. *South Carolina, The Prostrate State.* (reissued) New York: Loring & Mussey, 1935.

RUSSELL, C. E. *The Story of Wendell Phillips.* Chicago: Charles Kerr & Co., 1914.

SHERMAN, JOHN. *Recollections of Forty Years in the House.* Chicago: The Werner Co., 1895.

STILL, WILLIAM. *Underground Railroad Records.* Philadelphia: Porter & Coates, 1872.

VAN DEUSEN, JOHN G. "The Exodus of 1879," Washington: *Journal of Negro History,* vol. 21.

WARE, NORMAN. *The Industrial Worker (1840-1860).* Boston: Houghton Mifflin Company, 1924.

WESLEY, CHARLES H. *Negro Labor in the United States.* New York: The Vanguard Press, 1927.

WILSON, HENRY. *Rise and Fall of the Slave Power in America,* vol. 3. Boston: J. R. Osgood & Co., 1872.

WOODSON, CARTER G. *A Century of Negro Migration*. Washington: Association for the Study of Negro Life and History, 1918.

———. *The Negro in Our History*. Washington: Association for the Study of Negro Life and History, 1928.

Official Proceedings of Reconstructed Governments.

Official Proceedings of Pennsylvania Female Anti-Slavery Society, 1860-1870.

# INDEX